WILLIAM GOLDMAN

Adventures in the Screen Trade

A Personal View of Hollywood and Screenwriting

ABACUS

First published in Great Britain by Macdonald & Co (Publishers) Ltd 1984
This edition published by Abacus 1996

21 23 25 27 29 30 28 26 24 22 20

A CIP catalogue record for this book
is available from the British Library.

ISBN 978-0-349-10705-9

Printed and bound in Great Britain by
Clays Ltd, St Ives plc

Papers used by Abacus are from well-managed forests
and other responsible sources.

MIX
Paper from
responsible sources
FSC® C104740

Abacus
An imprint of
Little, Brown Book Group
Carmelite House
50 Victoria Embankment
London EC4Y 0DZ

An Hachette UK Company
www.hachette.co.uk

www.littlebrown.co.uk

lliam Goldman is the bestselling author of sev ks, including *Boys and Girls Together* and *Hype y*. He has written screenplays for *Butch Cassidy a1 lance Kid, All the President's Men, Misery* and *Ma1 lives in New York.

For Ross Claiborne

For Ron Shusett

contents

author's note

This book was begun at the greatest time of panic and despair in modern Hollywood history—late January of '82. Future film scholars may well term it "the *Heaven's Gate* era." And certainly that movie received more media coverage than any other contemporary disaster.

But only a few enlightened bookkeepers will know for sure if it lost more than, say, *Raise the Titanic!* or *Honky Tonk Freeway*.

During the holiday season of '81–'82, sixteen films were released by the major studios. Of those, only one—*On Golden Pond*—was a runaway success. And ten of the sixteen each lost more than ten million dollars. One major studio executive told me recently, "Of course the failures are upsetting. But there have always been failures. What's got us so immobilized now is that whatever it is that we're making, we're missing the audience by a wider margin than ever before. We don't know what they want. All we do know is that they don't want what we're giving them."

Perhaps the key word above is *immobilized*. By the end of February, only ten films will have begun production. At the same time a year ago, twenty-five had started shooting.

Again, this is the worst period within memory. By the time this book sees print, it may well be the best period within memory. The point being this: *Movies are a gold-rush business.*

Anyone interested in what follows had best commit that fact to memory. . . .

What follows, generically speaking, is a book about Hollywood. It may not come as a total shock to you if I say this is not the first attempt to mine that subject.

All I can provide that is different is my point of attack: I have been, for close to twenty years now, a screenwriter. I have seen a lot, learned more than a little—most of it, alas, too late.

In terms of authority, screenwriters rank somewhere between the man who guards the studio gate and the man who runs the studio (this week). And there is a whole world to which we are not privy. And I thought it may be helpful to know at least something about just what is taking place Out There. With that in mind, I've interviewed a number of people who work the other side of the street: studio executives, producers, directors, and stars. By the time we're done, it's my hope that you'll understand a good deal more about why you see what you see on the screen.

Because of my Hollywood work, I have seen films on three continents and in at least twice that many foreign countries.

But for me, still, always, it is the Alcyon. . . .

Certainly not a great movie theatre. Probably not even a very good one. But the Alcyon stands alone in memory because it stood alone on Central, even then an aging monopoly; if you wanted to go to the movies in Highland Park, Illinois, in the 1930's, it was the Alcyon—or it was no movie at all.

And the thought of no movie at all was just too painful.

Even when I was six and seven and eight, I was hooked. I suppose I still am, but the stuff I see today often vanishes, while the Alcyon remains.

Captain January. 1936. Shirley Temple. I was five and she was eight. My first time sitting there in the dark, I remember her curls so plainly. And could her dimples have been as large as they seemed? If the answer is no, don't tell me.

Tarzan Finds a Son. Late thirties and memorable because I went to see it twice on consecutive matinees. I don't think I liked it as much as I wanted to escape some visiting relatives, but the fact remains: I was the first kid on the block who had ever done such a lunatic thing. In this *Star Wars* era, nothing unusual. But the news swept the Elm Place Grammar School playground during Monday recess. "Twice? *How could you do it twice when you knew who won?*" I didn't have an answer. And I didn't like *Tarzan Finds a Son* as much the second time.

But I sure did like sitting there.

Not true of *Invitation to Happiness,* my first evening flick. I was eight and already a sports fan and, during an earlier matinee preview, *Invitation to Happiness* flashed on—

—a prizefight movie.

Fifteen or twenty seconds of solid slam-bang action were shown. I had to see it. It was only playing for two nights in the middle of the week and I understood the importance of school the next day. But I knew I had to go. Problem: I couldn't go alone. I launched a campaign of such ferocity that my parents gave in. Grudgingly, we trooped off to *Invitation to Happiness*—

—and it wasn't a prizefight movie, it was a *kissing* movie.

All they did was kiss, the hero and the lady. Those precious fifteen seconds of slam-bang action were there, all right, but that was the sum total of prizefighting. I never dreamed a preview would snooker you that way.

The kisses went on and on. I began to groan. Then I started counting. Eleven kisses. Now a quick buss on the nose, but that counted. Twelve. On and on they went, and by now I was counting out loud.

There were twenty-three kisses in *Invitation to Happiness* and I hated every one.

But I didn't hate the movies. Not then, not now. Too many memories involved. Movies help mark out our lives. Do you remember who you were when you first saw *Citizen Kane*? I do. Or *Casablanca* or *Singin' in the Rain*? If you give it a moment's thought, I'll bet you can come up with an answer.

I've been a fan for forty-six of my fifty-one years. Before I ever dreamed of entering the business, movies were an essential part of my life.

And whatever theatre I walk into today, part of me, a large part of me, is still going to the Alcyon. . . .

part one

Hollywood Realities

chapter one
The Powers That Be

It may well be pointless to try and isolate the great powers of the movie industry. Stars, studio executives, directors, and producers all circle in the same orbit, subject to the same gravitational laws.

I have divided these powers nonetheless, in the hope that it may simplify matters and shed additional light on the moviemaking process as a whole. Just remember that they are all joined at the hip, locked in an uneasy alliance, groping sometimes—but by no means always—toward the same mist-shrouded goal: a hit.

None of this is meant to imply that they like each other very much. Or trust each other, fully, ever. . . .

Stars

With one major exception, which will be dealt with in due course, as far as the filmmaking process is concerned, stars are essentially worthless—and absolutely essential.

Stars and studios coexist in an arena rarely glimpsed by screenwriters. When God chooses to smile on them, they make fortunes for each other. But money, as we know, doesn't cart happiness along with it. So if you choose to imagine these two mightiest of industry elements as snarly Siamese twins, you won't be far wrong. To understand why this situation exists, a little history may prove helpful.

Studios came first, and in the beginning they were not remotely ambivalent about stars: They *hated* them. It's important to remember that movies began as a fad—not unlike the Atari games today. No one knew what the future might bring—or if, indeed, there would even be a future—but the present was plenty lucrative enough for even the greediest executive.

April twenty-third, 1896—as much as any date, that can be taken as the beginning of the motion picture business. It marked the opening of the first theatre in New York that took money from the public in exchange for filmed entertainment. By the year 1910, there were over nine *thousand* theatres in operation across the country.

Movies, of course, were shorter then. D. W. Griffith, in one five-year stretch, directed over five hundred "movies." Not only were they of less duration, they were also a good deal more simplistic than what we are used to today; one early hit consisted in its entirety of nothing but a horse eating hay. (The filmmaker who created the horse movie followed up with another smash—some footage of a pillow fight between his two daughters.)

The audience could have cared less—they loved going to the movies. Clearly, these films were not directed at intellectuals or the upper classes. Movies then were for immigrants and the poor, who sought entertainment where they could get it cheaply.

And in this early booming decade, there were no stars.

Actors, mostly "legitimate" ones, were ashamed of this new medium. They snuck over to New Jersey and worked, but only for the bread—the last thing they wanted was their name attached to anything they did. Also, it was not glamorous labor: Actors were automatically given other chores to do, such as sweeping up, doing carpentry, etc. One early matinee idol shocked his employers by declaring, when he reported for duty, "I am an actor and I will act—but I will not build sets and paint scenery." Then again, it was difficult for the public to find a favorite: During this "buccaneer" period, theatres would often change entire shows—up to sixty minutes of short features— every day.

The resulting flood of product was, ultimately, responsible for the existence of Hollywood. All the major studios paid a fee to Thomas Edison for the right to make movies: The motion picture was his invention and he had to be reimbursed for each and every film.

But there was such a need for material that pirate companies, which did not pay the fee, sprang up. The major studios hired detectives to stop this practice, driving many of the pirates as far from the New York area as possible. Sure, Hollywood had all that great shooting weather. But more than that, being three thousand miles west made it easier to steal. (The more things change, etc., etc.)

In spite of the studios, certain performers began to become favorites. Of course they had no names. If you wrote to them, you would have to send off your fan letter to "The Butler with the Mustache" or "The Girl with the Curly Blonde Hair."

If a studio had a performer they used a great deal, they still would never give the public a name to associate with the face. And so it was that, in 1910, perhaps the most popular film performer in America was known as "The Biograph Girl," Biograph being the company that had her under contract.

But when her contract was up, another studio stole her away. There were, of course, the usual inducements—a higher salary, her husband came along with her with a directing contract of his own—all standard. What was not standard, and what altered the future of movies, was this: The new studio agreed to feature her name. And so, in 1910, a beautiful young girl with the mellifluous name of Florence Lawrence initiated the star system in America.

The peers of Carl Laemmle (the executive who had spirited away Miss Lawrence) were, of course, more than a little displeased. Why? Because they were afraid that once the public *really* began to identify with performers, they might be forced to pay them more. You can say what you will about the morals of these early titans, you can scorn them as little more than furriers. But boy, they sure weren't dumb. Here is what happened to salaries:

1912: Miss Lawrence was now the highest paid movie worker, making, by the end of that year, $250.00 per week.
1913: Mary Pickford signs for $500.00 per week.
1914: Miss Pickford re-signs for double her previous weekly fee.
1915: Miss Pickford re-re-signs, this time $2,000.00 weekly compensation.
1916: $10,000.00 per week—that was Charlie Chaplin's stipend. Plus $150,000.00 in bonus money for signing.
1919: Fatty Arbuckle became the first star in history to be guaranteed a salary of one million dollars per year. Minimum.

The war cry of the studios has been the same ever since: Every time the business is about to self-destruct, they can pinpoint the reason—it's the goddam greed of the stars. In the late sixties, the most recent crisis time till now, it was the Burtons' fault, each of them getting a million to co-star in such items as *The Comedians* and *Boom!* (The exclamation point didn't help the latter at the box office.)

Today, a million dollars is what you pay a star you don't want.

Personally, I don't blame the stars for grabbing every cent they can. They all know the studios are going to rob them of as much of a film's profits as they can. And no one forces the studios to pay what they do. Most of all, though, stardom just doesn't last. (For a gifted few, sure. But only a few.)

No one can say with mathematical precision who are the top ten stars. But Quigley Publishing Company has been taking a poll of theatre owners for fifty years now. And it's flawed: In the middle seventies, the star who was being offered the most money often wasn't even on their list, but that was because Steve McQueen wasn't working. Still, the Quigley poll is the best we have. Theatre owners, after all, should know at least a little bit about whose movies perform best in their theatre. Following is the Quigley list of the top ten stars of last year, 1981:

(1) Burt Reynolds
(2) Clint Eastwood
(3) Dudley Moore
(4) Dolly Parton
(5) Jane Fonda
(6) Harrison Ford
(7) Alan Alda
(8) Bo Derek
(9) Goldie Hawn
(10) Bill Murray

Now let's go back just five years. Here are the top ten for 1976:

(1) Robert Redford
(2) Jack Nicholson
(3) Dustin Hoffman
(4) Clint Eastwood
(5) Mel Brooks
(6) Burt Reynolds
(7) Al Pacino
(8) Tatum O'Neal
(9) Woody Allen
(10) Charles Bronson

In just five years, only two repeaters: Eastwood and Reynolds. This is five years before then—the top ten of 1971:

(1) John Wayne
(2) Clint Eastwood
(3) Paul Newman
(4) Steve McQueen

    (5) George C. Scott
    (6) Dustin Hoffman
    (7) Walter Matthau
    (8) Ali MacGraw
    (9) Sean Connery
   (10) Lee Marvin

Only Eastwood is still on from the '81 list. And only Eastwood and Hoffman still were around to make the list in '76.

This last list is from 1961. I know that twenty years is a long time. But we are talking here about the ephemeral quality of performers, which often manifests itself in their behavior and material. Also, twenty years isn't *that* long—not in the career of a professor or a doctor of internal medicine.

    (1) Elizabeth Taylor
    (2) Rock Hudson
    (3) Doris Day
    (4) John Wayne
    (5) Cary Grant
    (6) Sandra Dee
    (7) Jerry Lewis
    (8) William Holden
    (9) Tony Curtis
   (10) Elvis Presley

Now some of these people are dead, and some are retired. But a bunch of them are still there, but they're not making this kind of list anymore. Decline and fall can't ever be easy, but for a star it's torment. Because, when they are on top, they are so adored. Movie stars, as has been stated elsewhere ad nauseam, are perhaps as close as we come to royalty. So the distance of the drop is much greater than the rest of us may (or will) experience.

But more than that, *these people are role players.* They had lives, grammar school, high school, just like the rest of us. But they weren't contented with their parts. That's why they become actors. And when they become not just actors but stars, that's getting-what-you-wish-for time.

There's a cliché that goes "Be careful what you wish for, you might get it." The problem with stars is they get their wish but not for long.

Which is why it's crucial for a screenwriter to remember this: Never underestimate the insecurity of a star. Look, we're all insecure, we know that. Even brain surgeons probably get the shakes when no one's watching.

But movie stars? It's all but inconceivable. They are so blessed, and not just with physical beauty. They have talent and intelligence and command and an unending supply of self-deprecating charm.

We have read their interviews in the papers and we've seen them on the talk shows, and it's very hard to realize that what we are seeing are not the people themselves but the actors doing what they do best: acting.

George Segal may have put it best. I had watched him be terrific on a talk show, playing his banjo or whatever the hell instrument he plays, and joking it up. I asked him if he had always been able to enjoy himself that way.

He said, "That's like class: I prepare myself—I do an acting exercise. I tell myself I'm playing a character who's enjoying himself."

In my early days, whenever I met anyone who had worked with performers I revered, I would always pester them with the same question: What was that performer really like?

I already knew the answer, of course: They were the parts they played.

Alas, not so.

A man who worked with Bogart told me: "Miserable pain in the ass, always making trouble, always grousing that he had shit to say and everybody else had the good lines. Whined and bitched the whole shoot."

Bogart whining?

A man who worked with Cary Grant told me: "Cary was at his peak. I did two pictures with him and both times it was the same fight: He was convinced he had no charm and couldn't do a lot of scenes because the audiences wouldn't buy him. It was madness—here he was, maybe the most charming actor ever, and it was like pulling teeth. He was absolutely certain that his charm had gone."

Grant without charm?

I don't ask that question much anymore. I'm tired of the same surprise. I think I'm like most of us in that I want to believe the image. Don't tell me Clint Eastwood hates horses, I don't want to know it.

And what's this got to do with insecurity? Just this: From the star's point of view, it can get very scary. One example of what I mean, from an early day's shooting of *The Hot Rock*, a 1972 picture that starred Robert Redford.

We were working at a prison in New York and the shot simply required Redford, who had just been paroled, to exit a prison gate. He was dressed in intentionally ill-fitting clothes.

A bunch of prison workers were standing around while the lighting was finished. Some guards were watching, too, and one of them began talking to me.

"This is how it's done, I guess."

I said it was.

"Always take this long?"

I said it did, or longer.

Peter Yates, the director, was conferring nearby with Redford. They talked for a while, I assume about last-minute odds and ends.

"My wife would like to fuck him."

This remark caught me more or less by surprise and I turned to look at the guard: ordinary-seeming guy, maybe forty, in his prison uniform.

"I mean, you don't know what she would give just to fuck him."

Yates and Redford separated, Yates moving to the camera area, Redford to the gate.

And the guard, need I add, was not watching Yates. "She said to me today, my wife, that she would get down on her hands and knees and crawl just for the chance to fuck him one time. *One time.*"

Now, I had seen Redford act on stage: After his brilliant comedy performance in *Barefoot in the Park*, I was convinced he was going to be the next Jack Lemmon.

And I had known him a little socially. He was attractive and a wonderful storyteller and a good athlete and nobody ever said he was dumb—*but rooms did not hush when he entered them.*

Suddenly everything was different. *Butch Cassidy and the Sundance Kid* had opened, and Redford was an international cover boy. And here was this goddam guard using every word in his vocabulary to try to convey to me the extent of his wife's sexual passion for a guy who was basically a fine actor from California who had made some disastrous movies. (Anyone remember *Situation Hopeless—But Not Serious?*)

Well, if half the world suddenly thinks of you as this guard's wife thought of Redford, that's bound to be just the least bit unsettling. You've spent three decades walking along being one thing, and you're still that thing—part of you is—but no one's seeing that. You don't know for sure what the public is reacting to, but you do know it's not *you*. And you don't know how long the reaction will last, but you do know that chances are, it won't be forever.

Stars have to live with that madness.

I still remember the first day of my first trip to Hollywood: I met with some representatives of Paul Newman. We were talking about the scheduling of *Harper*, and I was worried whether Newman would be ready when Warner Bros. wanted to go with the picture. One of the men in the meeting said this after I voiced my concern: "Someday Paul will be Glenn Ford, but right now they'll wait for him."

It was my initial contact with the cruel kind of Hollywood remark that so often tends to deal with heat. Glenn Ford had been, a few years earlier, the number-one star in America and I wasn't aware that his career had stalled. And this was Newman's man forecasting his client's future. But he wasn't cruel, not in his terms. He was simply facing the reality that stars come and go.

Only agents last forever. . . .

WHAT IS A STAR?

Used to be an easy answer: A star was a performer who was billed above the title. But those were the days when billing meant something; now, more often than not, it's something that's doled out in lieu of a higher salary.

In other fields, it's easier to nail it down. Katharine Hepburn, for example, is a star in the theatre. Put her in a play and count your profits. Put Baryshnikov in tights, he's a star too. It doesn't matter if he's dancing Graham or Balanchine, just so he's dancing. Pavarotti and Itzhak Perlman, regardless of their program, are stars on the concert stage.

The most common definition I've heard out there lately is this: A star is someone who *opens*. (When a movie begins its run and no one comes, people in the business will say this of the movie, "It didn't open.")

A star may not guarantee you a profit—budgets can grow wildly for reasons totally out of their control—but they will absolutely be a hedge against disaster. A star ensures that, even if the movie is a stiff, *the movie will open*. One of the ways producers measure the appeal of a star is the amount of business a picture does on its first weekend. Is that too stiff a requirement, bringing the public flocking early to a disaster? Look at it this way: If you are a success financially, and you average fifty thousand dollars a year income for forty years of work, you are making a great deal *less* than what a star gets paid for three to eight weeks in front of the camera. I don't think staving off disaster is too much to ask from them. . . .

WHO IS A STAR?

Not as easy to answer as you may think.

Example: Back in the late sixties, *Life* magazine, then a weekly, had a performer on its cover who they said was the biggest movie star in the world. I was meeting that day with the head of one of the biggest studios. I asked if he'd seen *Life*. He said he hadn't. I told him what I've just told you. And then I asked if he'd care to guess who the performer was.

"Newman," he said.

No.

"McQueen?"

Not McQueen.

A pause now. "Can't be Poitier."

I agreed. It wasn't.

Now a *long* pause. Then, in a burst: "Oh shit, what's the matter with me, I'm not thinking—John Wayne."

The Duke was not on the cover.

The situation was now getting the least bit uncomfortable. "If it's a woman it's either Streisand or Julie Andrews."

I said it was a man. And then, before things got too sticky, I gave the answer. (It was Eastwood.)

And he replied after some thought, "They claim Eastwood? Eastwood's the biggest star?" Finally, after another pause, he nodded. "They're right."

The point being that if a studio giant couldn't guess the biggest star in his business, the territory is a bit murkier than most of us would imagine.

A lot of it has to do with playing hunches.

Example: In the early seventies, two big Broadway musicals were made into movies. *Cabaret* starred Liza Minnelli and was a big hit. *Fiddler on the Roof* starred Topol and took in twice as much money. But the prevailing wisdom was this: Minnelli was a brand-new star, Topol was carried by the property. Nothing much happened to his film career, but Minnelli starred in several big-budget failures until the disaster of *New York, New York* sent her scurrying back to the theatre, where she *is* a star—the biggest, perhaps, on Broadway.

But in movies, the answer to "Who is a star?" is "It's whoever *one* studio executive with 'go' power *thinks* is a star and will underwrite with a start date." (A superstar is someone they'll *all* kill for. . . .)

HOW DO STARS HAPPEN?

Invariably, by mistake.

And invariably that mistake is committed by another performer who is a bigger name at the box office. You may think of Robert Redford as a force of nature, but if Marlon Brando or Steve McQueen or Warren Beatty had said yes to the part of the Sundance Kid, Redford might well have remained what one studio executive told me he was when talk of hiring him first came up: "He's just another California blond—throw a stick at Malibu, you'll hit six of him."

If Albert Finney had agreed to play the title role in *Lawrence of Arabia*, Peter O'Toole wouldn't have happened. If Kirk Douglas had played *Cat Ballou*, forget about Lee Marvin.

Montgomery Clift deserves special mention.

(Clift, for me, is the most overlooked of the great stars. His was a talent that ranked right up with Brando's. I once met Burt Lancaster, and he told me a story of his first days with Clift on *From Here to Eternity*. One thing you should know about Lancaster: The man exudes physical power. Even today, if he went in the ring against André the Giant, I'd bet Lancaster. He told me, "The only time I was ever really afraid as an actor was that first scene with Clift. It was *my* scene, understand: I was the sergeant, I gave the orders, he was just a private under me. Well, when we started, I couldn't stop my knees from shaking. I thought they might have to stop because my trembling would show. But I'd never worked with an actor with Clift's power before; I was afraid he was going to blow me right off the screen.")

A recent biography of Clift reports that he turned down, in one short stretch, four roles: the William Holden part in *Sunset Boulevard*, the James Dean part in *East of Eden*, the Paul Newman part in *Somebody Up There Likes Me*, and the Brando part in *On the Waterfront*. These were all crucial roles in their careers—would these wonderful actors have become stars if Clift had given the thumbs-up sign?

Hard to say for sure.

It's easy to say, though, that without the aid and assistance of George Raft, there is no Humphrey Bogart. I know that's hard to believe today, since Bogart has become such a revered cult figure. But he scuffled for a decade or more in second-rate stuff. *High Sierra* began the turnaround, a part that Raft rejected.

Then came *The Maltese Falcon*. Raft didn't want to play Sam Spade because he didn't trust the first-time-out director, John Huston.

Finally, *Casablanca*. Would you have enjoyed that great entertainment as much with George Raft and Hedy Lamarr? Or Ronald Reagan and Ann Sheridan? They were all approached for the parts.

Stars happen when they have a major role in a major hit. If they're not lucky enough to be in the right place at the right time, it's back to the cattle calls and unemployment lines—or worse: television.

Remaining a star over a period of time is a different story altogether—a story of talent and intelligence.

Dudley Moore, from the beginning, was gifted and bright. Twenty years ago, he and three of his college peers were the sensation of the Broadway season in the revue *Beyond the Fringe*. Moore was then and is now a tremendous musician—pianist, composer—in addition to his charm as a performer.

But with all that, nothing much happened to him.

He made some movies in England—lead roles—but they stiffed. He came to America eventually and it was still the same story: too short, too "special," no chance. The best he got was a good supporting role in *Foul Play*. But Chevy Chase was the romantic lead in that movie. If you had said, back in '78, that Dudley Moore could be a romantic lead, they would have locked you out of The Bistro.

Then George Segal left *10*. Just before shooting, he walked the picture. With no time to waste, Blake Edwards chose Moore to replace him.

10 was a smash. Dudley Moore was a star.

At least that's what the backers of *Arthur* thought. And *Arthur* turned out to be even a bigger hit than *10*, so obviously they were right, right?

Sorry.

Arthur opened, but barely. It was, as they say in the business, "soft." But *Arthur* had, as they also say in the business, "legs." Word of mouth was wonderful, audiences kept coming in increasing numbers. It became, along with *Raiders of the Lost Ark* and *Superman II*, one of that summer's sensations. Moore was no star after *10*. (Miss Derek probably had at least a little something to do with its success.)

But he sure is now. . . .

WEALTH

Today's stars differ from their ancestors in at least one crucial respect: They are rich.

I don't mean to imply that Gable dined on gruel during his glory years. He was well paid, obviously; all the great pre-1950 stars were.

But they didn't share in profits of films. They were contract players: They did what they were told, not only because of the legal agreement, but because they needed the bread. Sure, they lived well, but today's stars have retirement money.

Bend of the River changed everything. In many ways, this little-remembered 1952 Jimmy Stewart Western is as important as any film ever in its effect on the industry.

Stewart's agent then was the remarkable Lew Wasserman, to-day the head of MCA-Universal. Stewart was already a major star. The studios were losing (or had lost) their contractual autonomy. And what Wasserman did was arrange for Stewart to take less than his usual salary in exchange for a percentage of the film's potential profits. It was a gamble that worked: *Bend of the River* was the number-two box-office film of its year, and Stewart cleaned up.

Nothing has been the same since.

Today, all stars command a percentage of the profits and, if they are superstars, a percentage of the gross, profits being like the horizon, receding as fast as you approach.

So, if you're Jack Nicholson and you make *One Flew Over the Cuckoo's Nest*, that's maybe ten million in your pocket. Same for Hoffman after *Kramer Vs. Kramer*. And all the others.

What this means is simple: Today if a star doesn't feel like working, he just doesn't work. He doesn't have to, not ever.

And what *this* means is simple: Since studios need stars, their desperation doubles and then some. They act like Siamese fighting fish in their frenzy to get a star's name on a contract. Stars are more powerful today than ever because they are rich—and the studios only want to make them richer, no matter what they have to put up with.

Which can be, on occasion, plenty.

"ADD ONE-THIRD FOR THE SHIT"

This is a Hollywood expression I have heard used mainly by production managers. Production managers, sometimes called line producers, are at the heart of any film. They are the men who make out the schedules, do the budgeting, and are on call every hour of every day, both before and during and after shooting. When there is a crisis, the man who must solve it is the production manager.

The expression refers to the actual cost of having a star on a film.

Stars, like Madison Avenue buses, never go out alone. There is, always, "the entourage." Marilyn Monroe toward the end, and Elizabeth Taylor at her peak, were famous for the number of people they added to the payroll. Secretaries, chauffeurs, hairdressers, makeup specialists, still others to care for their costumes, acting coaches, masseurs, various gurus, on and on.

Suppose the picture already has hired, say, makeup personnel. There is a certain standard ritual that follows. The production manager—and these men live and die by trying to stay within budget—will be contacted by the makeup specialist for the star. "Sorry, love to have you, but we've already got our people." Fine. Then the makeup specialist contacts the star or the star's agent and explains, often tearfully, that deep as is his (or her) devotion to the star, much as he (or she) would love to continue the association, the studio says no.

There will then be more phone calls, often rising in pitch. The small battle will go on until the preordained result: The star's makeup specialist will be hired, and at a much greater salary than they ordinarily command because the star insists on it. Therefore, there will be salaries paid for double (or triple) makeup personnel, many of whom end up with nothing to do.

Why production managers bother to engage in these little wars I can't say—because the studio rarely backs them up. Day after day, the production manager gets pasted. I suppose they hang in because they care. And maybe someday, some glorious future morning, they'll win one.

Beyond the entourage are the "perks." These can include the question of how much the star will get per week for spending money. (Thousands is the answer.) And how many free plane tickets will the star get from location to home? And how many of the entourage will also get plane tickets? And maybe the star already owns a trailer. And would like it a lot if you would rent the trailer. Fine, the trailer is rented. These things may not seem like much, but they are infinite in number. (Agents, often to justify their percentage when all they really do for a big star is make a phone call, are geniuses when it comes to devising new things to ask for. Which they can then tell their clients have never been gotten before. More than one star has used the same word to me in describing this perk or that: "It's precedential," they say.)

One must also never forget the top technicians. Some stars, as we'll see, have partner-producers; well, they go on the payroll. Or a pet cinematographer without whom they don't show. Or a friend who is a musician and will get paid a ton for any minimal assistance he may contribute to the composer.

Perhaps the largest percentage of the "one-third" that makes up "the shit" is star behavior.

As Mr. Fitzgerald said to Mr. Hemingway about the rich, stars are different from you and me. Yes, they get up in the morning, just like we do. And sure, they go to bed like we do too. But—big but—if they are hot, their day differs from ours in one simple way: From morning till, *they live in a world in which no one disagrees with them.*

In *Tinsel*, a Hollywood novel I wrote, I used an incident where a male star on location liked to wander around the set, ditty bag in hand, and take whatever struck his fancy. (He wasn't stealing as a kleptomaniac might. It was closer to *droit du seigneur*.) If he saw a pen he wanted, he put it in his bag. A watch, a pack of gum, anything. If the crew member called him on it, the star would make a joke, of course return the object, and the next day the crew member was gone. It got so that at the end of each day, the crew would simply report to the production manager what was taken that day and its value and the production manager would make reimbursement.

Well, that happened.

You may find that behavior immoral and I would agree with you; you may think it outrageous and I'd be on your team. But if you're sure it's rare, I'm afraid we part company.

In the contract era, of course, stars stayed in line. Oh, maybe Bette Davis would take suspension rather than play some part Jack Warner wanted her to, but movies in those days went over budget only rarely. (The same holds pretty much true for television today. One of the reasons for the low quality of performance on the tube is the preference for hiring "one-take" actors—people who can give you a reasonable line reading the first time. Television is strictly budgeted—producers are given just so much to bring in their product—and an actor who causes trouble can soon find himself condemned forever to doing dinner-theatre work in the boonies.)

Stories of star misbehavior have been a part of the Hollywood legend, I suppose, from the time Florence Lawrence first got billing. When they occur, they spread through the community with amazing speed. One is apt to hear the latest anecdote half a dozen times within a day of its taking place. Here are four. (I have named names in only two, not because I delight in being "hinty," but because the performers involved have recently died.)

One: A crucial beach scene is being shot. A cabin has been built on the sand and the weather, for reasons of plot, has to be brilliant sunshine. The setup involves the male star of the picture.

The first day—fog. No shooting at all. Just a lot of frustration and a great waste of money.

The second day—fog. Again no shooting, and now the frustration is turning sour. The whole crew is sulking, the director is being eaten alive by the studio over costs.

The third day—yes, fog again, but this time it seems to be lighter. And as the hours drag on, at long, long last, there seems to be a definite chance to shoot. If the fog will only continue to burn away.

Hours pass. The sky is definitely brightening and the crew races for position. They stare at the sky, literally praying for sunshine.

Finally the sun breaks through for a moment—

—and precisely at that moment the male star jumps into a dune buggy and goes for a long ride down the beach. The entire crew turns toward the director and on their faces he sees their message: *Do* something.

The director, helpless, turns away from the crew, stares out at the ocean, and cannot stop the tears of frustration from streaming down his face. (He swore, as he stood there, never to work with a star again.)

The sun goes away, the fog returns. So does the male star half an hour later. He hops out of the dune buggy and can't understand why everyone seems so unhappy. . . .

Two: Rehearsals of *Marathon Man* in New York. Dustin Hoffman and Roy Scheider are about to rehearse their first scene together. Hoffman has the vehicle role and is the more important of the two, but Scheider, coming off the lead in *Jaws*, is not chopped liver.

In the story, they play brothers. Hoffman is a graduate student. Scheider, whom he adores and thinks is in the oil business, actually works for the government as a killer and a spy.

Hoffman has just been brutally mugged in the park. He has written this to Scheider. Scheider suspects it was not an accident—bad guys are trying to get at him by threatening his kid brother. So he comes down from Washington to visit.

It's night, and Hoffman is asleep. Suddenly, he realizes he's not alone in his apartment, so he grabs a flashlight from his bed table and points it around the room, trying to catch the intruder. As he does this, he has a line of dialog:

```
                    HOFFMAN
                (very James Cagney)
        I got a gun, you make a move,
        I'll blow your ass to Shanghai.
```

Okay, rehearsal. A mock set is prepared. Hoffman lies down, closes his eyes, Scheider mimes opening a door, bangs his foot down to indicate the closing of the door, and Hoffman springs awake, mimes getting the flashlight, and says his Shanghai line.

Then rehearsals stop.

Hoffman says to hold it and he turns to the director, John Schlesinger, and tells him that he thinks it wrong for his character to have a flashlight in his bed table.

Schlesinger tells him we'll get to it later, let's continue rehearsing the scene, please.

Hoffman shakes his head. The character that he is playing, he feels, would not have a flashlight by his bed.

Now, if this had not been a star complaining, Schlesinger or any director would have told him that they were wasting rehearsal time, which was gold, since most movies don't bother with rehearsal. (The studios don't like it, they can't see rushes the next day, they consider it a waste of money. I think they're wrong—rehearsals *save* money, because you can work out problems without the intense pressure of a crew standing around doing nothing. Studios are, in this case, like the late Sam Goldwyn, who used to creep to the writer's building on the lot and was unhappy if he didn't hear typewriters clicking.)

But Dustin Hoffman is very much a star, and he has to be dealt with. Scheider stands quietly in the imaginary doorway, waiting.

A lot of people have flashlights by their bed tables, Schlesinger tries.

Hoffman isn't playing a lot of people, he is playing Babe and Babe wouldn't have a flashlight by his bed table.

Schlesinger makes another attempt: You've just been mugged, you're upset, you're taking precautions.

No sale.

Now a practical assault from the director: We *need* the effect of the flashlight beam bouncing off the walls to add interest to the scene.

Hoffman replies there won't be any scene worth anything if he can't play it, and he can't justify the goddam flashlight.

Through all this, silent and waiting, stands Scheider.

And that is probably my strongest memory of the situation—it took an *hour*, by the way—Scheider, waiting quietly, a perfect gentleman through it all.

Now, as stated, rehearsals are meant to deal with problems. And Hoffman is not only one of the best actors we have, he is also known to be a perfectionist. And maybe in his preparations he really couldn't figure out why his character would have a flashlight in his bed table.

But that sure wasn't my feeling in the rehearsal hall at the end of the day. Rather it was this: Hoffman was perfectly able to justify anything, he is that skilled; in my opinion, he didn't want the flashlight because he was afraid his fans would think him chicken.

I believed that then and still do. But that is the kind of thing one dares not mention to a star.

Three: A movie is shooting on a Hollywood sound stage and the female star is number one in the world. By half past nine, the first setup is ready. The star is in her trailer and the second assistant director goes about one of his functions: delivering the talent from the trailer to the set.

He knocks on the trailer door and says "Ready." Pause.

Then the star's hairdresser appears in the doorway and says the star is *not* ready. (Rule of thumb: Female stars are closer to their hairdressers and makeup people than to anyone else on the set. Male stars tend to buddy around with their makeup and wardrobe personnel.)

Anyway, the second assistant returns to the set with his message: The Lady is not coming. The director is sitting in his chair, waiting. They decide to give her a few minutes.

A few minutes pass. Now the first assistant director knocks on the trailer door. Again the hairdresser appears and says the same thing. The first goes back to the director and tells him: "She won't come out." (I think, by the way, that this may be my favorite star story. Sure, it's outrageous, but eventually it gets funny and, strangely, human.)

Now the director sits in his chair and begins to ponder. She won't come out: *Why?*

The obvious answer hits him: script trouble; she doesn't like the scene she's going to play. He contemplates that awhile. He opens the screenplay, reads the sequence—

—she has told him she *likes* the sequence.

Can't be script trouble.

He thinks some more. Of course, he could have gone to the trailer himself at this point, but he felt that would be wrong. First of all, there's protocol going against it—it's not his job to escort talent to the set. The director is boss on the set. That's where he belongs. Beyond protocol there lies the subtle and always shifting balance of power. If he goes to get her now, he's giving in. Just a little, but still. And if he gives in a little today, who knows how much he'll have to give in tomorrow.

But dammit, why won't she come out?

She's *the* female star, and not unknown for outbursts, but this is not the kind of thing she ordinarily does.

And now the real answer comes clear: She won't come out because of his not letting her see the dailies. They had had words about the problem before shooting. She always saw dailies to her pictures, but he didn't want her to.

For the following reason: As famous as she is, she is insecure about her looks, and after viewing dailies the first week, she is notorious for having the cameraman fired.

The director didn't want to deal with that problem, so before he took the picture, when they met, he suggested that she be the cameraman. She said she didn't know how. He told her, well, let's hire the best man available who *does* know how and let him do his job.

She asked are you saying I can't see dailies?

He replied that that was the case.

Now, she is powerful and he could have been discarded. But she gave in. Because (1) she wanted him to do the picture and (2) he was young and hot and he didn't care if he did the picture or not.

Time is passing. Word reaches the picture's production office that nothing is going on. The star is entrenched in her dressing room and won't budge. The production office calls the head of the studio. The head of the studio calls his top vice president and says go handle this.

So the top vice president goes to the trailer and knocks, announcing himself, and opens the door—

—except he can't, because now it's locked.

And from inside comes the voice of the hairdresser saying the star is not ready and won't come out.

The top vice president trots back to the office of the studio head and the studio head himself decides to get everything back on track.

But she won't unlock the door for him either. There is only the voice of the hairdresser saying "Not now."

At which point the head of the studio, his top vice president, the production manager of the movie, and various other notables gather around the director, who is sitting as before, waiting in his chair.

Roughly, their message is this: It's your ass if you can't get her out of her trailer and onto the set. So the director goes to the trailer and knocks, giving his name.

Go away.

It's me, he says; let's talk.

Long, long pause. Then there is the sound of the door being unlocked and the hairdresser opens it and beckons and the director goes warily inside.

Where his star is silently crying her eyes out. As he moves toward her she falls into his arms and collapses, wailing now. He holds her—for five minutes he stands there with her limp in his arms, weeping out of control.

And in those five minutes the director realizes that he has

been wrong about the script and wrong about the dailies. This kind of grief can only be caused by one thing: Her marriage had shattered. She had been secretly seeing another performer and obviously her husband had found out and her husband had guided her career and now it was all *pfft.*

The director tries to calm her. "It's all right. Just take it easy. I'm on your side. We can talk about it. Whatever you tell me, I'm on your team, believe that." On and on he goes and on and on she cries. But eventually the sobs lessen; she is regaining at least the start of control.

He holds her, gently reassuring her. Finally, she is able to talk. He asks her if she feels up to going into the problem.

She nods.

Good, he says, what happened?

And then, haltingly, she gives the secret to her torment: Her toy poodle died the night before.

The director, an animal lover, tells her he understands.

No, you don't, she says; you don't understand at all. He died eating.

Eating?

Now she is crying again but able to talk. And her poodle did not die of kibble or Ken-L-Ration. Rather, as a treat, she had given him a great big juicy lamb chop for dinner and gone away and let him enjoy it.

The dog, apparently overcome with its good fortune, enjoyed it too quickly. He choked on the bone and nothing the star or her veterinarian did could bring him back. Not only has the star lost her pet, it's her fault—she had no business giving it a lamb chop in the first place.

The next little while the star and director talked about the dog and what a loss it was, and the director remembers thinking that all the terms they used were as if they were talking of a dead child. It was insane, but it was undeniably sad. Or it was sad, but it was undeniably insane.

Eventually, he got her to leave the trailer. But it was hours before the makeup people could hide the damage done to her face by her tears. . . .

There were no tears shed in this fourth and last behavior story. It was angry and it made many newspapers. The story was never denied. That doesn't make it any less gossipy, but it does suggest that the incident may well have happened.

The surprising thing to me is that it concerned that most professional of stage stars, Al Pacino. Of all the stars, he is the one who most consistently returns to the theatre and whom I find consistently brilliant. Theatre is still run on fairly strict lines: If you're late or you miss performances, word spreads immediately, almost always to the detriment of the show, sometimes damaging it to the point of closing.

Anyway, Pacino was making *Author! Author!* and the company was shooting an exterior scene in Gloucester, Massachusetts. In the winter.

The windchill factor was way below.

The whole crew was ready for the shot. Ready and waiting. Pacino stayed in his trailer for over an hour. When he finally emerged, he walked into the setup and decided he didn't like the lighting. Something about it reminded him of the lighting from an earlier film of his, *Cruising.* He wanted the lighting changed.

Arthur Hiller, as gentlemanly a director as any now operating, exploded. He told Pacino he was thoughtless and that a hundred people had been waiting in subfreezing weather. He said all this strongly.

Pacino responded strongly in kind, told Hiller off, gathered up his entourage, then plunged into his limousine and was gone. (He returned hours later, when it was no longer possible to do the shot.)

Now, I have no idea what this action cost the film. Maybe a hundred thousand dollars. I would think at least fifty. Whatever it set the picture back, you can bank that the money was not made up for out of Al Pacino's multimillion-dollar salary.

Temperamental stars affect screenwriters only tangentially. On occasion, if a star is too difficult, a studio may choose not to get involved with him even though he or she may be ideal for the script you've written. More often, if a poisonous atmosphere invades the sound stage, if crucial people are not speaking to each other except through intermediaries, the quality of the film can be affected. This is no law—some of the happiest sets produced the unhappiest results, and vice versa. It may not hurt your movie, but it probably won't do it a whole lot of good either.

Some stars do misbehave, in infinite ways, but always for the same reason: They do it because they can. . . .

REYNOLDS, EASTWOOD, AND STALLONE

Burt Reynolds and Clint Eastwood are not just the biggest stars in America (and probably the world), they are a good deal more. With the results of the '81 Quigley poll, they are setting popularity records that far exceed Gable or Cooper or Grant or just about any other movie star.

Reynolds was voted the top star for the fourth consecutive year. Only Bing Crosby had held the number-one spot longer—he had lasted five years—and the way Reynolds's career is going, I will be surprised if he doesn't tie Crosby when the '82 results are available.

Eastwood's record is equally remarkable: He has now been one of the top ten stars for *fourteen* years in a row. John Wayne has held a consistent hold on the public's fancy longer—sixteen years. But since Eastwood seems more at ease with himself than any other star, again, I will be surprised if he doesn't surpass Wayne three years down the line. Reynolds and Eastwood are genuinely phenomenal.

So, in a somewhat different way, is Sylvester Stallone. The success of *Rocky* (then without the roman numeral) lifted him from as much obscurity as any talented actor wants to deal with, to the top popularity spot in the country—he was number one in 1977.

Then came *F.I.S.T.*, a big-budget film and a disappointment. Followed by *Paradise Alley* (which he also directed)—a disaster, but at least a low-budget one. Then *Rocky II*. And this past year, two films: *Nighthawks* was another big-budget film and another disappointment. Most recently, *Victory*—expensive and a total wipeout. This year's Quigley poll doesn't even list Stallone in the top twenty-five stars, much less the top ten. And what is his reward for this career in which he has demonstrated four times in his last five outings that there are no multitudes waiting out there to receive him?

Ten—million—dollars.

For that is the amount Stallone is being paid to write, direct, and star in *Rocky III*. Have you ever heard such madness? Can you believe that figure? Probably the largest amount of money ever paid a performer in the entire history of the civilized world. Isn't that insanity?

Me, I think it's a steal.

To try and make sense of that, I must now deal with the major exception that I mentioned in the first sentence of this discussion on stars.

WHAT IS THE MAJOR EXCEPTION?

Well . . . it's . . . it's something.

I mean it's there, it's just hard to isolate. And "something" may be about as close as I'm going to come.

Paul Newman, in discussing the careers of European versus American stars, put it this way: "One of the difficult things is that American filmgoers seem less able and willing to accept actors or actresses in a wide variety of roles—they get something they hook on to and they like, and *that's* what they want to see."

In the case of Stallone, they could care less about him as a labor leader or a soccer goalie. But let him be Rocky Balboa, the pug, and they'll stand happily in line for hours.

As I am writing this chapter, it is March and *Rocky III* won't be out till summer. I haven't seen it, haven't heard boo about it. But I don't just think it's going to be a hit, I wouldn't be surprised if it turned out to be bigger than the original. My reason isn't logical, but of all the sequels of recent years, *Rocky II* came closer to being a remake than any other. It was the same song, second verse, except this time the final decision of the fight was different. My guess is that Stallone, being the shrewd and skilled writer that he is, will ring in some innovations this time. (By the time this book comes out, *Rocky III* will probably be on cable, but I won't change this paragraph under any conditions. So we'll see what kind of studio executive I'd make.)

And though Stallone may be an extreme example, the same kind of point can be made about our two biggest stars. Eastwood has to beat up on people. When he doesn't, as in *The Beguiled* or the more recent and very sweet *Bronco Billy*, a film that he also directed, the audience is considerably smaller. *Bronco Billy*, for example, attracted less than a third of the audience than the Eastwood film that preceded it, *Any Which Way You Can*. Clint Eastwood is really only Clint Eastwood when he's the toughest guy on the block.

And Reynolds, in the four years he's been at the top, is only Reynolds when he can get his hands on the wheel of a car and have extraordinary adventures. When he acts an ordinary guy (*Starting Over*) or Cary Grant (*Rough Cut, Paternity*), forget it.

One final extreme example: In the four years of his self-imposed retirement, Steve McQueen was getting unreal offers. A million a week for three weeks in two different movies, back-to-back. Six million for a month and a half's work. He was *the* international star. Well, during that time he made one movie, *An Enemy of the People—*

—and no one would book it. (I think it tried a run somewhere—maybe Minneapolis—and expired before the first fortnight.)

The public didn't want McQueen in *Ibsen*, for chrissakes. They wanted bang-bang pictures; they had no interest in seeing him *act*.

I'm sure McQueen knew that before he started *An Enemy of the People*. Just as I'm sure Reynolds knows where his power lies. So why does he keep trying to expand his scope, why isn't he satisfied just doing Smokey?

I don't know Reynolds, but I've followed his career enough to be positive of this: *He's serious.* He got his first stage part in 1956 and was good enough a year later to get cast in a major revival of *Mister Roberts* at New York's City Center. And he was good enough a few years after that to get one of the top roles in *Look, We've Come Through* by Hugh Wheeler, a writer who was good enough to win not one but three Tony awards.

And look what Reynolds has been through. All those dreary tv series—*Riverboat, Hawk, Dan August.* And look at his earlier film doozies—*Navajo Joe* and *Sam Whiskey* and *Shark!* He was damn near two decades in the wilderness, doing crap because he had to; now, when he doesn't have to, why shouldn't he do what he pleases? (Why the studios continue to let him do what he pleases is a question we'll attack in the next section.)

So there is this strange "something," this nerve that is struck simultaneously in audiences all around the world. And when that happens, it's like discovering a vein of gold. Which is, of course, wonderful. But which also makes for a certain nervousness, because no one can predict the richness of the vein, or its breadth, or its depth, or when it will run dry. . . .

So, with the major exception aside, stars are essentially

meaningless. Studio executives know this—they know that *the picture is the star.*

But they are paying four million plus to Dustin Hoffman to appear in *Tootsie.* Of Hoffman's last three films, *Agatha* and *Straight Time* were disasters. The other was *Kramer Vs. Kramer,* for which he deserved every award he got. But don't tell me the picture would have stiffed if Redford or Nicholson had played the lead. The picture was the star. To repeat, studio executives know that to be true. They absolutely, positively, one hundred percent in their heart of hearts, in the dark nights of the souls, they *know* it.

They just don't believe it, that's all. . . .

EDUCATION

Most stars don't have much formal education.

(I know this must seem a bizarre and unimportant grace note, but please bear with me because I'd like to persuade you otherwise.) I think Barbra Streisand finished high school. I'm not sure Hoffman or Minnelli did. I think Jane Fonda may have had a year of college, Redford the same or less, Beatty the same or less, Travolta the same or less, Nicholson the same or less, many more the same or less.

Now, this doesn't mean they're not bright. I've never met a star who wasn't clever and shrewd and loaded with more street smarts than I'll collect in a lifetime.

What it does mean is this: early entry.

And when you come into show business early, there is one simple truth that applies to one and all: The business takes over your life.

At a time when a nineteen-year-old may be trying to figure out Joyce's symbolism in a course in contemporary fiction, the nineteen-year-old performer is trying to figure out how to get in to see an agent. And so, more than likely, is everyone he knows.

And when this nineteen-year-old attends a dramatic event, he may actually be thinking about it—but usually what he's thinking is that great theatrical cliché: "I could have played that part."

Once you're in the business, it permeates your mind. So

when our performer reads a script, what he thinks is "*I'd* be great here; and I'd *kill* 'em there; no, I don't want to play that scene the way it's written."

They are thinking of themselves in the part and how that part may work for them and what may be altered to make it work for them; because of early entry, that's mostly what they know.

How to make it work for them.

Which is not the same as how to make the project work as a whole. (Elizabeth Taylor was famous, at least in legend, for never reading an entire script, just her own lines. No one's had a more fabulous career; maybe she knew something the rest of us didn't.)

By now we're aware of the power of stars. The way that power most manifests itself is this: not in the material you see on screen (that's something the studio decides) *but in the way that material is treated.*

And I can give no better example of how that affects screenwriters than in discussing the movie that follows.

THE GREAT SANTINI

Speaking purely as a screenwriter, as someone who must deal with stars, no scene in recent years has rocked me as much as the basketball-playing scene in *The Great Santini.* I'll try and describe the lead-up to the scene, the sequence itself, and then why it took my head off.

The movie, written by Lewis John Carlino, from Pat Conroy's novel, starred Robert Duvall, Blythe Danner, and Michael O'Keefe (and the work of those three—father, mother, and son—was world class). Duvall played the lead role, that of a great Marine fighter pilot whose name is Bull Meachum.

But it's 1962 and there are no wars to fight. The movie opens in Spain, where we see Meachum in action during air maneuvers, then watch him with his buddies, making a wonderful mess of a fancy restaurant.

Bull is sent home to a new assignment, and his family meets him at the airport. Danner, O'Keefe—a high school basketball player—and three smaller children. As they wait for the plane to taxi in, Danner admonishes the kids to wait for their father to come to them, because he'll probably hold inspection, but when he alights, his arms go wide and they bolt for him.

Which is not to say Bull isn't tough. The family drives to a new rented house, and there he harangues them to shape up, calls them hogs: "Listen, hogs—" is his standard family greeting. You sense he cares, but that's from inside the actor and the character, not from the lines.

Now Bull goes to his new post. We learn several things— chiefly, that he's been passed over for promotion and that his new boss, who has requested him, loathes him. But the superior officer wanted Bull for a reason: The Marine squadron is in rotten shape and he, the superior officer, has no intention of being passed over when his time for promotion comes. So Bull is to bring the squadron up to speed.

Bull meets the squadron and, in a brilliant speech, scares the crap out of them. He tells them, "I don't want you to consider me as just your commanding officer. I want you to look on me as if I was . . . well . . . God. If *I* say something, *you* pretend it was coming from the Burning Bush." He finishes off by saying, "You're flying with Bull Meachum now, and I kid you not, this is the eye of the storm."

Then comes the basketball scene.

It's in the backyard of the rented house, Blythe Danner and the three youngest are sitting happily around, watching Duvall and O'Keefe play a game of one-on-one, the first to score ten baskets wins. It's all very idyllic, the family happily cheering on the underdog son. O'Keefe and Duvall engage in a little taunting family banter, the kid has the ball. He fakes, shoots, and scores.

1–0, for the son.

Duvall takes the ball out, maneuvers, scores.

1–1 tie.

O'Keefe takes the ball out, puts on another move, slips past Duvall—and just as he goes up for the shot, Duvall shoves him against a fence. The family starts chanting "Dirty," but O'Keefe says "No foul." His shot has gone in in spite of Duvall's tactics.

The son is ahead of the father, 2–1.

Now there is a quick dissolve: We're later in the game.

It's 8–6, in favor of the father.

As he scores, Duvall shouts out, "All right, who's for me?"

The answer is immediately evident: Everyone's rooting for the kid.

And tension is mounting.

Duvall's play, which has always been rough, is now far past that. This is combat, something he knows about. And he's winning.

And now, another dissolve.

The score is tied, 9–9.

Duvall takes the ball out. "Last shot of the game coming up," he says. He dribbles this way, that—

—and the kid steals the ball from him.

The boy bounces the ball, talking to the Bull. He says that none of the family has ever beaten him in anything, not checkers, not dominoes, not softball.

Don't goad him, the mother calls out to the son.

The boy still bounces the ball. He tries moving toward the basket, Duvall shoves him back. He tries another way, again he's shoved away. The rest of the kids are trying to cheer him on—

—and the kid fights off another illegal shove, shoots, scores.

Game over, 10–9, the son wins.

Duvall stands tossing the ball in frustration as his wife and kids rush to the boy, congratulating him. One daughter goes to Duvall and says, "You played a great game, Dad."

And Duvall says, "Get out of here before I knock every freckle off your face." Crushed, the girl bursts into tears and runs into the house.

Then Duvall says to his son that the game isn't over, you have to win by two baskets.

The kid says that those weren't the rules.

Duvall persists.

The kid is hesitant, willing to give in, but Blythe Danner goes to Duvall and says no, he beat you, don't try and cheat him out of it.

He throws the ball at her, tells her to shut up or he'll kick her butt.

Surprised, terribly hurt, she runs into the house too. Next he insults the remaining two small children and they take off.

The father and the son are alone on the court, facing each other, standing close. But the boy has changed his mind—he won't play on now, because his father has behaved so badly.

Duvall says, "Mama's boy, Mama's boy, bet you're gonna cry." And he takes the basketball and sharply bounces it against the kid's forehead, catches it, does it again, a third time, again and again, all the time saying, "Come on, let's see you cry, come on, cry."

The boy is deeply upset and he turns, walks past the father into the house. But Duvall follows him inside and then up the stairs. And all the time he's bouncing the ball against his son's head, going "One, two, three, cry. One, two, three, cry." And the first tosses, outside, were by no means love taps. But now he's really throwing hard, the ball careening against the back of the retreating boy's head. "One, two, three, cry."

Finally they're at the son's door. They face each other a moment. "You're my favorite daughter," Duvall says. "My sweetest little girl." The son finally explodes—"This 'little girl' just whipped you good, Colonel"—and hurries inside his room to be alone.

Obviously my retelling can't come close to conveying the power and brilliance of the scene. But please believe me, it was brilliant and moving, filled with the knowledge of family love, family frustration, hate, and the wisdom of showing the proximity of these moods, how the one seamlessly shifts into the other. And growing up and getting old, battles that can't be won or lost, only fought over and over till the grave.

I blessed Carlino and Conroy for their talents as writers and director, and I blessed Danner and O'Keefe for theirs as performers. But most of all, I blessed that great *character actor*, Robert Duvall. Because if you are a screenwriter, and you wrote this wonderful scene, there is one simple fact you must never forget—

—*no major star would ever ever ever in this world play it.*

Why?

Two reasons: One—the guy's a loser. And two—the guy's an unsympathetic son of a bitch after he's lost.

Now, I know and you know that the Duvall character is, if anything, heroic. And your heart breaks for him in the film. But we are not stars and stars don't think that way.

Oh, they wouldn't necessarily insist the scene be excised

from the film. But what they would do is gently insist on a few teeny-weeny changes. Let's divide the scene into its two main actions: the game and its aftermath.

Taking the first. They would absolutely lose to the boy. But you'd have to add this kind of sequence before the game began.

```
CUT TO


    DUVALL. He enters the living room of the house,
    basketball in hand. BLYTHE DANNER sits quietly in
    a chair.

                    DUVALL
            Hey, Blythe, baby, I'm going to
            play our eldest a little one-on-
            one, come out and watch.
                    (she says nothing, instead
                    stares  quietly  out  the
                    window, full of emotions)
            What's up, hon? Something wrong?


                    DANNER
                    (her words come in a tor-
                    mented burst)
            Oh, Bobby, I'm so worried about the
            boy--he's got such potential, he
            could really be a wonderful ath-
            lete, but every time he gets into a
            school game, something holds him
            back.
                    (shaking her head)
            The child just can't shake the
            feeling that he's not good enough.


                    DUVALL
            That old inferiority, huh?


                    DANNER
            I wonder sometimes if he'll ever
            lose it.
```

                    DUVALL
            You think I'm too hard on him?

                    DANNER
            No-no, you're a wonderful father.

                    DUVALL
            Of course you know he's never beat-
            en me.

                    DANNER
            And he never will.

                    DUVALL
                (a long pause; then, mean-
                ingfully--)
            Oh, I don't know about that, some-
            day it's bound to happen.
                (he reaches for her hand.
                She hesitates, takes it,
                smiles at him, and they go
                out to the court)

In other words, the star will lose if—big if—*we* know he could
win if he wanted to. As long as he can wink at the audience and
have them know his cock is still the biggest around, he'll lose,
and gladly.

And he'll bounce the ball against the kid's head all you want.
If you add a sequence before he does it that goes something
like this:

CUT TO

DUVALL. He enters the kitchen after the game,
pours himself some iced tea. BLYTHE DANNER stands
quietly in a corner.

                    DUVALL
            Some game the kid played, beating
            me like that, huh, Blythe? He'll be

a whiz in his school games now for
sure.
>   (she says nothing, instead
>   stares quietly out the
>   window)
Something wrong, hon?

                    DANNER
Oh, Bobby, I'm so worried about the
boy--he keeps everything inside.
He's all bottled up, afraid to express himself. There's a great human being locked inside, but I'm so
frightened he'll never be able to
show an emotion, anger, anything.

                    DUVALL
That old repression, huh?

                    DANNER
I wonder sometimes if he'll ever
lose it.

                    DUVALL
You think I dominate him too much?

                    DANNER
No--no, you're a perfect father.

                    DUVALL
Of course, you know he's never lost
his temper at me.

                    DANNER
And he never will.

                    DUVALL
>   (a long pause; then, mean-
>   ingfully--)
Oh, I don't know about that, someday it's bound to happen.
>   (he puts his ice tea down,
>   swats her on the fanny, and
>   goes back out)

Now the star will go out and bounce the ball against the kid's head as long as you want. He'll beat the kid for hours if you want that too. He'll follow the kid up to his room, hurling the most vilifying remarks imaginable.

Because now we know he's still the same neat guy you loved on the Johnny Carson show. And when the kid finally yells at him, hey, terrific—we know he's only been mean for the boy's own good.

Here is one of the basic lessons a screenwriter must learn and live with: Stars will not play weak and they will not play blemished, and you better know that now.

Sure, Brando and Pacino will play Mafia chieftains in *The Godfather*. But those are cute Mafia chieftains. They're only warring on bad Mafia guys and crooked cops; they're only trying to hold the family business together. Try asking a major star to play a *real* Mafia head, a man who makes his living off whores and child pornography, heroin and blood; sorry folks, those parts go to the character actors, or the has-beens. Or actors on the come who haven't yet achieved star status.

Of course De Niro will play a psychopath in *Taxi Driver*. Some psychopath—he risks his life trying to save the virtue of your everyday ordinary-looking child prostitute, Jodie Foster.

Lawrence Kasdan, Hollywood's hottest (*The Empire Strikes Back, Raiders of the Lost Ark*) and I think best (*Body Heat*) young screenwriter, had some wonderfully penetrating things to say in a recent interview:

> If I thought that was all I could ever do and that I would constantly be turning over these works of love to other people and having them changed, I don't know how long I could do it. . . .
> . . . The movie comes out and there's the pain that *your* movie never got made; there's this other movie instead. But everyone says you wrote it, and they blame you for it anyway. So you're getting it from both sides, from inside and outside.

Clearly, that's true, but perhaps it doesn't go far enough. Look, we are wonders, those of us still left walking on the earth. We can create leaders ranging from Churchill to Attila, singers from Caruso to Florence Foster Jenkins, writers from Shakespeare to Beverly Aadland's mother.

In the world of the screenplay, not only are you terribly limited as to what subject matter is viable; your *treatment* of that subject matter is infinitely more restricted by the power of the star.

Which is why I truly believe that if *all* you do with your life is write screenplays, it ultimately has to denigrate the soul. You may get lucky and get rich, but you sure won't get happy. Because you will spend your always-decreasing days doing the following: writing Perfect Parts for Perfect People.

And there's got to be more to the human condition than that. . . .

Studio Executives

Studio executives are intelligent, brutally overworked men and women who share one thing in common with baseball managers: They wake up every morning of the world with the knowledge that sooner or later they're going to get fired.

In the old days of the great studios, this situation didn't exist. The Harry Cohns and the Louis Mayers fully expected to be in their traces till they dropped. Their modern counterparts are under a totally different system: They must get results—*now*— or they're gone. There is perhaps more executive shuffling in any single year now than existed in the entirety of the nineteen thirties or forties.

And with this pressure always on them, always mounting, each "go" decision they make becomes excruciating—one of the reasons why, right now, no one in Hollywood wants to make movies. (As of June, 1982, film starts were down exactly fifty percent from a year ago.)

The "go" decision is the ultimate importance of the studio executive. They are responsible for what gets up there on the silver screen. Compounding their problem of no job security in the decision-making process is the single most important fact, perhaps, of the entire movie industry:

NOBODY KNOWS ANYTHING.

If there is a Roman numeral *I* to this book, that's it. (Actually, there are two Roman numeral *I*'s to this book, but I won't get to the second until the chapter on *Butch Cassidy and the Sundance Kid.*)

Again, for emphasis—

NOBODY KNOWS ANYTHING.

Not one person in the entire motion picture field *knows* for a certainty what's going to work. Every time out it's a guess— and, if you're lucky, an educated one.

They don't know when the movie is finished: B. J. Thomas's people, after the first sneak of *Butch,* were upset about their client's getting involved with the song "Raindrops Keep Fallin' on My Head." One of them was heard to say, more than once, "B. J. really hurt himself with this one."

The initial preview of *Star!* was such a success that Richard Zanuck cancelled any further previews and sent a wire to his father, Darryl, that said, "We're home. Better than *Sound of Music.*"

The Sound of Music was then the most popular movie in history, and *Star!* went on to become the Edsel of 20th Century-Fox: No matter how they readvertised it or changed the logo or the title, no one came. And Richard Zanuck has as keen a mind about commercial films as anyone.

They don't know when the movie is starting to shoot either. David Brown, Zanuck's partner, has said, "We didn't know whether *Jaws* would work, but we didn't have any doubts about *The Island.* It had to be a smash. Everything worked. The screenplay worked. Every actor we sent it to said yes. I didn't know until a few days after we opened and I was in a bookstore and I ran into Lew Wasserman and said 'How're we doing?' and he said, 'David, they don't want to see the picture.' "

They don't want to see the picture—maybe the most chilling phrase in the industry.

Now, if the best people around don't know at sneaks, and they don't know during shooting, you better believe that executives don't know when they're trying to give a thumbs-up or -down; they're trying to predict public taste three years ahead and it's just not possible.

Obviously, I'm asking you to take my word on this and there's no reason really that you should, because pictures such as *Raiders of the Lost Ark* probably come to mind. Which, I grant, was an unusual film.

Raiders is the number-four film in history as this is being written. I don't remember any movie that had such power going in. It was more or less the brainchild of George Lucas and was directed by Steven Spielberg, the two unquestioned wunderkinder of show business (*Star Wars, Jaws,* etc.). Probably you all knew that. But did you know that *Raiders of the Lost Ark* was offered to every single studio in town—

—and they all turned it down?

All except Paramount.

Why did Paramount say yes? Because nobody knows anything. And why did all the other studios say no? Because nobody knows anything. And why did Universal, the mightiest studio of all, pass on *Star Wars*, a decision that just may cost them, when all the sequels and spinoffs and toy money and book money and video-game money are totaled, over a *billion* dollars? Because nobody, *nobody*—not now, not ever—knows the least goddam thing about what is or isn't going to work at the box office.

One additional anguish executives must cope with is that hot streaks don't last. A recent newspaper article mentioned how the other studios were gloating over what was happening at Columbia.

Columbia had been sizzling, but then *Annie* went wildly over budget. And an expensive action film wouldn't cut together coherently. And everybody knew that the set of *Tootsie* was not where you wanted to spend your summer vacation.

And they had passed on *E.T.*

Columbia had had it, developed it for a million dollars, took a survey, and discovered the audience for the movie would be too limited to make it profitable. So they let it go. (Universal picked it up and may make back the billion they didn't earn by dropping *Star Wars*.)

David Picker, a fine studio executive for many years, once said something to this effect: "If I had said yes to all the projects I turned down, and no to all the ones I took, it would have worked out about the same."

In any case, do not send to know why studio executives have insomnia. It goes with the territory. . . .

WHO ARE STUDIO EXECUTIVES?

Mostly, today, they are agents.

Ex-agents, more accurately. And a lot of people interviewed for this book feel that that accounts, more than any single thing, for Hollywood's present plight. I'm not at all sure I agree with the conclusion, but I can summarize the wisdom behind it.

Let's begin with some agent jokes; there are *always* agent jokes in Hollywood and the most recent ones I've heard are these: A patient goes to see a surgeon about having a heart transplant. The surgeon says, "I'll give you a choice: You can either have the heart of a twenty-five-year-old marathon runner or a sixty-year-old agent, which do you want?" And the patient answers, "Easy—let me have the agent's." And the surgeon, dumbfounded, says, "Why would you pick the heart of a sixty-year-old agent over a twenty-five-year-old marathon runner?" And the patient replies, "I want one that's never been used."

Or this one: An agent and a bunch of other passengers are on a boat in dangerous waters and the agent falls overboard, and before anyone can do anything this giant shark comes swimming up, and when the shark is six feet away he veers off and swims in another direction, and one of the passengers says, "Did you see that, did you see what just happened, it's an act of God," and another passenger answers, "That wasn't an act of God, it was professional courtesy."

All agent jokes are based on that same premise: Agents are not noted for human kindness. Now, in point of fact, this is not true. (I'm serious.) Most of the major agents I've come in contact with are decent human beings.

But probably one can make a certain valid generalization about agents, and it's this: Their primary interest is not in the art object but in the deal. That's not criticism, that's basic logic—if a man makes his living off ten percent of his client's earnings, the more those earnings, the more meaningful his percentage. That's his job. As an agent.

But it's not his job when he changes hats.

Agents become studio heads primarily for one reason: No one else will undertake the occupation. It's *terrible* work. It's seven days a week, it's mornings and evenings, it's getting killed by agents who are still agents. It's escalating costs, it's getting killed by their boards of directors, who are screaming that costs are too high.

So why do agents accept the responsibility? Because, in many ways, it's better than being an agent. There's more power and generally there's more money.

So we've got an ex-agent running our studio. What can we say about him? A lot of good things. He's hardworking. He's shrewd as hell. He's got a lot of contacts in the business. He understands a great deal about how the business operates.

What he doesn't understand, generally speaking, is passion.

Just as in the old days, when he didn't care about the film as much as the deal, the same holds true now. He never, most likely, has worked on a film, never written one or produced one, most certainly never directed one. People are coming at him day and night with projects—"I must make this. You must give me my chance." The agent, being unused to working this side of the street, seeks help from two sources: (1) stars, because he understands them from his earlier life, and (2) the business end of the studio, the people who handle the selling of films. Because they *never* cared about passion, and because they, at least in theory, know what will sell and what won't. (We know that's not true, and the business people do, too, but obviously if they admit it, they get drummed from the corps; my God, what are business people *for* if they don't know.)

Business people do know one thing: what they can book into theatres in advance. Theatre owners often don't see the product they're buying until it's too late, so if they are given a choice between a Steve Martin musical and a movie about two English guys running in the 1924 Olympics, logic dictates which way they swing.

I think it's safe to say that today, more than ever in Hollywood history, the business types hold sway. They are kept in close touch on every conceivable project that the studio may contemplate. And what they say matters. Matters crucially. In the old days, a studio head might have said, "Let's make the goddam movie and hope the business guys know how to sell it."

Such words are not much uttered nowadays. . . .

THE THREE *S*'s

Hollywood has always been a caste-system town. An ancient survivor told me: "When I was a fifteen-hundred-a-week writer, it was understood I didn't associate with another guy who only got seven-fifty. And the twenty-five-hundred-dollar guys didn't want me contaminating them. And it's the same with the other jobs—top directors knew top directors, big stars didn't pal around with unknowns. Oh, maybe they'd keep them as gofers, but when it was a heavy social situation that needed attending, the gofers were gone."

Of course this holds true with studio executives. They tend to know each other—they may have worked at the same agencies at the same time. And naturally, they are all competitive, one with the other. Out of this situation comes their reliance on stars. And that need can be divided into thirds, which can be called the three *S*'s.

S Number One: Social

This is more than one executive or his wife being able to say, casually, "Just made a two-picture deal with Burt." Or "Clint just signed on, we go in April." This is important in and of itself. If you've got nobody to talk about, it can make for grim going at a cocktail party.

A deeper need for parity comes not from individual social needs but from those of a studio itself.

One example: When the Arthur Krim group left United Artists to form Orion, there were rumors all around the industry that the new United Artists people weren't in the big time anymore. This was dangerous to United Artists because it meant that major "elements"—stars, directors, producers—might avoid going to UA with their projects. (Studios rarely initiate projects anymore. A package of sorts will be put together and brought to them and they will decide whether to put up the money. This abdication of what was once the essential role of the studio is as big a change as any in Hollywood.)

Anyway, here's UA, shunned and forlorn. So what did they do? They bought, for the record-breaking sum of two and a half million dollars, Gay Talese's sex book, *Thy Neighbor's Wife.* There was great publicity and the studio announced they would make not one but two major films out of the material. (They have made, to this date, a grand total of none and things seem likely to stay that way.)

Now, the thing that made the Talese buy remarkable wasn't just the incredible sum. The book was famous long before publication, and the logical assumption would be, to grab such a property at such a price, you have to outbid competition. I mean, the reason you pay two million five has got to be that someone else bid two million four.

Well, the rumor around town was that nobody else bid anything for the Talese.

UA paid that amount for two reasons: The first, obviously, was to acquire the property. But the most important was the second: They were announcing to the Hollywood community, *"Hey, we're still here."* Probably they could have bought the book for half or less than half of what they spent. But that wouldn't have served their purpose—they *needed* to blow the money. It served to put them back up there with their peers.

A sadder example of this social need for equality was a move the Orion people made. They also had to prove they were still heavyweights, so they made a zillion deals. Including one where they gave John Travolta *control* of any movies he did for them. Travolta was then maybe twenty-five with two leads behind him. Giving someone with that lack of track record control only betrayed Orion's desperation. Which was sad, at least for me, because they were, when at UA, maybe the top group in the business. But maybe it was worth it to them, since they could then say, "Look, everybody, we've got John Travolta."

S Number Two: Shorthand

It speeds things up when you have stars. If you say, "We're doing a Goldie Hawn picture," you don't have to go on. The performer sets the framework of the product. If you say you've got *Chariots of Fire*, you're going to have to go on and on explicating just what it is that you're talking about.

This shorthand is especially helpful to the business people at the studio.

This past holiday season, UA had four pictures out in the marketplace. (A different UA group, by the by, than the people who bought the Talese book—who'd come and quickly gone.) It was a tremendous lineup and quickly describable: "We've got Peter Falk in a raunchy comedy, Richard Dreyfuss in a Broadway smash, Lemmon and Matthau together again with Billy Wilder, and Steve Martin in a musical."

It's no wonder with product like that, they were able to get fabulous bookings in the best theatres all around the country. And with those fabulous bookings what did they achieve? The four films—*All the Marbles, Whose Life Is It Anyway?, Buddy, Buddy,* and *Pennies from Heaven*—probably lost a minimum of fifty million dollars, maybe as much as seventy-five.

But they got booked in theatres. Which is the name of the game for the business people at the studios. Should we be surprised at the theatre owners grabbing those movies? Of course not, they'd have been out of their gourds not to. Should we be surprised at the failures of the films? A very faint maybe. Clearly, this is hindsight, which never fails. And again, nobody ever knows. But each of these films had a giant problem attached. Let's take them in the order in which they opened.

The Peter Falk film, *All the Marbles.* In description it still sounds terrific. It's a raunchy comedy in which Falk plays the manager of two gorgeous girls who are tag-team wrestling partners. It takes place, for the most part, in raunchy tank towns, with Falk always the hustler. And no one plays that kind of sleazy character better than Peter Falk.

The problem: The movie takes pro wrestling *seriously.* We know that when Bruno Sammartino enters the ring, he's pretty much a shoo-in. He may get pounded, he may be beaten almost senseless. But one way or another, he's going to triumph. Whether pro wrestling is actually rehearsed or not, I have no idea. But the outcome is not in doubt.

All the Marbles treated each match as if it were the pro football playoffs leading toward the Superbowl. The matches, we were asked to believe, weren't fixed or phony, any more than the seventh game of the World Series. Would an audience buy that premise? When I saw the movie they sure didn't.

The Richard Dreyfuss film, *Whose Life Is It Anyway?* This was certainly a famous show on Broadway: Tom Conti won the Tony for his performance, and then, with tremendous publicity, Mary Tyler Moore took over the part, for which she was also awarded. But it was never much of a commercial hit. I don't think it ever had a single sellout week. It was well reviewed—as was the movie—but perhaps the problem was the subject matter.

Whose Life deals with a young sculptor who is totally crippled in an auto accident. He's incapable of moving from the neck down. And the story is that of his right to have himself killed. *Coming Home* dealt with a cripple, too, and it did business. But it was a romance. And no matter how the ads for *Whose Life* tried to sell you that it was about life, it wasn't. The ads on *F.I.S.T.* tried to tell us it wasn't a story of a labor union organizer but about a *man.* But hey, that man was a labor union organizer. And *Whose Life* dealt with death. Would the audience want to see such subject matter? Maybe treated as a fantasy—*Heaven Can Wait*—but treated realistically? They never have.

The Lemmon/Matthau/Billy Wilder comedy, *Buddy, Buddy.* Lemmon and Matthau have proved a superb comedy team, most successfully in *The Odd Couple* back in '68. And Billy Wilder? Unquestionably one of the great directors and one who is most skilled at comedic material. In one half-decade, his comedies included *Sabrina, The Seven Year Itch, Some Like It Hot,* and *The Apartment.* But his last major success was *Irma la Douce,* and that in 1963. Problem: Could their commercial skills be resurrected? Alas, they could not.

The Steve Martin musical, *Pennies from Heaven.* Martin is a cult figure for young people, and his only previous movie, *The Jerk,* was one of the most successful comedies ever. Martin and Richard Pryor I would think are the top two young comics in the business.

But *Pennies from Heaven* was a musical. And it wasn't meant primarily to be funny. Set in the Depression, Martin played a down-and-out song plugger who eventually gets sent up for murder. The actors simply mouthed all the songs: The actual voices were real records of the Depression era.

So the emphasis on the musical numbers fell, naturally enough, on the dances. And the simple fact is that Steve Martin isn't much of a dancer. Oh, he tried, he executed steps, he obviously worked his buns off learning to be a hoofer. But it was a case of the dancing bear—it's not that he does it well but that he can do it at all. For the truth is, there has never been a Broadway musical in the history of the world for which Steve Martin would have been good enough to get cast in the chorus.

Problem: Can you have a musical succeed in which the main character can't thrill you? I happen not to think so. With Kelly or Astaire, *Pennies from Heaven* might have gone through the roof. The audience I saw it with began wanting desperately to love it, and they ended—those who didn't walk out—whipped and silent.

To repeat, this was hindsight. And I think if I had been the studio executive that had a shot at these projects, I would have grabbed them all. Maybe they didn't work on the screen.

But they sure sounded great in shorthand. . . .

S Number Three: Salvation

As stated, the knowledge of their eventual decapitation is central to the life of the studio executive. And as also stated, when that happens, they will "go indie-prod," which is both easier and more lucrative. So why do the executives care at all if their movies succeed? Because there is a giant caveat involved: the better they've done as executives, the longer their life span, the fatter the deal they can strike for themselves when they're canned. None of the *Heaven's Gate* group at UA got rich when they were told to get lost.

So it's essential to the studio executive to be, at least for a time, successful.

And since nobody knows anything, and since the studio heads today haven't got a lot of faith in their creative instincts (since they've never been creative), they turn, for salvation, to the one thing that got them where they are: stars.

If you have a slate of films that are low budget and successful, as Frank Price had recently at Columbia, you're obviously in great shape. But if you have a slate of low-budget films that stiff, you're not just a failure, you're a double disaster: Not only did your pictures die, you couldn't even attract "elements."

Well, you can't have that. Which is why the cry of every studio executive on the way to the guillotine has been the same: "You can't do this to me, I got you a Charles Bronson picture. I was the one who signed Stallone. Ryan O'Neal only did our movie because we have a strong personal relationship. Kris Kristofferson thinks I'm creative. Jimmy Caan told me personally he wants to work for me again. And so did Donald Sutherland. And Chuck Heston. Liza and Ali and I are buddies. And Lee Marvin and I have dinner together. And . . . and—"

—and the blade always falls.

One fact of movie life must always be faced: Stars are kept in orbit by studio executives who are trying to save their own jobs. . . .

THE NONRECURRING PHENOMENON

Studio executives, as we have observed, are totally responsible for what we see on the screen. I'm sure even the biggest stars have some pet subject or another they can't get off the ground—Jane Fonda has been trying for years to make a movie about industrial cancer, for example. We've also noted that they, like the rest of us, don't know what will work. But there is one thing they absolutely do know, and that is what *has* worked. Which is why it is safe to say that *movies are always a search for past magic.*

"Shit, if I could just get Richard Pryor and Gene Wilder together again, I'd be safe." (I know of one project in which the studio bought a book for a producer and had a screenplay written, which the studio liked, except they wanted one little change in the next draft: The main character had to be changed from white to black. Why? Because Richard Pryor is hot again, that's why.)

They know from their accountants what worked in the past, and they can give you the reasons why. Here is a list of films released in 1981 that took in twenty-five million dollars.

Raiders of the Lost Ark	$90,000,000
Superman II	64,000,000
Stripes	39,000,000
Any Which Way You Can	39,000,000
Arthur	37,000,000
The Cannonball Run	35,000,000
The Four Seasons	26,000,000
For Your Eyes Only	25,000,000

Ask a studio executive about these successes, and he'll say: "*Raiders?* Great adventure picture, great special effects, Lucas and Spielberg. Great adventure pictures always clean up. *Arthur?* Great romantic comedy; always room for a great romantic comedy. And the public was falling in love with Dudley Moore. The rest are really sequels to other hits in one way or another, and sequels always do great. *Superman II* was a sequel, so was the Eastwood, so was the Bond flick. *Stripes* was like *Meatballs;* there's always a market for Bill Murray in a comedy. And *Cannonball* was Reynolds in a *Smokey* rip-off. That everything?"

Well, it's *almost* everything, but what about *Four Seasons*?

Then our mythical studio man says this: "It was Alan Alda and Carol Burnett. They've got a lot of fans."

You respectfully point out that if they have so many fans, why have almost all their previous movies been failures?

There then follows a longer silence before you get his final answer: "*Four Seasons*? That was a 'nonrecurring phenomenon.' "

Remember that phrase.

What it means, of course, is this: It was a freak, a fluke, a once-in-a-lifetime occurrence. The deeper and more important meaning is this: "Get away, boy, you bother me." It's a nonrecurring phenomenon—*I don't have to think about it.*

And why don't they want to think about it? It's too frightening—they are responsible for what gets made and they can live with not knowing if what they make is going to work or not. But not even knowing the *kind* of thing to make—well, the earth opens.

Why haven't there been rip-offs of *Kramer Vs. Kramer*? (Tv has done a bunch, but not Hollywood.) Because *Kramer* was a nonrecurring phenomenon. And so was *Ordinary People.*

Four Seasons had nothing going for it—no movie stars, no violence, it wasn't even all that funny. It was just this lovely movie about—about *friendships,* for chrissakes. So its success both depresses and frightens studio people. The audience, *their* audience—well, it shouldn't have gone. And in point of fact it didn't, not in the beginning. Who did?

There is a lot of talk in Hollywood as to what happened to the *Sound of Music* audience. I mean adults over twenty-five and children under twelve. Executives refer to it as "The Lost Audience." It's gone, simple as that—lost and by the wind grieved, never to come back again, locked forever with their living-room tube. Well, they left their homes long enough to see *Four Seasons.*

And there's one other 1981 hit that I didn't list earlier, because it opened too late in the year for its fate to be known. It's March as I write this, and the ultimate success of *On Golden Pond* is still not certain: How it does in the coming Oscar battle will affect it, as will the effect that word of mouth exerts. But *On Golden Pond* is already more popular than *For Your Eyes Only*, the James Bond film. And it's also passed the Reynolds and the Eastwood and Bill Murray. In fact, it conceivably can catch *Superman II*, making it one of the fifteen most popular films in American history.

Naturally, it's a nonrecurring phenomenon.

Freak casting, they'll tell you. Hank and Hepburn, Jane and Hank, that's all she wrote.

I don't believe that. Granting the skill and charm of those three performers, I think the movie would have worked every bit as successfully with other actors of equivalent skill—say Jimmy Stewart and Bette Davis with Susan Sarandon as their child. Or Jimmy Cagney or Fred Astaire teamed with Irene Dunne or Ingrid Bergman. With Blythe Danner or Sissy Spacek as the daughter.

When I saw *On Golden Pond* I heard something so wonderful, something I hadn't heard in a movie theatre in years—the sound of middle-aged laughter. Well, you're not going to hear much of that in the future. Do you realize how many copies of *American Graffiti* the studios have churned out in the last years? Or *Halloween*? Or *Rocky*? The stomach turns. Well, *On Golden Pond* may be bigger than any of them. And I'm sure they'll never rip it off.

Because it would mean a total opening up of what constitutes a commercial film. And that's scary—so much more comforting to make *Death Wish XXIII*.

Maybe the most depressing comment made to me while I was interviewing for this book was by a bright studio guy who told me why *On Golden Pond* was breaking through. He said, "It's because it's got Jane Fonda in it."

Now, Jane Fonda is a very big star, but the same fortnight that *On Golden Pond* started, so did *Rollover*, another Jane Fonda film, only she wasn't the support in *Rollover*, she was the star—

—and it didn't open.

Total wipeout. Maybe twenty million down the tubes. This

with a name co-star and a name director. So why did the studio guy say Fonda made *On Golden Pond*? Because he was desperate to come up with something, anything, that wouldn't shake the foundations of what he knew to be true—what kind of film to make.

There's a whole world of subject matter that will never be touched by the major studios. Because the executives know the sort of film that may work. Just like the bright boys in Detroit *knew*, a while back, that what the American public really wanted was a great big glossy gas-guzzling car. And all that interest that was starting in Japanese cars?

Just another nonrecurring phenomenon. . . .

ALL NIGHT LONG

I don't know of any other movie that better illustrates the interrelationships of studio execs and stars than the Gene Hackman film *All Night Long*.

All Night Long is a fragile film, very short—it runs only eighty-four minutes and has a distinctly European feel, which is not surprising when you consider that the idea began with its ultimate director, the Frenchman Jean-Claude Tramont.

Tramont wanted to do a movie about people who work at night.

That was all he had, just that notion, but it struck a chord with the people at Fox, who said to go ahead and find a writer. They would develop it step by step.

Tramont found the wonderfully talented W. D. Richter (*Slither, Invasion of the Body Snatchers*), and Richter agreed to attempt a script. What Richter eventually wrote was the story of a man in crisis, a man named George Dupler. (The part eventually played by Hackman.)

George has worked, for twenty-plus years, in regional sales for a large pharmaceutical company. His wife is sort of a sludge, but not evil. His teen-age son also isn't much to crow over: The kid is done with school and, when he works at all, paints houses. George has the kind of life, then, that's okay if you're happy, terrible if you're not.

George isn't happy—all he ever wanted to do was be an inventor.

As the story opens, George has just been passed over for promotion. He takes the news badly: First he slugs his boss, then he throws a chair through a closed window. Because of seniority, he isn't fired; instead he is made the night manager of a huge California-type drugstore that is open all night long.

Now a distant relative dies, so George and his family pay a condolence call at the house of a macho-type fireman who also works at night. During the visit, George sees his son kissing the fireman's wife, Cheryl. The next day he confronts the kid and asks, are you having an affair with Cheryl? The answer is yes, but the kid adds that he loves her. George says to end it. The kid is upset.

That night Cheryl visits George in the store to talk about the situation. A few scenes later, George is at Cheryl's house, having a meal, when the kid rings the bell. George quickly sneaks out, hopefully without having been discovered.

But his son is convinced that his father is having an affair with the woman he loves—this news is spoken in front of George's wife—and George snaps. He packs up and leaves, taking a crummy room in a hotel.

Eventually, George and Cheryl actually begin an affair, but before it is consummated, she talks a little about her life. And her fears of being a failure. That's why her music is so important to her—she composes and her dream is to be a songwriter. But as she speaks about her music, it's sad. She's just a *neb*, poor Cheryl; a weak, sweet, quiet, pushed-around lonely lady. (She married her fireman husband only because he had saved her life: She said yes out of gratitude.)

When George and Cheryl are in love, he quits his job, rents a large space in a warehouse to be an inventor. He goes to a family gathering, bodily takes Cheryl off with him. But then she leaves—she hasn't the guts to stay.

Finally, she sucks it up and goes to the firehouse to talk to her husband, to try and take a stand. He's furious, shoves her around, and probably would do worse, when the alarm bell goes off.

George, it turns out, set the alarm. When the firemen are gone he pleads with her not to be afraid anymore. She hesitates, then slides down a fire pole into his arms and the two of them begin a new and, hopefully, better life.

Fox passed on the project.

Eventually it found its way to producer Leonard Goldberg, a giant television name (*Hart to Hart*, *Family*, etc.). Goldberg and his partner Jerry Weintraub (*Nashville* and *Diner*) had a deal at Universal that gave them the authority to make movies there whether Universal liked the movie or not—provided that the budget was low enough.

The budget of *All Night Long* could scarcely have been lower for these inflated times—three-million-and-change.

Universal didn't like it, felt they couldn't sell it, didn't want to do it. But for contractual reasons, they were not in a position to pass.

If Universal hated the project, Gene Hackman *loved* it. Hackman, an Oscar winner for *The French Connection* and one of our finest actors, was crazy to play the vehicle part of George. (Getting the script to Hackman undoubtedly caused no problem, since his agent is the most famous in Hollywood, Sue Mengers. Mengers had more than a little interest in the project, since she was married to the director, Jean-Claude Tramont.)

Hackman was so anxious to play the lead that he was willing to gamble: He would forfeit at least part of his up-front salary in exchange for a larger percentage at the other end; if the picture cleaned up, so would he.

Now, logic would dictate that since Universal didn't have any faith in the picture, they would have grabbed Hackman's offer. Since they felt the picture would stiff, why not keep costs down up front? Beyond that, if their feelings were correct, Hackman would essentially be doing the picture for nothing.

Universal insisted on paying him his regular salary. So the three-million-and-change movie was now going to cost four and a half.

With Hackman on board, the problems of casting the rest of the picture arose. Hackman's was the giant part—in almost every shot of almost every scene—but there were four major supporting roles: Hackman's wife, his son, the fireman, and of course Cheryl.

Cheryl was the most tricky. The creators felt that, sure, she was attractive, maybe even the belle of the block, but in the great world she shouldn't be a traffic stopper, because that would make the movie about a guy with hot pants. If this had been an English film, Julie Christie would have been wonderful—quiet, pretty but not too pretty, vulnerable. The studio suggested Loni Anderson, the sexpot on the tv series *WKRP in Cincinnati*.

Lisa Eichhorn got the part.

Eichhorn, a fine actress, had received wonderful reviews in the 1979 film *Yanks*. *Screen World Annual* selected her as one of the most promising new performers to appear that year, an honor Eichhorn shared with, among others, Bo Derek and Bette Midler. Probably Eichhorn has less instant star quality than these other two ladies, but the part of Cheryl, after all, didn't need star quality—not only is it a secondary role, the entire essence of the role is that this lady is the antithesis of a star. Shy, picked on, lost.

Shooting begins.

This is always a nervous time, but no giant problems arise. The first weeks go pretty much according to schedule.

Then comes the phone call.

Goldberg listens to the voice of agent Sue Mengers on the other end. Mengers parcels out this tidbit of information: Another of her clients would be interested in taking over the part of Cheryl. Who?

Only Barbra Streisand.

Goldberg hangs up, thinks awhile. There is no question in his mind that although both Hackman and Eichhorn are splendid in their roles, there is undeniably a certain chemistry that is lacking. Still, they're well into production.

No matter what, Goldberg can't just sit on the information. So he calls Universal and informs them that Barbra Streisand will do the Lisa Eichhorn part. Universal says, don't go anywhere, we'll get back to you.

Which they do. And now they *love* the picture. The sales force loves it, the advertising people are in ecstasy, fabulous.

Goldberg tries to explain that it's still the same little picture it always was, the one they so recently loathed, hated, and despised.

That was in another country, and besides the wench is dead.

All Night Long shuts down. For several weeks. Now, this is costly, because all the people who are on salary stay on salary, even though they're not doing anything.

But closing costs are nothing compared to what it takes to

sign Streisand. No one knows the truth outside of the people who made the deal, but the rumor around town is four or four and a half million dollars plus a gigantic contribution to her favorite hospital charity. That's a lot of money, but Barbra Streisand is something very special.

As the lyrics to one of the songs she sang in her breakthrough role, *Funny Girl,* proclaim: "I'm the greatest star." The lady just may well be. Oh, you can argue that Reynolds or Redford or Eastwood is bigger by a hair at the box office—

—but do they sing? (Actually, Reynolds did once, in a 1975 stifferoo called *At Long Last Love,* but probably it's not his favorite topic of conversation.)

Has any female soloist ever sold as many records as Streisand? Name her.

She doesn't choose to play Vegas anymore, but when she did, she killed them. She doesn't choose to do television anymore, but when she did, her specials went through the roof. And if she ever chose to return to Broadway, she'd outrun *Fiddler.*

The most remarkable thing about Streisand is that she can do it all—there is no area of popular performing where she isn't *it.* Redford would sell out on Broadway, too, if he ever came back, and so would Reynolds, but how would they do standing alone for an hour on the stage of Caesars Palace with a microphone in their hands? In films, she has been the unquestioned female star for fifteen years. Her movies may not always be successes—*Hello Dolly!* cost too much to get its money back—but they have almost always done business in the past.

(Remember the "almost," because now I have to talk about the handling of story material, something that may not seem germane but I think may prove to be.)

There is a famous, probably apocryphal, story about a Broadway actor who had a tiny blink of a part in *A Streetcar Named Desire.* He appeared only at the very end, and then to help cart Blanche away. Someone asked him, before the play opened, what *Streetcar* was about. And this actor replied, "It's about a man who takes a woman to a booby hatch."

All right, *All Night Long* is the story of George and his mid-life crisis—*but that's only because the writer wrote it that way. Gone With the Wind* is only about Scarlett and Rhett because that was the creator's decision, but you could have told about the Civil War through the eyes of Ashley Wilkes, in which case Scarlett would have been of secondary importance and Rhett nothing much at all. Or you could have done the whole thing centering on the Tarleton twins, minor roles who are with Scarlett at the beginning of the story, in which case *everybody* major now disappears.

Look, the story of *All Night Long* could have made a terrific Jane Fonda picture. A noble, decent wife whose husband leaves her but she goes on alone.

If you'd had Travolta, it becomes the son's story—a strong drama about a young man in love and on the brink of manhood who finds himself in dangerous competition with his father over the same object.

The fireman would have been great for Robert Duvall—a tough, expert guy in a dangerous line of work who finds his wife is sleeping with another man, and how does his macho soul come to grips with that?

Or easiest of all: Cheryl's story—it would make a super sex comedy. Start it this way: She's cooking up some concoction in her kitchen, fumbling and funny, when suddenly there's a flash fire and she's saved by this gorgeous fireman. Dissolve. They marry. He's still gorgeous, but not only is he crummy to her, he's away all night long. Enter this handsome teen-ager to paint the bedroom, he's confused, insecure—boom, they're in the sack. Only next comes something she hadn't counted on: He's got a real crush on her. Madness: She's a married lady much older than he is. Now another boom: The kid's father finds out and says, look, stop playing around with my son. She says sure, and the next thing you know, she's playing around with the father. She's in the sack with him and the son comes knocking at the door—instant farce. Men are flying in one door and out the other, with Cheryl at the center, trying to handle her husband with one hand, the kid with the other, and the kid's father with any parts of her body left over.

As a matter of fact, not only would this make a sex comedy, it would be a perfect part for Barbra Streisand.

And what is that?

Streisand's persona was pretty much outlined with *Funny Girl:* This is a lady who dominates. She wins every scene. And she may not be classically beautiful, but her energy and drive are enough to captivate the most beautiful of men—O'Neal, Sharif, Redford, Kristofferson. She can do musicals, she can do farce, she can do romantic comedy. Just let her dominate and you're home.

Remember *Up the Sandbox*?

It's maybe her most telling film performance, and also her sole disaster. What did she play? A put-upon, forlorn housewife with daydreams that don't quite work. Why did it fail? Because she may have been acting, but she wasn't acting *her* role. And what was the part of Cheryl? Nothing else but a put-upon, forlorn housewife with daydreams that don't quite work.

Why didn't the studio alter the film, once they'd shut down, to accommodate their star? And why didn't they add a bunch of musical numbers? (Cheryl, after all, is a songwriter in the story.) Because Barbra Streisand wanted to play Cheryl as written. (She was perfectly fine, by the way.)

So what the studio had done was to take a frail, three-million-dollar film and turn it into a fifteen-million-dollar film that was a total disaster and that, when you add in prints and advertising, probably lost them twenty million dollars.

Because what they were doing, in essence, was to pay Barbra Streisand four and a half million dollars *not* to play Barbra Streisand.

And if the same thing happened today, they'd do it all over again. . . .

Directors

Some of my best friends are directors. . . .

P.S.: EVERYBODY KNOWS DIRECTORS ARE IMPORTANT. IN MUCH OF WHAT FOLLOWS, DIRECTORS APPEAR CONSTANTLY.

SUFFICE IT HERE TO SAY THAT THEY ARE GOOD AND BAD, HELPFUL AND SUBVERTING, ENVIOUS AND SUPPORTIVE. WHATEVER THEY ARE, I FEEL SCREENWRITERS MUST SUPPORT THEM, BECAUSE DIRECTORS ARE UNDER ASSAULT FROM ALL QUARTERS AT ALL TIMES.

OVER THE YEARS I HAVE MET AND WORKED WITH A DOZEN PRIZE-WINNING AMERICAN DIRECTORS, AND THERE IS NOT ONE WHOSE "PHILOSOPHY" OR "WORLD VIEW" REMOTELY INTERESTS ME. THE TOTAL AMOUNT OF WHAT THEY HAVE TO "SAY" CANNOT COVER THE BOTTOM OF EVEN A SMALL TEACUP. (MORE ON THAT LATER.)

THAT THEY CAN SURVIVE THE SANDHOGLIKE PHYSICAL DEMANDS OF THE JOB FILLS ME WITH AWE AND ADMIRATION. THE BEST OF THEM ARE WONDERFUL STORYTELLERS. AND THOSE BEST DO ONE THING SUPERBLY WELL: THEY *HELP*.

EVERYBODY.

Producers

Producers may just be the least understood figures in the industry.

Part of this is due to terminology. Once, a movie was simply "produced by" so-and-so. No more. A simple reading of today's paper shows that now there are people who "present" movies. There are "executive producers," "associate producers." There are "executives in charge of production." One recent film had two "executive producers," two "associate producers," and one "executive in charge of production." Now, you may well ask, what in the world do all these terms mean?

I can answer in total honesty: I haven't the foggiest.

Some producers are simply money men. They arrange for, or come up with, the cash, and they take some kind of billing (and fee) for their efforts.

Others are packagers. They option a piece of material, interest an "element," make a deal with a studio, and head for points west. They literally will have nothing more to do with the picture than that.

Others are in that oldest of Hollywood traditions, the "son-in-law" business. The term is still valid, but with the collapse of the studio system, there aren't that many actual relatives by marriage on the payroll anymore. But there are lots of brothers or husbands. You want a star, he makes a deal that includes his spouse. The spouse gets billing.

Most often now, they are agents or ex-agents who are now the star's partner. In the former case, let's say an agent has a hot book; he'll make a deal with the studio to the effect of, sure, you can have it, but you'll have to pay me a little something extra or I'll go across the street. So they become "executive producers" or some other title more to their liking.

On *Butch Cassidy*, for example, the original material was purchased by Fox for Paul Monash. Monash was the producer of the film.

Then, when Paul Newman was signed, along came John Foreman. Foreman had been Newman's agent for years, had left the agency to become his business partner. In order to get Newman, guess what happened? Foreman became the "producer" and Monash suddenly was "executive producer." And what was their contribution to the film?

I still haven't the foggiest, because *Butch* was directed by George Roy Hill, and on a George Roy Hill film, George is the giant ape. Because of his vast talent, his skill at infighting, his personality, he runs the show. He has been known to banish writers from the set if he finds them intrusive; the same with producers.

None of this is meant to denigrate Monash or Foreman, who, I suspect, were terribly important to the finished product. What I'm saying is this: Screenwriters don't—at least this is true for me—deal all that much with producers. They hire us, we have meetings, they make suggestions, I go off and rewrite—that kind of thing. I have worked for some famous producers—Joseph E. Levine, Robert Evans—but the crucial aspect of their work does not often come in contact with mine.

One other reason that there is a lack of understanding about the producer's function is this: They have no effective governing body. (There is a guild, but it is not powerful or cohesive in the sense, say, that the Directors Guild operates.) If there were a strong producers' union, the buy-offs that permeate the trade might be eliminated. You can't suddenly decide, for example, to make someone who is close to the star an "assistant director." Not unless he's already an assistant director; there's a whole program of training that must be successfully completed. Or you can't make someone suddenly the "executive writer"—there's no such thing.

But as things now stand, anyone can walk around saying, "Yes, I'm a producer, I just bought a book." (Probably not adding that he just bought it at Brentano's.) In any case, the proliferation of terminology is something that drives quality producers up the nearest wall.

And there are quality producers.

If they are very smart, they are flexible enough to realize that their specific duties vary with the particular film. Sometimes they're on the floor constantly; at other times, if a production is running smoothly and on schedule, they'll stay away. But if their individual requirements alter more from one job to another than, for example, the cinematographer's, there are certain definites—

—their job is to get the picture made—

—and more often than not, they are the first ones on a project, and years later, after the selling has been done, they are the last ones off.

There is only one producer today to whom no laws apply, and that is George Lucas. Lucas is our Walt Disney: His name indicates a certain kind of subject matter and guarantees success. All the rest have to scuffle and suffer.

And wait.

Waiting is the curse of the producer's profession.

To illustrate this, it may be helpful now to zero in on one particular project, and I have chosen the Zanuck-Brown production of *The Verdict*, which is shooting today in New York City.

There is no *one* best producer. But it would be very hard to make a list of the top half dozen and not include the team of Richard Zanuck and David Brown. They make an interesting and unusual team. Longevity, for example: As both studio executives and producers, they have been together for going on a quarter century.

And they can scarcely be more different (except for the fact that they both are Stanford graduates). Brown, a native New Yorker, is sixty-five, gray-haired, and courtly. He comes to movies from the literary end. After receiving a Master's in journalism from Columbia, he began an editorial career. He was editor in chief of *Liberty*, managing editor of *Cosmopolitan*—the same magazine where his wife, Helen, has been so successful for the last decade. He was brought into the picture business by Darryl F. Zanuck, eventually rising to the post of executive vice president/creative affairs at 20th Century–Fox.

Richard Zanuck grew up at the studio. His father, the legendary Darryl F., was king there for close to thirty years. He produced his first success, *Compulsion*, when he was but twenty-four. At thirty-four, he became president of Fox, the youngest corporate head maybe ever. During his eight-year reign, three

Fox films won Best Picture awards—*The Sound of Music, Patton,* and *The French Connection.*

But we already know what happens to all studio executives, and in the early seventies, Zanuck-Brown became independent producers: They "went indie-prod"—Hollywoodese for being canned.

In the last decade, they have had their share of misses, but three of the hits, *The Sting, Jaws,* and *Jaws II,* are among the few movies in history to have taken in more than a hundred million dollars. Between them, there is precious little they don't know about the picture-making process.

The Verdict was a novel—not a well-known one—by Barry Reed. From the moment they acquired it, they were surprised to find a remarkable amount of star interest in their relatively obscure book. Performers such as Roy Scheider, William Holden, Frank Sinatra, Cary Grant, Dustin Hoffman, all let it be known in one way or another that they were aware of the project and please keep in touch.

The reasons behind the flurry of interest are, with hindsight, not hard to figure. *The Verdict* is a courtroom drama, and the main character, Galvin, is terribly appealing: He's a washed-up Boston Irish lawyer, a kind of burnt-out case, a boozer, a womanizer who, through his involvement with the trial, finds, if you will, redemption.

The Verdict also had one other thing going—a sensational and important subject matter: The trial is about medical malpractice.

It's at this point in a production—with or without any star interest—that a producer faces what is often the make or break decision: selecting who is going to write the script, who is going to direct. This is also the last time that a producer has total control. Whatever their vision may be, it is now bound to alter. From here on, it's no longer "their" movie, it's "ours."

Producers tend to keep lists. If they decide to go for a director first (which Zanuck-Brown did), they get out their trusty directors list and begin to ask questions. Who is available? Who is "helpful" (in the studio's eyes) in moving the project closer to actuality? Who can they stand? Who can they get to? And, most important of all: Who is *right* for the project?

Zanuck-Brown went after Arthur Hiller (*Love Story, The Americanization of Emily*). Hiller is much in demand. He's an excellent shooter, even-tempered, reasonable. And known in the business as a man who will deliver the script he carries onto the floor. Hiller was fascinated with *The Verdict* and immediately came on board.

Zanuck-Brown did not have to go after a writer next, because a writer came after them—the playwright David Mamet. Although his reception on Broadway has been limited, Mamet has had sensational success both Off-Broadway and in regional theatres all around the country.

He had not done much, if any, movie work to this point, but Zanuck-Brown knew him well; in fact, they had tried to get him to work on an earlier project of theirs that already had a director. Not only did Mamet not do this earlier piece, he had been so convincing that the material was fatally flawed that the director quit.

Now, you may think that this experience might have made Zanuck-Brown a wee bit reluctant to try Mamet again, but the reverse was true: Mamet had worked for weeks on the other piece and, at his own insistence, had taken no money. So they knew that when Mamet called and said he wanted to write *The Verdict*, they were dealing with not only a talent but a talent of proven integrity.

Hiller wanted Mamet. Zanuck-Brown wanted Mamet. Mamet was hired.

And that's when the waiting begins for the producer. All producers (Sam Spiegel may be the exception) try and have a bunch of projects moving forward concurrently. Because once a writer starts to write or a script is sent to a star, there's not a goddam thing to do but wait for the phone to ring. You can't constantly call someone who's doing a screenplay for you and beat around the bush before coming out with the biggie: When will you be done, when can we have it? When I do a job, I *know* the producer's going mad, I feel that pressure, and it's death when they call. All the up-front bullshitting about how the Knicks are doing or did you see *Dream Girls* is agony. And even though they say, "Oh, by the way, not important or anything, but how's it coming?"—of course they don't mean "How's it coming?"—you're bound to say, "Terrific, better than I'd hoped," because if you said, "Horribly, I'm fucking it up beyond repair," everyone would have cardiac arrest. *When's it coming?* is the subject not under discussion. All a phone call like that does is increase your insecurity and slow everything down.

Which is why good producers don't call. In the case of *The Verdict*, the wait was not agonizing: Mamet delivered promptly and skillfully.

Only Zanuck-Brown didn't like the screenplay. Brown says, "It was written in that terse, dramatic style that directors and actors love and that producers and executives rarely understand."

Only Hiller, the director, didn't like it either. They all felt it just didn't work. Hiller got off the picture. So instead of having a director and a writer, Zanuck-Brown now had no director and a script they felt deviated too much from the book they had purchased.

Now they went after another top writer, Jay Presson Allen (*The Prime of Miss Jean Brodie, Prince of the City*). They met with Allen, went over what they wanted, point by point.

Allen delivered her script and they loved it: It was exactly what they wanted.

Enter Robert Redford.

Redford was looking at some houses in Connecticut, and one of the places he saw was Jay Presson Allen's. He also saw a copy of *The Verdict*, asked if he might read it. Allen, who may have felt Redford was interested in directing, gave him the copy.

Redford then called Zanuck and Brown and asked if they might talk. When a star of Redford's magnitude requests a meeting, usually it can be arranged.

Redford told them he was really interested in *The Verdict*.

Ecstasy.

But then he said he liked the subject matter, not Jay Allen's script. He thought writer-director Jim Bridges (*The China Syndrome, Urban Cowboy*) would be good for the material.

Out Allen, in Bridges.

And the waiting began.

Bridges met with Redford, went off and wrote his own screenplay based on *The Verdict*.

Redford didn't like it.

Bridges went away and wrote another version.

Redford didn't like it either.

Months are going by. Zanuck-Brown have negotiated a deal

with Redford, which was finished but unsigned. Redford was announced for the project: The Fox brochure of its upcoming films listed him as the star. It was set—but it wasn't set-set.

On and on, the waiting.

Because of his childhood, because he was privy to the inner workings of studios in the Golden Era, waiting may be more frustrating for Zanuck than for any other producer. He says, "I remember as a kid, under my father's desk, under the glass on the top of his desk, was a big chart. And it had everybody that was under contract there. All the producers, and the directors, and the writers and actors and actresses. And it was so simple. I used to sit in on casting meetings, which would take all of about ten minutes. Not only casting, but putting the whole picture together. He would say, 'Well, we've got Julian Blaustein as producer, he's available next week. Put him with Henry Hathaway, he'll direct. And we've got Tyrone Power, he's going to finish his picture, give him a week off. And Betty Grable.' And that was the end of it. Nobody said, 'Can we make a deal with him?' They already had a deal. I'm not asking for a return to the old days. But some goddamned good pictures were made with that system."

Bridges is now writing a third version. Finally he turns it in; he's been on the picture nine months by now. Like the main character of *The Verdict*, Bridges is turning into a burnt-out case.

Strike three.

Redford is still interested in doing a movie about medical malpractice—but the main role, that of the lawyer, Galvin, that's the problem. He's a boozer and a womanizer and Zanuck and Brown hear that Redford thinks the character could be bad for his image.

Bridges, whipped, withdraws from the picture. Zanuck and Brown still sort of have a star. But they don't have a script the star will accept. And now their director is gone.

Then they hear that Redford is having meetings, without telling them, with his friend Sydney Pollack, about directing *The Verdict*.

And Zanuck snaps. He does two genuinely remarkable things. First he fires Redford. (Not strictly true, since the contract was unsigned. What he does is he calls Redford's agent and tells him they are no longer interested in having the agent's client in their picture.)

He also goes public with his anger, talking to the press about his ex-star's behavior.

So now Zanuck and Brown have achieved an extraordinary Hollywood reversal: They have taken a "go" project and turned it into a development deal.

Back to their directors list. Sidney Lumet. Sidney Lumet is now available and he's perfect. He's also on vacation in Venice. They contact him, he says he'll be glad to read what they've got. So they take the best of the Bridges scripts and send it to Lumet. And they also send the Jay Presson Allen script, because they liked it and, also, Allen is Lumet's partner.

Lumet never keeps anybody waiting—no director has earned a larger reputation for efficiency and organization. Lumet calls from Venice and says yes, he's very interested in doing *The Verdict.*

Which script, though?

The *Mamet* version, Lumet replies. Zanuck and Brown, needless to say, have not expected this answer, since not only did they not send it, they had no idea Lumet knew of its existence. But they agree to meet when Lumet was back in New York. (Back in their executive days, they had a not dissimilar experience with *Patton.* There had been six versions or so when George C. Scott said he would do the part if they would go with the very first version, written by Francis Coppola.)

In New York, Lumet explained what was wrong and easily fixable with the Mamet script. The story *The Verdict* has two parts: that of the trial itself, plus that of the man's redemption. Mamet had been less interested in the subject of medical malpractice than with the character. So what he had done was written *The Verdict* and ended it before the verdict. The trial's outcome was not included. He cared about the guy, not the courtroom conclusion.

Lumet and Mamet went to work, an ending was written. Paul Newman was approached and requested all versions. He liked the Mamet script, regardless of what Lumet liked, which wasn't the problem, since Lumet liked it too.

Lumet also liked Newman. When Lumet was announced, word seeped down that Redford was available. Lumet and Newman are finishing the movie now. The public's verdict on *The Verdict* will be within the next six months.

And those months are perhaps the busiest, and certainly the

most important, for any producer. Because those months contain the ultimate decisions on how the movie will be sold.

The selling of a film is so important that there are some bright industry figures who feel that a movie should be divided into two equal parts: the making of it and the marketing of it. I am not equipped to detail the latter. And the audience doesn't, and shouldn't, give a damn about it: A flick comes to your local, you go or you don't, that's it. But the selling is often more essential to the fate of the film than the quality of the film itself.

Let's just take two extremes as examples. If you have Burt Reynolds in *Smokey and the Bandit XII*, you are dealing with a pre-sold piece of merchandise. There is a huge audience out there waiting for it (or at least there has been in the past, and if you're the studio, since you live and die on past magic, you feel it must be out there still—*please*). So what you want to do is get it to that audience quickly and nationally. Often, such a film will go into as many as fifteen hundred theatres the first week. Fifteen hundred theatres means fifteen hundred prints of the movie have to be made, and a print can cost around two thousand dollars now, so you're spending three million dollars off the bat. To back that up, you spend maybe another five million or more for tv ads, print ads, etc. You don't need to build word of mouth; the earlier *Smokey* films have done that for you.

But what if you've got an art film—say, *Chariots of Fire.* Your job there is to spend as little as possible up front and pray that word of mouth will build. So you make maybe two prints, open behind Bloomingdale's and in Westwood, and pray. Gradually, if the movie begins to work, you add a few more cities. If the movie doesn't work, it disappears, and you haven't spent a lot of money.

Now, within these extremes there are infinite variations, and it's often here that a producer fights his ultimate battles, trying to convince the studio to release his film in a manner they consider best for their individual project.

Another giant battle for a producer is not how his movie is released but *when.* All the different media have a "target audience." For pop music, that audience is made up of kids from the ages of eleven to fifteen. That's the group the pop music moguls *must* reach. Television's prime-time target audience is a different age group—twenty-five to forty-nine.

For films, the target audience is different still: Movies must hit those between sixteen and twenty-four. That's the bulk of the popcorn buyers. No one knows for sure why, but the common wisdom is this: When a kid hits sixteen, he wants to get the hell out of the house, away from his folks. By the time people are twenty-four, a lot of them start getting married and having families, and the cost of a movie escalates for them—sitters, etc.

Which is why the most lucrative time for movies is summer; and after summer, Christmas. The target audience is out of school. Which is why so many expensive films come out at those two periods, competing expensively with each other.

Now, there is certainly logic behind that thinking. And more than a little madness. Because in the rush of product, some films are certain to be lost and left behind. One of Hollywood's leading producers, Daniel Melnick (*That's Entertainment, All That Jazz*), had some comments on that madness in a recent interview concerning a film of his that was scheduled to open in early '81 but, at the last minute, got shoved into the Christmas barrage.

> I wanted to release *Altered States* in January, because I felt there were no other major movies being released then and there would be an audience. I would rather go at a time when there are fewer people attending movies and offer them pictures they want to see, rather than to divide a larger audience with ten other desirable films.
>
> I think that as an industry we have very often shown the instinct of lemmings. To find ourselves releasing films basically twice a year and glutting the market is, I think, folly. I realize that historically Christmas and summer have had the highest attendance. But I think to some degree that's a self-fulfilling prophecy. We're all convinced that people go to the movies primarily at Christmas time, so we release our big pictures then. . . .

Obviously, Melnick lost his battle in *Altered States*. But you can assume that, like any quality producer, he didn't go quietly. A producer is really like Willy Loman trudging along with his suitcase under his arm, trying to convince people to buy what he's selling. Often they end up with no more success than poor Willy eventually found. (There are exceptions. Warren Beatty, a brilliant producer, had, as his first film, the famous *Bonnie and Clyde*. Only it didn't get famous its first time out. Controversial it was, but successful it wasn't. But Beatty—cajoling, kicking, screaming, God knows how—convinced the studio to give the film a major re-release soon after its original time at bat. The movie became a gigantic success, but had it not been for Beatty's unique skill, it might have been just another unknown cult film today.)

Studios have the money, and that's always where the power lies. I remember an early Sam Peckinpah film—still for me his best—called *Ride the High Country*. It opened in New York as the bottom half of a double bill with a European Mongol-type picture. It got some sensational notices, and when I saw it, I couldn't believe the way it was handled. I eventually tracked down an executive at the studio and asked why it had been dumped. He explained: "Sure we previewed it. And the preview cards were sensational. But we decided to send it out the way we did because that way we were sure to pick up a little money. We didn't believe those preview cards. *The movie didn't cost enough money to be that good.*" (Italics mine.)

Money today, as it always has been, is the essential glue that binds the movie powers to each other. But today the talk of money dominates as perhaps never before: The interest rates make it more prohibitive than ever for the studios to borrow money. And the money needed to mount a movie continues to escalate: The *average* cost of a major studio film today is over ten million dollars, a four-hundred-percent leap from just ten years ago. Everywhere you hear the cry: "We've got to do something to bring down the cost of pictures."

I don't see it happening.

Two examples from pictures I've worked on. *Stepford Wives* was probably released badly as far as the people involved in the making of that movie are concerned. It has some exploitable elements, but it wasn't *Halloween*. The best way to release it would have been slowly, praying for favorable word of mouth. The studio threw it on the market in hundreds of theatres immediately. Why? Because the studio's needs are not the same as the needs of the individual pictures, and right then Columbia needed cash flow badly—dollars, and *now*. *Stepford* got them some dollars. It was gone in a month, but it served the studio well.

The other picture I can't name for legal reasons that will shortly come clear. But in this second instance, the studio purposely set out to destroy its own product.

Madness? Not at all. (And not at all that unusual either.)

There was a change in studio leadership. The old management, the one that had given us a "go," was out. And when new management comes in they all do the same and, for them, the proper thing: They try to prove to their board of directors that the board was correct in firing the old bosses and bringing them in. And one of the ways you do that is you sabotage the old bosses' films.

This film opened in New York to record-breaking business and within a couple of weeks was gone. Not only did they louse up the booking, when they did advertise it, they kept changing the ads, a sure sign a picture is in trouble.

I later talked to an executive of the company who had survived the old regime. He said to me: "Look, we're a public company, so I wouldn't say we intentionally ruined the film. We would *never* intentionally ruin a film, we've got stockholders to report to. But I don't think it's a secret to say that if the old guys were still around, maybe we might have tried a little harder."

Okay, these films had one crucial thing in common: They were both, relatively speaking, cheap films. They did not have heavyweight directors, they certainly had no major stars.

We have already talked about studio executives and their thirst for stars. Well, producers want them too. Because if you have a star, not only is your picture automatically "important"—

—it's also expensive.

And the studio can't dump it, can't do anything but fight like hell for it in order to try and salvage their investment. (All that campaigning that went on recently for *Pennies from Heaven*? That movie was an instant stiff and everybody knew it by the end of its first week. But the studio kept ploughing money into the musical, praying somehow they might be able to generate some interest. *Pennies from Heaven* was a twenty-million-plus movie. If it had been brought in for five, you would never have known it had opened.)

So the Powers of the industry are sort of like the goony-goony bird that flies in ever-decreasing circles until it gets swallowed up by its own asshole.

I'm sure of two things about *Pennies from Heaven* for example: that there is no built-in Steve Martin audience and that, after its failure, Steve Martin's price will go up. That's the pickle the Powers are in: They want movies to be cheaper, while at the same time, every move they make only ensures that movies will become increasingly prohibitive.

By the end of the eighties, it wouldn't surprise me if we weren't all looking back on the good old days of a decade before, when *Heaven's Gate* was a cheapie. . . .

chapter two
Elements

There is no particular order to what follows. And none of it is meant to be factual, but everything, at least in my experience, is true. . . .

L.A.

I find Los Angeles a very difficult and potentially dangerous place to work in, and I think anyone seriously contemplating a career as a screenwriter ought to move there as soon as it's humanly or financially possible.

As to its being difficult and dangerous, that's entirely a personal reaction. I am aware of the number of brilliant writers, painters, and musicians who have thrived in the sunshine. I can't help it that from the very beginning the place has terrified me.

Part of it has to do with money. For the hardcover publication of my first novel, I was paid five thousand dollars. Such was the glory of its reception that, for my second novel, I was paid twenty-five hundred dollars. For *Harper*, my first Hollywood film, I received eighty thousand dollars.

So what's so terrible?

Obviously nothing in a monetary way. It was a fantastic windfall. But—and, remember, we are dealing with *my* neuroses here—there was something unsettling about the discrepancy. If you write a novel, and you get X for your labors, that sets up a value system: You put in a certain amount of effort, you receive a certain amount of reimbursement, just like any other worker. However, if you are lucky or talented enough to become in demand as a screenwriter, the amounts you are paid are so staggering, compared to real writing, that it's bound to make you uneasy.

It was on *Harper* that I first (not counting funerals) rode in a limousine.

Late afternoon. I got off the plane at LAX and started for the baggage claim area. Then I stopped. Dead. A uniformed man was standing by the gate exit, holding a cardboard sign with the name GOLDMAN written on it. It was a paranoid moment for me, because my last name isn't all that uncommon, and I stared at him, wondering what the hell to do. Should I approach him or not? No one had told me I would be met at the airport. What if I pissed him off? The scene might have played like this:

```
                ME
         (perspiring lightly)
   Pardon me, sir, but are you,
   chance, waiting for Willia
   man?


                HIM
          (affronted)
    No, you fool, who's William Gold-
    man? I'm here to pick up Max Gold-
    man, now get away.
```

Finally, I went up to him and said, "Pardon me, sir, but are you, by any chance, waiting for William Goldman?" and he smiled and said, "Yes *sir*, Mr. Goldman," and then he took my under-the-seat bag and led me to where the luggage would come belching down the chute. (I know everybody thinks their bags always come toward the end. Well, mine do. I sometimes am convinced that there is this insidious worldwide plot. All those bag-smashers have some kind of code, and one of their pleasures is to sneak my stuff out of line, hold it, chuckling all the while, before reluctantly letting go, never last but, say, fourth from last. I travel solely with an under-the-seat bag now, if it's at all possible. It's not a really soul-satisfying revenge, but it's the best I can do.)

Eventually, fourth from the end or so, my suitcase came clumping down and he bent for it, my driver did, easily beating me to the task, and then he said, "Just follow me, Mr. Goldman," and I did, hoping nobody I knew would see me.

We trooped out to the sidewalk. He put my stuff down, smiled, and said, "I'm just parked over there, sir, wait right here, I won't be a minute."

I waited until this giant Cadillac appeared. Before I could make a move, he bounded out from the driver's seat, raced around, opened the back door for me. "Watch your head, Mr. Goldman," he advised.

I got in. I sat back. He put my luggage in the trunk. Then he hurried around to the front, gave me a little kind of salute, moved in behind the wheel. (It's crazy the things you remember, but believe me, I remember all of this.)

What I remember mostly was sitting in the back of that big

alone, feeling very close to panic. "What the fuck am I do-g back here—I'm not Jackie Kennedy—I shouldn't be here—what does this have to do with writing?"

The motor turned over perfectly, he looked back to see that all was well, and then he skillfully began piloting the car into the stream of airport traffic—

—and I yelled "Stop!"

He stopped, glanced at me. "Forget something?"

"Can I sit up front with you?" I said.

He looked at me, I thought, kind of weirdly. "Of course, Mr. Goldman. Anything you want."

Before he could even start to come around and open things for me I threw open the back door, got in alongside. And then we began the drive to my hotel.

Dusk now. The end of it, just before it loses out to night. We're tooling along in the limo and I'm, naturally, lost: I have absolutely no sense of direction; even when I *know* where I'm going, I don't know where I'm going. On both sides of the street now are houses, cheek to jowl, contiguous. I can't make them out clearly, except they're all about the same height and, like I said, all huddled together. I turned to the driver and said, "Is this a housing development?"—

—and he burst out laughing.

Because we were right smack in the middle of one of the fancier sections of Beverly Hills. He explained that these were all half-million-dollar houses (probably two million today), and as he went on, I squinted out, trying to make it jibe, because I'm from outside Chicago—and in the Midwest, when people have money, they have property—and I couldn't help thinking, "Be careful: *These people are strange out here.*"

I bought a bottle of Kaopectate as soon as I reached the hotel.

No joke. For the first several years, whenever I was in Los Angeles, I went nowhere without a bottle of Kaopectate hidden in a brown paper bag.

The summer I spent working with George Hill on *Butch Cassidy,* I rented a house in Santa Monica for my family and I commuted every day to the Fox lot in Beverly Hills. I hate to drive. As I've indicated, I get lost, but worse, my mind wanders.

So most mornings that summer, I took a taxi to work.

Now that fact probably doesn't seem like it's worth a paragraph, except that in L.A., you just don't do that. It's bizarre, every bit as oddball as strolling the sidewalks of Beverly Hills.

I am not by nature flamboyant, but I think I have never been as colorful as during that *Butch Cassidy* summer, when I got out of the taxi each day, a script of *Butch* clutched in one hand, my bottle of Kaopectate in the other.

To repeat: Los Angeles terrifies me.

But my particular crazies are not why I find writing so difficult. It's more this: Everything's so goddam *nice* out there. Sure, they bitch about their smog, but unless you're a Hawaiian born and bred, the weather is terrific. And so many of the basic necessities of life are made so easy for you: The markets are often open twenty-four hours, nobody snarls at you in the stores when you're trying to buy something. It's all just . . . swell.

But writing is essentially about going into a room by yourself and doing it. Writing isn't about meetings and it's not about backhands.

And when you have sunshine. And the beach. And a pool. Or access to a pool. And the public tennis courts are open all the time. And the golf course is nearby. And the drive to Big Sur always beckons. Who the hell wants to go into a room and shuffle papers around?

Maybe you can do it breezing. I can't. . . .

The danger of Los Angeles comes with success.

(If some of you just groaned, "Is he crazy?—gimme some of that danger, lemme at it," I wouldn't blame you a bit.)

Sure, success is what we strive for; it's what's drummed into our little heads from the playpen on. And yes, success is better than failure. And "I been poor and I been rich and rich is better."

Here is an alphabetical list of eight successful movie people:

> Woody Allen
> Paddy Chayefsky
> Francis Coppola
> John Huston
> Nunnally Johnson
> Ernest Lehman

Joseph Mankiewicz
Billy Wilder

These were the first eight names that came to me when I asked myself which screenwriters I admire. I'm not saying they're the eight best: If I thought for a little longer, I could come up with eight more I admire just as much. But these will do. What they have in common is this: They all began as screenwriters in movies, but if the names are familiar to you, it's as directors or producers or stars. They all became hyphenates as soon as they could. Why? Strictly guesswork on my part, but I'll have to go with it. More money? Maybe. More power. Absolutely. But I'll bet the primary reason is neither of the above.

It's because *just* being a screenwriter is simply not enough for a full creative life.

And I'm not using the word *creative* in a loaded sense—I mean, shit, someone "created" *How to Stuff a Wild Bikini.*

Creative in the dictionary is defined as "having the power to create," and *create* means "to bring into being, to cause to exist."

The primary success available to a screenwriter is financial, and that's all well and good for bankers and businessmen, how else would they keep score? But if you are the kind of weird person who has a *need* to bring something into being, and all you do with your life is turn out screenplays, I may covet your bank account, but I wouldn't give two bits for your soul.

Those of us who were permanently altered by the little engine bringing the toys over the mountain, or Piglet getting rescued with the honey jar, or whatever else it might have been, never daydreamed, as we grew, of becoming Jacqueline Susann. We were after the giants—we wanted to make wonders.

Screenwriting isn't about that.

There is a Women's Liberation term called shitwork and it means work that when it is well done is unnoticed. Like dusting or cleaning. Rare is the husband who walks in from a hard day at the office and says, "Darling, the windows just sparkle, how lovely." But he may well walk in and say, "This place is filthy, what am I breaking my ass for, to come home to a zoo?"

Well, screenwriting is shitwork. Brief example: *Waldo Pepper. Waldo* was basically an original screenplay of mine. I say "basically" because the pulse of the movie came from George Hill, the director, and we worked for ten days on a story. So *Waldo* wasn't as "original" as *Butch*, but it was a hell of a lot more mine than any adaptation I've ever done.

Okay, we open in New York and three daily papers are split— two terrific, one pan.

In neither of the laudatory reviews was my name even mentioned. But you better believe I got top billing in the pan. I had screwed up George Hill's movie.

Nothing unusual at all about that—it's SOP for the screenwriter. That is simply the way of the world. You do not, except in rare, rare exceptions, get critical recognition.

But you do get paid.

And as you get hotter, you get paid more. (Now we're into the danger zone.) You don't get banished to Siberia at Chasen's.

And you get flattered in meetings. And at first you sit there thinking, "Can you believe this asshole, bullshitting me like that?" But the flattery continues as the heat rises. And at first, again, you remind yourself that none of the heat has to do with literary quality, it's because people lined up to see your last picture.

But eventually, inevitably, you say to yourself, "Since so many people tell me I'm a terrific writer, what's my voice against the multitudes? Forget my voice—they're right. I *am;* check my box-office receipts if you don't believe it—terrific."

And you're finished but you don't know it.

That child who wanted to bring something into existence is long gone. And the only way to save him is this: *You must write something else.*

Anything else.

Epic poems or rhyming couplets, novels or nonfiction, I don't care. But there has to be an outlet where quality matters, where the world is not measured by the drop in box-office receipts in the second weekend in Westwood.

Maybe I'm crazy; I may be dead wrong. Maybe you know people who have spent their lives doing nothing but writing screenplays. If you do, ask them about the road not taken. . . .

So why go to L.A. at all?

For the same two reasons I would urge a young playwright to

do his best to get to New York; one of the reasons being practical, the other emotional.

To begin with the practical: Simply put, they *know* things out there the rest of the country doesn't, and they get that information first. The movie business is a part of the fabric of life in Los Angeles, and that just isn't true anywhere else. It is, if you will, in the air.

Take, for example, *Porky's.*

It is now the first week in May '82, and since I began writing, *Porky's* has opened. With no stars. And no name director. And less than flattering reviews.

It's still too soon to say what the final fate of the movie may be, but it's certainly a freak hit, and there are many who feel it will end up as the most popular comedy in the history of American films.

Now, if you're sitting in Chicago, or Miami, and you saw *Porky's* in April and you sat there thinking, "I can do better than this," and you went home and set to work on a screenplay dealing with the sexual awakening of teen-agers, and you did a wonderful piece of work, really quality stuff, and you had an aunt who went to grammar school with a kid who now works in the legal department of the William Morris office, and you asked her would she get it to him, and she did, and he loved it, and he got it to a top Morris agent, and *he* loved it, you know what?

It would all have been an exercise in futility.

The Morris agent would read the script and think, "Too bad, if only I'd had it six months ago."

Six months ago? The movie just opened.

But they knew. They knew late last fall, the Fox people did, because they had test marketed the film and it had done sensationally. Now, they couldn't have predicted that it would become the present phenomenon. But they sure were aware they had *something.*

And everyone else in the business out there knew the same damn thing. And you better bet that before *Porky's* opened, every studio had at least two *Porky's* rip-offs in development. And when *Porky's II* opens—believe me, there will be a *Porky's II*—it will have been preceded by maybe three or four similar films.

The word on a film starts before the film starts.

"Hollywood" is basically a very small community, and there are precious few secrets. When a studio gives a green light to a project, before casting or crew is completed, a lot of people know the project well: Remember that the majority of films have been turned down already by the majority of studios. (Probably a slight overstatement, but only slight.)

Now, as principal photography approaches, there are hundreds of people working on it. And they know, collectively, housands of people, the majority of whom work in the picture business. And these technicians are talkative and, since everyone's a critic, opinionated. "The director's on the sauce, brace yourself." "The goddam girl's all wrong, shit, we could have really had somethin'." "I don't know, it all feels awfully good so far." And like that.

Then, when photography starts, any number of people are seeing the "dailies"—snippets of film that make up the previous day's shooting. Most important of these people are the studio executives, and I have found they are shockingly honest, if you know them, about their product. If a movie's a stiff, they won't come out and directly say that, but they will say, "Perhaps our hopes were a bit too high on that one" or "There really is more, I think, than we're getting on the screen."

And when they really like what they're seeing, they're thrilled—because, among other reasons, we all would like, from time to time, to be involved with something that isn't dreck.

And when they really like it, that word really spreads. (Obviously, "the word" isn't infallible. Sure, people in Sioux City knew that *Heaven's Gate* was in trouble while it was still shooting, and that turned out to be true. But in my experience, the movie that was in the most talked-about trouble—both real and imagined trouble—was the first *Godfather*. (There was a famous story, I suspect true, about Francis Coppola returning from a final location trip in preproduction and getting off a plane where a wire from his agent awaited him, saying, "Don't quit. Make them fire you.")

Once shooting is over and there is a rough cut of the film available, studios often have screenings for their own personnel. I remember a secretary at Paramount talking to me months before *Saturday Night Fever* was released. And remember that at this time, Travolta was just another poster pretty boy from a schlock tv series. And she said, "I saw *Saturday Night Fever* and I loved it and John Travolta is sensational, I don't care what anybody says." I was not surprised at the success of that movie, primarily because of that quick conversation. She didn't have to bring it up, I didn't ask her about it—she just plain loved the film and couldn't stop talking about it.

That may seem trivial to you, but there has yet to be a movie that was damaged by wonderful word of mouth.

After these studio screenings, most films have "sneaks," and that's when you really begin to get a strong sense of fate.

Two giant musicals are going to open in the next months or so—maybe a hundred million dollars cost between them, counting prints and advertising and publicity. They are *Annie* and *The Best Little Whorehouse in Texas*.

The reaction I've heard on *Annie* has been mixed. Some say "tremendous" and others say "bland." But everyone has said that it will do business. And so I suspect it will.

About *Whorehouse* I have heard—absolutely nothing. Not a syllable. Which leads me to suspect it's in trouble. We shall see.

The only reason I'm reasonably current is because I've been researching this book for a long time now and I'm making an effort to talk to a lot of people and ask a lot of questions. But ordinarily, since I live and work in New York, I'm pretty much like everybody else: I know what I read in the papers.

Out there, though, even an introverted loner at USC film school knows more than I do now. Sure, a lot of successful movie people live in the East or San Francisco. But how many of them started there? And how many of those were screenwriters?

It just seems to me to be common sense to start in the center, in the town where there is the most interest and activity. I think if I wanted a screenwriting career today, I would go along with Mr. Greeley. L.A.'s a great place to visit.

And there's no law that says you've got to stay....

Enough of practical matters. The emotional reason is at least as important.

I don't think most people realize—and there's no reason they should—the amount of demeaning garbage you have to take if you want a career in the arts. I mean, going off to med school is something you can say with your head high. Or being a banker or going into insurance or the family business—no problem.

But the conversations I had with grown-ups after college ...

"So you're done with school now, Bill."

"That's right."

"So what's next on the agenda?"

Pause. Finally I would say it: "I want to be a writer."

And then they would pause. "A writer."

"I'd like to try."

Third and final pause. And then one of two inevitable replies: either "What are you going to do next?" or "What are you *really* going to do?"

That dread double litany ... What are you going to do next? ... What are you *really* going to do? ... What are you going to do next? ... What are you *really* going to do ... ?

The first ("What are you going to do next?") implying failure.

The other ("What are you *really* going to do?") implying that my life's daydream wasn't a serious occupation.

That may not sound like much to you, and maybe it isn't, but, you see, I had a secret: I knew they were right. Maybe not about the seriousness of being a writer, but there was no doubt in my mind that I would fail.

I would have been crazy to think otherwise. I came from a businessman's family and I lived in a businessman's town. At Oberlin, I took the one class they offered then in creative writing. There were maybe a dozen of us, and the eleven others all took it for one reason: It was a gut course. I was the only one who wanted to write. All the others got grades of B or better. I got the only *C*.

In summer school at Northwestern I took another writing class. I don't know about anyone else's ambitions, but the result was the same: I got by far the worst grade.

At Oberlin there was a literary magazine and I was the fiction editor. There was also a poetry editor and an overall head of the magazine. Everything was submitted anonymously and every issue I would sneak in a story and the three of us would meet and I would listen while they both agreed whoever wrote this thing (my thing) was not about to get published. I was the fiction editor and I couldn't get my own stuff included.

When I came to New York in '54 I remember going to a party. I am not good at parties. My SATs in partygoing are among the lowest in history. But there was this girl there, a native—Sarah Lawrence, I think—and we were gamely going through the motions and she said where are you from and I said where are you from and she said where do you live and blah blah blah until she asked, "What do you do?"

I told her. "I want to be a writer."

And on that, she literally turned her back, but before she did there came a look on her face and she said it: "Oh, another one."

... Oh, another one....

When you are Jamie Wyeth and you are starting out to paint, well, Daddy did okay. But most of us are entering uncharted ground, and we have hope, but we also know the odds against us. Failure keeps us company.

And that's almost the only company we have. Because no one's going to do it for you. We have tunes in our heads, but what if they stink? We have color and composition dancing behind our eyes, but what if no one cares?

If you think we're a long way from Los Angeles now, I disagree. Every taxi driver out there is just an actor between jobs, that's in the city charter. And of course we know that every shop girl fantasizes being Streisand.

But you would be amazed how many screenwriters there are stocking the grocery shelves at Ralph's or waiting on tables in Westwood. They are multitudes, and even if you're the King of the Nerds, you can't help but meet them. And talk to them. And drink with them and bitch about the Industry and argue about craft. In other words, if you want to be a screenwriter and you live in Des Moines, that's a terrible curse to bear. It's a terrible curse in Los Angeles, too—but at least you're not alone.

And oh boy, when you're beginning, does that matter....

Agents

Agents are the Catch-22 of the movie business: Everybody starting out desperately needs one and nobody starting out can possibly get one.

My memory is that in the years I've been around the business, whenever I meet anyone interested in screenwriting, there is really only one question on their minds: How do I get an agent? No one starts out by inquiring after craft or the color of Paul Newman's eyes. It's always "I need an agent, how can I get one, how?"

Obviously, it's impossible.

But you can try. Intelligently. Before getting to that though, this question ought to be answered first: What can an agent actually do for you?

Nothing magical.

If you've written *Fire Maidens from Outer Space* or *Billy the Kid Vs. Dracula*, not even the legitimately legendary Lew Wasserman at his peak could have snookered David Lean into directing your efforts.

But the major agents can save incredible amounts of time. If, say, Sam Cohn of ICM wants to deal with Paramount, more than likely he will not call any of the numberless executives that work for the company, he will dial Barry Diller, the boss. And Diller will take the call. Because he knows not only Cohn's client list, he knows Cohn and he knows Cohn wouldn't be calling unless there was a project of genuine value to market.

Even the greenest of agents serve a tremendously valuable function—since very few people in the business will read a script that is unrepresented, because of legal reasons.

Let's say you've written a zombie picture and someone at UA reads it cold and, a year down the line, UA announces they're making a zombie picture. That's how lawsuits are born. Most studios, before they even go near an unrepresented piece of material, will send out a form to the writer that the writer must sign and return, thus clearing the studio, in theory, of potential legal action.

Agents also know as much scuttlebutt as anybody. More, probably. Not just which studios are looking for a love story—all studios are always on the lookout for love stories. But which star wants to change his image and try something else. And which director is getting killed with alimony payments and needs a job fast. And which studio executive is going to get fired, so don't go near him. (Because when he is fired, those projects he has accepted become anathema to his successors and forget about the movie ever happening.)

And all the decent ones, green or veteran, have a wonderful sense of career guidance. I've been with Evarts Ziegler for fifteen years, and whatever my career has been, he is enormously responsible for it.

"But what goddam good is career guidance when I haven't got a career yet?"

Okay, let's set about trying to get an agent.

(1) You better have something written that's as good as you can do. A screenplay, in proper form and—don't laugh—legible. If you have more than one screenplay, better yet. Not that you're going to show the agent two, not at the beginning. But if he reads one and is at least intrigued, he's liable to ask for another sample of your work.

(2) Find out who and where the agents are. How? Easy. Contact the Writers Guild of America, either the East Coast branch in New York or the West Coast branch in Los Angeles, and acquire their list of accredited agents. I am looking at such a list now. It is dated July 1981 and it is nine pages long and lists, I would guess, the names, addresses, and phone numbers of at least two hundred agents.

(3) Study the list. Really go over it and over it. Bewildering, but keep at it. On the first page, for example, there are only five entries. "Agency for Artists"—forget about them for now; and the same, again for now, with AAG—Artists Agent Group. But "Adams, Limited, Bret"—that may be of value. Bret Adams is a name. And that's what we're tracking down now—names.

Because any point of contact, no matter how distant, is infinitely preferable to no contact at all.

Do you have a lawyer? Probably you don't. Do your parents? No? Well, somebody in your family *must* have come in contact with a lawyer sometime. Call that lawyer. Ask did that lawyer go to grad school with anyone who ended up in some form of show-business law? If the answer is yes, throw yourself on the mercy of the lawyer you know to contact his old buddy from Virginia. If he will, fine; if he won't, and he probably won't, thank him anyway and think some more.

Did your mother go to high school with anyone who ended up as a performer? Probably she didn't and if she did, probably you knew that already. But did she go to high school with anyone who ended up working for a performer? Doubtful. But maybe she went to high school with someone who once did makeup for a local tv talk show. If she did, have her renew that acquaintance, or do it yourself. Nothing will come of it.

But if you want an agent, get used to frustration.

And rejection.

A lot of rejection.

But maybe—unlikely, but it's within the realm—somebody knew somebody who knows Bret Adams.

No? On to the next.

Buddy Altoni. He's next. Anyone have any way at all of getting to Buddy? How about Velvet Amber? Or Fred Amsel? Or any of the *B*'s or *C*'s or down the line.

No? Keep at it.

By the time you're done you will have come up with zip. But at least you're in show business, baby.

(4) Even if you luck out and make a contact, how can you know if the agent's any good?

Tough to answer, because I can't really define what a "good" agent is. As close as I can come, it's someone who believes you have talent and will hustle for you.

But you can find out who the successful agents are. *Being an agent is really about signing clients.* So find out who handles important clients. If you'd want to know who Lawrence Kasdan's or Alvin Sargent's agents are, all you have to do is call up the aforementioned Writers Guild and ask. You don't have to be a member. Just pick up the phone and dial. They'll tell you. It's a service they willingly perform.

There is a lot of information that is available to you. But Dan Rather isn't going to tell it on the nightly news. You have to think and act and, most of all, hustle.

Pester is the password here. Remember the character Lucy in

Peanuts? Make her your image. *She* wouldn't have any trouble getting an agent. . . .

One final suggestion: You're a writer, write a letter. You've already found out who handles either people who are successful or whom you admire, write the agent and tell him who you are and what you want.

I think everybody that's been in the business awhile gets "help" letters from young people. Here are two I've recently received:

> Dear Mr. Goldman:
>
> I've got this fantastic screenplay going that I've been guaranteed six hundred thousand dollars for when it's done, but I need the bread fast and I'm a slow writer.
>
> So if you'll do the rest of it with me, I'll cut you in for half. Have we got a deal?

Well, there's no coherent reply you can make to a letter like that. You can pray that the man with the butterfly net catches up to that kid before he does permanent damage, but that's it. It's loony tunes.

Here's the second:

> Dear Mr. Goldman:
>
> I am a young Australian writer—a newcomer both to New York and to the craft of screenwriting. In the past year and a half I have written three screenplays (more accurately, two and a half—the first was a one hour thing commissioned by an Australian director who had seen a short story of mine.)
>
> I also wrote a feature-length script of *Troilus and Cressida*, knowing full well that costume dramas are not a hot ticket with the studios. I was right, however, in thinking that the executives would be more likely to show interest in work from an unknown, if they recognized the subject. Thus I've been able to get *Troilus* read by production v.p.'s at Fox, Paramount and MGM. They were positive about the quality of my work, but the consistent refrain is that it would be too expensive to produce.

My other screenplay is a better prospect, commercially, being a spy thriller dealing with a paranoid who comes into possession of some important government documents. I sent it to MGM last week.

So you see, I am neither an absolute beginner, nor totally naive about the business aspects of screenwriting. Since I am without an agent, however, I do have a lot of questions about how to proceed from here. If you could spare an hour or so to talk to me, I would appreciate it. I promise not to ask for introductions to anybody or beg you to read my work.

There may be no great profit in such a meeting for you, but perhaps it would not be entirely disagreeable. I am not a fool nor (despite the evidence at hand) am I by nature a forward person. The tradition of older writers advising younger is both long and honourable, and I hope you will consider my request in that light.

I don't know what you think, but there was no way I couldn't meet with that kid. I had no way of knowing if he was telling the truth or not, he might have been a hustler from Sandusky. But the idea of assuming that studio executives would know the subject matter of *Troilus* was terribly appealing.

For whatever reason, the letter worked. We met, I answered questions for an hour, I don't think I did him any good, but he got what he wanted from me.

Obviously, I'm not an agent. But that *kind* of letter—thoughtful, serious, I think talented—might have triggered something positive in an agent as well. They do, after all, need clients to survive. It also might not have worked. If not, don't hate them.

Theirs is not an easy life.

Just a couple of reasons to indicate what I mean. I was calling Zig once not long ago, and it was late and I was bitching about something, probably the standard screenwriter's whine: "They don't appreciate me." Whatever. In the middle of my spiel, I could sense his tone changing and just like that I had a thought. And I stopped talking. He asked me why and I told him: "I just realized something: *Nobody ever calls you with good news.*"

And that, I suspect, is true. Clients just don't phone in or write and say thank you. Rather, they think, "That lazy son of a bitch, having lunch when I call, why isn't he out getting me a job, hell, he takes ten percent, why doesn't he *do* something." So there is that, the lack of gratitude that goes with the job. And there is something else, a truth they must live with every day of their lives.

Clients leave them.

Every agent knows that every client will, at some point, become dissatisfied. One top Hollywood agent I talked to almost never mentions a client's name without preceding it with an expletive. Most aren't that open. But the reality is a constant they must endure.

I was at a gathering once where a star was chatting socially with an agent not his own. And the star was being funny and charming and we all listened and laughed and then the star began to tell a story that had happened to him that day, on a taxi ride in from the airport, and—

—and the agent said, quietly but with amazement, "You mean they didn't send a limo?"

The star shrugged and said he didn't want one and went on with his taxi ride material. But I was watching and I saw the look that passed ever so briefly when the agent cut in with the limo line.

It did not surprise me when I learned, shortly afterward, that the star had changed agencies. . . .

Bread

Anywhere from $11,110 to maybe a million....

Meetings

Whoever invented the meeting must have had Hollywood in mind. I think they should consider giving Oscars for meetings: Best Meeting of the Year, Best Supporting Meeting, Best Meeting Based on Material from Another Meeting.

One studio, and this is typical, recently announced that they had one hundred and eighty-three projects in development. Do you know what that figure represents to people in the business?

Heaven.

Look at it logically. Of those one hundred and eighty-three projects, maybe ten, at the outside, will ever happen. And only one person at that studio has the final "go" decision. Well, what are all the other executives supposed to do with their time? How can they justify their salaries? And how can producers fill their days?

Meetings are everyone's salvation.

I suspect that those one hundred and eighty-three projects represent—at the very least—well over a thousand meetings.

Studios rarely initiate projects anymore. So let's say you're a producer and you think the time is ripe for making *The Little Engine That Could*.

So you take a meeting with your agent. The agent says, "Well, animation is awfully expensive nowadays, can you do it live action? I hear Eastwood is a train freak, he might be great for the engineer." The next thing then is to set up getting an option on the rights.

Now, once you've got the rights, you take a meeting with a studio executive. Could be lunch at the Polo Lounge, could be over breakfast coffee. You kibitz awhile about the Rams or the Lakers, and then you lay it on him: *The Little Engine That Could*.

And the executive, no fool, says, "Look, we're not into animation, go see Disney." And you say, "Who's talking animation, I'm talking adventure, suspense, a picture for everyone. And Eastwood might be available—I mean, everybody knows what a train nut he is."

Now you wait while the executive has a meeting with a fellow executive. And they spitball awhile, first trying to figure out what they can get for Richard Pryor. That out of the way, the first executive says: "Eastwood in a train picture, we know how loony he is over trains." The second executive says, "God knows *Silver Streak* took in a ton. And so did *Von Ryan's Express.*" And the first executive says, "On the money, only I think *The Little Engine That Could* will be bigger than both," and then, before his peer can bring up animation, he adds "Done live—action, adventure, the whole ball of wax." And the second executive thinks before saying, "Well, God knows it's a classic, I wonder what sales might say."

Now the executives set up a meeting with the top salespeople and they kick it around. "Sure, Eastwood loves trains and Eastwood in action is money in the bank, but this is kind of a kids' picture, would the two audiences conflict?" "What if they didn't conflict, what if they *combined?*—What if they turned out to be *Star Wars* plus *Every Which Way but Loose?*"

The salespeople ask for a little while to run a couple of surveys, check sales and title familiarity, etc.

The salespeople work their magic and eventually they might decide it was worth a shot. So they meet again with the executives and give their findings, and finally the first executive will have a second meeting with the producer, at which they discuss the parameters of the development deal. Including how much they'll pay for the writer of the first-draft screenplay.

Which is where we come in.

What this chapter is really about is this: behavior in meetings. There are really two kinds of meetings involved here: (1) the audition meeting, when they're thinking of hiring you, and (2) the creative meeting, when the script is done and everybody wants changes.

(1) THE AUDITION MEETING

The proper note to strike in the audition meeting is a mixture of shy, self-deprecating intelligence and wild, barely controllable enthusiasm.

This combo is not something the majority of us were born

with. It's not easy to come by, especially if you're young or starting out or, most importantly, if you need the job. If you do, if you actually *need* it, that fact must go with you to your grave, because they sense things Out There and they will never hire you if you are desperate. Because they then know you don't care about their project; you would take anything they offered.

You walk into the executive's office with your producer leading the way. Introductions follow. Then the standard circling chitchat: "Been here long?" "Actually, I was born in Westwood." "A native? Are they legal?" Chuckle chuckle chuckle.

During this sizing-up time, the executive is trying to answer one question: "Who is this asshole?" He knows you're not Mario Puzo because Puzo wouldn't be there talking about taking twenty-five thou for an iffy project like this. The executive undoubtedly has read something of yours—a treatment, a story maybe, an earlier unmade screenplay. And he's talked with the producer who has probably glanced at the same material.

But are you the one?

That's what they're trying to ascertain. Screenwriting is not something at which you necessarily improve: You may be as good as you're going to get your second or third time out.

Are you the one?

Are you the man in all the world most liable to bring to life this combination of a child's fantasy and a Clint Eastwood bang-bang picture? Because if you are, and you write a screenplay that captures the star, then the producer gets rich and the executive gets a big boost up on his career.

It may seem casual, but there's more riding on this meeting than you ought to think about.

Eventually, after five minutes are fifty, there will be a pause, and the executive will then ask it: "What do you think of the material?"

Do *not* say "I think it's my favorite book and will make the greatest movie since *The Battleship Potemkin*."

Something like this is much better: "Well, of course as you know I'm kind of new at this, I'll probably never know as much as you guys, but of course I've read the book and I wrote my senior thesis on Movement in Contemporary Juvenile Fiction, and this will probably sound stupid, but when the train gets the toys across the mountain, I cried—I don't mean buckets, but there were tears. I guess probably as literature it isn't *Alice in Wonderland*, and this isn't to knock *Alice*, but, well, it never moved me."

Are you the one?

You won't know till your phone rings. . . .

(2) THE CREATIVE MEETING

There is one crucial rule that must be followed in all creative meetings: Never speak first. At least at the start, your job is to shut up.

This transcendental truth came to me early on in my movie work and quite by accident. I was involved with a film that was, I thought, set. The studio had said "Go," preproduction was well under way. I was feeling pretty chipper because everything had gone as well as it could—a few skirmishes, an occasional outbreak of hostility, but bloodshed had been kept to a minimum.

And I get a call from the producer, saying, "Look, I'm in town, I'm free Saturday, save all day, we've got some things to talk about."

Save all day?

That was the phrase that echoed as I marched down to the Sherry for the meeting. I went to his suite, we ordered coffee, and I tried very hard not to let him know how nervous I was: I thought the script was okay and had no idea what he wanted or how in the world (or if) I could fix it.

Because of his "Save all day" warning, I bought a notebook. (Never enter a creative meeting without a notebook.) And I opened it and took out a pen and got ready to face the firing squad. I said, though I didn't know it, the magic words. "Tell me everything you have in mind," I said, and I took the top off the pen and prepared to write.

I didn't know it then, either, but the meeting was over.

Because suddenly, he was unarmed and I had this weapon with dread stopping power: my notebook. I was going to take down everything. *All* his wisdom. Record it then and there.

And, like most producers and executives, he had nothing

specific to say. They are generally not equipped to deal with the intricacies of a script—any more than I could deal with the problems they face.

What he offered was something like this: "I think we have to watch out in case there are any sags," he said.

I repeated "Watch sags" and wrote the words.

"Gotta keep the pace up."

"Pace mustn't flag," I said, and wrote that down.

"And our main guy has gotta always be sympathetic."

"Sympathy for hero."

By then our coffee had arrived, we poured and sipped and then we were into bullshitting about this and that. I was gone in half an hour.

I have followed this procedure in every creative meeting since. If *you* begin, they can counterpunch. Try never to give them the chance.

Allan Burns, a writer friend, recently emerged from a creative meeting in which the studio head had only this comment to make: "The script's got to be twenty-five percent funnier."

A few weeks later, the guy asked after the rewrites. Allan, who co-created *The Mary Tyler Moore Show* and can be funnier than most people, replied, "Well, I'm only eighteen percent funnier so far, which means I've got to be thirty-one percent funnier the rest of the way."

And the studio head didn't know it was a joke: What he said was, after some thought, "Sounds about right."

Usually, before you have a creative meeting, you are stroked. Quite rightly, I think, since most of us are so insecure. It's counterproductive from the producer's point of view to say over the phone, "Get out here, this script sucks." Because when the face-to-face confrontation begins, guns have already been fired across the water.

I recently submitted a script to a producer who read it and called me and said, "It's everything I hoped it would be, why don't you come on out here and we'll talk about details."

I flew to California, met with him, we ordered coffee, I got out my notebook, readied my pen, and said, "Tell me everything you want to say."

Did he ever. He told me "I think the script is downbeat and depressing and I *hate* the main character and it's all got to be done over completely."

I remembered those words very clearly—no need to write them down. But unpleasant as that meeting may have been, note two things: Nothing specific was mentioned, and nothing fatal was done to the structure. The rewrite I did required a lot of brute work, but that's the nature of the beast, we expect that. Since the structure could stay, my job became one of making the new script the same only different.

Most people in the business, being nonwriters, haven't the least notion about what's hard.

A friend of mine is struggling now with an adaptation of a novel in which he was instructed to keep everything just the way it was, except for one small change—make the main character, who is sixty-six in the book, forty years old. (Perfectly logical from a producer's point of view; not only logical but sound business practice. There are no bankable stars who are sixty-six; there are a bunch who can play forty.)

A change like that is agony. Because you can't really keep anything in the book. The problems and tensions of the novel shift epically when you lop a quarter century from the hero's age. The guy doing this job lives across town from me.

If the wind is in the right direction, I can hear his screams. . . .

Gareth Wigan, one of the powers at The Ladd Company, is the best I've met at dealing with script. The first odd thing about Wigan is that he's perfectly willing to spend hours in a meeting, going over your work shot by shot.

Wigan is English, so everything is couched with great gentility. And he will say things (often without referring to the screenplay) like this: "I think perhaps we lose the thread of the narrative near the top of page thirty-seven and don't get back on track till the middle of forty-two."

Frequently, that's the section where you were scrambling and hoped to skill your way past the problem. But when he says something like that, you're so grateful that you can talk as you would to another writer that you often answer, "I got lost there."

And then he will make suggestions. Can we cut the sequence? Can we bring a different character in to bolster things? Can we shift scenes around to aid the structure?

The reason I single out Wigan is not because he's any genius—though he's pretty damn smart—but because, at least in my experience, he is always totally prepared. He's done his homework.

You have no idea how often I've had creative meetings about a script, only to realize half an hour in that the producer or executive hasn't read my script at all.

Usually this happens when you're discussing a rewrite, and they make a remark about a scene that was in the first draft but is gone now. Except they don't know it's gone.

I don't know how frequently this happens in other industries, but it sure happens in movies. It's always a shock and impossible to handle. Because you can't say, "Hey, *putz,* that's not in the script anymore."

I had one meeting with the late Steve McQueen, involving a Western I'd written that, he told me over the phone, he liked a lot, and could we meet?

We met, and the then director of the project, Don Siegel, was also present. And this is about how it went.

> McQUEEN
> I want a campfire scene where the
> two guys get drunk and talk about
> the old days.

> SIEGEL
> He's got that--I think it's fine.

> McQUEEN
> I don't mean that kind of campfire
> scene, I mean a <u>campfire</u> scene.

We met like that for several hours and I still don't know why. But it was madness. Here I was, closeted with these two men whose work I've admired for years, and McQueen kept going on and on about things that he wanted in the script that were already in the script, and Siegel tried to do his best. I just sat there, nodded, took notes, prayed for it all to end. I wasn't surprised, a few weeks later, to learn that Siegel had walked the picture.

Not much more to say about meetings. Except that if we land Eastwood, there's a real shot that *The Little Engine That Could* just might work. . . .

Auteurs

I remember the moment I was first told about the existence of the auteur theory. I listened and listened as the explanation went on, and all I could think was this: "What's the punch line?"

(Briefly, the auteur theory came out of France, where a bunch of young, then would-be directors—Truffaut, Jean-Luc Godard, etc.—promulgated the notion that the director was the *author* of the film. Andrew Sarris of *The Village Voice* is the leading spokesman for the auteurist view in America.)

Maybe it's true in other places. Maybe Truffaut designs his own sets and possibly Fellini operates his own camera and conceivably Kurosawa edits every inch of the films he directs. They are all wonderfully talented men, and where the limits of their talents lie I have no way of knowing. In point of fact, I don't know *anything* about foreign filmmaking; nothing in this book is meant to cover their method of operation.

But I do know this: It sure as shit isn't true in Hollywood.

I have never met another fellow technician, not a single cinematographer or producer or editor, who believes it.

I haven't even met a *director* who believes it.

Godard, in a recent interview, said that the whole thing was patent bullshit from the beginning, an idea devised by the then young scufflers to draw some attention to themselves.

Well, then, if it's so untrue, why is the idea still around? Answer: the media. Every time a piece of criticism or interview refers to a movie as "Francis Coppola's *One from the Heart*" or "Martin Scorsese's *New York, New York*," the auteur notion is prolonged. And I suspect it's going to be with us for a while longer.

The word *author* has been defined as follows: "The person who originates or gives existence to anything."

The word *auteur* has come to mean this: It is the director who *creates* the film. (None of any of this is meant in any way to denigrate directors, by the way. They serve an important function in the making of a film, and the best of them do it well.)

But creator?

Look at it logically. Studio executives are not stupid, and they are, believe it or not, aware of costs. If the director creates the film, why does a studio pay three thousand dollars a week for a top editor? Or four thousand for an equivalent production designer. Or *ten* thousand plus a percentage of the profits to the finest cinematographers?

It's not because they're cute.

And it's not because they want to. They *have* to. Because that's how crucial top technicians are. Crucial *and* creative.

One example now, not because it's famous but because it's absolutely typical: *This is the way things are.* Peter Benchley reads an article in a newspaper about a fisherman who captures a forty-five-hundred-pound shark off the coast of Long Island and he thinks, "What if the shark became territorial, what if it wouldn't go away?" And eventually he writes a novel on that notion and Zanuck-Brown buy the movie rights, and Benchley and Carl Gottlieb write a screenplay, and Bill Butler is hired to shoot the movie, and Joseph Alves, Jr., designs it, and Verna Fields is brought in to edit, and, maybe most importantly of all, Bob Mattey is brought out of retirement to make the monster. And John Williams composes perhaps his most memorable score.

How in the world is Steven Spielberg the "author" of that? Why is it often referred to today as "Steven Spielberg's *Jaws*"? Am I ever not knocking Spielberg: He did, for me, a world-class job of directing that wonderful shocker.

But there's no author to that movie that I can see.

If I haven't mentioned Dreyfuss and Scheider and Shaw, it's not because they weren't crucial too. But there is a theory put forward by some (Gore Vidal for one) that the true influence of the director died with the coming of sound. In the silent days, Griffith could stand there and, with his actor's voice, he could talk to Lillian Gish or whoever and literally mold the performance with long, heated verbal instructions *while the camera was rolling.*

Not anymore. Now the director must stand helpless alongside the crew and watch the actors work at their craft. Sure, he can do retakes, he can talk to them before, but once the shooting starts, he can't move up and verbally be Svengali.

So why does much of the media continue with the notion that

the maker of the film is the director? Among lots of reasons, here are a few.

It's convenient. If you want to talk about *Jaws*, you can't mention all the technicians I named earlier. So shorthand is one reason.

Another is that most people who write about movies don't know much about the actual problems of making one. (No reason they should. *Our* job is to make movies, their job is to write or talk about them.)

Still another is that even if you're involved with the making of a film, it's damn near impossible to say who is responsible for what.

And don't forget publicity—they don't send production designers out on hype tours. It's the star or the director. So when the star says "I made up my part" or the director explains that he had this vision and *voilà*, it's now up there on the screen for you all to see and admire, that's what gets reported.

As I've said before—and please believe me, it's true (and if you don't believe me, ask *anybody* in the business for verification)—*movies are a group endeavor*. Basically, there are seven of us who are crucial to a film, and we all seven have to be at our best if the movie's going to have a shot at quality. Listed alphabetically:

> the actor
> the cameraman
> the director
> the editor
> the producer
> the production designer
> the writer.

In addition, there are times (*Chariots of Fire*) when the composer is as important as any element. But that varies. I think what made *The Exorcist* work was the remarkable makeup that Dick Smith created for the girl. Truly dazzling special effects are not easy to bring off, and sometimes that department makes the movie wonderful.

To elevate any single element in a film is simply silly and wrong. We all contribute, we are all at each other's mercy. To say that anyone is the "author" of a film is demeaning to the rest of us.

Besides it's being false, that's another of my chief quibbles with the auteur theory: It's demeaning.

I also think that it's dangerous.

Dangerous to whom?

To the director.

I believe that the auteur theory was responsible, just to take one example, for the collapse of the career of one of my favorite directors: Alfred Hitchcock. (You may not have known that there was a collapse, not from his reviews. But after *Psycho*, in 1960, oh, what a fall was there.) Let me spend the next few pages trying to explain what I mean.

As noted, the notion began in France around '54, and for a while it attracted all the seriousness of the annual meeting of the Flat Earth Society. But Truffaut and his peers were bright and gifted and energetic; they kept plugging away.

One of the things they had to do, since they were advancing a new theory, was to come up with new heroes—heretofore critically ignored directors who had, in their minds, "a personal vision."

Hitchcock, from '54 to '60, was on a truly wondrous streak: glorious entertainments. *Rear Window, To Catch a Thief, The Man Who Knew Too Much, North by Northwest*, and *Psycho*, among others.

Because of his skill and his tv program and his wizardry at personal publicity, Hitchcock became, along with Cecil B. De Mille, one of the two most famous directors in the business. In other words, a star.

But not taken very seriously.

He won some Oscar nominations, but never the Best Director award. He was a great molder of sophisticated thrillers. But not Important.

Just what the auteurists were looking for. Famous but ignored critically. With a personal vision. Perfect.

What they did in their writings was to elevate him. Let's say he was Ian Fleming before they began. Well, they didn't say he was John le Carré, they made him Graham Greene.

Ernest Lehman has been quoted in a recent interview on the subject of *Family Plot*, a 1974 film he made with Hitchcock.

By mistake a propman had two pieces of wood set up so that they looked vaguely like a cross, and the car goes downhill and crashes through a field, goes through a fence and knocks over the cross. Some learned New York critic commented: There's Alfred Hitchcock's anti-Catholicism coming out again. When I was at the Cannes Film Festival with *Family Plot,* Karen Black, Bruce Dern and I attended a press conference, and some French journalist had the symbolism in the license plate all worked out: 885 DJU. He had some *elaborate* explanation for those numbers. When he got through explaining it, I said "I hate to tell you this but the reason I used that license plate number was that it used to be my own, and I felt it would be legally safe to use." So much for symbolism.

The sudden firestorm of *serious* criticism concerning Hitchcock continued, reaching these shores shortly after the release of *Psycho.* I suppose it continues to this day, although for me it peaked in the mid-sixties with the publication of one of the genuinely ego-ridden books of the postwar world, the Truffaut/Hitchcock interview. It purports to talk about directing, but on every page the subtext tells us: "Aren't you fortunate that we're around to tell you these things?"

Anyway, Hitchcock was not unaffected by all this.

My God, who could be? I know if somebody came up to me and said, "Do you know who you really are, you're a modern Dostoevski," I would send him straight to Bellevue. But if people kept coming and coming, bright and serious young critics, and they said, again and again, "Only you, Bill, only you and Fëdor really understood the anguish of religious mysticism, look at the number of Christ figures in your novels, count the crosses referred to in *Tinsel,* the torture in *Marathon Man* is only a thinly disguised reference to the blood of Jesus and the torture *He* suffered—" pretty soon I'd start thinking, "Ah, well, who am I to argue against so many brilliant scholars? They're right. Of course they're right. It's me and Dostoevski all the way."

Following *Psycho,* in '63, came *The Birds.* Some nice shock effects, period. And from then on it really got bad—*Marnie, Torn Curtain, Topaz, Frenzy*—awful, awful films.

But they got great reviews from the auteur critics.

The reason is this: Once an auteurist surrenders himself to an idol, for reasons passing understanding, said auteurist flies in the face of one of life's basic truths: People can have good days, and people can have bad days.

Any movie by Chaplin, even shit Chaplin, is terrific. (I wish them all a very long life on a desert island with nothing but *The Countess From Hong Kong* for company.) *Any* John Ford, another of their favorites. And, of course, any Hitchcock.

I think the last two decades of Hitchcock's career were a great waste and sadness. He was technically as skillful as ever. But he had become encased in praise, inured to any criticism.

Hitchcock himself had become The Man Who Knew Too Much.

So yes, I think the auteur theory ruined him—or at least his belief in it. And I think that belief is dangerous to any director. I mentioned before that no director I ever met said out loud he believed in the auteur theory. But God knows what's silently eating away at them in the dark nights of their souls.

Is there then no American auteur director? Perhaps there is one. One man who thinks up his own stories and produces his pictures and directs them too. And also serves as his own cinematographer. Not to mention he also does his own editing. All of this connected with an intensely personal and unique vision of the world. That man is Russ Meyer.

I can't wait for Truffaut's book about *him*. . . .

Beginnings

The first fifteen pages are the most important of any screenplay. (To which Paul Newman adds: "Yes. And the final fifteen minutes are the most important of any *movie.*" Point well taken: When the end of a movie is the most exciting or emotionally involving part, then the audience troops happily out of the darkness, and that's how word of mouth is born.)

But for now, we can leave such things as word of mouth to our daydreams. For now, we don't care if they like the movie or not; we want somebody to make it.

And the beginning cannot be overemphasized enough. One obvious reason, of course, is statistical reality. Remember that a major star may read two hundred scripts a year, an executive twice that many.

Remember that poor executive? He's been at meetings and screenings and lunches all week; he's probably spent three or more hours a day with the phone growing out of his ear. Now it's Friday night and what accompanies him home?

Screenplays.

Groan.

A sludge pile of scripts. Heavy to carry, heavier to wade through. Maybe he puts it off on Friday. Maybe he even sneaks through Saturday. But he knows one thing: That pile isn't going to go away. So at some point he sinks into a chair, takes the first script, opens it. (He may—I know I would—peek at the last page, because if that page reads 180, he knows it's probably not a properly constructed piece of work, just as if it read 90—135 is about right.)

Now he may study the format: Does it *look* like a screenplay? Is it legible or some Xerox that is hard to read and slants across the paper? Finally, he will take a deep breath, turn to the fade-in. And do you know what he wants at that moment?—

—he wants to love it.

Truly. He wants his head knocked off, he's been doing this a long time, thousands of *Rocky* rip-offs, of *Star Wars* steals. It's been so long since he's been thrilled by something.

At last he begins to read.

Some screenplays are like Marley—dead to begin with. Westerns. Or disaster films. Or a movie about two octogenarians tending each other through their final days of leprosy. But maybe only five percent of screenplays fall into the Marley category.

But a much larger percentage than that are dead by page 15. Because by then an experienced reader will either be hooked or bored. And if he's bored, he may skip to page 50, read a few more pages, then on to the end, a cursory glance—

—and the ball game's over.

All right, what's a decent beginning for a movie? This is not:

```
FADE IN ON

NIGHT, A THICK DESERTED WOOD, AND A BEAUTIFUL GIRL
running for her life. At least she would be beau-
tiful if her face were in repose--but right now
panic distorts her features. She plunges on, the
branches of the trees slashing at her clothing.
She runs and runs and, with every step, her terror
grows. Now, suddenly, she stops, trying to hold
her breath as she turns, looks back, listens.

CUT TO

THE WOODS BEHIND HER. For a moment there is noth-
ing--then the unmistakable sound of growls,
heavy footsteps.

CUT TO

THE BEAUTIFUL GIRL as she involuntarily shud-
ders, begins to run again as we

HOLD.

THE GIRL IS GONE, we can hear her running on, but
now the growls grow louder, the footsteps too and
as we watch--

A DISFIGURED GIANT appears, stopping where the
girl stopped. His face has been hideously burned.
```

He looks around, growling and then, as the sound
of a female cry comes from up ahead, he begins to
lumber forward again as we

CUT TO

THE BEAUTIFUL GIRL and she's tripped over a log,
fallen heavily, the wind knocked out. One of her
legs has been cut and it's starting to bleed. Maybe the sight of the blood spurs her on or maybe
she's just a girl with a lot of courage, but she
ignores the pain, forces herself to her feet, runs
on, only now, if anything, she's going faster than
before and the tree branches are really cutting in
at her but she ignores it, goes racing through the
night as we

CUT TO

THE DISFIGURED GIANT, growling as he moves after
her, and he's strong, you can see the power in his
body, but with his enormous size there is also
something else apparent--a lack of speed and

CUT TO

A TREE BRANCH, whipping across the BEAUTIFUL
GIRL'S face, a slice of blood curls down her cheek
and it must hurt like crazy but she ignores it,
rushes faster than she's ever gone and

CUT TO

THE DISFIGURED GIANT, and maybe he senses he's
losing her, maybe not, but he throws his horrid
face to the heavens and a wild scream of frustration bursts from him and

CUT TO

THE BEAUTIFUL GIRL, and the sound is audible and
it's not close and she keeps on, keeps on and

CUT TO

THE DISFIGURED GIANT, lumbering forward, screaming again at the night and

CUT TO

THE BEAUTIFUL GIRL, and this time the sound is farther back--she's winning, she's winning and she knows it, but all that does is summon more energy and she's never run this fast, never in her life, and for the first time now, briefly, the panic is less, you can see that, and so what if the woods are thick, so what if her leg and her face are bloody, she's got a chance at survival and

CUT TO

THE WOODS, starting at last to thin out, we're coming closer and closer to the edge of the thick trees and

CUT TO

THE DISFIGURED GIANT, slowing, panting, he bangs a great hand against a tree in wild frustration and

CUT TO

THE BEAUTIFUL GIRL as ANOTHER DISFIGURED GIANT appears suddenly in front of her, and this one makes the first one look handsome and

CUT TO

THE BEAUTIFUL GIRL, screaming as the SECOND DIS-FIGURED GIANT grabs her, raises her high in his hands, throws her to the floor of the woods, and

CUT TO

THE SECOND DISFIGURED GIANT growling in triumph as he falls on her, pins her helpless, and she struggles, tries to twist and kick and

CUT TO

THE FIRST DISFIGURED GIANT, bursting onto the
scene--he too drops beside the BEAUTIFUL GIRL,
and as they commence to rip at her clothes--

DISSOLVE TO

It matters not where we dissolve, I suspect our world-weary
executive has already closed the script and reached for the next
in his endless pile.

Why? I mean, what's so terrible about these pages? It's got
action, suspense, shock, mystery, blah blah blah.

Well, among other things, it's television.

This paragraph contains all that I know about writing for
television. They need a hook. And they need it fast. Because
they're panicked you'll switch to ABC. So tv stuff tends to begin with some kind of grabber.

But in a movie, and *only* at the beginning of a movie, *we have
time.* Not a lot, but some.

Time to set up our people.

Time to set up our situation.

Time, if you will, to set up our particular world.

As I sit here I can only think of one first-class modern novel,
movie, or play that begins at full speed, and that's Malraux's
Man's Fate. Clearly there must be others, but not all that many,
which perhaps underscores the point: In narrative writing of
any sort, you must eventually seduce your audience. But seduce
doesn't mean rape.

Here's another beginning that makes a mistake of a different
sort, but one no less uncommon:

FADE IN ON

CENTRAL PARK. New York City. A glorious spring
dawn.

CUT TO

```
A COUPLE OF JOGGERS, moving quickly along. Ahead
of them is a hill and they start up it, then stop
dead, staring, and as they do--


CUT TO


THE TOP OF THE HILL AS FIFTY CAMELS come roaring
over the crest of the hill, bearing down on the
joggers.
```

More than likely, our studio executive will stop right there. He may even pitch the screenplay across the room. Why? I mean, it's kind of an interesting visual, fifty camels racing across the Sheep Meadow. You certainly don't sit there and say, "Oh Christ, here's another goddam Central Park camel opening."

And probably, if instead of Central Park the movie began in the Sahara, the executive would read on.

Or if the script was written say, by Woody Allen, he would most certainly continue. Because Allen is a pro, and he understands the realities of the picture business. If he wants fifty camels in Central Park, there must be a valid reason, a payoff somewhere down the line. But few of us are Woody Allen.

And this is an amateurish beginning.

Do you know what would more than likely go through the executive's mind when he read that? Something like this: "Fifty camels? Where are we going to rent them? And for how much? And where are we going to train them to run in a pack? And who's going to do the training? And for how much? And how do we get the goddam things to New York? What's the going rate on camel shipping? And once we get them there, is the city going to give us a permit? For fifty camels? In Central Park? *Is this writer crazy?*" And there would go your screenplay flying across the room.

When you write something, if the picture happens, someone must actually go about executing the details of the script. Hardworking technicians, like yourself. So if you get a flight of fancy that entails a sudden snowstorm blanketing Honolulu airport, there better be a good reason. A crucial reason. Because that is not an easy thing to recreate.

And movies are not made by elves and fairies. . . .

Having now shown you what I consider to be a rotten beginning and an amateurish one, it would be nice if I could write you a good one. But since I'm never quite sure what "good" means, the best I can do is put down what I think is the classiest opening I've done—one that, by the way, was never shot. The notion came from a recurring flying dream that the director, George Roy Hill, had as a child.

This was the start of *The Great Waldo Pepper*. (*Waldo*, remember, was the story of these daredevil flyers in the twenties, grown-up children who wanted to impress girls and be heroes and fly.)

```
FADE IN ON

THIS KID. Maybe he's ten, freckled and bright-
eyed. Very American-looking. And we're in CLOSE
UP, so we don't know where we are or when, but that
doesn't matter; what matters is that the KID is
concentrating on something just as hard as he can.
He's staring off and biting his lip and

CUT TO

A TEN-YEAR-OLD GIRL. CLOSE UP. And there are a lot
of boys who are going to lose a lot of sleep over
this one when she gets a little older. She's look-
ing up at something just now, we don't know what
yet, but she's so excited you can feel the pound-
ing of her heart. Now--

CUT TO

THE BOY. Not quite so close up this time. He takes
half a step forward, then hesitates, stops, and
begins kind of to rock back and forth, nervously
back and forth as we

CUT TO
```

THE TEN-YEAR-OLD GIRL, AND NOW ANOTHER GIRL THE
SAME AGE JOINS HER. This one is pretty, too, and
she, too, stares up at the same angle, and she's
just as excited as her friend, and they stand
there, side by pretty side, watching and waiting,
watching and waiting.

CUT TO

THE BOY. He takes a deep breath, slowly starts
running forward, and as he does

CUT TO

THE TWO PRETTY GIRLS, and whatever's going on,
it's just too exciting, they simply can't stand it
and, keeping their eyes on the running BOY, they
reach for each other's hands, find them, clutch
each other tightly as we

CUT TO

THE BOY, running faster now, picking up speed as
he tears across this enormous hill, coming closer
and closer to the edge of it, and beyond that edge
there's one hell of a sheer drop-off but that
doesn't seem to matter, because now the BOY is going all out and the edge is just ahead and

CUT TO

THE GIRLS, watching, clinging to each other,
their eyes wide, going wider and now

CUT TO

THE BOY, suddenly extending his arms out like
wings, launching himself off the edge of the cliff
and

CUT TO

THE GIRLS, waving joyously as the BOY soars over
them, changes his arm position, banks, flies back

over them a second time, waves down, then starts
to climb as the GIRLS continue to stare up at him,
their eyes filled with wonder.

CUT TO

THE COUNTRYSIDE AS THE BOY SOARS ALONG and, Jesus,
it's beautiful up there, green and sunlit and pure
and now

CUT TO

A DIFFERENT BOY, SOARING THROUGH SPACE.

CUT TO

A DIFFERENT GIRL WATCHING THAT DIFFERENT BOY, but
that same look of dreamlike wonder is in her eyes,
too, and

CUT TO

STILL ANOTHER BOY, running along the roof of a
barn, and when he reaches the edge he, too, starts
to fly and

CUT TO

ANOTHER BOY, poised in a treetop, but only for a
second, and as he glides into space

CUT TO

THE SKY, and it's full of flying children.

CUT TO

THE GROUND and the GIRLS are there, beautiful,
awed, waiting and

CUT TO

THE SKIES AGAIN, and now the BOYS are starting to
come in from unexpected angles, soaring up from

the bottom, zooming in from the corners, and the
GIRLS are clapping and waving and crying and everything's going faster, getting more and more
wild, it's all reaching a peak now, and the GIRLS
just love it, they do, you can see it in their eyes
as they watch their heroes and the flying dream is
perfect, and no one ever crashes, not ever, not
once, not here, not now. . . .

After this there was the sound of a motor and we dissolved to
Waldo flying into town, as he does now in the movie.

Why did I like that? It's hard to remember for sure, but I
guess I thought it was original. And unexpected. And also, in a
weird way, logical—

—I thought it set up the world.

Because the barnstorming pilots were just adolescents nour-
ishing a heroic fantasy that World War I had taken away. And
what this sequence was intended to do was show the daydream
at its best: girls, glory, freedom, etc. I still think it does.

George Hill disagreed, and this opening was gone by either
the second or third draft. I suspect I argued for it, but you can
only do that for so long: If your director either has no faith in a
sequence or just plain won't shoot it, it usually doesn't end up
on the silver screen.

My memory is that George felt the fantasy clashed with the
reality that was to follow. Plus, he had shot a lovely sequence in
The World of Henry Orient where the two teen-age heroines go careening around New York in slow motion, jumping high over
things, floating. *You mean 'careering'!*

Another opening I wrote that wasn't used was for *All the President's Men.* I'll describe what it was briefly, but first let me explain why I wrote it.

When I began researching the Woodward-Bernstein book,
before it was published, it seemed, at best, a dubious project.
Politics were anathema at the box office, the material was talky,
there was no action, etc., etc. Most of all, though, people were
sick to fucking death of Watergate.

For months, whenever anyone asked me what I was working
on, and I answered, there was invariably the same reply: "Gee,

('Careening' only happens to boats.)

don't you think we've heard enough about Watergate?" Repeated often enough, that can make you lose confidence.

Because, of course, we had. Heard enough and more than enough. Years of headlines, claims and disclaimers, lies, and occasional clarifying truths.

I decided my best shot was to try and surprise people.

So I opened, intentionally, with the most cornball shot in the world—the Washington Monument lit up at night. Then another totally predictable shot—the Watergate complex, also at night. Then inside the building to the Democratic National Committee offices and a bunch of men, quietly and expertly, starting the famous break-in.

I truly hoped at this point the audience would be groaning. "What are we doing here for chrissakes? We *know* it all already."

The robbery went on, tautly and expertly in silence—*only they had the wrong keys.* They goofed and had to leave the place, frustrated and angry.

The reason I opened that way was because people *didn't* know it all. The famous break-in was either the third or fourth attempt, and what I wanted was to have people suddenly looking at each other and thinking, "Hey, maybe I better pay attention, there's stuff here I hadn't heard about."

The opening was never shot because the movie always had a length problem and the feeling was we didn't need the red herring to start off with. And that was a very sound decision. If the original opening had been incorporated, and you looked at it today, I think you would wonder what the hell it was doing there.

At the time, though, at least in theory, it had a purpose. To set up a world, a world in which there would be traps and surprises.

In a sense, a screenplay, whether a romance or a detective story, is a series of surprises. We detonate these as we go along. But for a surprise to be valid, we must first set the ground rules, indicate expectations.

And that's what beginnings are all about. . .

Endings

Near the conclusion of *North by Northwest*, Cary Grant finds himself in something of a pickle.

His true love, Eva Marie Saint, is dangling helplessly in space on the face of Mount Rushmore. If she falls, *splat*. The reason she has not fallen is that Grant is holding her with one hand while with the other he grabs a rock ledge. Not easy. Watching all this is Martin Landau, the subvillain, who stands a few feet away, holding the precious statuette that contains valuable microfilm inside, said microfilm being of great danger to America should it fall into enemy hands. Grant, desperate, looks up at Landau and asks for help.

Landau walks over to Grant and, instead of bending down and aiding him, puts his foot on Grant's fingers and begins pressing down. He grinds his shoe down as hard as he can.

That's the pickle.

Now, between that moment and the end of this superb Ernest Lehman–Alfred Hitchcock collaboration, the following occurs.

(a) Landau is made to cease and desist.
(b) Grant saves himself.
(c) Grant also saves Eva Marie Saint.
(d) The two of them get married.
(e) The microfilm is saved for America.
(f) James Mason, the chief villain, is captured and handed over to the authorities.
(g) Grant and Saint take a train ride back east.

That's a lot of narrative to be successfully tied up. And I would like you to guess how long it takes in terms of screen time for it to be accomplished. Got your guess? Here's the answer—

—forty-three *seconds*.

Here's how they do it, from the moment where Landau is

117

crunching Grant's hand. The camera's in close up on the shoe and the fingers. A shot rings out. The shoe begins to slide away from the fingers. Next a cut of the statuette falling safely to the ground and cracking, revealing the microfilm inside. Now Landau falls to his death off Mount Rushmore. Now another part of Mount Rushmore, where Leo G. Carroll, a good guy, thanks a police officer who is holding a rifle. Behind Carroll is Mason, flanked by more officers. Now back to Grant and Eva Marie, him saying you can do it, her saying I can't, back and forth, quick cuts between them, and then a really brilliant shot of Grant pulling her up, only now he's not on Mount Rushmore, he's in the upper berth of a train, and he brings her to him, calls her "Mrs. Thornhill"—Thornhill being his last name, so we know they're married now—and as they embrace, a final shot of the train roaring into a tunnel as *The End* flashes on the screen.

I don't know a more adroit ending to a film.

Lehman wrote it that way for two reasons. "All the essentials were on the screen. And there was so much unexplained that the one shot of Leo Carroll and Mason and the authorities took care of. People might have asked, 'How did Leo Carroll get there? How did he find the authorities? How did they capture Mason?' If we had had more, it would have made us vulnerable to looking like an entire grocery shelf of open cans of peas."

I am not suggesting that you have to go like a streak when you're running for curtain. In *Butch Cassidy,* for instance, after they are shot and the Bolivian cavalry arrives, getting the cavalry into position takes sixty seconds. It could have been done in one: You could have seen the officer giving instructions (as you do) and then, instead of shot after shot of armed soldiers running up stairs, you could have just gone to the final shot when they're all in position; the same information would have been given.

But not the emotion. Because since, in theory, we're rooting for the heroes to get away, the awesome number of troops ranged against them has an impact that has nothing to do with numbers.

Endings, frankly, are a bitch.

A proper ending for a film is one in which an expectation is fulfilled for the audience. But once they get a sense of it coming, often they're ahead of you. You don't have to rush. But you must never waste even a single shot—because I think the ending requires the most delicate and thoughtful writing of any part of a movie.

Example of a misconceived ending: *Excalibur*.

The movie is the story of the Arthurian legend, and Excalibur, of course, is this magical sword that Arthur possessed.

Okay, we're into the closing minutes and Arthur is mortally wounded. He lies there bloody while a knight, Percival, drops beside him. Arthur says to take Excalibur and find a smooth stretch of water and pitch the sword into the water. Percival doesn't want to do it. Arthur says "Go."

So Percival goes. And he rides and he finds some pretty lake or whatever and he rides into it and he takes Excalibur, brings it up to throw it—

—but he can't bring himself to do it. We're in on Percival's face now and we see he's suffering. He's got his orders, but this, after all, is a magical sword. Finally, he turns his horse around and rides back to Arthur, still clutching the weapon.

Arthur is still expiring. How'd it go? he asks. Percival says, I couldn't do it. Arthur says, well, you've got to, because someday, when a worthy king comes by, Excalibur will rise again from the waters for him. Back, Percival gets on his horse. Back to the pretty lake or whatever. He hesitates, finally does what he's been told to do, and the sword magically disappears beneath the surface. Now he goes back to Arthur a second time, only Arthur's dead and gone, drifting mystically out to sea in some boat. Credits start to roll.

Why is that so terrible?

Because that entire first trip of Percival, where he can't bring himself to follow orders, deflates the ending of the movie dreadfully. You sit there (I did, anyway) getting pissed at the flick just when you're supposed to be most deeply engrossed: My God, King Arthur is *dying*.

And it was all so unnecessary. Percival could have made his objections and Arthur could have explained about some future king passing by and the sword rising for him, the first time. That extra ride to the water and back—and we're not talking about much more than a minute of screen time—was, for me, irritating and damaging.

I think I can guess why it's there. Excalibur is a very valuable article, and even when his dying King gives an order, noble Percival can't follow it. In other words, the creators of the film were setting up the sword.

But this is the *end.* If we haven't established after close to two hours that Excalibur is not your everyday weapon, we are in very big trouble.

This identical sequence would have worked just fine at the beginning of the film. Because then Percival's disobedience would have told us something we didn't know: Excalibur is the most valuable sword in the world. But to tell us something we already know at the end of a film is deadly.

Screen time is a most mysterious thing: The same scene must be written differently depending upon where it comes in the narrative, beginning or middle or end. Because the more information an audience has, the less additional information it requires. And the ladling out of when and where something is necessary is one of the requisite components to skillful storytelling.

As has been said for years, it's possible to conceive narrative as an endless piece of string. The writer makes two snips, one for the beginning, one at the end, and the placement of those snips may be as important as anything a writer does.

Narrative as *I* see it has nothing whatsoever to do with what *you* consider the story. We are moved by different things, interested in different aspects, confident in making different confrontations work. So we will cut the string in not remotely the same spots.

It's usual to note that in a screenplay, not only do you attack each scene as late as is possible, you attack the entire story the same way. The camera tells you so much so quickly that you are always forced to get on with it.

Jaws began with the shark snacking on the girl, but it didn't have to; *2001: A Space Odyssey* didn't begin in the future but thousands of years in the past. You could have done the same with *Jaws*—shots of little one-cell sea creatures and then structures a little more complex and then the tiniest minnow and then a bigger minnow and then a small fish that shockingly bites a smaller fish and then to piranhas and then, all the time with the music building, maybe a barracuda and then a small shark, music very loud now, and then a bigger shark until—climax, crash of cymbals—Peter Benchley's monster comes roaring at us on the screen.

Might have worked. Sure didn't hurt *2001*.

You must cut the narrative string yourself, with what you emotionally feel is sound. No one can tell you how or when. Because there are no rules.

To try and validate that, let me end this discussion with another film directed by the man who directed *North by Northwest*, Mr. Hitchcock. More specifically, *Psycho*, my favorite of his work and a film that a film freak recently referred to as "the greatest splatter film."

Two points about *Psycho*, one briefly dealing with screen time, and then on to its ending.

My guess is, when that movie is mentioned, everyone first thinks of the shower scene. Janet Leigh and what happens to her. But when we say "the shower scene" we don't mean the lady adjusting the water temperature before she lathers up and we don't mean Tony Perkins doing his household chores later, getting the tub all nice and tidy again. We mean this: the knifing. I don't know if there are that many more famous sequences in modern films. The impact, the shock, all of it. From first stab to last, it runs *seventeen seconds*. To repeat: Screen time is most mysterious.

Now to the ending. For me perhaps the most remarkable aspect of *Psycho* is this: I don't know of another major film that has as atrocious, as boring—as in all ways wrong—an ending.

In the last reel, Janet Leigh's sister, Vera Miles, goes into the main house and she's in panic and alone and she runs just where we don't want her to run—into the basement.

Now she's in a room down there and turns on a light revealing—sitting alone, her back to us—"Mother." She goes to the old lady, turns the chair (and I can still hear the audience scream), and in close up comes this chilling-in-the-deepest-sense shot of the skeleton with clothes on. Vera screams in terror, turns—and *whammo*, there's Tony Perkins in drag, the killing knife in his hands. More screams as he starts to attack, and then the hero, John Gavin, leaps into the room and the light bulb is swaying as he wrestles with Perkins and the music is blasting away and we have the fight intercut with Vera's hysteria and these shots of "Mother," her skull changing in front of us as the light bulb in the ceiling swings and swings. Fabulous.

It's sure as hell a high spot, and I'm willing to bet it's the last thing most of us remember clearly, but it's not the ending.

The ending is seven full minutes away.

And five of those seven minutes are taken up with one of the great snooze scenes, where the local shrink comes in and delivers this agonizingly primitive course in Freud, where he tells us that Perkins is a nut-cake.

Well, we've been pretty clued in to that fact by this time.

I can only guess as to why that doesn't mar the movie; I think the high points are so extraordinary that we're more than satisfied, we'll forgive anything. When I saw the movie, in 1960, I remember the audience screamed so much during the basement sequence that they were almost relieved there was nothing more to jolt them—there was nervous laughter and chitchat from the basement till the end. Nobody listened to the psychiatrist.

In any case, *Psycho,* for me, remains unique. The most important minutes of the film are totally soporific, and yet the film is still a glory. Amazing. Maybe Hitchcock is the only director who could have pulled it off.

After all, he spent half a century getting away with murder. . . .

Speed

I think screenplays should be written with as much speed as possible—and with even more deliberation.

By "as much speed as possible" I don't mean to suggest you should throw a bag over its head and do it for Old Glory. But I do believe that you should push yourself hard and continually.

What's important to decide here is your own specific pace. If, for example, when you're going well, you do one to two pages a day, when you write a screenplay, I would try and reach the second number. If you do seven to ten when you're rolling, try and get to ten.

The reasoning (if you can call it that) is, I believe somehow, that extra energy translates itself to the page, and from there to the reader.

Maybe it does, anyway. Maybe sometimes.

As an example of the "deliberation" mentioned above, I'd like to talk briefly about the writing of *Butch Cassidy and the Sundance Kid.*

I first read about Butch and Sundance in the late 1950's, and the story of the two outlaws fascinated me. I began researching them in a haphazard way; there weren't many books about them then, but there were articles and I would seek them out and read them. The more I read, the deeper my fascination became.

In 1963 I met a movie producer, Lawrence Turman (*The Graduate*), and talked to him about the material. He was tremendously helpful in trying to figure out a story line.

Because as colorful as the material was, it had inherent problems. It covered a number of years, it moved from continent to continent. Terribly sprawling. Now, if you're writing an epic, you can sprawl to your heart's content, but this was no epic; rather, I thought it was a personal story of these two unusual outlaws.

Eventually, I'd done all the research I could bear, I hoped I

123

had a story that would prove coherent, so I sat down and wrote the first draft in 1966.

It took four weeks.

When someone asks how long it takes to write a screenplay, I'm never sure what to answer. Because I don't think four weeks is what it took to do *Butch*. For me, eight years is closer to the truth.

In any case, before you begin, you must have everything clear in your head and you must be comfortable with the story you're trying to tell. Once you start writing, go like hell—

—but don't fire till you're ready. . . .

Subtext

You are standing on top of a hill with a snowball in your hand. You swing your arm back and let it go. If the snow is dry, the object that reaches the bottom of the hill will look very much like the object that left your hand. But if the snow is moist, if it's good packing, what reaches the bottom of the hill will have traveled the same path as when the snow was dry, but it will have accumulated size and weight.

That accumulation brings us to the problem of subtext.

This is going to be very brief, since subtext is worthy of many volumes of discussion. Probably no narrative work in any form of any quality can exist without it and, probably again, no narrative form can exist without it as easily as the screenplay. (Because the camera expresses so much of it for us.)

What is subtext? Just what the word implies. The text is what's written on the page. *Sub-* means "under" or "beneath." Subtext, then, is not stated in the words, but it is the pulse beating beneath those words; it is the unexpressed subconscious life that brings size and weight to your writing.

Three examples, the first from Raymond Chandler, in describing correctly, I think, decent movie writing.

A man and his wife are riding silently upward in an elevator. They are silent, the woman carries her purse, the man has his hat on. The elevator stops at an intermediate floor. A pretty girl gets on. The man takes off his hat.

This is not a scene about manners. It's about a marriage in trouble. The subtext tells us, with wonderful economy, a helluva lot about that married couple. If, for example, the couple's destination is a divorce lawyer, I wouldn't be a bit surprised. Wherever they're heading, they're not giddily enchanted with each other. And if, a few pages on, they have a wild fight, the simple act of his removing his hat for the pretty girl would make a logical and movingly human trigger.

The World According to Garp. More specifically, the scene where we first meet Robin Williams as the grown-up hero.

Mary Beth Hurt is sitting on the grandstand of the college athletic field, studying. In front of the grandstand is the running track. Robin Williams appears on the right-hand side of the frame, runs to the left out of the frame. Pause. Now he reappears, running backward. Then he leaves the track and begins running up and down the bleachers, right next to where she's studying, and he says something like I hope I'm not bothering you, and she says something like no, not at all, and he keeps on going up and down as they get into what it is she's studying.

This is a scene about neither athletics nor academics, it's about making love.

All About Eve, the glorious central twenty-five-minute party sequence. (It's where Bette Davis utters the now famous line "Fasten your seat belts; It's going to be a bumpy night." It's also where Marilyn Monroe scored so heavily as an aspiring actress, "a graduate of the Copacabana School of Dramatic Art.")

The setup for the party is this: Davis is a great, flamboyant aging (she's just turned forty) Broadway star. She is in love with Gary Merrill, her director, who is in love with her. As well as being talented, he is also thirty-two. Merrill has been in Hollywood, directing his first film, but now, the night of his return, is his birthday.

Davis is upstairs, dressed, her guests about to arrive. Thelma Ritter tells her that Merrill has already arrived and has been downstairs for twenty minutes, talking with Anne Baxter, Davis's secretary. Everybody loves Anne Baxter except Davis, whom Baxter is driving mad with her kindness.

Davis goes downstairs, interrupts Baxter and Merrill. Baxter leaves them. They have a fight: Why didn't he come upstairs? He explains gently that Eve is fascinated with Hollywood and they were just talking. She doesn't buy. He gets angry.

There are eight more scenes that follow in which a lot of narrative happens, important to the movie but not to this discussion. During the course of the party, Davis starts sober, gets increasingly drunk, and manages to insult everyone in the world near and dear to her.

She behaves outrageously, but you don't hate her. Because the sequence isn't about how Merrill was late, and it isn't about Davis being jealous of Anne Baxter.

It's about her terrifying fear of aging.
And it's funny. And it's sad.

You can categorize movies in infinite ways. One way that pertains here is this: There are three kinds of movies—

    (1) movies that aspire to quality and succeed
    (2) movies that aspire to quality and don't succeed
    (3) movies that never meant to be any good at all.

The third group, alas, comprises the majority of commercial films. It's hard to define this kind of film, but try this: movies for which the original pulse was either totally or primarily financial. Rip-offs, spinoffs, sequels, etc. This is the sort of film that we want to avoid, but few of us are so lucky.

And in this third group, subtext is not a word much bandied about. You don't fret a whole lot about subtext if you're writing *Halloween VI* or *Conan the Barbarian*.

But if you, as a writer, aspire to quality, it must be alive under every page you've done. Look at what you've written: If all that's going on in your scenes is what's going on in your scenes, think about it a long time.

Then repack your snowball. . . .

Protecting the Star

Bogart.

> ... I won't play the sap for you ... you killed Miles and you're going over for it ...

> ... I ain't sorry for you no more, you crazy, psalm-singing, skinny old maid ...

> ... you gotta get up pretty early in the morning to outsmart Fred C. Dobbs ...

> ... my health. I came to Casablanca for the waters ...

> ... of all the gin joints in all the towns in all the world, she had to walk into mine ...

> ... if she can stand it, I can: Play it ...

> ... we'll always have Paris ...

> ... here's looking at you, kid. ...

This is just a personal opinion, but I don't think any other star got to deliver as many memorable dialog lines as Bogart. With Gary Cooper we think "Yup." Gable got the famous "Frankly, my dear, I don't give a damn." Brando had "I could have been a contender," and Tracy—I can't come up with a single line to associate with that great actor.

But perhaps no line in any Bogart picture is as germane to this discussion as a wonderful zinger from *The Barefoot Contessa*, a 1954 movie written and directed by Joseph L. Mankiewicz and starring Bogart and Ava Gardner. Here's the line:

> ... what she's got, you couldn't spell, and what you've got, you *used* to have. ...

I'll try and set up the situation where the line appears. Bogart is an on-his-uppers movie writer/director. He is given a job and, in Spain, discovers Ava Gardner. In the course of the first hour or so of the action, they do three movies together, all of them vastly successful, and Gardner becomes the leading sex symbol of the world.

Nothing of a sexual nature ever happens between Bogart and Gardner because, when they meet, he is already in love with a script girl, whom he marries. The part of Bogart's wife is tiny, with no more than a few lines to speak in the entire film. Totally unimportant to the plot. (I suspect she only exists as a character because Mankiewicz wasn't interested in a Bogart-Gardner romance and the wife conveniently enabled him to ignore that problem.)

The scene where the line takes place is a big Hollywood-type party. Bogart is playing backgammon with his wife. Gardner sits and watches them.

Now a drunken blonde intrudes.

She is jealous of Gardner, whose personal sex life is a mystery. Who are you sleeping with, she asks. Great big sex number—she hasn't even got what I've got. Now comes that wonderful line—

> . . . what she's got, you couldn't spell, and what you've got, you *used* to have. . . .

—only Bogart doesn't say it, his *wife* does.

Mankiewicz is one of the masters, and the line works in the scene. But that was 1954; studios still had power. Today, that simply isn't the case.

And giving that line to the wife, in today's movie world, is not just incorrect screenwriting, it is lethal.

Today, you must give the star everything.

There is no single more important commercial element in screenplay writing than the star part. As we've seen over and over, studios crave stars, and more likely than not, what will make stars commit is not necessarily the quality of the project as a whole but the part they're going to play.

Some movies have three stars, but they are uncommon—*Gunga Din, 9 to 5.* A lot have two—"buddy" pictures, most romantic comedies. The majority have but one, and that vehicle role is what we're going to talk about now. How do you best go about protecting the star? There are no concrete rules here any more than anyplace else in the movie business. But here are some thoughts on the subject.

(A) GET THE STAR IN EARLY

There are exceptions to this—Paul Newman in *The Sting,* for example. But when Newman got that script, Hill was already committed to direct; Redford was aboard. They had done *Butch.* So I don't think it's illogical to assume that Newman was saying yes to a package, not an unattached script that came his way.

Stars count pages. If you're fifteen pages in and the star has yet to make an appearance, maybe you've misstructured.

(B) DESCRIBING THE STAR

If any part of your screenplay requires skillful writing, it's this. Because you've got to indicate a lot with a little. The reader must know the vehicle role has just appeared on the page. But you can't go overboard in loading on attributes. *Plus*, you've got to be, if at all possible, vague. Here is an example of a damaging description:

```
CUT TO

CHALK BROCKTON IN CLOSE UP.

CHALK stands silent, a dead cheroot between his
lips. Fifty years old, six foot four, you get the
feeling there's not a lot his blue eyes haven't
seen. Nothing nowadays surprises him anymore,
and nothing ever has made him feel fear.
```

What's so terrible about that? He's obviously not the water boy: Anyone reading it would know the star has just put in an appearance. And it fits the general mold for most star parts—

the Byronic hero. (The Byronic hero, to oversimplify, is this: a tall, dark, handsome man with a past.) So what's the problem?

Here's another star description that has the same flaw—this time the female lead.

CUT TO

DAHLIA GRACE IN CLOSE UP.

DAHLIA stands in the doorway a moment before join-
ing the party. She is simply beautiful, but there
is no ego about her. She has, instinctively, a
model's grace. Seventeen years old, blonde, very
tall, she is the most beautiful girl in any room
she's ever entered.

Dahlia's obviously some cutie. And she hasn't let it go to her head. (We like her for that.) Maybe she's even going to turn out to be perfect. (Remember, *all* stars are *always* perfect.)

The problem with both descriptions is this: They're too specific. Chalk can only be Eastwood; Dahlia, Brooke Shields.

Do you know what a studio executive might do if he had some interest in the Chalk Brockton script. He would try and get a reading from Eastwood's agent or, if he could, from the man himself. And if the answer came back in the negative, your script would suddenly develop all kinds of heretofore hidden but fatal flaws.

Which is why you must be vague.

Most stars are, relatively speaking, interchangeable. If you can't get Jane Fonda or Streisand, there's always Keaton or Streep. The same is more true of the men, because there are more male stars. Burt Reynolds recently announced that he would do a role originally slated for De Niro, not an uncommon kind of occurrence.

So what you must do is make your description something that can encompass any of them. Don't make Chalk fifty, don't make him tall. (Most stars aren't tall.)

This is a less damaging description for the man—

CUT TO

CHALK BROCKTON IN CLOSE UP.

CHALK stands silent, but he doesn't ever have to
say much; the man has presence. He's long since
been a kid, but he moves with the grace of a young
athlete. And he sure isn't old, but there's not a
lot he hasn't seen.

And then you can go on, if you want, and load up some adjectives. If you don't want, that's okay too. But we can go to damn near anyone with that description. Reynolds, Eastwood, Redford, Travolta, Pacino, De Niro, Newman, Bronson, Nicholson, on and on.

They all think they have presence because they do. They all fantasize they move with an athlete's grace because we all do. And they've all been around.

If you can, make your star description like stretch socks—one size fits all.

(C) EXPOSITION

Stars, without exception, *hate* carrying the plot.

And they're dead right—it's a bore. There are few goodies awaiting the performer who has to stand there and tell us the requisite information we need to get on with the story. But since that requisite information is what enables us to get on with the story, problems arise. What's a mother to do?

If the exposition has impact, that's terrific. If, say, John Wayne is explaining to a group of helpless settlers what lies ahead of them on their trek, it may go something like this:

WAYNE
Well, first there's the rapids.
They ain't known as Deadman's
Rocks for nothing. And if we get
past them, there's gonna be a month

on the desert, and we can only carry
three weeks worth of water, and
there's no water holes along the
way, so don't get your hopes up. The
desert ain't known as the Killer
Sands for nothing. Beyond the desert, if we get beyond the desert,
is Comanche country, the Bloodbath
Comanches run things there. Some
Comanches can be reasonable, but
no one knows about the Bloodbaths,
'cause no one's ever got past 'em
alive. Okay, let's mount up.

Don't worry about that kind of exposition. The scene will play off Wayne talking and then cuts to the helpless settlers, showing them growing increasingly disconsolate. The scene also reaffirms the superhuman qualities of Wayne. We sit there with our popcorn, marveling. Because we know he's going to get the settlers through.

But a lot of the time, there's no excitement under the exposition. It's just something you have to get past. Cary Grant was famous in his films for trying to get other people in the scene to do the expository talking. Grant was a brilliant listener, and often scenes would be shifted to suit him.

He was no fool. If you *can* give the exposition to a secondary character, *do it.* It's just another way of protecting the star.

Sometimes it's a bitch. I was the (I think) original writer on *Papillon.* (One line of mine, the last in the picture, is all that remains of my contribution to the film.) Anyway, it was a Devil's Island picture.

The problem was this: Steve McQueen was being sent via ship, along with a bunch of other prisoners, from France to the prison. And it was imperative that he know about Devil's Island before arrival. But he had never been there before.

Well, you couldn't have Steve McQueen going around asking a bunch of dopey questions. Stars don't like doing that a whole lot.

I don't really remember the solution, but I think we had another prisoner, more craven than Steve, badgering some guy who had been to Devil's Island before. And the veteran answered. And as the cowardly guy grew more frightened by what he found out, McQueen just sat there, quietly unperturbed. Listening confidently. No prison, not even one surrounded by sharks, can hold a movie star once he sets his mind to escape.

Recently a major star said the following, and it sums up this point (and a lot more about their needs) as well as anything:

> I don't want to be the man who learns—I want to be the man who *knows*.

(D) MOMENTS

I believe it was the late Rosalind Russell who gave this wisdom to a young actor: "Do you know what makes a movie work? Moments. Give the audience half a dozen moments they can remember, and they'll leave the theatre happy."

I think she was right. And if you're lucky enough to write a movie with half a dozen moments, make damn sure they belong to the star.

Let's go back to the Mankiewicz line from *The Barefoot Contessa*, the one the wife says to the drunken blonde. There is no way that happens in the eighties. Either the line would be gone or it would be said by the star. And since it's such a strong line, it wouldn't disappear.

But the star would *never* come up to you and say, "I want that line." His agent might, or if the producer was the star's gofer, he also could bring you the message. But if it was a face-to-face, it would happen either in rehearsal or during a preproduction script discussion. And the dialog might go like this:

                    STAR
                (casually)
            Listen . . . about the party scene
            . . . I've got a problem. . . .

                    ME
                (panicked)
            Problem? I thought you liked the
            party scene.

STAR

Hey, I'm crazy about the whole
script, why else do you think I'm
here?

ME

Right, right.

STAR

Let me drop the shoe: You know that
zinger my wife says to the bimbo?

ME

Sure.

STAR

Well . . . I can't justify that
line. . . . I don't know who the
woman who says that line is--but
she's not my wife.

ME
  (the light bulb has now gone
  on--or should have. The
  rest is rote)
Not your wife.

STAR

Look, my character, at least the
way I see him, is he's this direc-
tor-writer and he's seen it all.
And he hates all the smart-ass Hollywood crap.

ME

That's what I was trying for.

STAR

Good. Well, the reason I marry my
wife is because she's--I don't
know, different, maybe even pure.
None of the smart-ass stuff has
touched her.

                              ME
          Pure, right.
                             STAR
          Okay--maybe I'm too obtuse to get
          it, but the woman who comes out with
          that zap line--I would never have
          married her. I don't like her.
          She's just like all the rest, and
          that line fucks up my character-
          ization.

                              ME
          I hate to lose that line, though.
          But the last thing I want to do is
          mess with your characterization.

                             STAR
          Just thought I'd mention it is all.

                              ME
             (excited)
          Wait a sec--

                             STAR
          --what?

                              ME
          What if _you_ said the zinger? That
          way I could keep the line. Could you
          justify yourself saying it?

                             STAR
             (thinks a bit)
          I could give it a whack. . . .

    And a good whack it will be. Because not only is it a strong
line, the star is absolutely right. He should have the dialog. It's
a nice moment and, sure, we want our secondary roles to be as
distinctive as we can make them. But movies are not Chekhov.
There are not nine people we root for.

Studios need stars and screenwriters need studios, and that, said John, is that.

One final example of protecting the star. Before Steve McQueen broke through in *The Great Escape* (1963), he scuffled like other actors. One of his earlier efforts, in 1958, was a low-budget horror movie, *The Blob*, in which the following badly conceived scene occurs.

McQueen and his girl friend are sitting in a car. The Blob is menacing the neighborhood, and strong action is needed. McQueen asks the girl if she wants to go along, because tracking down Blobs can be dangerous. She says yes, and then adds that what they need are some other people to come along and help them. He asks, who? She says, what about your friends? He says, wow, what a good idea. End of scene.

Not much protection there.

Forget the fact that when the star goes after the monster, he would much prefer to do it alone. More important is that, in this scene, the secondary part does all the thinking and the star is this lump. One way to improve things would be this—assuming we need the girl along to be frightened and the friends to be eaten:

```
                    SECONDARY PART
          I'm afraid to go after the Blob,
          Steve.


                    McQUEEN
          We don't know where it is; you're
          safer with me.


                    SECONDARY PART
          Just the two of us alone?


                    McQUEEN
          Who said alone?
             (and as he winks--)
CUT TO

HIS THREE FRIENDS, ready to follow the star.
```

Probably a better way still would be to cut the car scene entirely and just open on the friends and the girl, with McQueen saying something like "It's not going to be any picnic, going after the Blob; any of you don't feel up to it, I won't hold it against you."

To repeat: sock in the vehicle role, give the star everything you possibly can. And don't worry yourself about it being too much.

No matter what, it won't be enough anyway. . . .

Believing Reality

I was riding in a car one afternoon with the Canadian director Norman Jewison. The next day, his daughter was to turn twenty-one. A large celebration had been planned, almost all of it to take place outside.

It was gloomy that afternoon, the threat of rain growing. If it rained the next day, the party would have to be considerably altered with very little notice.

We were driving along and Jewison said, "I wonder what the weather's going to be like tomorrow?" As he said this, he flicked on the car radio, and the *instant* he spoke the word *tomorrow*, the voice on the radio replied "Tomorrow's weather is for heavy rains, flooding at times, etc."

In other words, if you had closed your eyes and listened, you would have heard two run-on sentences without so much as a pause in between.

Jewison and I turned to each other and simultaneously said, "A movie moment."

What we meant was—and this cannot be stated too often or too strongly—that the reality of a movie has almost nothing to do with the reality of the world that we, as humans, inhabit.

But every movie—from a Robert Flaherty documentary to *Raiders of the Lost Ark*—sets it's own special reality. And once those limits are established, they may not be broken without the risk of fragmenting the entire picture.

Let me talk about a scene from *Raiders*, a wild adventure story full of sensational action.

Harrison Ford is the hero and he has just discovered the lost ark. It's in a giant archaeological dig run by the Nazis. Ford is sneaking out of the place in disguise. He is of good cheer, having discovered the location of the ark, but he's also blue, because Karen Allen, the heroine, has been blown to death in an explosion.

As he sneaks out, his discovery becomes possible, so he quick spins into a nearby tent—and there, alive and bound and gagged, is Karen Allen.

139

Not good.

Then Lawrence Kasdan, the screenwriter, does a terrific reversal. Ford starts to untie Allen, and as he does this, they talk, and as they talk, he realizes that bad as her situation may be, she's better off left there. So he ties her back up, gags her again, and goes on his way.

The whole scene could not be more charming. But if Ford had escaped with Allen, the movie would have been damaged. Because the entire weight of the plot would have then rested on a monumental coincidence and would not have been acceptable—because nothing in that movie, not a single one of the previous adventures, had used coincidence totally as a device.

Of course it's possible that he might have stumbled into her tent—just as it's possible that Jewison might have his question answered instantly by the radio weatherman; it might have been real, but it would not have been believable.

Believing reality is always a tremendous problem. Because the screenwriter runs dead into the problem of audience expectation and what they will and won't accept. Two examples now, one invented, the second a problem I had to try and deal with.

Let's make up a caper film, the kind where the hero has to accomplish something that is clearly not capable of being done. We've all seen a million of these, ranging from *Seven Samurai* to *Mission Impossible.*

Paul Newman is our hero. And his job: to get to the most famous and richest woman in the world, never mind the reason; maybe to kidnap her, or exchange information, or whatever, it doesn't matter—getting to her is the problem.

Because this is not Christina Onassis, someone he might meet at Studio 54 and say "Hi, my name's Paul Newman, we have to talk."

If she's available, of course, his job is too easy, and there's no movie. Our rich and famous woman must be totally inaccessible. Not only must she never see or talk to strangers alone, she also is constantly guarded by an enormous number of trained men. Plus, she lives, let's say, in a walled castle that is forever heavily patrolled and contains maybe six hundred rooms.

How is Paul Newman going to accomplish his task? Obviously, first and foremost, *he must have a plan.* And not just any plan:

It's got to be intricate as hell, and it also has to be something he can't pull off himself.

He needs, crucially, a gang. And not just any gang; he must recruit a group of specialists who may not be totally trustworthy, but their talent is of such international repute, he must take the risk.

Now, the first part of the movie, then, is always taken up with the gathering of the accomplices. Here is a list of some of the people he might go after:

(1) an architectural freak who specializes in castles and has blueprints of the entire six-hundred-room edifice, down to secret passages, if any

(2) an embittered ex-guard who was fired from the castle and wants revenge; what he supplies is total knowledge of when shifts change, etc., etc.

(3) a beautiful girl who will have an assignation with the head of security for the castle so he won't be around when all hell breaks loose

(4) an explosives genius who can detonate a series of blasts to serve as cover

(5) a whiz at burglar alarms so that wires can be cut at the precise second of the raid

(6) the world's greatest driver who will handle the business of the getaway car.

There are half a dozen more possibilities, but these six will do. Newman will conscript them, train them, practice the plan to perfection.

Since we've all seen this kind of thing so often, I won't go on. But it's safe to say the rest of the movie will be the execution of the plan and mishaps that occur before Newman is triumphant.

I don't know about you, but I buy this picture if it's skillfully made. It may not be real as my world is, but for me it's totally believable.

Now let me suggest a different plan—or rather, no plan at all. Newman just decides to go in and get to the fabulous woman.

So, early one morning in daylight, he scales the wall of the castle. Just decides to go up and over.

Not so smart.

But what if he's not only dumb, he's unlucky: A guard sees him climbing the castle wall. And this guard quickly passes the word to the very central control room of the castle, where another guard receives the message.

Only he doesn't do anything with the information, this guard in the control center. Doesn't act on it in any way at all.

Now back to Newman. He's scaled the wall, but since he didn't do any preparation, he doesn't know where the hell his quarry is, the rich and famous lady. So he walks around the entire castle, poking here and there.

And no one, not a single guard, spots him. (I think, by this time, you might have left your seat for the candy counter.)

Newman finds an open window. He climbs in—

—and sets off an alarm. Only no one pays any attention to it.

He finds the doors to the room locked, so now Newman goes back outside and shinnies up a drainpipe to the second floor. He's looking for another unlocked window.

Here comes a maid. She unlocks a window and leaves. Newman crawls inside. This time, he finds himself in a room where the doors are unlocked, so he opens one and enters the castle itself.

Since, as already stated, he hasn't any notion of the setup of the castle, he starts to kind of idly wander around. (By this time you are back from the candy counter and, I think, you are either laughing or starting to get ticked off at the insult to your intelligence that is taking place on the silver screen.)

Newman keeps on wandering, here, there, following one corridor into another. People see him, castle employees. They don't think much of it, maybe some of them nod to him as he meanders around.

Fifteen minutes later Newman stumbles totally by accident on to the quarters of the rich and powerful woman he is trying to see.

But, of course, she is always guarded.

Only now she isn't, because as Newman arrives, the guard decides it's time to walk the dogs of the rich lady. He goes off with the dogs to watch them pee.

At the same time, the rich lady's maids decide it's time to clean another part of the castle, so they go. (If you had eggs in your hands, my guess is that by now you would be throwing them at the screen.)

At last, Newman opens the rich lady's door and there she is, snoozing in bed. He opens the curtains to her suite. She wakes, quickly buzzes for help—

—only no one hears. This lady's got an elaborate buzzer system, but when she needs it, no one's minding the store.

Newman is now face-to-face with the richest and most famous woman in the world—mission accomplished.

The truth now: Have you ever heard anything so totally unbelievable?

Well, it happened: That's exactly how Michael Fagan paid his little visit on the Queen of England in Buckingham Palace not long ago.

Of course it's unbelievable—but it's also real. It makes fabulous newspaper reading. But it has nothing to do with proper movie storytelling, and true as it may be, if you handed it in as a screenplay, you would find yourself thrown out without ceremony as a very uninventive writer of fantasy.

My problems in dealing with a sequence for *A Bridge Too Far* had nothing to do with fantasy; I was trying to describe an event that a great British combat general referred to as "the single most heroic action of the war."

The action involved a river crossing.

The most effective way to capture a bridge is to attack both ends at once: This divides the enemies' resources and generally initiates panic and confusion. The bridge in question, a gigantic structure, was being attacked by Allied forces at one end only, and the Germans were so deeply entrenched that no advance was possible.

So a plan was initiated to send a group of men in boats, under cover of night, across this wide, swirling river, to the other end of the bridge, behind the Germans.

The boats were to be loaded with combat troops and rowed across where the troops would get off and the boats would return to the Allied side, where more men—*a second wave*—would get in and row across and join the fighting.

The plan developed logistical problems, the boats didn't arrive in time for the night crossing, so it was now to be done in daylight. And when the boats finally arrived, they turned out to be dangerously flimsy—plywood bottoms and canvas sides and there was a shortage of oars.

Now, the first wave had one thing going for it: smoke cover. A barrage of tank fire was to lay down a giant smoke screen to help the men get across. Major Julian Cook was to lead the first wave (Robert Redford played the part in the film), and when the boats were finally assembled and dragged to the water and the men began to row, something terrible happened: A wind came up.

And it blew away the smoke-screen cover.

So there they were, in these tiny boats, on this vast river, heading into God only knew what. It didn't take long to find out: The Germans were ready and considerable carnage followed. But Cook led his charge and a lot of men died, but he got across and the boats returned and took the second wave across and eventually, with both sides of the bridge being attacked simultaneously, the Germans were defeated.

I think there is no question that we are dealing with valor here of a very high order when we discuss Cook's crossing—

—but that was *not* what the British general was referring to as "the single most heroic action of the war."

He meant *the second wave.* Sure, the first wave was a tremendous undertaking. But they *didn't know* that the Germans would be waiting for them and they *thought* they had smoke cover.

The second wave, standing there, watching it all, *knew* when their turn came they were going to get slaughtered. But when the boats returned, they got right in and rowed into the bloodbath.

If you saw the movie you saw Redford leading his men, and it was a splendid piece of action. But you did not see the second wave—

—because even though it was true, I didn't know how to make it believable.

Look, when John Wayne is in a movie, he doesn't arrive at the Alamo the day after the fighting. He is *there*, superhuman, beating up on as many Mexicans as the budget will allow for.

I didn't have John Wayne but I had Robert Redford and the same logic holds. The star must be in the center of the action.

I could have written a scene involving the second wave of men waiting their turn. And one of them could have said, "Boy, what those guys are going through is no picnic, but they didn't know what they were dealing with; we know, and that means our job is going to require much more bravery."

And the audience wouldn't have believed it, not for one minute. What's so brave about standing around on a riverbank, safe and unfired upon, when your buddies are out there in the middle, getting shelled to death? And what's the star supposed to be doing during all this, besides maybe running up and down the embankment, shouting encouragement—"Row, you guys, we're coming."

Some star. That's the Elisha Cook, Jr., part.

I tried as hard as I knew to use the second wave, but I failed. The single most heroic action of the war, and I couldn't figure out how to include it. The moral I guess is this: Truth is terrific, reality is even better, but believability is best of all.

Because without it, truth and reality go right out the window....

Enduring

I personally do not believe that you can tell if a movie is "good" or "bad" when it comes out. All you can be sure of is this: Does it "work" or not? For audiences.

Perhaps it was possible once to make a sound judgment as to quality. But now, with the enormous amounts of money spent on advertising, with the unending "hype" that accompanies each release, the film itself becomes obscured.

As an example of what I mean, I'd like to discuss the Best Picture race for the Oscars of 1976. Understand this about the Oscars: You may think the program is silly or long or whatever, but Out There they care about it. They take it seriously and no one has the least idea who'll win. When I was researching this book, I asked everybody whom they were voting for, and truly *everyone* said the same thing: "*Chariots of Fire*, but it hasn't got a chance."

Understand this, too: That nervous guy who is giving an acceptance speech for Best Black and White Short Subject, that guy whom you are hooting at in the safety of your living room as he rambles tortuously on, thanking his mother and his first-grade teacher who introduced him to the wonders of film—he may seem like a jerk to you, but you are very likely watching the high point of his life.

The '77 race was touted as being a toss-up between two films, *Rocky* and *All the President's Men*.

And it seemed to me absolutely certain that *President's Men* had to win. For the following reasons:

(1) It was wonderfully reviewed.
(2) More important than that, it did business.
(3) More important than that, it was a Significant picture. No less acute observer of American politics than then Governor Reagan of California said he thought the movie eventually cost Gerald Ford the presidency against Jimmy Carter, because the film's release in April of '76 and its long run

flushed to the surface again all the realities of Watergate that the Republicans had tried so hard to bury. We are talking then about a movie that may be one of the few that just might have changed the entire course of American history.

Rocky got the award.

Impossible to say why, but the following reasons may have relevance:

(1) It was well reviewed—but not as well as *President's Men*. I don't know that Canby of the *Times* ever wrote a worse notice than the one he gave *Rocky*.

(2) More important than that, it did spectacular business, millions more than *President's Men*.

(3) More important than that, perhaps more important than anything, was this: *Rocky* satisfied the most basic Hollywood dream—dreams can come true.

   If we sit on the right drugstore stool at the right time, as Lana Turner supposedly did, Fame will find us. Sylvester Stallone's phenomenal emergence from obscurity with a picture that he invented and starred in was too much for the voters to resist. They gave their hearts to Stallone and their votes to his picture.

This is all hypothetical, remember, but I think if the same vote were taken today with the same people voting, Rocky wouldn't stand a chance.

Why?

Impossible to say for sure, but following *Rocky*, Stallone went through a period of public misbehavior; a certain arrogance showed in his interviews and personal appearances. In other words, he wasn't the sweet, humble guy whom the publicists had going around saying earlier, "The story of the movie is the story of my life."

Also this: *Rocky* won three awards and was nominated for a bunch more. *Rocky II*, which also did fabulous business and got decent reviews, didn't gain a single Academy nomination.

Granted, it's a sequel. But *Godfather* won the Oscar in '73 and its sequel did the same thing a couple of years later—and it got *more* nominations than the first one did.

Rocky today is sort of in the same genre as the James Bond movies, popular films but not prizewinners. So am I saying if the vote were taken today that *All the President's Men* would win?

Not at all: Today I think the votes would go to *Taxi Driver*, the third film up that year.

Why?

Again, impossible to say for sure. *Taxi Driver* was well received back then, and it did business, too—but my guess is that the Academy was made uncomfortable by the violence.

Today, with the Hinckley madness all around us, with poor Jodie Foster being always in the press, that violence of *Taxi Driver* has a terrifying ring of truth.

I would bet anything on *Taxi Driver* today.

But not three years down the line. Because television is going through a wild upheaval; they are doing incredible things to try and get ratings. Cable has the networks panicked. (A recent show that never got aired was a cinema verité notion about divorce. There were actually ads in L.A. papers for couples going through divorce proceedings. The idea of the show was that they would simply have their divorce on the tube, all the fighting and hatred would pour into our living rooms. We could be voyeurs, comfy and warm, seeing other people's real anguish for free. As I said, this divorce show didn't make it—

—or at least, it hasn't made it *yet.*)

I'm guessing that in 1985 or so, *Network*, Paddy Chayefsky's apocalyptic view of the battle for ratings, and the fourth picture up that year, would take it all. It's feeling less and less apocalyptic all the time.

But so is *Bound for Glory*, the fifth and final contender back in '77. It dealt with the Great Depression, not such close reality back five years ago.

Today, though, the country is in economic chaos. No matter how hard the government tries to convince us that things aren't so bad and are getting better, we know things are that bad and are getting frighteningly worse.

And if the country continues its slide, I would guess that maybe by 1990, *Bound for Glory* will be the one they'll be studying in film schools.

Movies are not like vintage wines. If you drink, say, a '62 Lafite or a '68 BV Cabernet, and then you drink them each again five years later, of course they won't taste the same. Not only will you be different, older, in a different mood, perhaps in a different surrounding, but the wine is alive and constantly changing.

Movies are just these strips of celluloid running through a machine. If you can find an adequate print, *The Great Train Robbery* is exactly what it was when Porter directed it eighty years ago.

I am continually dumbfounded by the effects of time. I recently looked at three movies, one I saw alone, *La Dolce Vita*, and two accompanied by teen-agers: *Star Wars* and *Bambi.*

I was never crazy about *Star Wars* when it came out, but I loved the excitement of the audience reaction. This time, the audience reaction was actually this: embarrassment.

The young people I saw it with thought it was corny and badly acted, but their embarrassment was because this was the same movie they had gone berserk over, seeing it again and again, just five years before.

Bambi, of course, was an (ugh) Disney film. Disney films don't have the hold they once did; in point of fact, most kids avoid them.

Bambi took all of our heads off. Because, primarily, they don't make movies like that anymore—animation stinks these days because of costs. It's all jerky and when the mouths move they don't coincide with the words and the color is bland. My guess is that *Bambi* works better now than it did when it came out in 1942, and I think it's only going to improve as the quality of animation continues to deteriorate.

La Dolce Vita I suppose surprised me the most. Fellini of that period, before his excesses took over almost totally, is for me, along with Bergman, the great director of my time. And *La Dolce Vita* was, when I first saw it, a masterpiece.

Now it doesn't work at all—I wanted to hide my head during some of it. It's still the same technical achievement. But the subject matter of the movie—the wild, shocking, debauched Rome of the sixties—well, today it's no more shocking than *Captain Kangaroo.*

None of this is to indicate that (a) I'm remotely correct in my judgment or (b) if I see it again twenty years from now I won't find it a masterpiece again.

Not only is my judgment always suspect, my whole point here about the effects of time is open to question.

The *New York Times*, for example, recently ran a long article about how special effects were changing movies. One of their points was that special effects can overwhelm a film. Essential beyond all else, they said, was not the visual show but the story.

To prove that point they picked a couple of classics that endure because of story line. One of the movies was *Bambi*, forty years young. The other was *E.T.*, which, at the time of the article, had been released for twenty-two days. I don't mind anybody raving over *E.T.*

But before we start praising a movie for it's endurance, I think we ought to wait till it's been around at least a month. . . .

The Ecology of Hollywood

(or, George Lucas, Steven Spielberg, and <u>Gunga Din</u>)

Hollywood has never been short of boy wonders.

Joseph L. Mankiewicz received his first Óscar nomination when he was twenty-one years old. Stanley Donen was twenty-four when he co-directed *On the Town*. Most notable, I suppose, is Orson Welles, who received four nominations for *Citizen Kane*, a feat never accomplished up to that time. Welles was twenty-five.

But nothing in memory comes close to the dominance of George Lucas and Steven Spielberg.

Both are extraordinarily talented, have been working successfully for a decade or more, and are still in their thirties. And when I say "dominance," consider this: Lucas and Spielberg have been crucial to the five most successful pictures in history.

Star Wars and *The Empire Strikes Back* belong to Lucas. Spielberg directed *Jaws* and *E.T.* The fifth, *Raiders of the Lost Ark*, was a collaboration, Lucas being the inceptor, Spielberg calling the shots.

Not only have these films made the two among the richer young men in America, the four released prior to this year have all won various prizes and awards and been nominated for a lot more. But none of the four has won the Oscar for Best Picture.

E.T. will change all that.

This is the middle of '82, and next year's awards are nine months away. And half the films for this year have yet to be released. I don't care.

There's no doubt in my mind that *E.T.* will win.

So?

Just this: What the five films have in common, besides their worldwide appeal, is that they are all comic-book movies.

If you think I am putting down comic-book movies, you could not be more wrong. Not only have I written my share of

151

them, my favorite movie of all time is a comic-book movie: *Gunga Din*. (I have seen it sixteen times, still start to cry before the credits are over, and will return to it shortly.)

But first, the matter of definition.

Having used the term "comic-book movie" several times now, I think it's only fair that I tell you precisely what it means—

—except I can't do that.

Primarily because we get into matters of personal taste: What I find a comic-book movie you may totally disagree with, and you may be right. For example, I think *The Deer Hunter*, that searing indictment of American involvement in Southeast Asia, was a comic-book movie, and I think *Bambi*—yes, I know it's an animated cartoon—is not.

But if I can't give a precise definition of what the hell I'm trying to say, at least I am able to give a few parallels, which should help set the parameters of what I'm after.

Food: empty calories. (Not, underlined *not*, junk food, which has a pejorative connotation. Please remember that in none of this am I making a critical judgment against the comic-book movie.) But as an example of empty calories, put down potato chips.

Television: The only prime-time entertainment series that is not a comic-book program is *M*A*S*H*. Not because of its outstanding quality, but because every scene in *M*A*S*H*, no matter how wildly farcical, is grounded in the madness of death. That is what gives it its tone, that is the heart of the piece. You can make *M*A*S*H* into *My Mother the Car* easily enough. Just keep those same wonderful actors and stick them in a giant Army training camp here in the States. And the wounded are simply guys hurt in fights or drunken-driving accidents—of which, by the way, there are more than plenty near any major Army post.

And what you've got then is a bunch of goofy surgeons grousing because they're stuck in the service and not out in the civilian world, making a fortune. It might be just as funny, and just as successful, and absolutely would be exactly like every other series on the air.

Music: bubble-gum songs. Billy Joel, Elton John, etc. The

kind of singer-songwriter who basically appeals to pop music's target audience, the teenyboppers who buy albums. (The Beatles began as bubble-gum musicians—"I want to hold your hah-hah-hand" and the like. Then they changed. Lennon, in his solo albums, did not write bubble-gum music; McCartney, the most successful songwriter in history, still does.)

Now let's try and take some of this and apply it to comic-book movies. None of these are meant to be strict rules, but more often than not I think they're true:

(1) Generally, only bad guys die. And if a good guy does kick, he does it heroically.

(2) There tends to be a lack of resonance: Like the popcorn you're munching, it's not meant to last.

(3) The movie turns in on itself: Its reference points tend to be other movies. If, for example, there had been no Saturday afternoon serials, there would have been no frame for *Raiders of the Lost Ark*.

(4) And probably most important: The comic-book movie doesn't have a great deal to do with life as it exists, as we know it to be. Rather, it deals with life as we would prefer it to be. Safer that way.

Let me briefly explain now my feelings about *Bambi* and *Deer Hunter*.

Does anyone remember, say, the last part of *Deer Hunter?* Saigon is going up in flames and Robert De Niro, an ordinary guy with no contacts in high places, is out of service and back in Pennsylvania. He hears about his old buddy, Christopher Walken, who's still back there.

Shazam—De Niro's in Saigon. Now the entire world is trying to get out, but somehow De Niro gets in.

He finds Walken. Do you know what Walken has been doing all this time? He's been playing that game of Russian roulette with real bullets. (The Russian roulette ploy was made up by the movie's creators, by the way; it didn't happen in reality.) For months and months, Walken has been taking on all comers in this loony tunes Russian roulette, and guess what?—

Whappo—he's undefeated, untied, and unscored on.

It would take a computer a while to give the odds against that happening, but never mind, because now we're into the confrontation scene.

De Niro versus Walken at Russian roulette.

If you looked at the billing of the picture on your way in, did you ever doubt who was going to win?

Zap—De Niro is unscathed but Walken dies—with a touch of the heroic smile on his lips.

All this was exciting, and I enjoyed it every bit as I used to be enthralled by Batman having it out with the Penguin—

—and precisely on that level.

What *Deer Hunter* told me was what I already knew and believed in: No matter how horrid the notion of war, Robert De Niro would end up staring soulfully at the beautiful, long-suffering Meryl Streep.

So I say in spite of its skill and the seriousness of its subject matter, we have here a well-disguised comic-book movie. Nothing shook my world.

Okay, *Bambi*.

If the shower scene in *Psycho* was *the* shocker of the sixties, and for me, it sure was, then its equivalent in the entire decade of the forties was when Bambi's mother dies.

And what about that line of dialog: "Man has entered the forest"?

And the fire and the incredibly strong antiviolence implications. (The National Rifle Association would probably picket the movie today.)

I know it was a cartoon, I know Thumper had one of the great scene-stealing roles, I know there was a lot of cuteness.

But I left that movie changed.

It had, and has, a terrifying sense of life to it, and not life as we like it to be. You may think I'm crazy and you may be right, but *Bambi* still reverberates inside me.

Now let me circle back to *Gunga Din* and make strictly a judgment call: It is my absolute opinion that in every conceivable way—direction, script, star performances, special effects, emotional power—it is infinitely superior to any of the five Lucas-Spielberg prizewinners.

Gunga Din was released in 1939, and when it came time for the Oscar balloting, it received a grand total of zero nominations.

Granted, 1939 was an exceptional year for Hollywood. (I am going to start playing games now, but please bear with me, I hope and believe there's a point to it all.) You probably don't remember the Oscar winner for '39, but let me list five movies and then you guess:

> *Golden Boy*
> *The Hunchback of Notre Dame*
> *Intermezzo*
> *Juarez*
> *The Private Lives of Elizabeth and Essex*

To help you along, a few refreshers: *Golden Boy* introduced us to William Holden; *Intermezzo* to Ingrid Bergman. Charles Laughton played the Hunchback, Paul Muni starred in *Juarez*, and Bette Davis was Elizabeth, one of her more famous performances.

The envelope please.

Answer? None of the five. In fact, none of the five even got a Best Picture nomination.

But here are the five that did:

> *Goodbye, Mr. Chips*
> *Mr. Smith Goes to Washington*
> *Ninotchka*
> *Of Mice and Men*
> *Stagecoach*

Again, please, the envelope.

Same answer: none of the above. (They nominated more than five pictures back in those days.) And one of the five I didn't list was *Wuthering Heights*.

Which also didn't win because '39 was also the year of *The Wizard of Oz*.

Which also didn't win because *Gone With the Wind* did.

Pretty impressive year.

So impressive that in spite of my passion for *Gunga Din*, I can't complain. It's a glorious adventure film; I may prefer it to any other, but I don't think it belongs up there with the prize-winners.

And I don't think any of the Lucas-Spielberg films do either.

The subject here, remember, is the ecology of Hollywood. Ecology, as I am using it, means balance.

Hollywood has always made great comic-book movies. *The Great Train Robbery* was not intended as a sonnet, and let's not forget that early wonder that was these two little girls having a pillow fight.

But traditionally the money made from pillow-fight pictures was ploughed back in, and sometimes what emerged was *Citizen Kane*.

Several years ago, a studio head told me this: "If I've got to come up with a slate of sixteen pictures a year, I know going in that four of them are turkeys. I just hope they're not too expensive and I don't lose too much on them. Eight or nine are going to be programmers—decent enough entertainment if I'm lucky; money-makers. *The last three I have hopes for.*" (Italics mine.)

He meant, he went on to explain, quality; the kind of movie he might be proud of.

Now, I assume it's clear by now that 1982 is not 1939 in terms of quality.

But let's go back twenty years: *Lawrence of Arabia* won Best Picture. I thought it was a great epic and deserved everything it got. But the following pictures didn't even get nominated:

> *Birdman of Alcatraz*
> *Days of Wine and Roses*
> *The Miracle Worker*
> *Long Day's Journey into Night*
> *Sweet Bird of Youth*
> *David and Lisa*
> *The Man Who Shot Liberty Valance*
> *Freud*
> *Lolita*

I'm not suggesting any of them should have been nominated; I'm just saying that's a pretty good list of non–comic-book pictures. In a year that was not considered anything special.

That was twenty years ago, now let's try again. Another unremarkable year, but these were some of the non–comic-book pictures that came out in '72:

The Godfather
Cabaret
Deliverance
Slaughterhouse-Five
A Separate Peace
Play It as It Lays
Lady Sings the Blues
The Heartbreak Kid
Fat City
The Candidate
Jeremiah Johnson

The summer movies of '82 are now half done, and by the time you read this, most of them will have blissfully faded from your memory. But this is what's come out so far: *Conan the Barbarian* and *Rocky III* and *Poltergeist* and *Hanky Panky* and *Dead Men Don't Wear Plaid* and *Annie* and *Star Trek II* and *E.T.* and *Firefox* and *Grease II* and *Author! Author!* and *Blade Runner* and *The Thing* and *Megaforce* and *Tron* and—

—and they're *all* comic-book movies.

Okay, let's put as positive a light as possible on things: Summer, after all, has always been the time for kids' pictures because that's when the kids are out of school. And Woody Allen has directed a film and George Hill has directed a film and there's a strong advance word about *An Officer and a Gentleman.*

You can be as Pollyanna-ish as you want; me, I think it's scary.

Why? Because in the entire first five months of this calendar year, there were almost no films you can think of that *also* weren't comic-book movies. A few: *Victor/Victoria* and *Diner* and *Missing* and *Shoot the Moon.*

Maybe you can come up with some others; I can't. And none of the above four did the kind of business that tends to win at Academy time. Which is why *E.T.* will take the Oscar: There's nothing else.

And why do I find this all scary?—

—because the basic ecology of Hollywood is, I'm very much afraid, radically changing.

Remember that italicized quote from the studio head: "*The last three I have hopes for*"? Well, those "last three" aren't being made anymore. The money made from *E.T.* is only going to give us, if we're lucky, something like *Mandrake the Magician.*

Jaws began the present cycle: It did business far beyond what anyone dreamed possible. Then *Star Wars* shattered all the records set by *Jaws.* And now every executive in Hollywood is trying to figure out how the hell to topple *Star Wars.*

Which, of course, is only right and proper: It's their job. But in their quest, they have altered the tradition of ploughing back profits in pursuit of an entire range of different sorts of films. Right now—today—comic-book pictures are only breeding more comic-book pictures, something that has *never* happened to this extent before.

Will the ecology shift back to what it's been? "Absolutely," the studio executives will tell you. When? "When the public demands it."

Of course, there's a certain element of truth to that—but basically it's a cop-out. Change will only come when the executives stop ignoring the churning in their guts. These are bright people, never forget that. They don't personally enjoy the movies they're okaying. Do you think they're happy going home and saying to their families, "Hey, guess what, a great thing happened today, we decided to make *Megaforce.*"

The ecology can only shift when these people decide that there's got to be more to life than a remake of *The Creature from the Black Lagoon.* When they suck it up and decide to find material like *Ordinary People* and *Cuckoo's Nest.*

But this summer's three big pictures so far are *E.T., Rocky III,* and *Star Trek II.* So, for the present, I think we may as well prepare ourselves for seven more *Star Wars* sequels and half a dozen quests involving Indiana Jones. By the end of the decade, we may well be seeing *E.T. Meets Luke Skywalker.*

As Bette Davis advised us, I think we all ought to fasten our seat belts. Because it looks from here like we're entering a long and bumpy night. . . .

part two

Adventures

Introduction

I suppose what follows is the most autobiographical part of the book. I have had some wonderful times in the movie business—*Butch Cassidy and the Sundance Kid,* rehearsing with Laurence Olivier—but scratch a screenwriter and you're bound to find horror stories, and some of those are in here too.

The movies are taken in chronological order—with the exception of *A Bridge Too Far.* I've saved it for the end because it was, without question, the most unusual experience I've ever had....

chapter three
Charly and
Masquerade

Cliff Robertson got me into the movie business, in late 1963. I had been a published novelist and failed short-story writer since 1956; I had been a movie nut all my life. But looking back on it now, I truly don't believe the thought of combining my writing career with my love of movies had ever surfaced. I grew up before the prominence of "film schools." Like my peers, I assumed that the directors did it all, and when they came up dry, the actors made up their lines.

My meeting with Robertson was no more circuitous than most people experience when there is a shift in career direction, but it probably ought to be mentioned here, because if I have managed to maintain any sanity at all after nearly two decades of movie work, it is mainly because of this: I was a novelist first and I am a novelist now, but one who happens also to write screenplays.

My first three books had all been, relatively speaking, short. And, like a great fool, I thought it might be interesting to tackle the problems of a genuinely long piece of work. All of my friends at this time in New York seemed to be coming apart at the seams. I discussed this with my beloved editor, Hiram Haydn. I said I was distraught with the world around me, that I wanted to write about it at length, but that I hadn't the least notion what the hell the shape of the book would be. He told me just to put it down, everything down, and eventually we would find some kind of order in the chaos.

So, for my sins, I began *Boys and Girls Together*. (Note to fledgling writers: Under threat of torture, *never* write a long novel. I once met James Clavell, who only writes monsters, and asked him how he got the courage to start when he knew what was going to happen to him before he reached page 1,500. His answer was simple: Each time he began he genuinely believed *this* one was going to be short. And that once he was into it and it began expanding, he was trapped.)

I wrote for maybe a year and a half and I suppose I had six or seven hundred typed pages, the piece perhaps two-thirds completed, when I stopped to do two Broadway shows, a play and a musical. Both died bouncing, which was not a lot of fun. (Note to fledgling writers: Never *never* write for Broadway. Nothing is as wracking as a show that stiffs in New York. Because of the immediacy. When a novel dies, or a movie, it's usually at least a year between when your work is over and disaster overtakes you. But in the theatre, you've just finished that week and you have no defenses. If you ever have an urge to write for Broadway, be kind to yourself and write a long novel instead.)

After my mourning period, I returned to *Boys and Girls Together* and discovered, to my genuine horror, that I was, for the first time in my life, totally and completely blocked. Perhaps only other writers can understand the panic that takes hold then. You go to your desk, you sit for two hours, six hours . . . and nothing. A week, a month . . . nothing. You try to trick your demons, perhaps by going to the movies instead of to work, and casually, after a double feature or two, you slide in behind your typewriter at the end of the day when there's absolutely no time to write anyway, so all the pressure is off.

. . . nothing.

You read what other writers have done to win their similar battle.

Doesn't work for you.

Nothing works for you.

And then you enter into despair. Because drying up permanently just may be the ultimate nightmare if what you do for a living is battle empty pages. For almost without exception, this happens to every writer. Few of us drop in our traces. Mostly, our energy goes; we fiddle awhile, try this, that, and then it's over, and how do you fill the rest of your days? (Please understand that I am aware of the melodramatic content of these last paragraphs, but in a very real sense, the end of creativity is for a writer not unlike Altsheimer's Disease: You don't know for sure it's going to happen, but you know it's there. Waiting.)

At any rate, I was in that mood of impotence when I read a very short article one morning in the *Daily News* dealing with the Boston Strangler. All the paper reported that day was a new theory that had begun to gain credence: Perhaps there were two Boston Stranglers, not one.

I was living then on Eighty-sixth Street and my office was two short blocks uptown and on that trip that day, something happened to me that never occurred either before or since: A novel literally dropped into my head. Full blown. Based on the simple idea that what if there were two stranglers and what if one of them got jealous of the other.

At my desk I scribbled down one note after another, each of them shorthanding a scene. Done, I looked at it and didn't know what the hell I had. Because what I wanted to write was the last four or five hundred pages of *Boys and Girls Together* and what I held in my hands sure wasn't that. Was it another trick? Was it something to take me further from where I desperately needed to go? What if I started this one, got halfway through it and came up dry again? Much worse off than before, doubly blocked.

I talked about it with some friends and thought about it before deciding if I flew through the strangler notion—it was to become *No Way to Treat a Lady*—maybe it would unblock me. But as a hedge against disaster, I gave myself ten days only to do the strangler book. At the end of that time, if I was done, terrific; if not, pitch it.

In order to give myself added confidence, I wrote the book with as many chapters as I could. Even if a chapter was no more than a paragraph, I could start another page at the top. I could get moving. Get something, anything, under way.

I got it done in the allotted time. It looked a little weird—160 pages and 53 chapters. But it was a book that eventually got published under a pseudonym, Harry Longbaugh, the real name of the Sundance Kid. This was six years before the Western came out, but I had been researching the material for a good four years and I loved his name.

Enter Robertson.

He called and asked if we could meet. We did so that evening. He explained that the quality work of his career to that time was mainly on television, and when movies came to be made of the tv shows, he had not gotten the parts. *The Hustler* and *Days of Wine and Roses* were two roles he'd lost out on. So in this case, he explained, he'd optioned the basic material, a short story by Daniel Keyes entitled "Flowers for Algernon." (The resulting movie, *Charly*, won Robertson an Academy Award for Best Actor.)

Robertson went on to explain that he'd gotten hold of my strangler "treatment" and liked it. I remember thinking, "Treatment? That was a *novel*." But probably the odd look of the thing, all those chapters, accounted for his thinking. None of this is important, except to note that I entered the movie business based on a total misconception.

He gave me a copy of Keyes's story and asked if I would read it and, if I liked it, write a screenplay. I said of course. He left. I read the story as soon as he was gone. It was a glorious piece of work about a retarded man who becomes, briefly, a genius because of a scientific experiment. The experiment, however, fails, and at the end Charly is retarded again.

It was midnight now and I said to my wife, Ilene, that I'd finished it and she said how was it and I said just wonderful and we talked for a few minutes more all very calmly until suddenly it hit me—

—I didn't know what the hell a screenplay looked like!

Madness.

I tore down to Times Square, where there was an all-night bookstore. There aren't shelves full of books on screenwriting even now, but back then, what we have today seems like a gusher. I nervously asked the clerk did he have any books on what a screenplay looked like and he sort of nervously waved me back in the general direction of the rear of the place. *Everyone* was nervous in Times Square at two in the morning, then and now, in bookstores or on the streets. The other few customers eyed me strangely and I suppose I gave as good as I got. God knows what they were doing there, pushing, dozing, maybe bookworms with insomnia or other budding screenwriters; they went their way, I mine. I don't know how long I took, but there was one copy of one book with the word *screenwriting* in the title so I grabbed it, blew away (truly) the dust, clocked the contents table, flicked through until I finally got to the pages that showed what a screenplay looked like.

More madness.

To this day I remember staring at the page in shock. I didn't know what it was exactly I was looking at, but I knew I could never write in that form, in that language.

The book is gone from my library now, lost probably in some move or another, but the form is still clear, and what I would like to do now is take a famous scene—I have chosen the shirt scene from *Gatsby*—and put it in the form that so threw me.

For those who may not know the plot, it's simply this: Gatsby, a bootlegger, is showing Daisy and his friend Nick around his famous house. Gatsby and Daisy knew each other before. Daisy is married now. Gatsby is still terribly and obsessively in love with her. Here goes—

100. EXT. THE LAWN OF GATSBY'S HOUSE. DAY. 100.
ESTABLISHING SHOT.

GATSBY leads NICK and DAISY toward his
mansion. It has never seemed larger or
more impressive. DAISY stops for a moment, looking around, admiring it all.

101. EXT. THE LAWN OF GATSBY'S HOUSE. DAY. 101.
MED. SHOT.

GATSBY glances at her. Excited, doing
his best to control it. After a moment,
they move on.

102. INT. THE MUSIC ROOM OF GATSBY'S HOUSE. 102.
DAY. ESTABLISHING SHOT.

The room is enormous, ornate. Done in
the style of Marie Antoinette. GATSBY
leads NICK and DAISY through.

103. INT. THE MAIN SALON IN GATSBY'S HOUSE. 103.
DAY. ESTABLISHING SHOT.

Another ornate, impressive room. The style here is Restoration. GATSBY, NICK and DAISY wander through, continuing their tour.

104. INT. THE MAIN SALON IN GATSBY'S HOUSE. 104. DAY. MED. SHOT.

GATSBY hasn't once ceased looking at DAISY. It is as if he is reevaluating everything in his house according to the response it draws from her well-loved eyes.

105. INT. THE MAIN STAIRCASE IN GATSBY'S 105. HOUSE. DAY. ESTABLISHING SHOT.

The staircase is as large and impressive as everything else we've seen. GATSBY leads them up. At the top of the stairs is a door. He opens it, beckons them inside.

106. INT. GATSBY'S BEDROOM. DAY. ESTABLISH- 106. ING SHOT.

The room is simple, in sharp contrast to what we have seen before. There is a dresser on which is a toilet set of pure dull gold. There are two hulking cabinets. A bed. Little more.

107. INT. GATSBY'S BEDROOM. DAY. C.U. 107.

DAISY, with delight, takes the brush from the toilet set and smooths her hair.

108. INT. GATSBY'S BEDROOM. DAY. MED. SHOT. 108.

GATSBY begins to laugh hilariously. He has been so full of the idea of having her here for so long, has waited at such

an inconceivable pitch of intensity
that now, in his reaction, he is beginning to run down like an overwound
clock.

                    GATSBY
            (still laughing, he looks
              at NICK)
        It's the funniest thing, old
        sport. I can't--when I try to--

109. INT. GATSBY'S BEDROOM. DAY. MED. LONG 109.
     SHOT.

     GATSBY recovers, goes to the two hulking
     cabinets, opens them.

110. INT. GATSBY'S BEDROOM. DAY. C.U.   110.

     The cabinets hold his massed suits and
     dressing gowns and ties, and his shirts,
     piled like bricks in stacks a dozen
     high.

111. INT. GATSBY'S BEDROOM. DAY. MED. LONG 111.
     SHOT.

                    GATSBY

        I've got a man in England who buys
        me clothes. He sends over a selec-
        tion of things at the beginning of
        each season, spring and fall.

112. INT. GATSBY'S BEDROOM. DAY. C.U.   112.

     GATSBY takes out a pile of shirts and be-
     gins throwing them into the air where
     they land on the bed. Shirts of sheer
     linen and thick silk and fine flannel,
     which lose their folds as they fall in
     many-colored disarray.

113. INT. GATSBY'S BEDROOM. DAY. MED. SHOT.   113.

NICK watches GATSBY throwing the
shirts, watches DAISY as she admires
them.

114. INT. GATSBY'S BEDROOM. DAY. MED. SHOT.   114.

GATSBY takes another pile, throws them
into the air toward the bed.

115. INT. GATSBY'S BEDROOM. DAY. C.U.   115.

The shirts fill the air, shirts with
stripes and scrolls and plaids in coral
and apple-green and lavender and faint
orange, with monograms of Indian blue.

116. INT. GATSBY'S BEDROOM. DAY. C.U.   116.

Suddenly, with a strained sound, DAISY
bends her head into the shirts and begins to cry.

> DAISY
> They're such beautiful shirts.
>   (she sobs on, her voice muf-
>   fled in the thick folds)
> It makes me sad because I've never
> seen such--such beautiful shirts
> before.

This scene from the novel (the writing is mainly Mr. Fitzgerald's) is one of the most moving in a desperately moving book.
We know damn well Daisy isn't weeping over the beauty of the
cloth or the quality of the tailoring, she's mourning what's happened to her life.

Not only is this one of the high points of the book, it works
on film. It worked in the recent version when Redford played
the title role. My God, it even worked with Alan Ladd in the
lead. But it sure doesn't work here. Why?

Because the form of the screenplay is basically unreadable. Everything
brings your eye up short. All those numbers on both sides of

the page and those Christ-awful abbreviations and the *INT.*'s and the *EXT.*'s and on and on.

None of that has any bearing on what we are talking about. It has nothing to do with screenwriting, nor with the selling version of the script.

Those are all for the other technicians when the movie actually shoots. The shot numbers, for example, are for the schedule maker. If we're going to shoot Gatsby's bedroom, he will indicate that tomorrow's work will entail shots 106 through 116. Which lets the production designer know he better damn well have the bedroom set finished. And wardrobe can read this and think, ooops, better get those damn shirts folded and the suits and dressing gowns on hangers.

All that matters *emotionally* to the scene is the hairbrush and the shirts. The sight of her delightedly touching her hair with his brush sends him slightly out of control, and he begins flinging the shirts in the air *because there are no words*. He tried to talk, couldn't finish his thought, so to do something, anything, he begins grabbing and throwing his shirts.

Back in Forty-second Street of course, at two in the morning, I was a long way from Gatsby. I bought the book and taxied home, wondering how in the world I was ever going to try and write a screenplay.

Some weeks later, I got a call about *Masquerade*.

Masquerade was sort of a gentle spy parody (the James Bond craze had hit) concerning a failed soldier of fortune who gets involved with trying to protect the child heir to the throne of an Arab oil country. He doesn't protect him very well, adventures ensue, all ends reasonably happily. Rex Harrison was to play the lead but he dropped out, Robertson replaced him.

Dialog had to be altered to fit the new star, and to my astonishment (because he hadn't read the *Flowers for Algernon* script yet) Robertson wanted me to do the altering. I met with the English producer Michael Ralph, and after the standard case of writer's panic, I went to England to attempt the job.

Five points quickly to be made about that experience.

One: Since the picture was already well into preproduction— locations, casting, etc., were pretty much set—most of what I did was what I'd been hired to do: fuss with the dialog. This basically reenforced my misconception that screenplays *were* dialog, that talk was the crucial contribution the writer could supply.

Two: A single sequence might be mentioned. Two-thirds of the way through the picture, Robertson finds himself trapped in a large circus cage that is set in the middle of a barn. (The circus people are in on the kidnapping and have trapped Cliff and imprisoned him.) Next to Robertson's cage is another large cage containing a monstrous and very hungry vulture. Now the circus people leave for a conference, but one of them stupidly leaves a large ring of keys on a nail maybe ten feet away.

Robertson spots the keys, and when the villains have left him, he tries reaching for the keys, but it's obviously hopeless. Then he realizes the monster bird is sitting on a couple of long bamboo perches. Sucking it up, he reaches into the bird's arena, tries slipping one of the perches out. The bird, naturally, has a certain territorial sense and pecks the hell out of Robertson's hands. But he perseveres and, knuckles bleeding, frees a piece of bamboo, reaches with it for the ring of keys.

Still too short.

Balefully, he eyes the vulture, takes a breath, and goes back into the cage again, hands getting zapped worse than before. It really smarts, but there's nothing else he can do, and after great effort he grabs the second piece of bamboo, ties it to the first, goes to the bars of his cage, reaches just as far as he ever can, tries to get the shaky bamboo pole around the rings, can't quite get it, tries again and again until God smiles, he lifts the ring of keys from the nail, raises the pole up so that, at last, the keys slide along it, and when they're close enough he grabs them, puts them in the lock of the cage—

—and they don't fit, they're the wrong keys.

I guess this was the first reversal I ever wrote, but it sure wasn't the last. Because that's what a lot of screenwriting is: putting new twists on old twists. The audience is so quick, so smart, they grasp things immediately, and if you give them what they expect, if they reach the destination ahead of you, it's not easy for them to find it in their hearts to forgive you.

Three: I went to Spain with the production when shooting was about to begin, in case there were last minute adjustments that needed doing. The day before principal photography, I was walking in the hills with the director and the production designer. The purpose of the walk was to discuss a location for a vehicle crash. We found the spot and stopped.

The plot involved simply the capturing of Robertson by the villains. He was being driven along the road in a limousine and the villains were to roar out from hiding in a wine truck, surprising the driver. There would then be the crash and the capture.

The designer pointed to the side road and the hiding place and started to talk. "What I thought we might do is this," he said. "Here comes the Cadillac limo. Now we cut to the wine truck starting to block the route. Then cut back to the driver, surprised, trying to avoid the collision. Then back to the wine truck. Then we have the sound of the crash and we cut to the limo on its side, wheels spinning, and inside the driver is unconscious and Robertson is stunned. They pull him out, dump him in the wine truck, and drive off."

To which the director replied, "I think that's perhaps the most clichéd description of a crash I've ever heard in all my life."

Silence for a while. The designer pulled on his cigarette. These were two very English men, and very proper. "You really think it's that terrible, do you?" the designer asked.

"Absolutely the worst," the director answered.

Now the designer flicked away his cigarette and turned to face the director. "I have a suggestion, then," he said. "Give me . . ." and now he paused for emphasis. *"Give me two fucking Rolls-Royces I can destroy and I'll give you the greatest fucking crash you've ever seen."*

They went on chatting and I went on listening and what it was, of course, was the first discussion of budgets I'd ever heard. (Not only couldn't we buy and destroy two Rolls-Royces, we couldn't even destroy the Cadillac: I found out later it was rented and had to be returned unscratched.)

I had always assumed, until then, that what you saw on the screen was what was meant to be on the screen.

Wrong.

A crucial if not *the* crucial problem of every film today is what it will cost. And within that context, how can you make what you've got to spend look like something. "It's all up there on the screen" is a common expression in Hollywood, and it has a positive meaning: We can see where the money went.

Masquerade was, as stated, of the James Bond genre, but it didn't have a James Bond budget. A Bond film would have wrecked two Rollses. Or whatever else they felt would be telling: They're meant to be expensive, part of their appeal is their scope.

Masquerade wasn't like that; nor are most pictures. That's why producers and directors fight like hell for every penny they can get to spend. Probably it's fair to say that nobody shoots what they really want, not all the time.

They shoot what they can afford.

Four: My first day on the set.

Probably I have been more excited in my life, but not often. Watching a movie, a real live movie, actually being made was something I'd never dreamed of, even six months before.

(I suppose it was similar to the first time I ever went backstage in a Broadway theatre. I was in my middle teens and visiting New York and a cousin of mine had gone to high school with Judy Holliday, who was starring in her greatest hit, "Born Yesterday." After the matinee my cousin escorted me backstage to Miss Holliday's dressing room. We were introduced, I doubt that I managed to get out more than "Hello" and "Thank you" before I was ushered out. The entire encounter may have taken five minutes, more likely two.

To me, today, it still seems like hours. I'd never met an actress, much less a star. I have no artistic sense whatsoever. Even my stick figures stink.

But I could draw that room. I remember every goddam thing about it. The size, the color of the walls, the pictures hung there. I remember the bright lights on her dressing table, all the jars of makeup, the color of her hair, the texture of her skin, the angle of her neck as she looked up and smiled so sweetly at me. A lot of people believe Judy Holliday died years ago.

I am not among them.)

Back to that Spanish morning in 1964.

A shot was being set up when I got there and I remember being surprised by two things most of all: the heat of the lights and the incredible number of people on the set. It wasn't a big picture, but there had to be over a hundred technicians.

I asked if it would be all right if I stood where the camera was pointed for a moment. No problem. I moved into the lit area. The lights literally were blinding. I turned around in a little quick circle.

It was the closest I would ever come to being a movie star.

I got the hell out of everyone's way and waited while Robertson was called. The setup was a very simple reaction shot. Robertson was supposed to walk to a spot, turn his head, look off, and react to what was supposed to be there. The director and Robertson talked briefly. Robertson got ready, closed his eyes (they are very blue, and the lights can be a problem), and the director said "Go, Cliff" and Robertson went.

He walked to the proper place, stopped, looked off, reacted as he was supposed to. The director said, "Very good, Cliff, cut, print"—

—and then it was like this army attacking.

Dozens of men charged forward and work began for the next setup in a slightly different location. Which meant this: Everything had to be moved.

And it took, literally, hours.

I didn't know that was how movies were made. I thought you did this shot and when it was right you did that shot and when it was right you did the third and that was how the day went.

Wrong.

What happens on a movie set is this: nothing. Not for the stars, not for the director, not for most of the people you think of when you think of movies.

Let's say Clark Gable walks into a room at Tara and says "Good morning" to Vivien Leigh and she looks up and says, "I'm not speaking to you, Rhett."

Well, that kind of sequence can take a *day*. You shoot that little scene, if you want to skimp, in three ways. The master shot encompassing his entering and talking and her replying. Then we do his close-up of the scene with the camera just on him. Then we do her close-up with the camera just on her.

Now, I don't suppose it's giving away secrets to say, at this point in time, that there really wasn't any Tara or any room inside. That was all built on sound stages. With walls, probably, that "fly"—are movable. Okay, we do the master shot. And it's lit in a certain way and they go jabber jabber and do it a couple of times until the director is satisfied.

You just don't quickly move to Gable's close-up. You've got to tear the room apart, at least the part where Miss Leigh was, because that's where the crew is going to be. And walls have to be moved and lights have to be taken down and moved and put back up and then relit and altered so that it exactly matches the lighting of the master shot. If it was early morning when the master shot was supposed to happen, it can't look like dusk when we do the close-ups.

Unless you're the cinematographer, who is busting his chops to get the look duplicated, it is the snooze of all the world.

Back on *Masquerade,* I remember the boring crash of reality coming down. "This is how they make a movie? Where's the *magic?*"

There ain't none. I've said this before and I believe it now: The most exciting day of your life may well be your first day on a movie set, and the dullest days will be all those that follow.

Five: This was my first experience in working with a movie star, and one morning Robertson and I were strolling along the beach in Alicante, Spain, where the movie was headquartered. My job was pretty much over, his about to begin, and we were in conversation when a friend of Robertson's came hurrying up, talking very quickly about Acapulco, where Robertson had done a turkey with Lana Turner.

No actor I've met has more social grace than Cliff Robertson; the man is immaculately polite. But suddenly he was distant and cold and the Acapulco man was soon behind us as we continued on. Whether he sensed my surprise or not I have no way of knowing, but a few moments later, Robertson began to talk quietly. "I don't think I ever met that guy in my life," he said. "And if I did it might have been a quick hello with a bunch of other people. But when your face is familiar, people have an edge on you—they know who you are, you don't know them, and sometimes they try to take advantage."

True. Over the years I have been with people who, say, will Dustin Hoffman you to death. It's "Dusty" this and "Dusty tells me he's very interested in" that. While I've sat there knowing the man has never talked to Hoffman in his life. It always surprises me, the lying, but probably the stupidity is mine: Stars are golden, they give off heat, and we all want to be closer to the fire.

Robertson added one more line then. Quietly. "You don't want to be rude but you have to be careful—there are a lot of strange people out there."

True again, sometimes agonizingly so: When John Lennon took his final walk into the Dakota, one of my first thoughts was of walking in the morning with Cliff Robertson in Alicante, Spain.

I returned then to New York and continued my first screenplay, *Flowers for Algernon*. It wasn't easy, but I wasn't getting paid for it to be easy, and what kept me going was my affection for that wonderful Daniel Keyes short story. That affection is all that ever keeps you going on an adaptation, and if you don't have it, or if you lose it, you are in very deep trouble.

Finally it was done and I sent it off to Robertson. The next event of consequence was when I found out that I was off the project and Stirling Silliphant was doing the screenplay. (And wonderfully, too, without a scintilla of mine in the finished work.)

I couldn't believe it. Getting canned is always two things, shocking and painful. I was rocked. I'd never been fired before. No one ever told me specifically what was wrong with my work. But if I were forced to guess, I would say, odds on, my screenplay stunk.

I got in touch with Robertson, asked for a chance to try again, which was probably stupid of me and embarrassing for him: Down in the movie business is definitely down.

So there I was, my first picture, and *ka-boom*. Cashiered. Unseated. Out. If you get the idea that I am trying to indicate that it was an unsettling experience, you are correct. But looking back on it now, I could not have asked for a better educational tool, considering what was to come. . . .

chapter four
Harper

Harper, my next screenplay, was when I first began to learn at least a little about the craft of screenwriting.

It was also, inadvertently, when I began to learn about how movies actually happen. *Boys and Girls Together* had been published, to calamitous notices. (The *New York Times* said "a child of nine could understand this book before he could lift it." From there, the review got really bad.) However, a producer, Elliott Kastner, had optioned it for films.

I met with Kastner to talk about the book—I was not to be the screenwriter, which was plenty okay with me—but before we got into discussing any notions about how to turn a six-hundred-plus-page book into a one-hundred-twenty-page script, he began talking about a movie he'd recently seen, a very successful Western called *The Professionals.* "I'd like to do a movie like that," he said. "I'd like to do a movie with balls."

I suggested he read some of the Lew Archer detective books by Ross Macdonald, and if he liked them, I'd reread them and try and do a screenplay for him. He called the following Monday and said he was very much interested and that he would option whichever one I said.

There were probably ten Archer books published by this time, and like an idiot I started with the most recent and worked my way back. "Like an idiot" pertains to the fact that as the series went along, Macdonald was increasingly leaving the roots of the tough-guy Hammett-Chandler tradition where he began and was getting more interested in character complexity, less with plot.

I finally chose the first Archer book, *The Moving Target,* which

177

Kastner optioned, and I set to work. The script I wrote was dialog heavy because I still thought that was the crucial element. (The resulting movie, by the way, was very successful for a lot of reasons, none of which I can take much credit for. Television had preempted the private-eye format, and there hadn't been a movie like *Harper* for years, so it had freshness. It also had some kind of a cast for a detective flick—among the performers were Lauren Bacall, Julie Harris, Arthur Hill, Janet Leigh, Strother Martin, and Robert Wagner giving what I still think is far and away the deepest emotional work he's yet shown. Not to mention just wonderful work by Paul Newman, who simply shouldered the script and rammed it home.)

I don't believe Newman was the first to see it—my memory is Sinatra turned it down. Newman was in Europe when he was sent the project, and he showed quick interest.

Because we couldn't have caught him at a better time. He was making a dog of a period piece, *Lady L*, and he was running around in tights and having a miserable time. *Harper*, very much in the American tradition, felt very appealing to him.

Kastner did then what any adroit producer does at such a time: He hustled. A young director acceptable to Newman showed a willingness to do it, so Kastner took him and they flew to Europe to sew up Newman while his interest was high.

Imagine Kastner's surprise when the meeting took place and it turned out the young director didn't like the script at all, said it was rotten, and what they should do was pitch it all and start over, doing something in the genre but not this piece of shit. (*Piece of shit* by the way is the standard terminology in Hollywood for a project. If you ask a producer what he's working on, more than likely he will say, "Well, I've got this Western piece of shit I'm working on" or "this piece-of-shit comedy.")

Kastner managed to stifle the director before total disaster overtook the project. They left Europe with the director out but Newman, perhaps a bit ruffled, still interested. Eventually, another young director, Jack Smight, did the picture with terrific pace and skill.

When *Lady L* was done, Newman returned to his home in Connecticut and Kastner took me up to a crucial meeting: Changes were needed and were they the kind of alterations I could accommodate. (If I hadn't, by the way, I would have been gone and someone else would have done them. *If* Newman's interest would hold. Stars like Newman get offered everything practically every day, and if a situation begins to get messy, they can get turned off. Quickly.)

Paul Newman is the least starlike superstar I've ever worked with. He's an educated man and a trained actor and he never wants more close-ups. What he wants is the best possible script and character he can have. And he loves to be surrounded by the finest actors available, because he believes the better they are, the better the picture's apt to be, the better he'll come out. Many stars, maybe even most, don't want that competition.

We walked the back lanes of Westport and it all went well. But what I remember most about it was that Newman carried a handful of pebbles and I noticed that whenever a car drove by, he was always in the act of tossing a pebble into the woods, so that his back was to the street. It's hard not to notice Paul Newman and he was doing all he could to talk and not be stared at.

With Newman set, Kastner and I drove back to the city and on the way he said, "You don't know what happened, do you?" I said I didn't. He told me the following: "You just jumped past all the shit."

And he was right. I was no longer a *putz* novelist from New York. Now I was a *putz* novelist who had written a Paul Newman picture. Any first credit in Hollywood is tremendously meaningful. When that credit involves pleasing a major star, you can square that import.

Now for my education.

The shooting script for *Harper* began like this:

FADE IN ON

LEW HARPER'S FACE in CLOSE UP. He is tough, bright and poor. A good man in a bad world.

PULL BACK TO REVEAL

HARPER standing in front of the impressive closed gate to an impressive estate. Behind him is his car with the motor running; like its owner, the

car has been around too. He speaks into a microphone set in the gate.

                    HARPER
          My name is Lew Harper. To see Mrs.
          Sampson.

After a pause there is a click. After the click,
the gate swings open. HARPER gets back in his car
and starts to drive forward.

CUT TO

HIS FIRST VIEW OF THE SAMPSON HOUSE. It is enormous, surrounded by a vast expanse of lawn. Among
other things VISIBLE are a tennis court, a swimming pool with patio and pool house, a large garden filled with flowers.

CUT TO

HARPER, driving along, taking it all in.

This is a perfectly adequate opening to a movie. (We don't
know it's a detective story yet.) What we do know is a guy in a
beat-up car is expected, for some reason or another, at a mansion.

It doesn't tell us much more than that but at least it's direct.
If something interesting happens soon, we'll be interested; if
not, not.

And that was how the movie opened when production began.
I was back in New York when I got a call from the coast saying
they needed a sequence immediately to cover the opening
credits.

What?

Just a credit sequence and fast. Whatever it was, they'd shoot
it. Get it in the mail. I hung up. Get *what* in the mail? I sat at my
desk and did what any hopefully professional writer would do
when he is asked to do something he doesn't know how to do.

I panicked.

I mumbled, cursed, paced around. No ideas at all. This was a detective story, and traditionally they don't start until there's a case, until the detective meets his client and finds out what he's supposed to do. I could have always had him getting the phone call when he's told to go see Mrs. Sampson, but the thought of credits running over a phone call with snappy dialog like "Yes, this is Lew Harper" or "Fine, I'll be there" made my eyes glaze over just thinking about it.

And there wasn't any time. So in desperation I decided, what the hell, he had to get up in the morning, everybody gets up in the morning, what's special about our guy? Not all that much, maybe, but it was the best I could come up with. This is what I wrote and sent that day, and what was the eventual opening of the movie.

IN BLACKNESS, there is the loud metallic ticking of a clock.

FADE IN ON

LEW ARCHER'S EYES. The eyes blink. Again. Again. Now—

PULL BACK TO REVEAL

HARPER lying alone in bed in his small crummy office. It's early morning. Across the room is a tv set, on but blank, no programs yet. An alarm clock is on a table nearby. HARPER lies there, wearing underwear shorts and shirt. The clock continues to tick. HARPER continues to stare. At nothing.

CREDITS START TO ROLL

Now the clock goes off like an explosion. HARPER half rises, swipes at the clock with his hand and

CUT TO

THE CLOCK, the sound dying suddenly as it hits the floor.

CUT TO

HARPER, out of bed now. He goes to the blank tv
set, turns it off. Now he moves to the window, lets
the shade fly up. WE CAN SEE his office more clearly now--it doesn't look a bit better.

CUT TO

HARPER, still in his underwear, running water in
the sink, splashing it on his face, coming to
life.

CUT TO

THE TINY KITCHEN AREA. He's shaved now, wears
pants and a short-sleeved shirt not tucked in. A
tie is draped around his neck. There is a hot
plate, water is boiling. Beside the water is a
Chemex-type coffee maker. He takes a paper filter, folds it in half, folds it one more time, puts
it into the Chemex. Then he takes a coffee can,
pours coffee into the filter--

--only the can's empty. No coffee left. Unhappily
he stands there a moment, looks down--

CUT TO

A WASTEBASKET. He lifts the lid. Inside is yesterday's coffee filter, the used grounds still
there.

CUT TO

HARPER. He hesitates a moment, then reaches into
the wastebasket, takes out the used filter and old
coffee grounds, puts them into the Chemex, and as
he starts to pour boiling water in--

CUT TO

A FILLED CUP OF BLACK COFFEE. HARPER stands beside
it, shirt tucked in now, tie tied. He picks up the

cup, takes a swallow--and then the horrendous
taste of the stuff registers; it's like something
you might drink in the Black Hole of Calcutta. He
puts the cup down, walks past a framed photograph
of a pretty smiling woman close to his age, kind of
salutes the picture as he moves round a corner.

CUT TO

HARPER, standing by his closet. He takes out a gun
and shoulder holster, starts to strap it on.

CUT TO

HARPER leaving his office, closing the door. He's
wearing a suit coat now. The office door has a sign
reading ''Lew Harper. Private Investigations.''
Down the corridor of the old building, a JANITOR
is mopping the floor.

CUT TO

A LOS ANGELES FREEWAY and a battered blue Porsche
convertible driving along.

CUT TO

HARPER in the Porsche. He puts on sunglasses,
drives on.

CUT TO

THE PORSCHE, taking an exit ramp. There is a sign
reading ''Santa Theresa. 90 Miles.'' The Porsche
turns in the direction of Santa Theresa.

CUT TO

A FANCY STREET in Santa Theresa. The Porsche turns
up toward a gate. A SERVANT stands by the gate with
a dog.

> HARPER
> Lew Harper. To see Mrs. Sampson.

The SERVANT presses a button. The gate opens.

CUT TO

A LONG TREE-LINED PRIVATE DRIVEWAY. Maybe half a
mile or more in length. At the end of it is the
SAMPSON mansion. As it starts to come INTO VIEW--

CREDITS COME TO AN END.

The first time I saw *Harper* in a Broadway theatre was when
my education began. (I had already seen it once, at a screening,
which I'll get to shortly.) I sat there with my popcorn, waiting
for the picture to get going—which was when he gets his assignment from Mrs. Sampson. At least that's what I thought.

The credits came on. Paul Newman lies there, the alarm
clock goes off, he knocks it away, gets up, turns off the tube,
lets the shade fly up, goes to the kitchen, picks up the coffee
can. Nothing unusual so far.

Then, when he tipped the coffee can and found it empty, this
sound began in the theatre. It was laughter and it built when he
opened the wastebasket and saw the used grounds. And built
more as he hesitated, making up his mind. Now when he
reached down, plopped it into the Chemex, the theatre was
really loud. This was not one of those wonderful sudden
shrieks of laughter, such as when Woody Allen sneezes on the
cocaine in *Annie Hall.*

If you're in the movie business, you try to pay as much attention as you can to audience reaction; you try to read it. And as I
sat there, surprised at what was going on around me—I'd seen
the picture, remember, with a few people, and the credits were
just that, credits—I wondered what it was the audience was reacting to. It sure wasn't any zippy dialog of mine, because there
was no talk at all.

Then, when he looked at the filled coffee cup, the sound
seemed to be peaking. But it wasn't. For when he finally took
that first swallow and practically gagged, the theatre exploded.

I still just sat, listening to the people. The appreciative laughter continued practically till he drove up to the mansion. And
once the plot began, everything played at a much higher level

than I'd imagined possible when I first saw the movie at the screening.

Why?

Obviously, I can't be sure of the answer. The audience certainly knew a lot more about him than the way the movie originally opened. They knew he lived alone, in a pit of an office. They knew he went to sleep with the tv for company. They knew he didn't sleep well, not when he's up before the alarm. They knew there was a woman, because of the photograph, they knew he felt something for her from the way he saluted her, they knew she wasn't with him, he was very much alone. And they knew a lot more, too—yes, he was a detective, not a successful one, and he carried a gun, so he didn't seem like someone to take lightly. The battered car told a lot about him.

But mainly it was that business with the coffee.

Whenever anyone talked about *Harper* to me in the weeks that followed, that was the moment they remembered—drinking that horrible stuff. (Just like the jump off the cliff is what people always mention first in *Butch*.) And the laugh that went along with it, that was a laugh of affection.

In a detective story of this type—*The Maltese Falcon, The Big Sleep*—all you really have going for you is your main man: You see everything, the whole world, through his eyes, he keeps you company every step of the way. And if you don't like being with Sam Spade or Philip Marlowe, not all the plot skill in the world is going to make it a happy journey. If you are turned off by your host, forget it, it's over. And what the coffee moment really turned out to be was an invitation that the audience gladly accepted: *They liked Lew Harper.*

From that moment forward, the script was on rails.

Four brief memories from that Warner Bros. film.

First: I was called to California for the start of shooting. And before we began on that opening day, Jack Warner himself visited the set.

He was the last of the titans, of the legendary studio heads who ran things in the so-called golden age of film; the Mayers and the Thalbergs had long since gone. I had heard stories about them all, not many flattering. They were brutal men, gut fighters, etc., etc.

Mr. Warner, when he appeared that day, was immaculately dressed. He had an aide with him, and the purpose of his visit was simply to wish everybody luck. He shook hands with Newman and with Jack Smight, the director, both of whom he knew. Then he said hello to a bunch of the rest of us, his aide preceding him, telling him who we were and what our names were. It was all over quickly, a final wave and he and his aide were gone.

Shooting started.

Hours later, alone, I was wandering around the lot. I'd never been on a Hollywood film studio before and when I came to the Western street, lined on both sides with false fronts of saloons and general stores and all the rest, I was in hog heaven. I love Westerns, and Warners' had made a bunch of them, and I looked around and around, lost in memory, trying to remember which store front I might have seen in which movie. I have no idea how long I stood there by myself, but eventually I realized I wasn't by myself anymore.

Mr. Warner, also alone, was standing down the street, staring at me. I didn't know if I should be there or not, I didn't know if I'd committed some gaffe that would irritate the man, I didn't know anything except I felt like a ten-year-old getting caught in the wrong place by the school principal.

He looked at me for a long moment before he kind of shook his head and smiled and said, "Goldman, what the hell are you doing here?"

I was relieved he wasn't angry and we talked for a few minutes, maybe about the street, maybe about the old days, maybe about a million things. The truth is, I don't remember a single word of what was said.

I was simply stunned that he'd remembered my name. . . .

Second: Late in the movie, Robert Wagner is revealed as one of the villains. Newman, as the detective, forces the revelation. Wagner, boyish and innocent-seeming, is supposedly involved with the film's ingenue, but Newman suspects that instead his real love is an aging drug-addict singer. Newman accuses Wagner of being less than he should be; Wagner, convincingly, pleads his case. Newman seems to believe him, Wagner is relieved. Then Newman goes on to say how happy he is that Wagner is innocent, because the drug-addict singer is slime.

And then Newman launches into this long speech about just how loathsome and despicable she is, and the speech goes on and on, insult following insult until Wagner can't take it anymore, his true love is being sullied, and to make Newman shut up, he pulls a gun.

Okay, they shoot the master shot.

Now it's time for Wagner's close-up. The camera is on *him*, and all Newman has to do is stand out of range with the script in his hands and read his string of insults. The camera rolls, Newman reads, and suddenly, as actors say, Wagner fills the moment—

—on camera, in close up, Robert Wagner starts to cry. This is, let me tell you, a bonus. And it's genuinely exciting.

And no one is more excited than Newman. In fact, he's so excited at what's happening with Wagner that *Newman* begins fucking up his lines. All he has to do is stand there and read and he can't get the goddam words out right.

It didn't matter, thankfully. They got the shot. Wagner was so deep into what he was doing that the crying continued. After the shot was finished, everyone ran to Wagner and milled around, congratulating him; it was that thrilling.

Wagner said a moment like that had never happened to him before. And he also added one more thing: It was the first time in his experience that a major star had actually stayed around and stood there off camera, reading the lines with him, acting along, as it were. Usually, when the star is done with his shot, it's off to the dressing room, and the remaining performer gets to act with the script girl reading the star's lines. Script girls are very important on the set, they work like hell—but they are also noted for a certain woodenness when it comes to reciting dialog. No question that Newman's presence helped Wagner fill the moment.

And if you ever see the movie, the moment's right there. That's not glycerine on Wagner's face as he pulls the trigger. Those were very real tears. . . .

Third: There are some stars of whom you just never hear anything bad. Newman and Lemmon and Heston and Peck, of their generation.

And Wagner, maybe one generation down, is another. Still

another is—or sadly, was—Natalie Wood. Wagner and Wood had been married, but by the time of *Harper* they were divorced and going very separate ways.

One afternoon, when he wasn't needed, Wagner wandered off the set and I went along. Nearby, on another sound stage, *Inside Daisy Clover* was shooting, starring Natalie Wood. Wagner went in and I followed, watching as, far away at the very front, she was doing a take of a musical number.

I continued to watch. Wagner did, too, climbing several steps up a ladder. There were several takes and then she was released, and I don't know if it was accident, design, whatever, but when she left the set to go to her dressing room she passed by the ladder and the following dialog took place.

> WAGNER
> (from above)
> Hi.

> WOOD
> (stopping, looking up)
> Oh. Hi.

> WAGNER
> That looked good.

> WOOD
> You think?

> WAGNER
> I do. Yeah.

> WOOD
> Hope so.
> (little smile, starting off)
> Bye.

> WAGNER
> (watching after her)
> Bye.

I stood there like a gnome watching him watch her, and they were, of course, very famous faces to me; I'd read about their courtship and their marriage and their troubles and divorce, and certainly that was not very telling dialog.

But the subtext sure let you know a lot.

Their subsequent remarriage pleased a lot of people, just as her obscene drowning sent a lot of people into shock. From all I could gather, they were as well liked as any in the Hollywood community.

There are a lot of dreadful jokes about movie funerals, the most famous, I guess, dealing with Harry Cohn, the head of Columbia and perhaps the leading ogre of his era. At the services, someone expressed surprise at the number of people present, to which the reply came, "Give the public what they want and they'll turn out."

No jokes surrounded Natalie Wood. I suspect few deaths in recent years have upset so many. Thirty years a star and a lady every year.

Remarkable. . . .

Fourth and final memory: The screening of *Harper* that I previously referred to was another learning experience for a screenwriter. My wife, Ilene, and I were living in Princeton at the time and we drove in for it. I was, obviously, excited. My very first real movie. *Masquerade* had come out, but that wasn't mine, not like *Harper* was.

(I don't attend screenings if I can avoid them, by the way. I suppose I average one every two years. I don't think they're helpful—sneaks, yes, enormously, but not screenings. You sit there with a few other people, all of them in the business, and no one's a real audience. George Abbott, the legendary Broadway director, once said, "You can't tell anything about what you've got until there are hot bodies out front." By "hot bodies" he meant people who paid their money to see the show. Theirs was the reaction that meant something.

And I think movies would be better if more company executives sat there with the people. Some do, but most don't. They leave their offices and walk into a small room and tell the camera operator via intercom that they're ready and then the movie rolls and often they talk through what's going on up there and when it's over they're quickly back in their offices. For me, that has *nothing* whatsoever to do with moviegoing.)

Anyway, we arrived at the building where the screening was to take place early, and we wasted a few minutes outside because, my God, you don't want to be the first, and then we elevatored up to the screening room. There was a publicity guy guarding the door, and I said my name was Goldman and he looked at a small list in his hand and then eyed me, truly, with suspicion.

"What're you doing here?" he said then.

I hadn't expected the question and couldn't come up with anything, but Ilene, with emphasis, said, "He's the *writer*."

The publicity guy didn't budge or change expression. "Yeah?" he said finally. "Well, what're you doing here . . . ?"

chapter five

Butch Cassidy and the Sundance Kid

As mentioned earlier I first came across the Butch Cassidy story in the late fifties, researched it on and off for eight years. In the beginning I had no idea that I would ever write it, and it never crossed my mind that when I did put it down, it would be in the form of a screenplay; this was all long before Cliff Robertson came into my life.

By the time I did the initial draft, in the mid-sixties, I was already into movie work, so the idea of trying to make a movie of the piece did not seem forbidding. Plus, I've never been a great fan of Western novels, horses scare the hell out of me, and to do the additional research required to make a novel authentic was out of the question. The movie came out in '69 and is still with us today on television.

Looking back on it from a distance of perhaps a quarter century, I still think now what I thought then: It is a glorious piece of narrative, original and moving.

The whys of that I'll get to in a moment, but let me just give the bones of the story here. There are three main characters, the two title roles and Etta Place, the Sundance Kid's mistress. F·itch led an outlaw gang, of which Sundance was a member.

When a murderous and implacable Superposse was sent to kill them, Butch and Sundance barely escaped and Butch decided to head for South America where life, in theory, would be a bit less precarious. The three went to Bolivia, where eventually the men were killed.

Why the movies never told this story before, I can't say, but my guess is because of the last third of the narrative, the South American section: Butch did something Western heroes simply do not do—he ran away.

If I speak primarily about Butch, it's because there isn't a great deal known about the Sundance Kid or Etta. Sundance was a phenomenal gunman who may have been born in New Jersey. That's about it. Of Etta, there is even less: She was either a schoolteacher or a prostitute who traveled with them, left before they died. (There are numbers of photographs of prostitutes in the Old West. There are also some pictures of Etta: She looked like Jeanne Crain, and even the young whores then looked old. To me, she had to be a schoolteacher.)

Butch is pretty well documented. A good Mormon boy, he was born Robert Leroy Parker in Utah in 1866. (He took the alias of Cassidy after his boyhood idol, Mike Cassidy, who first got him interested in robbery.)

By the 1890's, Butch was the head of the largest, the most successful, and the last great outlaw gang—The Wild Bunch, the Hole-in-the-Wall Gang. The remarkable thing about this was that Butch was no gunman at all: He never killed a man until late in life, when he was serving as a payroll guard in South America. He was neither particularly big nor strong, never much of a fighter. Nor was he the brains of the outfit; they had a resident intellectual, Elza Lay, who did as much of their planning as anyone.

Now, The Wild Bunch consisted of some of the most murderous figures in Western history. Arrogant, brutal men. And yet, here running things was Cassidy. Why? The answer is incredible but true: People just *liked* him.

Everybody liked Butch. Sometimes (and I could never figure out how to get this into the narrative) when he was being followed, he would ride up to a farm and say, more or less, "Look, I'm Butch Cassidy, there are some people after me, I'd really appreciate it a lot if you'd hide me for a while."

And they would. There have been only two American out-laws who were outsized legends during their careers: Butch was one, Jesse James the second. But people liked Butch before he was famous. This next anecdote is true—and it *killed* me not to be able to find a place to use it.

When he was a young man, Butch was in jail in Wyoming. He came up before the governor with a chance at parole. The governor said, "I'll set you free if you promise to go straight." And Butch answered—really he did—"*I can't do that.*"

The governor, naturally, was a bit taken aback, but before he could say much, Butch came up with the following offer: "I'll make you a deal," he told the governor. (This is a convict offering the governor a deal, remember.) "I'll promise that if you let me go, I'll never break the law in Wyoming again—"

—and the governor *accepted* the deal, set Butch free—

—and Butch never again broke the law in Wyoming: If his gang did a job there, he refused to go along.

You've just got to admire someone like that. I did, anyway. I still find him fascinating.

The period in our history we have glamorized as the "Wild West" was actually very short—it began with the end of the Civil War, died with the turn of the century. A total of approximately thirty-five years. Butch pulled his last job in this country in the fall of 1901.

One of the organizations he had picked on more than once was the Union Pacific Railroad, owned by E. H. Harriman. Harriman got fed up and, at great expense, formed the Super-posse. He put them in a special train, outfitted them with whatever they needed, and paid them well.

In real life, the instant Butch *heard* about the existence of this new enemy—the half-dozen finest lawmen together and out to get him—he took off immediately for South America. The Superposse never actually chased him, since he and Sundance and Etta were long gone.

The trio spent some days in New York in 1902—we have wonderful photographs documenting their visit. One of Butch's weaknesses was he loved having his picture taken.

Butch and Sundance died seven years later, and in that time they led a remarkably varied life, robbing, rustling, ranching, taking various aliases as their needs dictated. My image of them during this time was as if Willie Mays, instead of retiring, had gone to Japan to play baseball and become home-run champion again.

Butch and Sundance did what Gatsby only dreamed of doing: They repeated the past. As famous as they were in the states, they were bigger legends in South America: *bandidos Yanquis.*

And probably that fact—recapturing their past—is what I found so moving about the narrative. We all wish for it; they made it happen.

One more thing. As a writer I believe that all the basic human truths are known. And what we try to do as best we can is come at those truths from our own unique angle, to reilluminate those truths in a hopefully different way.

I believed, back a quarter century ago, that it was not possible for two people truly to know each other. No matter how close the husband and wife, the father and son, the lover and beloved, we are locked inside ourselves. In Butch and Sundance I had two friends who lived through decades together, who traveled tens of thousands of miles, only to die bloody in a country where no one knew their names, where they barely spoke the language—

—it seemed a wonderful vehicle to say something about our lack of knowledge, about our hopeless and terrible and, sadly, permanent loneliness. . . .

I feel now that Butch was by far the most important screenplay, for me, that I ever wrote or will write, not because of the success of the film—

—but as a learning experience.

The film work I'd done had either been dialog rewrites or adaptations of novels. And in an adaptation, obviously, you've got the source material to move you along.

Butch was an original.

I had to find the story.

Which story, though? Which incidents? There was so much wonderful material. I mentioned the scene where Butch made the deal with the governor of Wyoming to let him out of jail. I *loved* that. I don't know if I've ever come across a better introduction to a character.

But it had problems.

Logically, in order to get *out* of jail, he had to be *in* jail first.

Which meant he would have to be arrested. And tried. And sentenced. And serve at least some time.

Now add this: For the scene to have any credibility, Butch would have to be young. No governor would dare let so famous an outlaw free. But my story dealt with two guys who were already legends.

If you had asked me, a year before I began writing, what sequences I was positive would be in the screenplay, I would have come up with two: the shoot-out at the end and the scene with the governor.

But I couldn't make it fit. I fiddled every goddam which way; it kept falling out of the picture. I wanted it in. Desperately. I figured, "Well, what if I had him arrested quickly and then dissolved to a year later and made the governor an old friend and bullshit, bullshit, bullshit."

Stunk. Wrong. Silly.

There is a wonderful phrase of William Faulkner's that goes something like this: "In writing, you must kill all your darlings."

The scene with the governor was certainly a darling of mine, but eventually I realized I had to kill it. Because, probably not consciously, I was approaching what I believe to be the single most important lesson to be learned about writing for films and this is it:

SCREENPLAYS ARE STRUCTURE.

As I said earlier, there are two Roman numeral *I*'s to this book—the first being that nobody knows anything. Well, this is the other, in well-deserved caps:

SCREENPLAYS ARE STRUCTURE.

Yes, nifty dialog helps one hell of a lot; sure, it's nice if you can bring your characters to life. But you can have terrific characters spouting just swell talk to each other, and if the structure is unsound, forget it.

Writing a screenplay is in many ways similar to executing a piece of carpentry. If you take some wood and nails and glue and make a bookcase, only to find when you're done that it topples over when you try and stand it upright, you may have created *something*, but it won't work as a bookcase.

The essential opening labor a screenwriter must execute is, of course, deciding what the proper structure should be for the particular screenplay you are writing. And to do that, you have to know what is absolutely crucial in the telling of your story——what is its *spine*?

Whatever it is, you must protect it to the death.

Sometimes the spine is pretty simple to locate—as in a private-detective movie. There is no story until the detective—Lew Archer, say—is called on to solve something. Archer meets his client early on, takes the case, *invariably* is given some information about the case by the client, and then begins to act on that information. He goes and talks to people. One interview leads to the next, on and on, you throw in a little action when things get slow (I think Raymond Chandler said something to the effect that every time he felt in trouble, he had a guy come barging through a door with a gun in his hand). Eventually, something is solved, though often not the original event that triggered the story.

Butch was not so simple.

The original thing that moved me—and whatever that is, it must *always* be kept tattooed behind your eyelids—was the story of these two guys whom I liked, but they were pretty much aimless. They drifted from job to job, unlike Lew Archer, who is always totally directed. Not only were they aimless, there was something worse to deal with: When they did act, they did something no one had ever done before—they went to South America.

Now today, looking back on it, with the success of the film a fact, that doesn't seem like much. But it was, for me in my job, the crunch. (The first time the script was shown, only one studio showed the least interest. And I remember an executive of that studio saying to me that South America had to go—that Butch and Sundance, in order for the movie to work, had to stand and fight the Superposse. Right here. In the Old West. I tried explaining that they really did go to South America, that what was so moving to me was these two guys repeating the past, then dying alone in a strange land. He replied, "I don't give a shit about that—all I know is one thing: *John Wayne don't run away*.")

So justifying the shift in locale was a *huge* problem—because not only don't movie heroes run away, they especially don't in Westerns because *Westerns are based on confrontations.*

Butch had another problem: For an action picture, it had almost no action. At least not action in the Western-movie sense: shoot-outs and fistfights between hero and villain, massive barroom brawls and stampedes with the heroine's life in danger. Following is a list of such moments in *Butch*, together with the screen time used:

Sundance shooting the saloon owner's belt off—	4 seconds
Butch kicking Logan in the balls and knocking him out—	9 seconds
Sundance knocking out the Superposse member (probably you forgot this moment was there)—	6 seconds
The jump off the cliff—	7 seconds
The mine owner getting shot by bandits—	2 seconds
Butch and Sundance killing the bandits—	40 seconds

In other words, up until the final shoot-out, the first hundred minutes of the movie contain approximately one minute of standard Western action. (You could call the various train and bank robberies action, but I wouldn't agree: There's never a sense of jeopardy; it's fun and games time.) There was hopefully a great deal of tension under a lot of the movie—but not the kind of physical action we expect in a Western.

Another problem: Not only did it not have enough violence to be considered an action film, it also wasn't funny enough to be a comedy. First of all, I'm not that skilled at comedy. More than that, if the movie was *too* funny, the ending wouldn't work. We wouldn't care enough that they died, and since I felt that sadness—since more than anything that was the emotional core of my interest—I had to make the audience care too.

Do you know the game that goes like this? "If Jackie Onassis were a car, what kind of car would she be?" Or "If Jimmy Carter were a vegetable, which vegetable would he be?"

Well, if *Butch Cassidy* had been a performer, that performer would have been Jack Benny.

I saw Benny toward the end of his great career when he did a short engagement in a Broadway theatre. And he was superb. Those fabulous takes, his unique sense of timing, he had it all. And the audience was knocked out—

—but he wasn't all that funny.

Sure, there were laughs. But not like Bob Hope gets laughs, or Rodney Dangerfield. Jack Benny was, is, and always will be one of my favorite comedians. Never more than that night in the theatre. And whatever I felt, so did everyone around me. After all, how often do you get to see a master? But it wasn't his comedy that won us—

—we enjoyed being *with* him. No matter where he led us, we wanted to follow along.

And that, I ultimately realized, had to be the spine for the movie—the relationship between Butch and Sundance. And I don't mean just *liking* them. I'm sure that when the people responsible for *Attack of the Fifty Foot Woman* sat around spitballing, they said to each other, "Hey, we've got to *like* the fifty-foot woman, at least a little, so we can feel something when she cashes in. Maybe she likes elephants or giraffes, something to make her seem human."

Butch and Sundance shared almost every scene in the movie, and just like Jack Benny was special, so their relationship had to be special: No matter where they led us, we had to want to follow along. (And the movie had to work off the give and take of the two stars. If they'd been Newman and Brando or Redford and McQueen, the acting would have been fine. But I don't believe the audience would have risen to the film in the same way.)

All I had, then, were the two guys. And it was my job to make them as inviting, and at the same time as unusual, as I possibly knew how.

As I've said, the most important minutes of any *screenplay* are the first fifteen and what I'd like to do now is talk about the structure of the first quarter hour of the screenplay, the first four scenes.

SCENE ONE: BUTCH CASING THE BANK.

Very short scene. A guy walks up to a bank that is very modern-looking and ugly and heavily barred. (The guy is Butch and he's an outlaw, but we don't know that yet.)

He looks at the bank sourly, then talks with a guard.

                    BUTCH
          What was the matter with the old
          bank this town used to have? It was
          beautiful.

                    GUARD
          People kept robbing it.

                    BUTCH
               (walking off)
          That's a small price to pay for
          beauty.

Not much unusual here. What it really is is a statement of theme: *Times are changing and you have to change with them—if you want to survive.*

(I happen not to believe Butch's final retort—I don't think he'd say it and I think it's smart-ass. There's a lot about the screenplay I don't like, the smart-assness just being one of them. I also find there are too many reversals and that the entire enterprise suffers, on more than one occasion, from a case of the cutes.

But the quality of the dialog is not at issue here; proper structure is what we're after and I feel the first scenes will illustrate my point.)

The first little scene is crucial for theme statement—something that gets repeated again and again as the story moves on.

SCENE TWO: SUNDANCE PLAYING CARDS.

Now I think we're starting to move into strange terrain. But it doesn't look like it at first. It looks like the standard cornball card game we've seen a zillion times.

We're in Macon's Saloon, and Macon, written as a strong, tough guy, is involved in a game of blackjack. A stranger is dealing. The stranger is also winning. He cleans out the table and Macon accuses him of cheating.

We don't know yet that the dealer is the Sundance Kid, but the Kid knows who he is. And he also knows three things: He hasn't been cheating, his honor and integrity have been insulted, and he is also the fastest gun in the history of the West.

Make this a John Wayne movie and you're into a "When you say that, smile" situation. Direct confrontation. Wayne, more likely than not, would pick up the card table and clobber the enemy.

What does the Kid do? He just sits there, silent and sad, while his tormentor stands, guns ready, and says, basically, get the hell out of here.

Now Butch comes tearing up. The Kid tells him he wasn't cheating. Butch could not care less about Sundance's being unjustly accused. He wants out. The Kid is stubborn: "If he invites us to stay, then we'll go."

And what does Butch do next? He tries to undermine Sundance's confidence. "You don't know how fast he is. . . . I'm over the hill—it can happen to you." Anything to avoid a confrontation. Butch knows who the Kid is and what he is capable of; there's no way the Kid's going to lose.

Finally Butch, with no other cards to play, tells his secret— the Kid's name. "Can't help you, Sundance," he says. And we still don't know what that means—

—but Macon, the guy who's accused the Kid, sure does. That's why he's written as a hero: big, rugged, powerful. It can't be Donald Meek across the table, not if the next moment's going to work. And that moment is panic: "I didn't know you were the Sundance Kid when I said you were cheating. . . . If I draw on you, you'll kill me."

Now the reader is hopefully saying, "What's with this Sundance Kid anyway? I never heard of him, but maybe I better pay attention."

Macon backs down, invites them to stick around, but they've got to be going. There wouldn't be any gunplay at all if Macon didn't ask for it:

```
                    MACON
          Kid?
               (a little louder now)
          Hey, how good are you?
```

CUT TO

Butch, between Sundance and Macon, but not for long, because the minute Macon asks his question, Butch gets the hell out of the way fast as we

CUT TO

Sundance, diving left and dropping, and his guns are out and roaring and as the sound explodes--

CUT TO

Macon as Sundance shoots his gun belt off and as it drops

CUT TO

Sundance, firing on, and

CUT TO

the gun belt whipping like a snake across the floor as Sundance's bullets strike. Then, as the firing stops--

CUT TO

John Macon, breathing the biggest sigh of relief anyone ever saw and

CUT TO

Sundance, standing now, his guns quiet.

CUT TO

Butch and Sundance. Butch glances at Macon's gun
belt for a moment, then shakes his head.

> BUTCH
> (to Sundance as they head
>   for the door)
> Like I been telling you--over the
> hill.
>   (and they are gone)

So now we've seen the Kid in action and we know one thing:
You don't want to mess with him. The man is a bomb, capable
of exploding at any time. Handle with care.

Although we learn something about Butch and the two men
together, this is essentially Sundance's introductory moment.

SCENE THREE: THE RIDE TO HOLE-IN-THE-WALL.

This is the first time they've been alone. And it may not seem
like much, but there's a lot we learn.

Butch hates what he's doing: "How can I be so damn stupid
as to keep coming back here?"

This is not news to Sundance: "What's your idea *this time*?"
Clearly "this time" means he's heard this kind of bitching before.

And now—essential—the first mention of where the movie's
going to take us: this lunatic destination, Bolivia.

Sundance is no genius: "What's Bolivia?"

Butch is not afraid of Sundance exploding around him. "Bolivia is a country, *stupid*."

Butch is also no genius: "Bolivia is a country, *stupid*—in Central or South America, one or the other." I mean, he's the one
who brought up the subject, and his knowledge of geography is
anything but encyclopedic.

Sundance has a crucial setup line: "Why don't we just go to
Mexico instead?" Crucial because it gives Butch a chance to explain about Bolivia, and also because it wasn't unheard of for a
Western movie to deal with Mexico. All the Alamo retellings,
the Villa stories. In other words, Sundance is saying, "Well,

moving someplace foreign isn't all that weird." He's greasing a path we have no idea we're going to follow.

Butch's reply is not just the most important line in the scene but one of the most vital in the movie. He talks about the California gold rush—which everyone knows about. And then he says, "When I *say* Bolivia, you *think* California."

That line gives the reader something to cling to. It makes comprehensible, even kind of logical, what's going to come.

And just as Butch isn't afraid of Sundance, Sundance doesn't have a lot of respect for Butch's notions. He laughs and says, "You just keep thinking, Butch, that's what you're good at."

At this point, we're eight minutes into the movie and what do we know? Times are hard, maybe a change wouldn't be a bad idea. Sundance is famous and deadly. But we don't really know a whole lot about Butch yet. Or who and what they are.

And what makes their relationship different and special.

SCENE FOUR: THE KICK IN THE BALLS.

Just as the blackjack game was Sundance's scene, this is where we really meet Butch Cassidy.

He returns to Hole-in-the-Wall to find that his leadership has been usurped. He has headed a famous gang, but now the giant, Logan, has assumed control.

Butch tries first what he always tries first: to talk his way out of trouble. That attempt fails.

He is forced into a knife fight and we're into one of the staples of Western films: *mano a mano,* good versus evil, honorable virtue versus unspeakable vice, maybe to the death. But just before combat, Butch begins talking about what rules they should follow, and while Logan is distracted, Butch kicks him full out in the balls.

I don't know if anyone who never saw the movie in a theatre can appreciate the reaction the kick-in-the-balls moment got. There was this huge gasp, followed by the enormous laugh of relief and surprise. Especially, I think, surprise.

Western heroes didn't fight sneaky. Gary Cooper would have turned in his badge before he stooped to such a thing. Can you imagine Randolph Scott doing it? Or Gene Autry?

And then after the fight Butch not only doesn't show any anger, he decides to do exactly what his enemy had suggested they do all along. He is, above all else, a totally practical man doing his best. A leader, without rancor, as affable a fellow as you're apt to meet. I think, after this, you really like him.

This scene underscores again the theme: Everything's harder than it used to be. And there are probably other odds and ends I could mention.

But what the scene does, most of all, is set the Butch-Sundance relationship. From here on, hopefully, we know we're into something different.

Logan, of all people, sets it in motion. He has told Butch that he gives the orders, then suddenly he says, "This don't concern you."

He means, of course, Sundance.

Logan goes on, ordering Butch to tell Sundance to stay out of their fight. So far we're merely underscoring what we've seen in the card game: Sundance is Dangerous.

Butch's reply though is odd: "He goes his own way, like always."

Now, a few moments later, Logan has his knife out and Butch begins to take off his jacket. He goes to Sundance, who is remote, seated on his horse, above it all.

Logan is a massive man, incredibly powerful. Butch makes an attempt at a joke: "Bet on Logan." Sundance replies: "I would, but who'd bet on you?" Then comes what for me is the essential exchange of the picture.

> LOGAN
> (calling out to the Kid)
> Sundance—when we're done, if he's
> dead, you're welcome to stay.

> BUTCH
> (quietly, to Sundance)
> Listen, I don't want to be a sore
> loser or anything, but when we're
> done, if I'm dead, kill him.

> SUNDANCE
> (this is said to Logan but
> in answer to Butch)
> Love to.

When we were in preproduction and rehearsal, there was more pressure over this exchange than any other—the producers insisted it be altered: The audience had to know, they felt, that in the crunch, Sundance would come to the rescue.

I said I thought that ruined everything.

They wouldn't go away: Do you expect the audience to believe he's just going to sit there and watch Butch get killed?

I said Butch didn't get killed.

They wanted something—a wink, maybe, some indication from one hero to the other, anything that would make it clear: "I won't let you get hurt."

Director George Roy Hill was on my side and we carried the day. I can't articulate even now why I felt so strongly. The producers had an absolutely valid point.

But the spine of the picture was the two guys. And they had to be appealing, sure; but they also had to be different and special. They were *all* we had going for us. And I truly believe that Butch's not asking for help and Sundance not offering any was what cemented their relationship.

From here on, I hoped, the audience would be asking, "Who *are* those guys?"

Two quick remembrances, one of rehearsal, one from opening week.

In the middle of the movie is a twenty-seven-minute sequence where Butch and Sundance are chased and almost captured by the Superposse. As a result of their narrow escape, Butch decides it's time for South America.

In the middle of the chase is a short scene where they go to see an old sheriff, Bledsoe, to ask his help in getting them to enlist in the Army and fight in the Spanish-American War. Bledsoe, who is a friend, tells them they're crazy, it's too late, that they're both going to die bloody and all they can do is choose where.

During rehearsal, Newman was bothered not by the length of the chase but by the fact that it was misstructured. His contention was that the scene with Bledsoe should not be where it was but at the end—Bledsoe should be the icing on the cake, the one that finally makes them believe they must leave the country.

Newman is totally pro, always prepared, always giving. (Dur-

ing shooting when his people were upset that Redford was being given too much of the picture, too many close-ups, etc.,
etc., Newman couldn't have cared less.)

He is also, to use an image he says of himself, a terrier. When
he gets hold of something, he simply will not let it go. And he
was absolutely convinced that the Bledsoe scene was out of order.

George Hill was equally convinced that it was not; if the
chase as it was didn't make them want to get the hell out, an old
sheriff *telling* them wouldn't make any goddam difference. Hill,
a Marine pilot who served in both World War II and Korea, is
not known for giving ground easily.

We rehearsed for two weeks, and on the first day, Newman
idly mentioned that he thought, perhaps, we might shift the order of the Bledsoe scene. Brief discussion. Negative decision.
On to the next.

The following morning Newman appeared, having done a
good deal of thought at night. The Bledsoe scene was definitely
wrong. It was not wrong, Hill replied. More discussion, a bit
more heated. (The rehearsals of *Butch*, by the way, were as en-
joyable as any time I've had in movies. Katherine Ross was ach-
ingly pretty and tended to be quiet. Redford was funny, in a
counterpunching way. The rest of us were nothing if not vocal.
Such was our sound that an article appeared in a Los Angeles
paper stating that rehearsals were so violent that the movie had
been postponed.)

Logistically, we were alone, seated around a table in the middle of an enormous sound stage. Far across this basketball-
court-sized room, a guy who I suppose might be called a gofer
sat in a chair, waiting to be called on if anything was needed to
help rehearsals along. He was old, and he dozed a lot. There
wasn't much for him to do.

Every day now, the argument between Newman and Hill took
up more and more time. The word *Bledsoe* began to lose all
meaning, we were that punchy. Newman would not give up and
Hill would not surrender. At one point Redford suggested we
retitle the whole fucking movie *The Bledsoe Scene.*

On and on Newman and Hill would go at it. Each day Newman would bring in fresh arguments buttressing his position
and Hill would one by one do his best to demolish them. Once

they were into the Bledsoe scene, *nothing* could make them stop.

Almost nothing.

Toward the end of the first week, Newman and Hill were at it again, tearing into each other, back and forth, on and on—until we were all aware of this strange, new, and altogether remarkable sound.

The gofer, way across the room, in his sleep, had let fly with this whopper of a fart. Newman and Hill registered the event, paused briefly, then went back into combat.

But the fart continued.

Now they paused a second time, all of us staring at this old sleeping guy. Newman and Hill turned back to each other again—

—the fart went on and on. (All true, I swear.)

Now we were all silent.

Still it continued.

Everyone was now aware of the fact that we were in the presence of a phenomenal physical feat. Amazing. We all had to break after that. The old guy slept on, eventually lapsing into silence. He never knew that he alone had the power to put the Bledsoe scene to rest, at least for that day....

Butch opened in New York to what might optimistically be called "mixed" notices. *The New Yorker,* for example, entitled its review "The Bottom of the Pit."

I think all of us involved liked the film a lot. We thought we might have something, and Hill and I, I know, were both in despair. What helped change my mood was something that happened the first weekend it was in release.

A rotten October afternoon, drizzling and cold. A friend of mine was waiting in line to see it, and as the preceding show broke, a number of people piled out of the theatre. And one of them, a guy who'd just seen the movie, stopped and looked at the others waiting in the rain. Then he cupped his hands and shouted out the following: "*Hey—it's really worth it.*"

And hey, when I heard that story, I thought for the first time that we really might have something after all....

chapter six
The Thing of It Is . . .

The Thing of It Is . . . was the screenplay I wrote following *Butch Cassidy*. It's a movie that never got made. Not remotely unusual. What made this experience unique for me is that this was a movie that not only almost but didn't happen—

—it didn't happen *twice*.

The first time began with Robert Redford. *Butch* had been shot but was months from being released, and his career was still in the scuffling stage.

Someone, I think Natalie Wood, had given him *The Thing of It Is . . .* , an unknown novella of mine. He'd read it, liked it, wanted to do it as a movie (assuming he reacted positively to the screenplay). But since there was no studio interest in the project, and neither of us was remotely bankable, the suggestion was to get a director and a female star and then approach a studio. In other words, if we could pull it off, we could beat the system.

The initial step, of course, was that I write the screenplay "on spec." In other words, without a contract, do it for free. I said I would immediately, for three reasons.

One: Writing "on spec" was something I'd always done. I wrote my first novel, *The Temple of Gold*, in 1956, and it was not until *Magic*, twenty years later, that I had a contract for an unwritten book. The reason I worked that way was probably neurotic: I had (and still have) the wild fear that I'll get halfway through a book and then want to stop. But if you're under contract, you can't.

Two: I knew Redford a little, had had a wonderful experience with him in *Butch*.

Three: He was perfect for the part. Briefly, *The Thing of It Is* ... is a tough romantic comedy. It concerns a young couple who go to Europe with their only child to try and save their marriage. The wife is a stunning-looking WASP type who has married Amos, the husband, against her family's wishes. She is rich, and he, when they married, wasn't.

Worse, he was in the arts. A songwriter. When the story opens he has become enormously successful, having written a "Hello Dolly!"-type smash with a title song that is the number-one hit in the country.

Except it's a rotten song and Amos hates it. But he is a secret-keeper, Amos is, and that's one of his secrets. Another, more important, is that even though his last name is McCracken and he looks gentile as hell, he is, in fact, half Jewish. Not only was Redford the right age and all the rest, he was also, at this time in his career, a sensational comic actor. As I mentioned earlier, he had scored a tremendous success as the male lead in Neil Simon's *Barefoot in the Park* on Broadway, a role he repeated in the somewhat less-well-received film version. For the part of Amos—quirky, funny, secretive—I couldn't think of anyone better.

Now, in order to "beat the system," what was necessary was a male star, a female star, and a director. I wrote the screenplay. Redford liked it.

One down and two to go.

For director, I went to Ulu Grosbard, whom I knew, who I also knew had read and liked the book, and who had just done the lovely film for Frank D. Gilroy's Pulitzer prizewinning hit, *The Subject Was Roses*. Grosbard said yes.

Two down, one to go—

—oops.

Strange things began to happen. The movie of *Butch* had opened by now, and Grosbard began having trouble getting together with Redford to discuss the script. Grosbard was perplexed—we all lived in New York, we didn't need plane tickets to get together. Time dragged, as it does, on, and nothing was happening. It didn't make sense for Redford to avoid Grosbard, because not only had he okayed Grosbard before I ever went to him, Redford was the one who wanted to do the movie in the first place.

Then Redford called me one day from a pay phone in the Salt Lake City airport. What he said was basically that since *Butch* was now a huge hit, he didn't think "his fans" would accept him as Amos, since Amos was "kind of weak." So good luck with the project, but he was out.

I don't know what happens to people when it happens, but it sure happens fast.

I called Grosbard and told him. We now needed not just a female star, but a male star as well.

By the end of the week, literally, we had Elliott Gould, who at this time, in 1970, had gone from *Bob & Carol & Ted & Alice* to *M*A*S*H* and was rated one of the five biggest stars in the business.

Two down, one to go. Again—

—oops.

I met with Grosbard and he told me that he was now leaving the project because he felt he had a moral obligation to direct *Who Is Harry Kellerman and Why Is He Saying Those Terrible Things About Me?*

But Gould really wanted to do our project, and his agent, David Begelman, famed in song and story, wanted him to get it done. Begelman also represented Faye Dunaway, got the script to her. She said yes.

Now all we needed was a director.

I met with Begelman to talk about who would be good for it. I said my first choice in all the world was someone I'd never met, Stanley Donen. Donen, an American living in England, had directed or codirected some of my favorite films: *On the Town, Singin' in the Rain, Seven Brides for Seven Brothers,* and most recently a wonderful tough marriage comedy, *Two for the Road.*

"Stanley would only be perfect," Begelman told me. "Except he's crazy."

I explained I'd already dealt with some pretty whacko people on this project already, one more wouldn't bother me.

"You don't understand," Begelman explained. "I don't mean Stanley's *difficult.* I mean he's *insane.* He cracked up over in England. Total nervous breakdown. He'll never be able to direct a movie again."

So much for Stanley Donen—or so I thought.

Enter Mark Rydell.

I didn't know Rydell. But he was then (he'd just finished *The Reivers* with Steve McQueen) and is now (most recent work: *On Golden Pond*) a gifted director, skilled with actors and possessed of a wonderful eye. We met in New York, discussed script changes, etc. Good standard meetings. And after they were over, he agreed to do the movie.

So at last we had the three crucial elements: Gould, Dunaway, Rydell. I won't attempt to describe my relief, but it was considerable. What had begun as a request from one acquaintance to another to try and beat the system had now become draining. (This whole process, from Redford's request to Rydell's agreeing, had taken maybe eight months.) And with the many shifts of personnel, the project had become obsessive. I found myself unable to do any writing of my own. The monkey was unquestionably on my back, and until the movie was under way, it wasn't going to leave me. But now, at last, we were set.

Oops—

Rydell called from California, said he'd had second thoughts, and didn't feel he wanted to direct the picture.

Panic in New York. Phone calls were made, entreaties, assurances were given Rydell that it really would all work out. Please would he think about it.

He thought about it, decided he had acted perhaps hastily, and agreed, again, to do the picture. With all the elements again intact, Begelman made a deal with a distributing company to take on the picture. (I don't want to get into the technical details of The Deal here—primarily because I don't understand them myself—but the arrangement was that the company would give us the money to make the movie but that we would only get paid upon completion of the film. Which was fine with everybody.)

Then Rydell called from California again to say finally and irrevocably that he had made a mistake when he changed his mind to do the picture and had now changed it again. He was out.

Hysteria in New York. More phone calls, more entreaties. Wouldn't he please reconsider one more time?

He did. He at last definitely and irrevocably said yes. He would direct the picture.

With one small proviso: I was no longer to be involved. He had someone he wanted to fix the script. It was my screenplay based on my novel but I was forced out.

What I know now that I didn't know then was simply this: I was having my first experience with a "writer killer."

There are a lot of directors in Hollywood who are writer killers. Some of the best directors in Hollywood are writer killers. I don't mean to indicate that these men don't like writers. In point of fact, some of their best friends are writers.

But what writer killers do is they work with you on a project, and they ask for apples and you try and give them apples, then they say no, pomegranates would be better, so you try and write pomegranates. Then that doesn't satisfy them and it goes on, rewrite following rewrite, until your mind is fucked around. You are frustrated, confused, maybe useless. Now, it's conceivable they're just such perfectionists that they never stop second-guessing themselves. It's also conceivable they wanted to bring in a friend all along—I don't know.

Many, maybe most, of the Hollywood community has a certain contempt for screenwriters. And they're not necessarily wrong: Most of us are not very good. But writer killers are the worst, because usually they are talented, usually they are bright, and I don't think that consciously they always know their objective.

Which doesn't mean they don't achieve it.

Perhaps the best example I can give of the subconscious contempt concerns an experience I had with Sydney Pollack on another project that never happened. We were talking one day and as usually happens in meetings, you drift away from the subject, circling awhile, and Pollack told me how much he loved *Boys and Girls Together*—he had been one of the directors who had tried to lick the problems of the book. David Rayfiel—his closet writer, the one he usually brings in—had done the adaptation.

We were so faithful to your book, Pollack told me. We treated it with such care. God, we were faithful.

And then he found a copy of the script.

Let me just read you a scene, he said. To show you how faithful we were.

I didn't want to hear it—I don't like my writing, don't reread it myself, and the thought of having someone else reading my lines to me was something I wanted to avoid.

No no, Pollack said, you'll really love this. You'll see how faithful we were.

I couldn't stop him.

He found a scene, started to read it—and it was a scene that wasn't in the book, between two characters who never talk to each other in the book.

I asked him to stop.

He wouldn't. He kept reading on and on, reading this terrible scene that had nothing to do with my novel. All on the pretext of showing his faithfulness.

And he simply would not stop.

I don't know to this day if he realizes the contempt in what he was doing. Maybe if I could have shown him some scenes I'd redirected from *Jeremiah Johnson*, for me his best film—maybe if I'd forced him to watch stuff I'd done to his work, with different locales and different actors and different camera shots—maybe he might have understood.

But only maybe.

When I was forced off *The Thing of It Is . . .* I guess I snapped. I am not, by nature, Homeric, but I had some kind of rage building. I didn't care about the movie, I didn't care about anything.

So I self-destructed the project.

Okay—if they were going to force me off my own movie, fine. Do it. But I insisted on being paid first. I was told that would explode the deal, which was based on no one being paid till the movie was done.

I didn't care. I just didn't care. I demanded payment immediately. Then I took my family and we fled on vacation. While we were gone, the explosion took place. *The Thing of It Is . . .* was dead.

Dissolve, as they say Out There.

A year later, my telephone rang. It was Stanley Donen, whom I'd still never met, and he was in New York, could we talk. We did, and I told him how much I'd always wanted to work with him and he said much the same to me, and then he wondered did I have any ideas?

Now, Donen was the director who Begelman had told me had gone insane in England and would never be able to direct again. Stanley didn't seem insane to me. I gave him *The Thing of It Is* ... and while he was reading it, I kind of tippy-toed around, trying to ascertain the state of Stanley's mental health.

It turned out he was fine. He hadn't had a nervous breakdown—he hadn't even had an upheaval—what he did have was an agent who wasn't David Begelman.

Begelman's behavior, by the way, is not remotely unusual. Not that agents are all liars. But since no one knows what will work, agents are constantly and rightly promoting their own clients. Had I been less of an idiot, I would have checked Begelman's statement when he made it. But he was so powerful, so bright and persuasive, I never thought to do so.

Besides, we were both New York Knick fans and I figured that counted for something.

Donen wanted to direct *The Thing of It Is* ... so the second act was under way. He gave the script to Robert Evans (then married to Ali MacGraw), who was at the peak of his career as head of production at Paramount. *Love Story*, a genuine phenomenon, was primarily Evans's baby.

Evans kind of liked it, was willing to develop it, but of course it all came down to casting. If we could get two leads he approved of, we were under way.

Then we got lucky: Mia Farrow had an obligation to Paramount for a picture, she was right for the part of the beautiful WASP wife, and she agreed to do it.

So all we needed was the man.

James Caan was willing to do the script. We told Evans. "No penis extension," Evans said. (I still don't know what that means.) Caan was gone.

Donen and I met with Alan Alda, who would have been the best of all possible worlds. Alda said yes, he really wanted to play the male lead. Evans said no—again the mysterious penis extension was at work. Good-bye, Alda.

So Donen and I went to England to work on rewrites, with Mia Farrow as our lady, but no man.

Then we lost Mia Farrow. She was preempted by another

film and gone. Donen and I continued working in London, the mood not too cheery. We had Donen, but we were back to square one on casting.

Until Ali MacGraw entered the picture.

MacGraw was, at this time, the top female star around, having gone from nowhere to *Goodbye Columbus* to *Love Story*. But she hadn't found a part that excited her sufficiently. Evans told Donen that if we could strengthen the female lead, we had a shot at MacGraw.

So we did what we could. Since the story was of a married couple in trouble, we couldn't make it a one-star vehicle. But we added scenes, shifted focus and emphasis where we could, and sent it off.

Alas, the lady was not pleased. That pretty much ended it. Donen went his way, I mine. MacGraw decided to do *The Getaway*, where she met and married Steve McQueen, left Evans.

Nobody beat the system. . . .

chapter seven

The Stepford Wives

"I think Nanette might be rather good for the part of Carol, don't you?"

"She's a wonderful actress; I think she'd be fine."

That innocuous dialog, spoken casually between myself and director Bryan Forbes—he asked the question, I made the reply—was, at least for me, genuinely memorable. It marked the only time that I realized, early on before shooting, that a project I was involved in was more than likely doomed.

What follows will try and make some sense of that. In general, what we are dealing with here is perhaps the most perplexing problem the screenwriter faces: his relationship with the director.

One can, if one wishes, divide the process of making a movie into three parts: prior to shooting, shooting, and postproduction. (There are those that claim the process should be divided in half: making the picture and selling the picture. There's a lot of wisdom in that view, but it has nothing to do with writing scripts, so a mere mention here will have to do.)

The first of the three parts listed above generally takes the longest time. (Always remember that movies are these great elephantine husks that hundreds of people at various times are trying to lug toward the finish line. It's at least two to three years between the first glimmer of doing a movie and its appearance at your friendly neighborhood theatre.)

More often than not, the movie begins with the producer. He reads a book, a treatment, an outline, sees a play, overhears a remark, whatever. Something tells him that a movie is lurking in the vicinity. Once he has acquired the rights to the project, which can take a lot of time and legal hassling, more often than not, again, the producer will then hire a screenwriter.

In my own case, from the first phone call to the first draft being submitted takes six months. I'm not writing all that time. But usually there's research to be done. And then finding a structure. And then all the things we writers are most brilliant at: finding reasons not to get to it. Eventually, though, we do, the producer reads the script, suggests changes, changes are made.

And then it goes to the studio.

The studio executives read, meet, mull, meet some more before deciding thumbs up or down. Most of the time, the answer is in the negative.

Statistically, in my own case, I suppose half of the screenplays I've written have actually seen production. And I am being dead honest when I tell you this: I have absolutely no more idea as to why some of them happened than why some of them didn't.

Of course it's more than possible that my work wasn't much good. But remember, executives are not necessarily in pursuit of quality.

One of the movies I wrote that never happened the studio truly liked—but it was antimilitary and they were preparing at the same time a giant war movie, one in which they needed a great deal of Army cooperation. And they were frightened that an antiwar film would damage that cooperation.

Another never happened because there was only one star who was conceivable for the part in the studio's eyes—and he passed. They never sent it out again.

Another died because the producer and the studio head hated each other and had for a quarter century. The producer's deal—this was his initial project—stated that he could develop a property, but to go into production he needed the head's okay. (I obviously didn't know of their personal conflict when I wrote the screenplay. If I had, I never would have begun, because the picture was dead from the first fade-in.) The producer liked the script, the studio head said it was garbage. The producer, who then left the studio, asked to take the script with him, paying all costs. The executive said he wouldn't hear of it. (If the producer had been able to take the script to another studio and get it made, and it had turned out all right, that would not have rebounded greatly to his enemy's prestige.) Because of their personal loathing, the script lies lost and forlorn on a shelf, along with you wouldn't believe how many others.

Why they occasionally say yes is far beyond my knowledge. But when they do, the producer has a "go" project.

And then, oh then, enters the director.

This also takes a tremendous amount of time—because the directors you want are always busy. A rule of mine is this: There are always three hot directors and one of them is always David Lean. Today it's Lucas, Spielberg, and Lean. A few years back: Coppola, Friedkin, and Lean. A few years before that: Penn, Nichols, and Lean.

Well, you can't get them. Many producers don't even want them—the more powerful the director, the less so the producer. But all movies are soft until principal photography—there is no such thing as an absolutely firm "go" before that time—so a giant director makes the producer's likelihood of getting the project off the ground that much easier.

Once a director is hired, he enters permanent and meaningful combat with the producer. They smile at each other a lot but maybe mongooses smile at cobras on occasion.

Anyway, they meet, pledge loyalty, and next the scriptwriter is brought in for additional meetings. Changes are made in the screenplay. Finally, casting begins. Just as you never get the director you want, you also don't get the star. Reynolds is committed for the next two years, Redford is hiding out in Utah, Eastwood runs his own show, De Niro usually works with Scorsese, on and on.

Somehow, miraculously, casting gets done, and then there are more meetings, more changes. And two crucial men are hired: the cinematographer and the production designer. What the movie looks like on the screen, these two are the gentlemen responsible.

At this point, every day more and more people sign on. The caterer, the script girl, a hundred and then some. And a start date is given for principal photography. And on that day, the first part ends.

Shooting can take from eight to forty weeks. And during this second part of the filmmaking process, the director is at his most evident. (And because this is also the time when the press comes in to do publicity pieces, it helps account for the omnipotence of the director. *Cosmopolitan* does not send reporters to meet with the producer when he's there alone at the outset. *People* doesn't spend a lot of time in the editing room after the shooting is done.)

The period after completion of shooting—the postproduction work—is the most technical of all. It takes months to cut and dub and loop and score and whatever else they do. I don't know what they do, but whatever it is, it's brutally hard and totally important.

The writer, then, usually only deals with the director on the second half of the first part of a film. Sometimes you have a voice in the selection of the director—"*Shit, not him!*"—sometimes you don't. Most of the time when you finally do meet, it is two total strangers shaking hands.

I feel the screenwriter must be just as supportive of the director as possible. But it's often hard to know just where you can be most helpful. I try to have seen everything the director's done before we begin. Because *no* director can do everything. Francis Coppola, for example, if you look at the two *Godfathers* and *Apocalypse Now*, has a fabulous sense for the epic. But it should be equally clear, if you look at *Finian's Rainbow* and *One from the Heart*, that he's no wizard when it comes to musicals or light comedy. So if I were working with Coppola on preparing a script—and I should only be so lucky—and I got an idea for something dealing with size, I would quickly tell him. But if the idea pertained to a musical moment or something lightly comic, I would never mention it.

Because if I did, and he hated it, terrific. But if he liked it, you're down the tubes. He'll shoot it badly or, worse, incorrectly; the moment won't work; and it will damage whatever's come just before it and, more than likely, everything that will follow.

The greatest enemy of every movie is this: There is never enough time. So when you meet with a director, you try and shorthand things, get to know each other in a way you wouldn't dream of if you were cruising the Caribbean together. Did you like this movie? Did you like that moment in another movie? You didn't? Why? Have you read this book? Bergman's my favorite, which of his stuff do you like best? (If he doesn't like *any* Bergman, you may as well get off the trolley then and there.) What do you like to eat? Which hotels are your favorites? Which restaurants? How old are your kids? (If he's gay, you tend to know that already, so you don't ask that question.) What did you major in? Are you a sports nut? Etc. Mutual friends? Etc., etc.

Now, all the while you're circling him, he's moving too. (I hate the script, can he fix it? I like the middle but the opening stinks, will he change that without a fight? Shall I fire him now or wait awhile? Etc., etc.)

This is all cordial, and it seems like time wasting, but it isn't. I'm trying to find out where he's coming from, he's feeling me out as quickly as he can.

And *neither* of us wants to get down to the business at hand: improving the goddam screenplay. I don't trust him—where the hell was he when I was alone for six months in my pit?—does he have the least conception how many times I wrote and rewrote the opening, trying to bring it to life?—is he trying to ruin my baby? (Sometimes yes, sometimes no, I can't tell at this stage. But I don't trust him, not a little. And I shouldn't.)

And he shouldn't trust me either. (People keep secrets from each other.) It's an accepted fact that all writers are crazy; even the normal ones are weird.

The writer-director relationship is an adversary one, at least when you're starting out with someone you know only from his work on screen. It can be pleasant, it can be hateful, but it never can be easy. But even at its worst, I feel it's my job to be supportive, to give him anything I can that will help the movie or, at the very least, won't screw it up.

And even after almost ten years, I still wonder if I was too supportive on *The Stepford Wives*.

Ira Levin's novella, on which the film was based, came out in the early seventies, when the Women's Liberation Movement was *the* hot topic on all the tv talk shows. Betty Friedan's *Feminine Mystique* had opened the floodgates, Gloria Steinem was a magazine cover girl, and all across the country people were echoing Freud's great unanswered question: "What do women want?"

The story takes place in the lovely Connecticut suburb of Stepford. A postcard town. Quiet, safe, not much to do at night. Many of the husbands in Stepford belong to the Men's Association, which meets in a large, protected building. They do a lot of good works to keep Stepford as fine a place to live as you could ask for. They meet quite frequently, these husbands do—bright, successful men, many of them in scientific fields, computers, plastics, etc.

But the Stepford wives don't mind their husbands' absence. They are a bunch of genuinely adoring women. They cook for their men, they raise well-mannered, happy children, they are passionate about housekeeping.

They are also passionate about their mates. No migraines in Stepford when a man needs bedding down. And if the sex is good for the husbands, from the husbands' point of view it ought to be pretty all right too—

—because the Stepford wives are *gorgeous*. I mean, you never saw such bodies. Not a Twiggy in the town. Raquel Welch would have been *average*-looking. These girls are Playmates come to life. And they don't dress to hide their virtues. In their summer shorts and T-shirts, in their tennis whites, you could have an orgasm just standing by the checkout counter at the A&P (shopping being something else they love to do).

Into this atmosphere moves a young couple, Joanna and Walter. Joanna is a bright, determined, reasonably aggressive girl who wants to be a photographer. Housekeeping she can endure; child-raising, too—but what she really wants, please God, is a career all her own.

Joanna isn't too ecstatic moving to Male Chauvinist Pig heaven. But she does the best she can, makes a friend—and then she realizes that something very strange is happening in Stepford.

The women change.

They become obedient, their bodies blossom, they live only to make their husbands happy. Joanna thinks maybe it's the water or something else crazy.

What it is, of course, is murder.

All those scientist-wizard husbands murder their wives and replace them with perfect plastic substitutes they create in the Men's Association. By the time Joanna realizes the truth, it's too late, and the movie ends with Walter married to another suddenly voluptuous, totally subservient Stepford wife.

The role of Carol was one of the three female leads. She is the robot who lives next to Joanna.

Nanette Newman is an English actress in her mid-forties. A good actress too. An attractive brunette. But a sex bomb she isn't.

Okay, now we get back to the crucial dialog in the car. Bryan Forbes was set to direct the film. We are still in the getting-to-know-each-other circling stage. If anything, I am a little more tense than usual, which, as my wife will tell you, is pretty tense, for a very good reason: Bryan Forbes is what is called Out There a "hyphenate." He is a writer-director. Since he got his first directing job, he has written every movie he's been involved with. (I didn't know it then, but he would totally rewrite *Stepford* too. Almost totally. The last quarter of the movie is mine. I think he would have changed that, too, but he ran out of time.)

Okay again, we're driving in the car, talking about casting. Names are tossed this way and that. And then the fatal (for me) words were spoken.

> "I think Nanette might be rather good in the part of Carol, don't you?"

Instant death. Why? Well, forget the fact that she was English; that might be a little jarring but there are lots of English women living in Connecticut.

The main thing was this: She destroyed the reality of a story that was only precariously real to begin with.

Look, this is a movie about insane men. Insane and so frightened of women, so panicked that their wives may begin to assert themselves, that they resort to murder. And if you are so insanely desperate, so obsessed with women being nothing but subordinate sex objects, if you are willing to spend the rest of your days humping a piece of plastic—well, shit, that plastic better goddam well be in the form of Bo Derek.

You don't commit murder and make a new creation to have it look like Nanette Newman.

Not only that, by having Nanette Newman in the part, the whole look of the film had to alter. Forget the tennis costumes. Forget the parade of Bunnies walking through the A&P in shorts on their perfect tanned legs. She can't wear the clothes. Which is why if you ever see the movie you will understand why all these women in the summertime in Stepford, Connecticut, walk around in long dresses to the floor and big brimmed hats on their heads.

What could I have answered when Bryan's question was put to me? Well, I could have said, "Bryan, she's English. And this is a very American piece."

I could have said that, but it would have been dicey. In the first place, she was a more than fine enough performer to act the role. And, as noted, there is no law barring the British from New York suburbia. But most important, Bryan knew it was an Americana piece and he was English, so he already felt, perhaps, somewhat uncomfortable as director. Throwing his background up at him would have done nothing—you can't say the actress is wrong because she's English when you're working with a director who is also English.

What I could *not* say was the truth: that she wasn't sexy enough, that casting her would possibly kill the picture right there. Why couldn't I say that?—

—*because Nanette Newman was his wife.*

What else could I have done? I might have run to the producer, Edgar Scherick, and told him everything. But *Stepford* was a troubled production—we'd had difficulty finding a director. Preliminary casting had turned out to be a bitch. And since everything is soft till principal photography (never forget that), the last thing Edgar needed was a hysterical writer predicting Doomsday because a good actress was suggested to appear in the movie. Besides, being his wife meant security for Bryan, his family would be around, he wouldn't be as much a stranger in a very strange land.

And even if I was right, even if Nanette meant a change in the look and the reality, that didn't mean the movie wouldn't work. *Nobody knows what movie will work.* (Never, *never* forget that.)

So I said what I said. I like to think I at least took a long pause before answering.

She's a wonderful actress; I think she'd be fine.

I'm still not sure....

chapter eight
The Great
Waldo Pepper

And sometimes you do it right and it still doesn't work. That was *The Great Waldo Pepper*.

The emotional beginning of *Waldo* rested with the director, George Roy Hill. Sometimes, back when we were working on *Butch* in '68, we would digress and George would talk about his lifelong love: old airplanes. Hill had been a Marine pilot in both World War II and Korea, but his heart was then and forever with the Jennys and the other flimsy machines surrounding the period of the First World War. He owned one of these planes, flew it across country, never minding when the cars below went faster than he did in the sky.

Often, when you begin a project, you fantasize about getting this star or that. You almost never do. *Waldo* was an exception: The only star we wanted was Redford; no other performer was mentioned. He was involved with us almost from day one. He wanted to do the part and, when he got the final script, agreed to do it.

And he was wonderful.

Now, Robert Redford at this time was not just the biggest star in the world. He was a phenomenon. In the period preceding *Waldo*'s release, he had starred in *The Sting, The Way We Were,* and *The Great Gatsby*. Plus the enormously successful re-releases of two other hits: *Jeremiah Johnson* and *Butch*. No star, at least in my time in movies, has ever had such heat focused on him.

And it is my firm belief that because of his presence in the film, giving a superb performance in a role tailored solely for his talents, that the movie was a commercial disappointment.

In order to try and make sense of the above, it's necessary to know a little of the plot of the movie and the world it dealt with: barnstorming.

The barnstorming era—often referred to as "the short-pants period of flying"—began roughly with the end of World War I and ended with the Depression. When peace came, the Europeans immediately grasped the potential future of commercial aviation, which is why so many of the great foreign airlines were founded around 1919.

No such thought occurred in America. Planes had been useful in taming the Hun, but that was done. Interest in aviation dwindled and all but stopped, not to be reborn until the Lindbergh flight in '27.

During that interim, it was the barnstormers who kept flying alive in America. They were either pilots who had served in the war or young men who wanted to fly. Planes, hundreds and thousands of them, were left in crates, just waiting to be assembled.

What the barnstormers did, at least in the beginning, was to give people rides, sometimes at a dollar a minute. Many if not most people at this time in America, especially in the Midwest, had never seen an airplane, much less ridden in one.

So for several years, in the late teens and early twenties, a plane would appear in rural areas and it would buzz a town and then land in a field. A crowd would gather and the pilot—a genuinely romantic figure, a man who would usually claim, modestly, that his war experiences were nothing really all that remarkable—this white-scarfed figure would make his pitch and then take people up for rides. And at the end of the day he would more than likely tie his plane down by the side of a barn, away from the wind, in case a storm came up. After which, if he was lucky, he would be given a free meal by some farmer, do his best to seduce any local wenches, and be off into the skies again the following dawn.

It was a frolicsome time, and the barnstormers would outsmart others in their trade, trying to get the best towns for themselves.

Then, in the early twenties, people began getting tired of it, so the pilots often banded together and did stunt shows to gather crowds. These shows were dangerous, and often people were killed in crashes.

Then, when Lindbergh happened, flying started to become Big Business. Those barnstormers still alive often drifted to Hollywood, where they did stunts for news cameras or stunt work for war movies. Most of them ended up broke, or crippled, or dead.

When Hill and I worked on the story, we found that the structure of the piece almost dictated itself. It fell, naturally, into three acts. The first, the fun-and-games act, had Waldo Pepper, our hero, engaged in hustling and lying about his past and taking people up for rides and having his way with women.

The second act was the air show act. Fun and games are gone. The air show stunts get increasingly spectacular and hairy. Finally a girl (Susan Sarandon, and was she terrific) dies during a show. Waldo, who is innocent, is blamed and barred for life from flying.

Act three: Hollywood. Waldo, who really only lives to fly, is an outlaw now, doing stunt work under an assumed name. Finally he gets a chance to do battle with his hero, a great German war ace. They fight it out in the skies, with no bullets, both of them lost souls, trying to recapture a past that for Waldo never was. The movie ends on the climactic air fight where they tear each other's planes apart, with the cameras rolling.

Now, this is, relatively speaking, dark material. *Oedipus* it isn't, but it's a long way from *Animal House*. Waldo, a brilliant pilot who never got his chance in the war, is hounded from his passion, first by public apathy, then by an unfair legal judgment, finally by the forces of commerce—the Powers That Be in aviation don't want barnstormers around; they're dangerous when you're trying to convince the public to travel in safety aloft.

But the movie begins brightly. "Rollicking adventures," etc., etc. Not only was the fun-and-games act a way of getting the audience with us, it was also historically valid. Our problem was this: How do you indicate to an audience that bad times are coming?

The solution was simple: The credits would be moody, mournful, dark. What we had was a beautiful sad tune playing while what we showed were the faces of young dead pilots accompanied by a series of still shots of terrible plane crashes. Planes in trees, planes stuck in rooftops, like that. We were alerting the audience to be ready for what was to come.

No picture I've been involved with aroused the expectations of *Waldo Pepper*. A giant star in a romantic adventure, a major director working from the single deepest passion of his life, the most spectacular aerial stunts maybe since *Wings*. I received calls from people in the business and the word was this: *Waldo* would pick up all the marbles. Hill and Redford had worked together twice before: *Butch* and *Sting*. *Waldo* would complete the trilogy.

I saw the sneak in Boston. Hill was there, some Universal executives were there, the place was packed. We were all nervous—normal at such a time. The movie began. The credits were lovely, the audience was properly quiet. Then the fun-and-games act began—

—and they loved it. Roars of laughter. They "fell about," as the English would have it. That sound of a group of strangers rising to your work—it's rare and it's one of the things you live for if you're in the movie business.

Now the movie elided into the second act of its story, the part that dealt with air shows. No problem—the audience was still with us. There were stunts, other air maneuvers—we still had them.

Then we came to the most sensational stunt of all—a midair plane-to-plane transfer. From the beginning of our story talks, we knew we wanted such a moment; it's an incredible sight to see, especially if the camera is set in such a way as to remove the possibility that we might be faking it.

The plot set up was this: Susan Sarandon played the girl friend of Redford's buddy. She begins the movie as this kind of wide-eyed innocent and, before our eyes, becomes obsessed with being the " 'It ' Girl of the Skies." A star.

The stunt the pilots agreed to try to draw a crowd was to have a plane fly right down the main street of a small town with Sarandon standing on the edge of one wing. Then, with the whole town watching, her clothes are rigged to come off. She's supposed to stand there frozen and helpless (the barnstormers did this kind of thing, by the way) and then the plane is to come back to the field outside town and land and all the locals will come running and take rides and spend money and a happy time will be had by all.

Only Sarandon freezes in fear on the wing end, and the plane can't land, because her weight makes the machine lopsided, and if it comes down like that, it will crash. Redford is not flying the plane, he's waiting back at the field, but when the plane comes close he realizes what's happened and he jumps into another plane, gets someone to fly him up close to Sarandon's plane. The two machines maneuver in the sky. Redford gets ready to switch from his plane to Sarandon's, grabbing hold on the opposite side of the wing from her, because if he comes up next to her, his added weight may cause her plane to go out of control and crash.

Dead silence from the audience. The two planes come close, Redford's about to make the plane-to-plane transfer, but the planes are parted by the wind. Again they maneuver together. Again the winds part them. Tension, as they say, is mounting. (The actual stunt, by the way, was done by a sixty-eight-year-old man who got it on the first take.)

But the audience doesn't know it's a sixty-eight-year-old man. All they know is this: Susan Sarandon is clutching the wing of one plane, and Bob Waldo Pepper Redford is going to risk his life to save her.

And he makes the switch! Thousands of feet up, a figure grapples his way from one plane to another.

Everyone's stopped with their popcorn now, staring at the screen. I was staring, too, probably just as caught as they were. The transfer is a really chilling moment because it's shot from above and you can see the ground far below. No cuts to faces, no way to fake it. *They're up there.*

Now the stunt *really* begins to get hairy. Redford makes his way slowly to the center of the plane, shouts to the pilot. Put the plane in a shallow dive to give it added balance—he's going to make the move out to where Sarandon, speechless, stares blankly out.

The plane begins a shallow dive. Redford, inch by dangerous inch, starts toward Sarandon, only now he's talking to her, telling her it's okay, everything's going to be fine, he's coming.

No response from Sarandon. No sound but the sound of the

motor and the wind. Redford is twelve feet away from her now, now ten. Talking soothingly, telling her that all she has to do is take his hand, grab hold tight, just take his hand, take his hand.

Eight feet away from her now. Now six. He reaches out his strong arm, still talking to her, still telling her it's okay, everything's going to be fine.

Sarandon blinks a couple of times. He's getting through to her. The fear, which had her so totally, is beginning to break.

On Redford comes, talking, arm out. Closer and closer. Take my hand. Just take my hand. Five feet. Take my hand. It's all right. We'll laugh about this later. Four feet. Almost there. Still he talks, his strong voice soothing. Take my hand now. Please, that's all you have to do. Take my hand. Take my hand. Now we're on Sarandon. His meaning registers. The fear retreats even more. Now we're on Redford—so close he can almost grab her, talking to her every moment. Now we're on Sarandon again and at long last she reaches for him—

—and now we're on Redford, stunned, alone on the wing. She's fallen. We hold on Redford's face a moment, distraught, stricken; he's come so far, risked his life, tried so hard. But she's gone.

So was the audience.

At first there was just this buzz. You could see people turning to each other, asking questions. Where's the girl? What happened? Then the buzzing stopped—they realized where the girl was. Dead. And after the buzzing ended, there was silence in the theatre. But not the silence of a group held in suspense. No.

They were furious.

They felt tricked, they felt betrayed, and they *hated* us. The most violent sneak reaction of recent years probably belongs to *Rolling Thunder*, where the audience actually got up and tried physically to abuse the studio personnel present among them. These people in Boston were much too civilized for open warfare. They just sat, sullen. For the first hour of the movie, they were in love with us, and in that instant when the girl went off the wing, the affair ended.

We'd tried to prepare them. We'd begun with death. We'd had people getting injured early on. We talked about pilots dying, we showed crashes. We knew it was a demanding moment and, academically speaking, we'd prepared for it properly.

They didn't want to know about "academically speaking."

Waldo Pepper had let a girl die. Only he wasn't Waldo, he was the golden boy of the middle seventies, he was *the* hero of his time. Errol Flynn didn't let girls die from the wings of airplanes and neither, goddammit, did Robert Redford.

I truly believe that if Jack Nicholson had been in the part, he wouldn't have been as good as Redford, but the movie would have worked for audiences. Because there is, inherent in Nicholson's persona, something dark. They would have expected trouble with Nicholson. Or Pacino. Or De Niro. Or the Redford of today. We know he's not just a golden boy anymore. We saw his serious side in *All the President's Men,* we know it from his Oscar-winning directing work in *Ordinary People.* But the Redford of 1975—alas no. Waldo was and is, for me, a quality adventure film. And usually a movie like that, especially one with a major star, finds a major audience.

But the Bostonians who angrily left the theatre were typical of audiences all across the country when the picture was shortly released. We had given them something they didn't want. No matter that we did what we could to forewarn them—we could not shake their expectations.

There is an Eisenstein dictum that says: "You must go where the film leads you." For a movie to work for a mass audience, they must be willing to let you lead them toward *your* destination.

They wouldn't follow us with Waldo. No matter how we tried. . . .

chapter nine
All the
President's Men

"Have you heard about these two young guys on the *Washington Post*?"

That question was asked me over the phone early in the winter of 1974. By Robert Redford. And it began my association with *All the President's Men*.

I had not heard, at that point, of Carl Bernstein and Bob Woodward. Redford explained that they were young reporters (both in their late twenties when the break-in took place at the Watergate complex). And that they had been doing sensational work on the story and had written a book. He had taken an option and asked me to read it.

The version that I read was well prior to publication or even the proofing stages. It was a Xerox copy, full of half pages and cross-outs, and it weighed a ton. I went through it quickly and I knew well before I finished that it was not a job I could conceivably turn down.

Nobody wants to be connected with a garbage film. I find it hard to believe that at the early meetings involving *The Green Slime* or *Jesse James Meets Frankenstein's Daughter* that the creative teams really thought they were in the *Citizen Kane* derby.

What you pray for is this: (1) a movie that people will remember and (2) a movie that people may actually go and see.

Movies with that double potential come along not too often, and when one does, and you're offered a shot, I think you have to take it.

I had no idea whether anyone would want to see a picture about Watergate, but Redford, then the number-one star in the world, was not just going to produce it, he was committed to playing the Woodward part, so obviously that didn't hurt. But the Watergate story had been so important to the country for so many months that I felt if it could be pulled off, people might remember.

Now, there were problems.

(1) Watergate had been so heavily dealt with in the media that a lot of people, rightly, were already sick of it.

(2) Certain kinds of subject matter were viewed with less than glee by studio executives: sports, for one; politics, for another. And *All the President's Men* certainly was a political story.

(3) The book had no structure that jumped out at me. And very little dialog.

(4) There were all those goddam names that no one could keep straight: Stans and Sturgis and Barker and Segretti and McCord and Kalmbach and Magruder and Kleindienst and Strachan and Abplanalp and Rebozo and backward reeled the mind.

(5) Great liberties could not be taken with the material. Not just for legal reasons, which were potentially enormous. But if there ever was a movie that had to be authentic, it was this one. The importance of the subject matter obviously demanded that. More crucially was this: We were dealing here with probably the greatest triumph of the print media in many years, and every media person who would see the film, if there was a film—every columnist and commentator and reviewer—would have spent time at some point in their careers in a newspaper. And if we "Hollywooded it up"—i.e., put in dancing girls—there was no way they would take it kindly. We had to be dead on, or we were dead.

(6) Redford himself. He was not to be a hired hand on the project. Being the producer meant that a lot of directors might shy from the job, since they don't like having their star be their boss.

Plus this: He wasn't just the star, he was the co-star. The Bernstein part would have to be equal. At least that. Because if you are a star, and your co-star is your producer, your part can disappear pretty quickly in the cutting room.

And we needed a *star*. If we had gone with a relative unknown—say, Robert De Niro at that time—not only would it have thrown the balance out of whack, Redford was very much aware that people would say he was afraid of an equal and wanted it all for himself. There were only two equals who had the proper ethnic qualities for Bernstein—Hoffman and Pacino. If we couldn't land either one of them, we were in trouble.

(7) And this turned out to be one of the great jokes—my wife remembers my telling her that my biggest problem would be somehow to make the ending work, since the public already knew the outcome.

Was ever a man so naive?

Before I went down to Washington to meet with the authors, I began my preliminary research, and one of the things I found that I hadn't known was the inept quality of so much of what went on.

The famous break-in of June 17, 1972, the event that triggered everything, was *not* their first attempt. The burglers had tried several times before, and they kept goofing it up. Once, they got trapped and had to hide for the night in an empty room in the complex. Better than that, another attempt failed because the keys they had made to get them into Democratic National Headquarters didn't fit. Now, they had had these keys made in Miami, and after their bungle some of them *went back* to Miami to have keys made all over again.

The reason I suppose I liked that stuff was my obsession with the likelihood that everyone assumed they knew everything about Watergate. So I felt whatever I could bring in that was surprising would help us.

Anyway, still winter, I shuttle to Washington to meet the *Post* editors and, most particularly, Woodward and Bernstein.

It was not a good meeting and I suspect it was my fault. Bernstein was late, but when he arrived the three of us began to talk and I remember talking about the incompetence of so much of what went on, and I said, "It's almost like a comic opera."

The look on Bernstein's face when "comic opera" came out was not one of joy. The story had taken him from being a young, not all that successful reporter and had already given him a certain amount of fame and was soon to make him rich. And here was this Hollywood asshole talking about it being something less than serious. (Not my intention, obviously, but it was not the best phrase for me to use on a first meeting.) At any rate, although I met with Bernstein a couple of times in the months that followed, his contribution to the film was, for a while, nil.

And that doesn't make him wrong. When a movie company takes a property of yours, it's not yours anymore. I think it was Hemingway who advised "Take the money and run." Not without wisdom.

Woodward, on the other hand, was available to me constantly. I cannot overemphasize his importance to the screenplay. When he was in New York he would call and we'd often meet. When I was in Washington, he gave me everything I needed in the way of knowledge and support.

And I needed plenty. Because it was an incredibly complicated story and trying to find the handle was a bitch. He'd been working on it for close to two years and I was new. Forget, for now, trying to make a screenplay; I was struggling just trying to get the events straight.

If Gordon Willis, the cinematographer, was the hero of the film, Bob Woodward was the hero of the screenplay. I hacked away at the morass of material and finally reached one conclusion: Throw away the last half of the book.

Bernstein and Woodward had made one crucial mistake dealing with the knowledge of one of Nixon's top aides. It was a goof that, for a while, cost them momentum. I decided to end the story on their mistake, because the public already knew they had eventually been vindicated, and one mistake didn't stop them. The notion behind it was to go out with them down and let the audience supply their eventual triumph.

If I ended there, and I began around the break-in, I didn't have a whole structure but at least I had the start of one. I fiddled with the rest of the narrative, tucking things in as best I could, and then Woodward came to my office. I asked him to list the *crucial* events—not the most dramatic but the essentials—that enabled the story eventually to be told.

I think there were thirteen of them and he named them in order. I looked at what I'd written and saw that I'd included every one. So even if the screenplay stunk, at least the structure would be sound.

Then I went to work writing.

In August of '74 I delivered the screenplay to Redford in Utah, where he has a home and a ski resort. My family came along, we rented a house in the area. The month was to be spent working.

He read the first draft, liked it well enough, and copies were sent out. Obviously to Warner Bros., which was the studio that was to make the film—if they liked what they read. (If they didn't, they could have gotten rid of me and brought in another writer of their choice, but that would have been very damaging in terms of time. I'd been working for six months at least by August, and it wasn't the kind of material another screenwriter could have whipped off easily.)

And copies were sent to the editors of the *Washington Post*, who were portrayed in the movie. And, of course, to Woodward and Bernstein. I'm not sure as to whether we were legally bound to give them copies or whether it was done for goodwill and courtesy, but it was done.

Now Redford and I began to wait. We met each day usually near his house, and we talked about changes and who would be best for director, etc. But mainly he talked and I listened.

It was a very strange time. We had known each other now for half a dozen years, had worked on three pictures together— *Butch, Hot Rock, Waldo Pepper*.

Shortly after *Butch* opened he was on the cover of *Life*, which identified him as "Actor Robert Redford." I remember him saying to me that each time he looked at the cover he had to look twice because he was convinced it said "Asshole Robert Redford."

Well, he wasn't an asshole anymore. Now he was a phenomenon.

He'd also become secretive. Not only did I know him, our wives knew each other, so did our kids. And he had asked me to come to Utah for the month to work with him—

—and he wouldn't give me his phone number.

In order for me to contact him, I would have to call his secretary, and she would then call him and he would then call me.

None of this mattered, of course, once we heard from Warners that they liked the screenplay and we were a "go." The movie was to become a reality. *President's Men* had been the most difficult and complicated movie work I'd done till then and I felt a greater sense of accomplishment at that moment than ever before.

If only I could have ridden off into the sunset then and there.

One of the things I have tried to avoid in this book is to re-write history. Some of what you're reading comes from talking to people, but the greater amount comes from memory. And I've blocked a lot of what happened between August of '74 when the news came from Warners and the following June when photography actually began.

The rest of this chapter is material I've been unable to block, no matter how hard I've tried.

It's still August, Redford begins the search for a director.

But we still haven't heard from the *Washington Post*.

And we still haven't heard from Woodward and Bernstein.

The first director we sent the script to—who must remain nameless for legal reasons—said yes.

Incredible.

Then things started getting funny. Phone calls weren't re-turned, meetings were delayed. Many weeks later I was finally told—who knows if it was true?—that the director was involved in litigation against Warner Bros. and had only said yes in or-der to do any little thing he could to take out his vengeance on the studio. He never had any intention of directing the film, he just wanted to cost Warner's time.

By the time this news surfaced, we still hadn't heard from Woodward and Bernstein.

But we had heard from the editors of the *Washington Post*—

—and they *hated* all the jokes I'd put in their budget meet-ings.

A word now about just what a budget meeting is. The *Post* had two of them a day. And the main purpose was to budget space for articles—especially front-page articles. If you are a re-porter or an editor, you want your stuff to appear on "page one above the fold."

When I was spending time at the *Post*, they were decent enough to allow me to attend their budget meetings. (They were all decent, by the way. Courteous and helpful as much as their very busy schedules allowed.)

Okay, I go to my first two budget meetings and they were, of course, fascinating. But afterward, the top editors came up and told me that they weren't as funny as they usually are. Because one of the editors—Harry Rosenfeld, the part played by Jack Warden in the movie—was out that day. They assured me that when Rosenfeld was back, and he would be tomorrow, I'd get a different picture.

The next day Rosenfeld was back and was, as advertised, hysterical. In these meetings, the various editors—metropolitan, national, foreign—all argue with each other about the importance of their stories and the prominence their stories should receive.

And every time one of these guys would tout a story, Rosenfeld would zap him. Funny, funny jokes. And sitting in a corner of the room, I copied down Rosenfeld's lines in my notebook.

And in the screenplay, when I wrote the budget meeting scenes, I used Rosenfeld's lines.

Which infuriated them, because now they felt they looked like a bunch of clowns.

So that was the *Washington Post*'s reaction.

Still nothing from Woodward and Bernstein.

It's now fall, I'm back in New York, in my office, and the phone rings. It's Redford. He says that Bob and Carl are with him and why don't I come on over.

I go on over to his apartment, elevator up, ring the bell, go inside. My mood was pretty good as I remember. And I had absolutely no warning bells going off in my head that I was about to begin experiencing the worst moments of my movie-writing life.

Redford's in the living room. Woodward's in the living room. Bernstein's in the living room.

And there is a script on the living-room table.

I say hello to Redford, shake hands with Woodward, shake hands with Bernstein.

And now there is this silence.

And that script is still on the living-room table.

Then Redford said really the most extraordinary thing: "Listen—Carl and Nora have written their version of the screenplay." (Nora being Nora Ephron, a writer, then Bernstein's girl friend, whom he was later to marry and divorce.)

I just stood there.

Probably I blinked.

But I sure couldn't think of anything to say.

As a screenwriter, I test very high on paranoia. I'm always convinced of any number of things: that my work is incompetent, that I'm about to get fired, that I've already *been* fired but don't know yet that half a dozen closet writers are typing away in their offices, that I *should* be fired because I've failed, on and on.

But all those nightmares—and on occasion they've all happened—are within the studio system. The producer goes to the executive and says, "Goldman can't cut it, let's get Bob Towne." And then the executive calls Towne's agent and a deal is struck and money changes hands and the first I hear about it is when my phone doesn't ring when it's supposed to.

But for two *outsiders*, a hotshot reporter and his girl friend, to take it upon themselves to change what I've done without telling anybody and then to turn it in to the producer—a "go" project, remember—

—not in this world possible.

But there was their script on the living-room table.

I stood silently, staring at the thing, and I wanted Redford to scream at Bernstein, "You asshole, get out of here, don't you know what you've done?"

Redford said, "I've gone over it a little and I think you ought to read it."

I wanted my producer to defend me—I'm eight months on the project now, and I've done a decent job—Warners said yes. I wanted to hear "You're a dumb arrogant fuck, Carl, and I'd like you to shove that script where the sun don't shine."

Redford said, "I think there might be some stuff in it we can use."

I'm up to here with Watergate, I'm going crazy with when did Haldeman talk to Mitchell and how can we fit Judge Sirica into the story and how can Erlichman be the perfect neighbor everyone described him as being and still do the things he did; I had fretted and drunk too much and stayed up nights because I couldn't make it work until finally I did make it work and I wanted acknowledgment that a terrible breach had been committed.

Redford said, "We all want the best screenplay possible, so why don't you look it over, we're all on the same side, we all want to make as good a movie as we can."

I said I couldn't look at a word of it until I had been told I could by lawyers. And I left as soon as I could.

I can make a case for my producer's behavior. After all, this was now a famous book, Woodward and Bernstein were the media darlings of the moment, and we needed all the help we could get from the *Washington Post*. A pitched battle with Bernstein wouldn't have been an aid to moving the project forward. I could go on longer and make a better case. Redford was in a bind, no question.

But I still think it was a gutless betrayal, and you know what else? I think I'm right.

Lawyers were called in, and eventually it was decided I could read the Bernstein/Ephron version. One scene from it is in the movie, a really nifty move by Bernstein where he outfakes a secretary to get in to see someone.

And it didn't happen—they made it up. It was a phony Hollywood moment. I have no aversion to such things, God knows I've written enough of them—but I never would have dreamed of using it in a movie about the fall of the President of the United States.

One other thing to note about their screenplay: I don't know about real life, but in what they wrote, Bernstein was sure catnip to the ladies.

One important positive moment came out of that, a moment so meaningful to me I've separated it here. When I next met Woodward to talk about the movie, he said the following, word for word: "I don't know what the six worst things I've ever done in my life are, but letting that happen, letting them write that, is one of them."

I was and am grateful.

The Bernstein/Ephron episode did not stay secret long. God knows I didn't talk about it, but Washington, like Hollywood, thrives on the gossip of its main industry.

It was eventually common knowledge that I had written a dud. Later, after Hoffman had been signed, *Time* wrote an article about the progress of the movie and mentioned the lack of quality in what I'd done, even though, as they pointed out, it had snared Dustin Hoffman. I wished then for the first and only moment of my life that I subscribed to *Time* so I could cancel.

I was at CBS once in the news department and Walter Cronkite was walking along a corridor. The guy I was with knew Cronkite and introduced us, which pleased me because during this Watergate time, when everyone was lying, he was among the few Americans you could trust. Following is the entire conversation:

```
            MY FRIEND
   Walter, this is Bill Goldman who's
   writing All the President's Men.

               ME
   How do you do, sir.

            CRONKITE
   I hear you've got script trouble.
      (and he continued on his
       way)
```

Spring of '75 was the most stomach-churning time I've ever had writing anything. I had been on the movie now for over a year, not as daisy-fresh as I might have been. And by now I was dealing not just with the producer, a director had been signed: Alan Pakula.

Alan is a gentleman. We had mutual acquaintances in the business and they said nothing but good things about him as a human being. Neither can I. He is well educated (Yale) and serious about his work. He had been a top producer for years before he became a director—*To Kill a Mockingbird,* which he produced, was nominated for the Best Picture award for 1962. His biggest success as a director had been *Klute,* which got Jane Fonda her first Oscar. He's wonderful with actors.

But I, alas, was no thespian.

I've only met Warren Beatty once, and that was at a large gathering where everyone was shaking hands with everyone else and there wasn't much time for conversation. Beatty had just finished working with Pakula on *The Parallax View.* As Beatty and I shook hands I managed to get out that I was soon to meet and work with Pakula.

Novelists are always using the phrase "enigmatic smile." It's a staple. In all my life, I have only seen one such enigmatic smile. It came on Beatty's face and he said this: "Just make sure you've got it before you go on the floor."

I didn't know what he meant then, and although I wanted to pursue it, it wasn't possible in the crowd.

Had I known then, as they say, what I know now.

Pakula and I began with a series of meetings. Now, when a writer meets with the director of a movie that is gearing up, there is really only one subject: improving the script. Cut it, change it, fix it, add, the whole point is to make it better.

As I've said, I like to think of myself as being very supportive at this time. I don't want to be on the floor, so if you're going to get the best I can give, this is when.

We would meet and discuss a scene, any scene, it doesn't matter, and I would ask if it was okay, and if it wasn't, how did he want it changed, what direction? For example, I might ask, did he want this shorter or longer?

He would answer, "Do it both ways, I want to see it all."

Both ways?

Both ways.

I might ask, did he want me to rewrite a sequence and make it more or less hard-edged.

He would answer, "Do it both ways, I want to see it all."

Both ways?

Both ways, absolutely.

But why?

And now would come the answer that I always associate with Alan: "Don't deprive me of any riches."

God knows how often I heard that. "Don't deprive me of any riches."

What I didn't know then, of course, was simply this: Alan is notorious for being unable to make up his mind. So here I was, thirteen, fourteen, fifteen months on the Watergate story, and when things should be closing down in terms of script, irising in, if you will, it was going all over the goddam map.

I didn't know what the hell he wanted. So I was writing blind.

Alan is also genuinely creative. One day he spitballed a wonderful little scene for Bernstein and his ex-wife. He just ad-libbed it and I wrote it down and typed it up and felt very good about the whole thing; at least I'd pleased my director.

Mistake.

In doing so, I had also displeased my producer.

Redford was very much aware that his two greatest successes had been in "buddy" movies: *Butch* and *The Sting*. And here he was, locked in with another male co-star.

He had always wanted a love interest in the movie. I think he always knew a romance didn't belong in the picture and this picture always had a length problem. It wanted to center on the two reporters and there was more than too much for them to do.

But now Hoffman had a scene with a girl and Redford became obsessed. I can't remember at the time whether Woodward was married or not, but he was involved with a lovely girl named Francie.

And now "Francie scenes" entered my life. Redford didn't want *one*, he wanted *three*, to show the growth and eventual deterioration of a relationship under the pressure of the story. It wasn't an incorrect idea, it was just incorrect for this movie.

At least I thought it was.

But he was my producer and he would appear again and again with new and different notions for three Francie scenes. I don't know how many I eventually wrote—a dozen, probably closer to two.

And it was miserable, because I didn't believe a goddam word I was writing. And I suspect my belief showed in the quality of my work.

So every day for months I would go to my office to write one of two things: either scenes for the director, who wouldn't tell me what to write, or scenes for the producer, which I didn't have a lot of faith in.

Plus I was dealing with their problems with each other. Redford was disgruntled with Pakula's lack of decision. Pakula could have cared less about the Francie scenes.

I think it was the existentialist philosopher Sören Kierkegaard who wrote about man's condition on earth being one of being caught between "insoluble tensions."

Sören didn't know it, but he was talking about me.

I've never written as many versions for any movie as for *President's Men*. There was, in addition to all the standard names, the "revised second" version and the "prehearsal" version. God knows how many. And by now the media are really gearing up to cover the film. And I'm fifteen months hacking away and tired of it all but I'm still writing these insane scenes for the star that everyone knew would never see the day and probably wishy-washy stuff for the director, who won't tell me what he wants. I didn't want to deprive anybody of any riches, I just felt impoverished and wondered if it all would ever end.

It ended when the phone stopped ringing.

When they started shooting, maybe a week after I'd delivered my who-knows-what version, I found out Pakula had brought in someone else to be in Washington with him.

There is a very funny line, attributed to the late Peter Sellers, who was asked to answer the question "What would you change if you had your life to live over?" And Sellers replied, "I would do everything exactly the same except I wouldn't see *The Magus.*"

The Woodward-Bernstein book became a famous and successful film. I saw it at my local neighborhood theatre and it seemed very much to resemble what I'd done; of course there were changes but there are always changes. There was a lot of ad-libbing, scenes were placed in different locations, that kind of thing. But the structure of the piece remained unchanged. And it also seemed, with what objectivity I could bring to it, to be well directed and acted, especially by the stars. It won a bunch of Oscars and numberless other awards besides.

And if you were to ask me "What would you change if you had your movie life to live over?" I'd tell you that I'd have written exactly the screenplays I've written.

Only I wouldn't have come near *All the President's Men.* . . .

chapter ten

Marathon Man

I don't remember much clearly about *Marathon Man*. I wrote, in a compressed period of time, two versions of the novel and at least four versions of the screenplay, and after that, someone, I suspect Robert Towne, was brought in to write the ending. So all in all, it's pretty much a maze.

What I do remember clearly, as clearly today as then, is Olivier.

The part Olivier wanted to play was that of the Nazi villain, Szell, who is living in considerable luxury in South America. Circumstances force him to come to New York to retrieve a fortune in diamonds.

He wanted the role, obviously we wanted him. The problem was would he be physically able to or, more bluntly, would he even be alive? The man has been dogged by a series of hideous ailments over the past years, killing ones. But the man is also a bull, and each time he somehow survived.

When *Marathon Man*'s director, John Schlesinger, first went to visit him to discuss the possibility, he came away filled with doubt. Olivier, he reported, was then almost totally incapable of movement; one side of his face worked—that was all. Beyond the question of his recovery was this: Would he possibly be able to pass the physical that all leads must take for insurance purposes prior to a film?

All answers came in positive, and rehearsals began in a large room in what had once been the Huntington Hartford Museum above Columbus Circle. Schlesinger and I and a number of others arrived early. There is always tension at such a time, but now there was more than normal: A new problem had arisen.

The Olivier role called for him to be bald. In his past, the character had been nicknamed "the White Angel" because of his glorious white hair. In the script, in order to help disguise himself, Szell shaves himself bald. Now a delicate moment was at hand: Olivier was old, he had been desperately ill, he didn't look all that terrific anyway—and no one wanted to bring up the subject of having his hair shaved. (There were rumors about his health flying everywhere and this would only add to it; "I just saw Olivier and his hair has fallen out. He looks worse than I've ever seen him. *Bald.* How much longer can he last?")

A barber was hired for the day, but he was hidden in a room downstairs. For all anybody knew, maybe Olivier didn't even want to play the part bald. Christ, we all have vanity, and this was once one of the world's matinee idols.

Rehearsal time approached. The barber was waiting below. But who the hell was going to ask this legend about getting disfigured?

There were no volunteers.

On time, Olivier moved silently and alone into the large room. We all made our hellos. Olivier carries none of his greatness with him. He is famous for taking directors aside early on and saying, "Please, you must help me. Tell me what you want." Most stars like to be thought of as being private people, being shy. We even grant those attributes to Woody Allen, this in spite of the fact that he must be the most visible celebrity in New York.

It's not an act with Olivier. He never has considered himself to be all that much as a film actor. On the stage, obviously, he is Something. In films, he thinks of himself as being just another player.

He also never refers to his great career as a director. No mentions of *Henry V.* Orson Welles, another great director, reputedly has on more than one occasion, when he first came on the floor to act, looked around, then nailed the director with probably one eyebrow raised and intoned, "Is *that* where you're going to put the camera?"

Anyway, after we greeted each other there was this very long pause. Broken by Sir Laurence, who said, "Would it be possible for me to be shaved bald now? I think it might be best to get it done."

Relief, may I add, abounded.

During lunch break we found ourselves together and I didn't know what to say, so I fumbled something about was his hotel all right, did he like New York? Did he know it well?

"Not all that well," he answered. "I was here I think in '46 and in '51 and '58, but I'm not that familiar with the city."

I nodded, wondering what to say next when suddenly it hit me—Jesus Christ, '46 was his *Oedipus*, one of the two performances in all my life I wish I'd been able to see. (Laurette Taylor in *The Glass Menagerie* was the other.) And '51—that was the two Cleopatras, the Shaw, and the Shakespeare he performed in with Vivien Leigh. And '58 was his phenomenal work in Osborne's *The Entertainer*. He never referred to the plays, just the years.

But those weren't dates we were talking about; that was theatre history.

During a break that afternoon, he was telling a story about being mugged. I was a good distance away, staring out the window like a fool, listening to every word.

The point of the story was he was in his home in Brighton, watching television with his family. And what was on television was one of his Shakespeare movies. He went downstairs for a moment, and when he was on the lower floor, the mugger clobbered him and he shouted. But on television upstairs, what was going on was a soliloquy, and his children just thought there was Daddy below, doing the speech along with the tube.

Well, when he told that story, when he told about being struck and shouting—Olivier really shouted.

I spun from the window, startled by the sound, startled and at the same time thrilled. Because there it was, and I was in the room with it: the famous Olivier stage cry, the sound that has mesmerized audiences for half a century. I stood still, frozen by the power.

Sure he was old, and God yes, the Fates had been dogging him. But even now, when he wanted to let it fly, it was there.

William Devane, a fine American actor with a lot of stage experience, played another of the villains in the story. He rehearsed his first scene with Olivier and it all went quickly and Devane was just terrific.

When they broke, I cornered Devane, who is bright and very articulate, and I told him how wonderfully he had done and asked what it was like, rehearsing with Laurence Olivier.

"It doesn't matter," Devane replied.

I didn't know what in hell he was talking about and said so.

"This is rehearsal," Devane said. "It's nothing. When the camera starts to roll, he'll give me a little of this, he'll give me a little of that, and you'll never know I'm in the movie. No one's going to be watching me—that's Olivier, man."

Dustin Hoffman loves to improvise and he's expert at it. He and Schlesinger and Olivier were sitting around a table, going over the penultimate sequence in the movie, where Hoffman has Olivier at gunpoint and they begin a long walk. Hoffman said, "Let's improvise it for a while."

Olivier said he'd really rather not. Improvisation is not something he likes to do, it's not part of traditional English theatrical training.

Hoffman jumped up. "Let's put it on its feet and improvise."

Olivier resisted again.

Schlesinger said he thought that since we were there to rehearse, why not try it.

Olivier got up. Slowly.

He was, as I've indicated, recovering from whatever terrible disease had recently crippled him. His hands, even now, were bandaged. (I don't know the specific nature of this particular ailment; someone said it was the nerve disease that had killed Onassis, but I can't vouch for that. And when I say his hands were bandaged, I don't mean totally swathed. But there were Band-Aids crisscrossing his skin and all Scotch taped in place, perhaps to hide the sight of swelling.)

He was protected brilliantly in the movie. There is only one moment where you can tell how frail he really was. It's at the end of the sequence in the diamond district, when he was to try and run for a nearby cab, perhaps two paces away. If you watch closely, you can see the struggle he had to put out to get to the cab. Even then two steps were almost too many.

But now, as he stood slowly in the rehearsal hall, we were months before the shooting of the diamond scene. Hoffman mimed a gun and said "Okay, get going" and they started to walk around the rehearsal hall.

Olivier tried ad-libbing, said again and again that he really wasn't skilled at it, could someone give him his lines, and Hoffman said, "You're doing great, just say anything, come on, we're getting somewhere."

So they walked.

And walked. And kept on walking.

I don't know why all this was allowed to happen. Improvising is a part of Hoffman's vast technique, and perhaps that was the reason. But Olivier, in spite of himself, scares the shit out of other actors. (I know of one giant star who insisted on Olivier being in a movie with him. This man was and is a friend of Olivier's. The movie was well into shooting when Olivier's role began, and the night before his first appearance, the star who cared for him and insisted on him was awake the entire night in, quite simply, panic. He was nursed through that night by his producer, who told me it was so sad, seeing this star all but helpless because he was going to have to act with Olivier the next day.)

And I think part of this was because of Hoffman's need to put himself on at least equal footing with this sick old man.

And I don't know why Schlesinger didn't stop it. Perhaps, as he indicated, to see what might come out of it that might help the sequence.

But I also have to think that Schlesinger knew that Olivier wouldn't give him any trouble: Hoffman was the star, Hoffman had the vehicle role, if anyone was going to bring him to grief, Hoffman was that man, and to go directly against his star's wishes so early on might not be a move of great wisdom—I'm not talking about the improvisation, I'm talking about the walking that went along with it—because inside of a few minutes, Olivier's ankles were beginning to swell.

But on they walked. And improvised. And Hoffman was terrific. And Olivier did his best. And Schlesinger watched it all.

And Olivier would not sit down. Would not. Give in.

He could have stopped, he could have asked for a chair, he could have requested a break.

But he walked.

And now his ankles were bulging. Pain is impossible to quantify. What lays me up may be something you can deal with easily. No one can say how much anyone is capable of enduring. But watching it all take place, seeing the old man grow increasingly pale, was something I knew then I'd remember. And I mean forever.

Truly skilled actors are rare. Of those, a few are blessed with brilliance. And of those, fewer still have even a shot at greatness. Most (Burton, Welles, Barrymore) blow it.

Every century or so, we are blessed with a tiny handful, and as impossible as their task may be, *staying* great is that much harder.

Olivier made his first stage appearance in 1922—he played Katherine in an all-boys production of *The Taming of the Shrew*. I doubt he was a great Katherine. But watching him as that awful improvisatory afternoon came to an end, I think I glimpsed why Olivier has been able to endure in that incredible rarefied atmosphere for so many decades. He was sure as shit great for me that day, and he'll be great on the day that he dies.

Assuming he allows that to happen. . . .

Last Olivier story.

He and Roy Scheider were rehearsing a scene. In the story they are very close to violence, but both are still trying to figure out what the other one knows. The dialog went like this:

> OLIVIER
> We must talk. Truthfully. Are you
> to be trusted?--
>
> SCHEIDER
> --No--
>
> OLIVIER
> --Was that the truth? Or are you
> trying to upset me?--
>
> SCHEIDER
> --I know why you're here--and I
> know that sooner or later you're
> going to go to the bank--
>
> OLIVIER
> --perhaps I have already been.

Schlesinger interrupted them. He said, "Larry, that's supposed to go fast, and after Roy says the line about the bank, you're taking a pause before 'Perhaps I have already been.' Don't take the pause."

Olivier said "Of course," and they started into the dialog again. And then he stopped. "I have a problem about not taking the pause."

We waited.

"I'm trying to find out information. Roy says, 'I know why you're here.' And I need to find out what that means. Then Roy says, 'I know . . .' And I'm listening. Then he says, 'I know that sooner or later . . .' And I'm still listening. Now he says, 'I know that sooner or later you're going to go . . .' And I'm *still* listening. Finally he says, 'I know that sooner or later you're going to go *to the bank.*' That pause I'm taking is to give me time to register the information about the bank."

"I understand," Schlesinger said. "But we've got to get rid of the pause."

Olivier turned to me, then. "Bill," he said, "could I suggest an alteration in the line? Would it be all right if I changed it so that the line went, 'I know that you're going to go to the bank sooner or later?' You see, then I could register the word *bank* while he was saying 'sooner or later' and I wouldn't need the pause."

Obviously it was fine with me and the line was altered and we went on without the pause. And probably this two minutes of rehearsal explained at length doesn't seem like much put down in black and white.

But that moment—when the actor of the century asked me would I mind if he switched six words around—is the most memorable incident of my movie career. Olivier. Calling me "Bill." Olivier. Asking *me* would I mind.

That's high cotton. . . .

chapter eleven
The Right Stuff

The Right Stuff became, literally, a nightmare.

It began—innocently enough, as they say—in early October of '79, when a producer friend of mine called from California and told me to go out and get the Tom Wolfe book that dealt with the *Mercury* space program.

I had little or no interest in the subject matter. I'm not a space buff and I assumed that the story, so heavily detailed in the press, especially *Life* magazine, was pretty much known.

But I went out and bought the book. Then my producer friend called back and said he'd lost out in the scramble for the material to the producing team of Chartoff-Winkler, but that I should read the book anyway because it was terrific.

I started to read the book. For my own pleasure.

There is a universe of difference between reading a book on your own for yourself and reading a book that someone has asked you to read to consider making it a screenplay. You want the same thing in both cases: You want to be thrilled. But when you're maybe going to have to turn the piece into a movie, there is a constant governor at work. A scene may work wonderfully in a book, but part of you is always thinking, "Can I use this? Will this play? When I compress, will this stay in or is it off the narrative spine?" Endless questions intrude. But nothing intrudes when you're on your own—it's just you and the writer, you put yourself in his hands and hope he takes great care of you.

I read *The Right Stuff* just as a reader. I had been told it was terrific, but that proved to be an understatement. It was just a masterly piece of work, one of the most exciting reads I've had in a decade.

But I sure didn't think it was a movie.

It's 436 pages long—no problem. *A Bridge Too Far* ran 650 plus. But whereas *Bridge*, for example, focused on a single event, the Battle of Arnhem, Tom Wolfe ranged all over.

Part of that is because the book is oddly constructed: Wolfe originally planned to write the entire saga; starting with the first seven astronauts, he was going to take the story all the way to the moon. But when he got as far as *The Right Stuff* takes him, he or his editor or somebody said, "Hey, this is a book right here."

So, for example, the first forty-plus pages deal with a character who was of no significance as far as the *Mercury* program was concerned, but someone who played a figure in later flights. The seven *Mercury* astronauts don't enter until close to page eighty. And although they are well handled, they are not the most exciting part of the story Wolfe tells.

The real excitement deals with Yeager.

Charles Yeager was one of those legends. A West Virginia kid who enlisted in the Army air force in 1941, at the age of eighteen. Wolfe describes him this way: ". . . he was the boon-docker, the boy from the back country, with only a high school education, no credentials, no cachet or polish of any sort, who took off the feed-store overalls and put on a uniform and climbed into an airplane and lit up the skies over Europe."

By the end of the war he was a twenty-two-year-old phenom-enon. He trained as a test pilot in '46 and '47, and on October the fourteenth of 1947, Charles Yeager flew the plane that broke the sound barrier.

An amazing character, dazzlingly brush-stroked by Wolfe. He would have made a wonderful central figure for a movie.

But the astronauts didn't begin until a dozen years later and Yeager had nothing to do with them. In other words, there were at least two central stories in the book and they truly didn't touch at any point.

Next I got a call: United Artists had bought the book for Chartoff-Winkler and would I talk with them? That event took place in early November, of course at the Sherry Netherland Hotel.

Robert Chartoff and Irwin Winkler have been best friends forever, and partners for damn near as long. Their producing career provides a fascinating split. In their first decade, they

were connected with an awesome number of either critical
or commercial disasters, or, most often, both. Here's a partial
list:

> *Double Trouble*
> *The Split*
> *The Strawberry Statement*
> *Leo the Last*
> *Believe in Me*
> *The Gang That Couldn't Shoot Straight*
> *The Mechanic*
> *Busting*
> *S*P*Y*S*
> *Breakout*
> *Nickelodeon*
> *Valentino*

Then, in November of 1976, came *Rocky*.

It not only won them the Best Picture award, it made them,
forever, rich beyond the dreams of avarice. These numbers are
approximate, but *Rocky* cost barely over one million and took
in, worldwide, probably close to a hundred million. When
money comes in over the transom like that, no bookkeeper in
Hollywood can hide it all.

With their success, the quality of the Chartoff-Winkler films
altered abruptly. Among their productions since, as well as the
Rocky sequels, have been *Raging Bull* and *True Confessions*. So
when we shook hands in the Sherry that November day, I was
meeting one of the top producing teams in the business.

I told them what I thought—that it was a wonderful property,
that I wished them joy, that I didn't know how to make it into a
movie.

And then Winkler totally turned me around. He spoke very
quietly and he said that probably we should forget the Yeager
material and go with the astronauts, starting with their selection, then their training, then the Alan Shepherd flight, followed by the Gus Grissom fiasco, and climaxing the movie
when John Glenn circled the earth.

What he had done, of course, was give me my structure for
the movie. Five acts: selection, training, Shepherd, Grissom,
Glenn.

But even more than that, Winkler had set something going in my head. Because, for the first time in my career, I wanted to write a movie that had a message. I wanted to "say" something using *The Right Stuff* as a narrative vehicle. I wanted to "say" something positive about America. Not patriotic in the John Wayne sense, but patriotic none the less—

—because the hostages had just been seized in Iran.

I think it's difficult today, in this terrible time in America, to remember back even three years and reconstruct just how terrible, in a perhaps different way, things were then.

Jimmy Carter was president—I had voted for him. This gets pretentious but I have to say what I feel—I think Jimmy Carter eventually flew directly against the heart of the American dream. The message America has always beaconed across the world might be put this way: "Careers are open to talent." An individual can go, in one lifetime, as far as his luck and skill will take him. And no one will look down on him because he began poor, unlike, say, in England, where you are what your father and grandfather were.

And the message Carter was sending from the White House was this: "The world is too much now—one man can't do more than I'm doing."

On December the seventh of '79 my deal with Chartoff-Winkler was finalized, and I noted in my journal that the date was a good symbol for a patriotic movie. I didn't want to preach in the film—I'm a believer in the old movie adage "If you want to write a message, use Western Union."

But the astronaut story paralleled the lack of confidence of the hostage crisis. The Russians were ahead. We were second rate. They put a dog in space. Our rockets exploded on the launching pad. Then, slowly, we began to get it together. When Alan Shepherd was lobbed into the skies for fifteen minutes, small as that feat was compared to the Russian achievements, it *meant* something to the American people. And when John Glenn finally orbited four times around, we went crazy. We had, in our minds, caught up. We were America again.

As the hostage crisis dragged on—as Carter began wrapping himself in the flag and running for reelection, hiding in the Rose Garden—I became increasingly obsessed with what *The Right Stuff* presented. I told Chartoff-Winkler I wanted to say something positive about America. I told the heads of UA I wanted to say something about America. All the answers were the same: "Swell, right, go to it."

I did my months of research. I went to California and NASA in Houston and to Canaveral in Florida, where I saw a rocket launching and, yes, the ground really does shake and your clothes vibrate like crazy.

To be sure everybody was in sync, I did something I've never done before: As I was about to begin writing, I sent a note to the producers explaining, yet again, what I was after. Here is the note:

BOB AND IRWIN—IRWIN AND BOB

A REMINDER TO US ALL:
THE MOVIE MUST BE REAL. NOT A DOCUMENTARY BUT REAL. WE MUST RECREATE THAT WORLD AND TIME OF THE LATE 50'S AND EARLY 70'S SO THAT THE AUDIENCE UNDERSTANDS WHY THE FUSS MADE OVER THE ASTRONAUTS HAPPENED. AND WHAT THEY MEANT TO US ALL.

ONLY IN THAT WAY, I THINK, CAN WE INDICATE TO THE AUDIENCE TODAY THAT WE ARE STILL, IN SPITE OF OUR FAULTS, A GREAT COUNTRY.

REMEMBER, THIS IS TO BE A MOVIE THAT, IF WE'RE LUCKY, SENDS THE PEOPLE HOME WITH A GOOD FEELING ABOUT AMERICA.

NOT SUCH A BAD THING TO TRY AS THE 80'S UNVEIL.

BILL

In May, I sent the first draft to Chartoff-Winkler. They said they liked it but they wanted me to add a section of basically daredevil material to the early part of the script before they gave it to UA.

In June, the new material added, UA was sent the screenplay. Chartoff and Winkler said they were pleased with it, but producers often say that.

UA said they liked it, too, and I had to believe them—because we became a "go" project with a twenty-million-dollar budget and no stars.

Trumpets, please.

Next, naturally, came the hunt for a director. Everybody's first choice was Michael Ritchie (*Downhill Racer, The Candidate*, a lot more). He wanted to do the project. Negotiations began. I hadn't ever worked with him but I knew him and thought him perfect; he is fast, prepared, good with men, and achieves a wonderful documentary look to his films.

Then his latest picture, *The Island*, was seen by Winkler, among others, and the feeling about *The Island* was disastrous—tasteless, unnecessarily replete with gore, the pits. Ritchie was out.

John Avildsen, who had directed *Rocky*, was next. In June, Avildsen was one-hundred-percent committed. Then came contract problems. Avildsen was out.

Enter Phil Kaufman. I knew Phil and I liked him. More than that, we had both been fired from the same project, so we had spilled blood together, always a good sign. Well, almost always. Phil is bright, serious, a good writer, a sports fan, always a good sign. Well, almost always. He had directed a few pictures, and only one of them—a remake of *Invasion of the Body Snatchers*—had done much commercially, but that had been a UA picture. They approved him.

On July twenty-first, we had our first meeting out in California. The meeting was preceded by a lunch with the producers and some UA brass and we talked about a lot of things but not the picture. Then Phil and I excused ourselves and went into a room alone.

Within two minutes, I was into the nightmare.

I mentioned at the start how fortuitous the timing was, since there was going to be a rocket launching in Florida and I knew they didn't happen often and I knew he would be as impressed as I'd been. He said, "I'm not going to Florida, but there are some air shows up in Northern California I thought I'd catch." Then I gave my pitch about the chance of making this patriotic movie and he said, "I don't want to do that, patriotism's too easy, Ronald Reagan's patriotic and who wants that?"

The entry I have in my journal for that day says: "Kaufman meeting—disaster." But in truth, I don't know which of his two remarks proved the more devastating.

The one about patriotism seems clearly the more potent. But the one about air shows meant old airplanes, and old airplanes meant one thing to me—

—Yeager.

Phil's heart was with Yeager. And not only that, he felt the astronauts, rather than being heroic, were really minor leaguers, mechanical men of no particular quality, not great pilots at all, simply the product of hype.

Well, now.

There is no way I can explain to you the size of the chasm between us but I will try. Let's suppose you were hired to do a movie about the Dallas Cowboys. Roger Staubach. Tony Dorsett. "Too Tall" Jones. They were your heroes. And your job was to make them as central and splendid as you could.

And you did that.

And everyone said fine.

Then a director came aboard who said this: "The Dallas Cowboys are minor leaguers—there hasn't been a *real* football hero since the days when everybody played the whole game, sixty minutes, offense and defense. Tony Dorsett stinks. Roger Staubach sucks. There hasn't been a real football hero since Bronko Nagurski, and he's who I want to glorify."

Now, I'm not saying that's wrong; in this example I've given, I happen to agree—Bronko Nagurski was the greatest football player who ever lived.

But that's not what I was hired to write.

I was supposed to tell the story of the astronauts. And I did. More than that, I wanted to say, using them as a vehicle, that America was still a great place, and not just to visit.

What Phil wanted to say was that America was going down the tubes. That it *had* been great once, but those days were gone, and wasn't that a shame.

We met for three days, and we went over the script. The version UA said yes to ran 148 pages. Do you know how many pages remained in the version Kaufman wanted to make?

Six.

One scene was all that would remain, a bitter fight between an astronaut and his wife.

On the twenty-fourth of July, Phil and I met with Chartoff and Winkler and I tried to explain the wee differences that existed between the director and myself. Chartoff and Winkler did what all bright producers do: They tried to make peace. What they said was sure, here and there maybe it's not the same, but in general you guys really agree with each other. I could not, I simply could not, make them understand.

But I had an ally—Phil. He's a writer, too, and he knew full well what I was talking about. And finally, with his help, the situation surfaced.

We agreed to think about things and meet again three weeks later, and what everybody would do was take a few notes and try and come to an agreement.

We were to talk for three solid days in August. I went back to L.A. to begin. The first problem surfaced when it turned out we wouldn't have three days, because Winkler had made plans to go vacation in the South of France in the middle of the second day.

And Kaufman's notes turned out to be a thirty-five page treatment of the film. I will quote here only the first and last lines; here is the beginning:

"This is a Search film, a quest for a certain quality that may have seen its best days. . . ." (That quality, by the way, is bravery in the sense that Wolfe uses it in the book: the right stuff.)

The last page lists a bunch of movies we should all be seeing: *The Searchers, La Dolce Vita, Grand Illusion,* and half a dozen more. His final comments on them said this: "Many of them have a rambling form—but a compelling theme; they are episodic. 'Truth' is found along the way. *And in all of them, it seems, we detect the passing of a higher quality.*" (Italics mine.)

We talk about Phil's notes on Monday and now something new has been added: Not only do Phil and I disagree, but Chartoff and Winkler disagree, Chartoff basically siding with Kaufman, Winkler with me. Then, at the peak of all this, Winkler takes off for the Riviera. (Chartoff and Winkler, by the way, ended their partnership pretty much at this time, and I have no way of knowing if *The Right Stuff* contributed to that severing. But there was a lot of emotion flying around the room while we went at it.)

At five-thirty the next morning, I had my nightmare, waking terrified because in the dream I was falling to my death.

Soon after that I did something I never conceived could happen to me: I left the picture. It was something I'd never done before and knew I'd never do again. (Ho-ho-ho, read the next chapter, it gets easier.)

Anyway, there was anger, and there were lawsuits, and everything was eventually settled. Not amicably, but guns are no longer being fired across the water.

UA dropped the project, and The Ladd Company picked it up, and Kaufman has written the movie and is directing it now. It should come out at Christmas.

This has been by far the hardest chapter of the book to write. I regret the experience so totally. There were no villains, we all behaved I think as well as we could, and yet it happened and I still don't know why.

The UA executives at this time were not exactly riding a hot streak—some would get canned for *Heaven's Gate.* And I wondered did they meet with Kaufman before he took the job? If they did, what did he tell them?

But it's obviously wrong to blame them for the ensuing disagreements—because I've *never* met with a director and discussed the script before he took the job. The director says yes and then you meet. Always. And always there are disagreements, but that's not only to be expected, it's not a bad thing—bright directors can make tremendous contributions to a script.

Chartoff-Winkler were doing their job—trying to get a picture made. And Kaufman had a vision of what he wanted on screen.

But it had nothing to do with mine, and I often found myself wondering in the ensuing months why I was hired in the first place. Since what I wrote so obviously didn't matter.

I mean, here we were, an expensive "go" project, and no one said, "Hey, let's try and make the script work." I may have never felt, in movies, such impotence as during *The Right Stuff* meetings. Whenever anyone asks, "How much power does a screenwriter have?" my mind now goes only to those terrible days in Los Angeles.

The answer, now and forever: in the crunch, none.

Could I have stayed on the project? If he needs the credit or the job, any screenwriter can throw a bag over anything and do it for Old Glory.

But whatever I wrote would have been, I think, useless. I wouldn't have believed a word of it and I would have known, as I hacked away, that everything was doomed to fail because it was so clearly not what Kaufman wanted.

I still feel sad. But ultimately, one nightmare was enough. . . .

chapter twelve
Grand Hotel

Grand Hotel was a movie that I very much wanted to write, that I was contracted to write, that I then found out I couldn't write: It is the story of losing confidence.

The film, of course, was to be a remake. The original MGM version won the Oscar as Best Picture fifty years ago, and it still probably has the quintessential all-star cast: Garbo, Crawford, Barrymore, Barrymore, on and on. I had seen this version and Garbo was beautiful, Crawford was a revelation, But it seemed to me to be hopelessly dated.

I got word that Norman Jewison (*In the Heat of the Night; Fiddler on the Roof; The Russians Are Coming, the Russians Are Coming*) was interested in doing the remake and wanted to meet. I thought I ought to see *Grand Hotel* again, and that was done. Garbo was still beautiful, John Barrymore was even more romantic than the first time—but it seemed more dated than ever.

Meetings are part of the Hollywood mating dance. (Maybe Woody Allen's best punch line is "All the good meetings are taken.") Mostly, at least in my experience, they are bullshit. I have met some dazzling salesmen and been impressed with their acting technique, but usually they are futile: If you have a strong opinion going in, it's not likely even the legendary Skouras Brothers in their prime can make you change it.

The *Grand Hotel* experience—it covered five years of my life—was unusual at least in this respect: It provided me with both the best and worst of meetings.

They came in that order. Jewison was staying at the Sherry Netherland Hotel in New York. (Practically everyone in the movie business, for reasons passing understanding, stays at the

Sherry when they come to Manhattan. I have known of studio executives who have stayed at the Park Lane, another fine establishment, who felt they had to explain why they weren't at the Sherry before any talk could get under way. The subtext being, of course, that they were still the "A" team, even though they had been banished, for the moment, to Central Park South.)

Jewison is a tough, feisty, funny, no-nonsense director, so we got right to it. I said I thought the picture had something from the past that couldn't be successfully given breath. I knew this version would take place at the MGM Grand Hotel in Vegas, an incredibly successful operation, but I didn't think that was enough. No one had shot at the Grand, no one had ever seen its size or interiors, so that was a plus. But about the only one I could think of.

Then Jewison took over. He wasn't interested in resurrecting the old classic. He didn't want to find a modern equivalent for the Garbo part or any of the others. He just wanted to use the title and the same kind of multistory approach as the original.

And he wanted to do it as a musical.

A great big high-style glossy, classy musical, the kind Metro was the master of in the old days. Musicals were out of fashion—this was April of '77—because making them had become prohibitive. But since this was to be a Metro movie about a Metro operation, that didn't matter so much in this case. We had a real shot at doing something wonderful, something not seen in years, and if we were lucky, maybe we might come up with a movie people could mention along with the legendary Donen-Kelly-Minnelli works of the forties and fifties.

I almost came out of my chair I was so excited. It had crossed my mind by this point, after ten-plus years in the trenches, that if I was anything, I was a genre writer. I didn't want to write the same kind of movie over and over.

And the one kind of movie I most wanted to try that I had never been given the chance to attempt was a musical.

We began throwing little vignette ideas at each other, and some of them were rotten but some of them weren't. Then I realized that the narrative of this kind of film wouldn't have to have all the main characters introduced early on. You could have some stories that went from start to finish, but others could begin a third of the way through and end half an hour before fade-out. I made a diagram for Jewison on a piece of scratch paper, trying to show what I wasn't articulating as clearly as I wanted, probably because I was so excited. The diagram looked something like this:

_____

_____

_____

_____

_____

I talked for a minute and then stopped, looking at the piece of paper. I realized what I'd done, subliminally, was make a music staff.

From there the meeting *really* took off. Metro wanted the musical made. Jewison wanted to make the musical. Jewison wanted me to write it. I was desperate to oblige. Agents were called. Deals were struck.

Heaven.

Then it began to rain. A Metro executive (literally) woke up from a sound sleep and realized that Jewison got final cut on his pictures, and what if he decided to ridicule the Grand?

Now neither Jewison nor I ever dreamed of ridiculing the Grand. We wanted to make this wonderful bubble, an entertainment, very pure and very simple, with the best musical talents we could find. An exposé of the dark side of Vegas's underbelly was not what he had in mind. Nor did we want to mock the ladies in curlers or the men in leisure suits. And we weren't after a tract that preached the evils of gambling. We dreamed of *Gigi*. Of *An American in Paris*. Of *Singin' in the Rain*. This message was conveyed to the Metro brass.

They said that of course they believed us, but we didn't understand one thing: The Grand Hotel was not just another flophouse on the Strip.

No. It was Unsullied.

It was Pristine.

The diamond in the Metro crown.

And they wouldn't give Jewison final cut.

Now, final cut—total approval over the finished film—is the most coveted goal a director can aspire to. A lot of directors say they have it. But in point of fact, they don't. Jewison had it; he'd done a dozen pictures and only one—*Gaily, Gaily,* for which he'd gotten probably his best reviews—had failed. When you're a director, you can alter your fee, you can fuss with every clause in your contract—but your right of final cut is sacrosanct.

More cannons were fired across the waters.

Finally Metro came back with this: Okay, you win, we'll give you final cut. Total and absolute and irrevocable final cut.

With this one small proviso: Anything that takes place *outside* the hotel is yours to do with whatever you please, but we'll keep control over any stuff that happens to take place *inside* the hotel.

Jewison countered that, since, as they well knew, 99 percent of what we planned took place inside the Grand, they weren't giving up a whole hell of a lot.

They replied that we didn't understand what we were dealing with. The Grand was special.

Unsullied.

Pristine.

The diamond in the Metro crown.

And what if we didn't put things in the script that appeared on the screen and they were helpless to stop them.

What kind of things?

Oh, say, what if we dressed the hotel executives so they looked like idiots? Or what if the boobs on the chorus girls sagged in an unsightly way? Even if we approve the script, you could damage the reputation of the hotel. We'll give you final cut. We'll give it on everything outside. *Plus* we'll give it on everything inside—unless we feel it's detrimental to the reputation of the hotel. We know you won't do anything detrimental, but if we feel something detrimental is there, of course we'll have to change it.

In other words, Jewison said, you'll give me absolute and total final cut over everything—unless there's something you don't like, which you'll then alter.

Now you've got it, replied Metro; what could be fairer than that?

We were entering, of course, Cloud-cuckoo-land. There is a wonderful Hollywood expression I first heard used by Robert Evans. I asked him, during the casting period, if a certain actor was signed. (In other words, yes or no?) Evans told me, "Absolutely, he's set. But he's not set-set." (In other words, absolutely yes, he isn't signed.) Jewison wanted what he had had for ten years. Final cut. Metro was offering exactly what he wanted. Final cut. Unless they wanted to change something.

Total stalemate.

Which was when I got my ho-ho-ho genius idea.

I decided what I would do was write a screenplay different from anything I'd ever tried: a total piece, *including everything*. Everything in *every scene*. If, for example, two hotel executives were talking, I wouldn't just write the setting and who they were and what they said. I would also include precisely how they were dressed, how their ties matched their immaculate suits perfectly, the tasteful paintings in the background on the wall behind them, *everything*. All chorus girls would be totally described, with each glorious boob pointing, if necessary, north.

The point being, if everything was put down, and precisely put down, and if Jewison agreed to accept and shoot only what was written, there would be no way to double-cross them and bring scandal down around us all. The script, as I could conceive it, would probably be totally unreadable and would certainly be as long as the *Oxford English Dictionary*, but I hoped it would move the project along.

Would Jewison accept my notion, though? I called him in California. He thought about it, finally deciding that the air of distrust around the movie was not the best of all possible atmospheres to try to make a movie in, so yes, he could live with my idea. If it wasn't in the script and he shot it, then they could change whatever they pleased. Because he would make damn sure that what he wanted was in the script.

Now I had only to convince Metro.

I flew to California, optimistic as Candide. Into disaster.

It took place in Los Angeles on a Saturday morning. My memory is, at a house Jewison was renting. Present were Jewison and Pat Palmer, his partner and producer, several Metro executives. Plus Norman's agent, Stan Kamen, and mine, Evarts Ziegler. These are two genuinely remarkable men. Not only did they both survive the rigors of top academic educations, they were both alive and well after probably fifty combined years of very hard agenting labor. They sat, Zig and Kamen, in a corner of the room, close together, out of the way.

There was the standard nervous chitchat, because the meeting could not begin until the arrival of the crucial figure, Frank Rosenfelt, the head of MGM.

More talk, blah blah blah, tension mounting. Now *no one* wants to be at a meeting in L.A. early on a Saturday morning. So the hour adds a certain discombobulation to the waiting.

Finally, out front, there is audible the closing of a car door. Rosenfelt has arrived.

Now there is the sound of the opening and closing of the front door of the house. Rosenfelt is inside.

Inside the house, yes, but not yet in the room. And you must picture what happened next. All the rest of us are standing in the living room, waiting. Rosenfelt is out of sight, moving along the corridor toward where we all stand.

And while he is still *out of sight,* he begins to speak, his voice booming, growing louder as he grew nearer. But no one can see him yet. We can hear him, though, and his words are forever etched on the inside of my eyelids.

"I just want you to know," this voice begins, *"I want you to know I'd be taking bread out of my children's mouths if I gave final cut on this picture."*

And he's *still* not visible.

I glanced at Zig and Kamen then, seated off in their corner, and their heads were shaking side to side, in perfect wordless unison. They knew what I didn't: that incredibly, before the meeting had started, it was done.

Rosenfelt entered the room, we all shook hands and managed to make it together for an hour. But it was futile. I flew back to New York, leaving, sadly, the Grand. Still Unsullied. Still Pristine. Gleaming like a diamond in the Vegas night.

In the movie business, the wheel is always in spin; projects die, are buried, then miraculously rise. (Bo Goldman's script of

Shoot the Moon, supposedly, was written ten years before the movie was made.)

So it was with *Grand Hotel*. In early '81, Jewison called me and said he'd been approached again to do the musical. Did I think I could reawaken my enthusiasm? I asked him about final cut. He explained there had been a couple of changes. One being that the hotel and the movie studio were now separate entities, which I never really understood. More important, David Begelman was now in charge of the studio and he and Jewison had a long and good relationship. Jewison felt Begelman could offer him sufficient controls to make the situation manageable.

I told Norman I would get back to him.

There were reasons, pro and con. The negatives were these: It *is* hard to get your passion back. We had wanted it so badly in '77 and felt we were kicked in the teeth. I was four years older, with different interests and feelings concerning the movie business. Most of all, though, the project had been shopped.

Metro really wanted to make the movie. If it stunk, no one would blame the hotel. But if it worked, and movies are a worldwide operation now, you couldn't ask for a better piece of publicity for the Vegas Grand or its sister up in Reno. In every country, the Grand Hotel would be a known commodity. Great for business.

And any number of directors and writers had been involved in these intervening years. I suspect the reason the movie didn't happen was that eventually the directors had said no for the same reason Jewison did. This was a big and important movie for both the hotel and the studio, and you didn't want to entrust it to the boys responsible for *Reefer Madness*. And if you want a Sydney Pollack or a Mike Nichols, two of the many directors who had been in and out, you have to give them what everybody else gives them: control.

To me, then, *Grand Hotel* seemed just the least bit tired.

But—

—I still wanted to work with Norman Jewison.

—Jewison still wanted to do *Grand Hotel*.

—It was still, I thought, a good idea for a movie. I still wanted to do a musical film.

—And, of course, the Grand was still there.

Unsullied and Pristine.

Yes, there had been movies about Vegas before. Sure, we'd all seen flicks about gambling. And God knows hotels weren't virgin territory for a background.

The Grand, though, truly was Special. Maybe the biggest hotel in the world, maybe the most successful hotel in history. All ours to show for the very first time.

So, did I want to do it?

Absolutely yes.

As much?

Probably, hesitantly, no.

I called Jewison back and told him my thoughts. We decided, what the hell, let's give it a whack. Deals were struck, Jewison and I met, went over our old story notions, decided which held and which didn't. We came up with some new ideas. He knew whom he wanted to do the score: Alan and Marilyn Bergman (*The Way We Were, The Windmills of Your Mind*) for lyricists. Marvin Hamlisch (*A Chorus Line*) for music. He set about contacting them.

I set out for Vegas. I had researched the Grand earlier, but that was before the tragic fire. And the last time, the personnel had been a bit hesitant about answering questions. It was crucial for me to know as much about the operation as I possibly could.

This time everyone was wonderful and open. I spent a week taking in as much as I could. The shows, from both the audience and backstage points of view; the kitchens, the casino operation, the room operation, the Eye in the Sky. Everything I needed they gave me. I learned about the jai alai fronton and the promenade of shops. All kinds of new notions popped—wouldn't it be terrific if we shot here? Hey, we could set a wonderful scene there. Really a terrific time for me. We're talking about a two-thousand-room hotel with a casino the size of a football field and I was getting to understand it—if not all of it, at least enough.

Now, the Grand (and I think most of the other major hotels on the Strip) has an interesting wrinkle. The biggest, most ornate suites are *not* for rent. They are kept empty for the highest rollers. And when one of them comes to town, they are given these gigantic suites free. As a perk. Often along with their meals and free shows. Whatever they want. Just so they'll gamble at the Grand and not, say, at Caesars Palace across the street.

I wanted to see these gigantic suites, and toward the end of my stay, I asked if I might be given a tour. No problem. A polite young man who worked in the reservations office took me up to the very top floor. There's a private guard at the desk by the elevators, always on duty. We moved past him and I was shown one suite, then the next. Finally, when I was studying maybe the biggest suite of all, the guy said the magic words: "This is the one Mr. Ashby used."

Hal Ashby is a major Hollywood director (*Shampoo, Coming Home*), and though I'd never met him, we had mutual acquaintances and I was surprised to find he was such a major gambler. I said as much.

"No, no," the reservations man said. "He didn't *sleep* here, he *shot* here."

I was entering the quagmire. He shot a scene in this suite? I asked. In this hotel?

"He didn't shoot just a scene in this hotel. He shot a *movie.*"

Gasping now. A whole movie?

"I wouldn't know if it was a whole movie or not. But he was here a long time."

How long?

"I'm not really sure. Eight weeks maybe. Maybe twelve."

This was the first I had ever heard of *Lookin' to Get Out*, a movie Ashby was directing with Jon Voight and Ann-Margret. I didn't know the name of it then, of course, but I did know this: I was shocked, I was pissed, but most of all, for the first time on this project, my confidence was shaken.

Writing is finally about one thing: going into a room alone and doing it. Putting words on paper that have never been there in quite that way before. And although you are physically by yourself, the haunting Demon never leaves you, that Demon being the knowledge of your own terrible limitations, your hopeless inadequacy, the impossibility of ever getting it right. No matter how diamond-bright your ideas are dancing in your brain, on paper they are earthbound. If you're trying a screenplay, you know it's never going to be Bergman. If it's a novel, well, what kind of a novelist can you hope to be when Dostoevski was there before you. And Dickens and Cervantes and all the other masters that led you to the prison of your desk.

But if you're a writer, that's what you must do, and in order to accomplish anything at all, at the rock bottom of it all is your confidence.

You tell yourself lies and you force them into belief: *Hey, you suckers, I'm going to do it this one time. I'm going to tell you things you never knew. I've—got—secrets!*

When I was trying *Harper*, one of my confidence builders was that there hadn't been a tough-guy detective movie in years. If I'd found out that Clint Eastwood was doing a Dashiell Hammett, I could have handled that. I would have told myself, what the hell, there have been lots of tough-guy detective movies in the past, there is always room for another if it's good enough.

But when I found out, after years of working on *Butch Cassidy*, that another movie was planned called *The Wild Bunch* (the name of Cassidy's gang), that was a blow. There was always room for another Western—but you couldn't be the *second* Butch Cassidy film. In Hollywood, often success comes not from being best but from being first.

I went back to my room at the Grand and called Jewison. He was just as stunned, I think, as I was. It was crazy—because the same company that was distributing the Ashby film was distributing ours.

But there was no point in going out the window. The important thing was to read *Lookin' to Get Out* and find really what similarities the two films had.

Back in New York, I read the script to the Ashby film: He had, indeed, shot everything in the hotel. The same locations we wanted to use. All. My reaction on finishing, it, though, was probably less depression than bewilderment.

Because, first of all, the script was written to shoot at Caesars Palace. Caesars had apparently taken one look at it and said "nothing doing," so Ashby went across the street and got the Grand's consent.

The Unsullied Grand.

That pristine diamond of the Metro crown had refused to trust us in '77, and here they had okayed a script that had, among other things, a scene where one of the male leads waits outside in the corridor so his buddy, inside, can get a blow job from a whore.

And as far as putting their executives in a bad light, one of the main plot points of *Lookin' to Get Out* hinged on the hotel's top man not being able to recognize the voice of a good friend, thereby giving imposters the run of the hotel.

Okay. The idea for *Grand Hotel* was already a little tired. And Ashby had shot everything we wanted to use. Still, our stories were completely different. And most important of all, we were doing a musical, a full-fledged musical set in Las Vegas—no one had done *that* for a while.

Then I found out that Francis Coppola was shooting *One from the Heart*, a full-fledged musical set in Las Vegas.

I was, to put it bluntly, in despair. *My secrets were being stolen away.* Every time I thought about the movie, the presence of Ashby and Coppola blocked any hope I had at vision. Whenever I thought of a musical moment, I wondered if Coppola had come up with the same idea; every book scene went flat because I knew that wherever we put it in the hotel, the audience would have been there already.

When I write, I must convince myself that it's going to be wonderful. (There is a character in a great play by Tennessee Williams, *Camino Real.* She's the Gypsy's daughter and she's a whore, but in her heart, each moonrise makes her a virgin.) I'm like that—each moonrise makes me a virgin, too—I'm going to write it and this time, *this time,* it won't be crap. When I don't have that confidence, I'm in big trouble.

I don't think I realized finally quite how big my trouble was until I read the *Variety* review of a movie starring Peter Falk called *All the Marbles.* Falk played a character who managed a lady tag-wrestling team, hustling his ladies up the rungs of the wrestling world, hoping for a shot at the world's championship.

Guess what? They get their chance.

Now, guess where the big match takes place? Bingo—at the Grand Hotel.

Variety then went on to explain that the last half hour of the film took place at the Grand. And that the match itself took place where the logo of the Grand was on the ring mat, so that every shot was a plug for the hotel. *Variety* had one word for this self-promotion—

—"shameless."

That word in that review was the final nail in my coffin. (It didn't matter when I next found out that the Bette Midler movie *Jinxed* also had scenes at the Grand. And it also didn't matter that the Falk picture took place at the Grand in Reno. Because they look alike. It was the same as if someone had said to me, "Don't worry that there's this other movie in the Anaheim Burger King, ours is in Cucamonga."

I met with Jewison, Hamlisch, and the Bergmans. They were all bright and they had wonderful ideas and they weren't bothered by all the other movies. But the musical people hadn't been through the same grinding-down process I'd experienced. And Jewison was about to begin directing a Burt Reynolds–Goldie Hawn film, so he was busy for the next nine months.

I had to go into my room and do it. Try, somehow, to make *Grand Hotel* come to life.

And I couldn't.

I had one final meeting with Norman. It was, at least for me, very sad. We wished each other well, that was that.

Looking back on the experience six months later, I feel it was the right and only thing for me to have done. At least it was right for me.

Could I have written the script?

Absolutely.

I could have filled 135 pages. If you'd lifted it, it would have felt like a screenplay. If you'd looked through it, it would have resembled a screenplay.

Would it have had any quality at all?

Doubtful.

My confidence was all—all—gone. The moonrise could not make me a virgin. When I am hired to try a movie, I may turn in a garbage script. But at least I know that, rotten as it may turn out, it was written by the best me available.

At the end, on *Grand Hotel*, I wasn't there. . . .

chapter thirteen
A Bridge Too Far

Until the reviews came out, *A Bridge Too Far* was probably the best experience I've had in films. And, as I said in the introduction to this section, the most unusual. What made it so unusual, from my point of view, was this: It was the only time that a picture was actually into production *before* a first draft screenplay or so much as a word of it was seen by anyone.

This kind of risk is unheard of for a studio-financed picture. But *Bridge* was not backed by a studio; rather it was one man using his own money, the producer Joseph E. Levine.

And if that isn't risk enough, remember this: We are not talking about a cheapie here. Levine knew from the outset that *Bridge*, a mammoth undertaking, was going to be expensive. But I doubt that he could have guessed that, when things were at their most desperate, he was going to be personally on the line for twenty-two million dollars. . . .

Joseph Edward Levine was born in the Boston slums in 1905. He was the youngest of six children and his father, an immigrant tailor, died when Levine was four. He endured one of those classic horrendous childhoods, moving always from tenement to tenement.

His mother called him the *broytgeber*—the bread giver—and he was always working, selling paper, shining shoes, stealing wood, so the family wouldn't freeze in the New England winters. The slum stink draped across his early years, and there seemed no escaping.

There was also no food. Weekly, he would go to the rabbi for religious instruction and the rabbi would always eat black bread during these sessions and never offer any. The rabbi also had a stick, and whenever Levine made a mistake, the rabbi would strike him on the wrist. One day the rabbi made a mistake and hit too hard, whereupon Levine grabbed the stick and hit the rabbi, which put an end to his theological studies.

At fourteen he quit school. All he had to offer was energy; he became an errand boy in a dress factory and worked his way up to being a traveling dress salesman. But he didn't like it. He opened a dress shop when he was twenty—called LeVine's—and did all right for a few years. But he didn't like the dress shop any more than being a traveling salesman. He tried New York, scuffled, drove an ambulance before he knew his way around the city. Back to Boston and into the restaurant business. But always he was looking for something.

Finally, forty-five years ago, he found the picture business.

An art house, more precisely—the Lincoln Theatre in New Haven. The first two movies he showed were *Un Carnet de Bal,* the French classic, which did well with the Yalies, and *How to Undress in Front of Your Husband,* which not only "dropped dead, some people threw eggs at the screen." Art films and exploitation films—he has been allied with both ever since.

Eventually he moved from exhibiting films to the distribution end. *Paisan, Open City, Bicycle Thief, 8½*—he brought over some of the best pictures ever. By his own reckoning, *A Bridge Too Far* was the four hundred ninety-second film he had either produced, coproduced, financed, presented, or distributed.

But the one that made him famous was *Hercules.*

It's a little difficult to explain to an audience today the impact *Hercules* had in 1959. The movie business was undergoing yet another crisis of confidence—studios were retrenching, long-term executives were being laid off—and television was the chief villain. The movie executives hadn't the least idea how best to cope with it—but they knew that tv had stolen their audience. Levine's importance in the history of this period may well be that he proved that the new despair-ridden movie business was, as a *Fortune* magazine article about him said, "really the old movie business under new conditions—and a pretty good business at that."

The *Hercules* story began in New York when Levine, who was basically a New England distributor, had a talk with a Metro employee who told him of the existence of the Italian sun-and-sandal epic. No other company would touch it for America, but

Levine *knew* as soon as he heard the title that it was for him.

So, on the strength of the title and the Metro man's recom-
mendation, Levine flies to Rome the next morning to see the
movie. He goes to the Metro offices in Rome and sits alone in
the freezing basement screening room, watching the picture.
His reaction?

"Lemme tell you something—if you thought *Hercules* was a
stiff when you saw it—and it *was* a stiff when you saw it, not one
of your all-time cinema greats—my God, you should have seen
it when *I* saw it—the color made you sick it was so terrible but
the color was sensational compared to the sound. See, they had
loused up the sound track something awful. There's a ship-
wreck scene, and the mast of the ship—this *huge* mast—it comes
crashing down to the deck. Well, when it hits there is dead silence. Nothing. Then a little later, Steve Reeves—you remember Steve Reeves?—didn't sound so good when he talked but
terrific muscles—anyway, a little later Steve Reeves is having a
love scene with a girl and *CRASH*—here comes the sound of
the goddam mast hitting the deck. It didn't get any better after
that, either, I can assure you. Anyway, I bought the American
rights for $120,000 and went to work."

The "work" consisted of what most industry figures agree
was the most aggressive campaign any film ever had. If you
think Paramount did a job selling *Gatsby* or *King Kong*, that was
bush-league stuff compared to what Levine did. He spent triple
what the movie cost him on newspaper ads alone. He bought
billboard space and space in comic books. You couldn't turn on
the damn radio without hearing someone hawking this muscle-
man movie.

And he went directly to the enemy—television—and spent
another quarter of a million dollars on advertisements. Not
only did he have these tv ads, he showed all the best stuff from
the movie on the ads, secure in the knowledge that no one
would dream there wasn't more of the same awaiting them at
the theatre.

Then he ordered over six hundred prints—which isn't uncommon today, but it sure was then—and he gave a party for a
thousand people at the Waldorf-Astoria for another forty
grand.

Now, out in Hollywood the executives are looking out from
their foxholes and they can't believe it. This independent from

Boston is going crazy—they *know* he's crazy because they've all seen the picture. It was available for a year but they all passed on it. Their business was to judge public taste and they knew nobody was going to want to see *Hercules*.

They were only wrong by twenty million dollars, which is what the picture grossed.

Levine never stopped running throughout the sixties, and long before *The Graduate*—his most prosperous enterprise—shattered everybody's concept of what the audiences were looking for in a hero, Levine had become the most famous and the most successful independent film producer in the world. And probably because of that word—*independent*—he has never been much loved in Southern California.

It's kind of ironic that Levine, maybe the archetypical Hollywood mogul, has always been acutely uncomfortable in Hollywood. He goes rarely, only when he has to, and usually he stays in his hotel suite, conducts his business as quickly as possible, and, as quickly as possible, takes the next plane out. He's a Boston boy and he always will be. He also defies the mogul tradition in that he is neither fast talking nor cigar smoking; he's a slow talker moving up to medium when excited, and a lifelong nonsmoker—pipes and cigarettes, as well as cigars.

He is an enormously antiestablishment figure that the media have fixed in the public mind for their purposes. (Once when a national magazine referred to him as a chain cigar smoker, he called the writer and asked why he'd written that, since it was so blatantly untrue. The writer said, "You don't smoke cigars? You really don't?"—pause, then—"Well, you should.")

Eventually, at the peak of his fame and success, Levine sold his company and retired. It didn't take, he still had all that energy. So, edging into his seventies, he decided to make a comeback. The vehicle he chose was Cornelius Ryan's posthumous bestseller, which began with this opening sentence:

> Shortly after 10 A.M. on Sunday, September 17th, 1944, from airfields all over southern England, the greatest armada of troop-carrying aircraft ever assembled for a single operation took to the air.

In other words, Levine wasn't making it easy on himself. But he was determined to finance as big a movie as any ever made.

And to see that the film was in profit before it ever reached the screen.

Not your everyday gamble. And to risk all that at his age becomes even more remarkable when you remember the poverty he came from, because most wealthy men who started poor cling to their money with ever-increasing determination as the years go on. Levine had enough money to take the challenge. But, as he's said, "If it had gone bad, I would not have been rich anymore."

In 1974, he set out to make it all happen. . . .

As if the size of the Ryan epic weren't enough—it dealt with the greatest airborne operation of World War II—the specific subject matter didn't make anything a lot easier or more commercial.

Briefly, the story Ryan told dealt with the Battle of Arnhem. Montgomery, the British military leader, came up with a plan to end the war by Christmas of '44. Put as simply as possible, Montgomery's notion was to airlift thirty-five thousand Allied paratroopers, mainly American, three hundred miles and drop them behind German lines in Holland, where they were to capture and hold a series of vital bridges.

Simultaneously, a British armored corps of thirty thousand vehicles was to crash through the German lines, cross the successive bridges, and race over the final and most crucial one, Arnhem Bridge, which led them straight into the industrial heart of Germany, thereby crippling the German forces and bringing surrender. It was a brilliant and audacious plan—

—only it failed.

In other words, this wasn't *The Longest Day*, where everybody got to leave the theatre waving the flag. This was a tragedy. Happy endings did not abound. It was a miasmal, mistake-filled conflict that the Allies lost.

Not your most commercial idea.

And Levine's choice for director, Richard Attenborough, was not a commercial one either. Attenborough had won awards with his first two pictures, *Oh! What a Lovely War* and *Young Winston*, but they had failed at the box office.

I had seen both films, liked *Young Winston* and thought *Lovely War* brilliant. Not only that, the former showed tremendous skill at dealing with size and scope, while the latter had a marvelous incisive eye toward handling antiwar material. So I was thrilled at the chance of working with Attenborough, and I wanted very much to write *Bridge*. And he wanted me to do it.

Richard Attenborough is by far the finest, most decent human being I've met in the picture business. But our first meeting was dreadful. It took place in London, where I was on my way back from location in France for *Marathon Man*. We talked for quite some time and it was pleasant as could be.

Except that afterward, his impression was that I didn't want to do the movie and mine was that he definitely didn't want me to do it.

Eventually, we tried again, this time in America, and our misconceptions were put to bed and we began to work. This was in the summer of '75.

The Battle of Arnhem is almost totally unknown in America, but in England, probably because the British cherish their disasters so, it is the second most famous encounter of the war, topped only by Dunkirk.

So I returned to London and every day for several weeks I read books in the morning and night and talked with Attenborough in the afternoons. There are so many books about Arnhem in England that it seemed to me at the time that every man who was involved must have written his memoirs about it.

Our problem was in trying to find a story line.

The Ryan book is well over 650 pages of not the largest print. It is filled with fabulous material. And these other books added still more stuff. I would tell him about something I'd just read and ask did he want to include it, and more often than not, the answer was yes, if we can. The heroism displayed was remarkable—on both sides. Arnhem will probably go down as the last major battle in which any of the old romantic notions of war still held true. The Bulge, which followed it, was vicious and dirty by comparison.

The movie was always intended to run close to three hours—it was impossible to tell the story in less time.

But *which* story? There were so damn many.

It became clear that there was no way I would be able to finish a first draft screenplay before late fall of '75.

Which presented a terrible problem for Mr. Levine.

From the first time I met him, he was totally convinced of

one thing: *A Bridge Too Far* was going to open on June 15, 1977.

"We will open June fifteenth of '77," he said.

That was fixed, for whatever reasons, in his mind. And since he was, in effect, the studio, we knew that June fifteenth was going to be our release date.

We also knew that this three-hour story was going to take approximately six months to shoot. And it had to shoot in Holland, because that's where the bridges were.

Because of the weather conditions in Holland, it was crucial to be finished with photography by October of '76. Counting back six months, that meant we had to start in April of that year.

But my script wouldn't be done till, say, November of '75. Well, you can't risk a giant undertaking without top personnel who have had experience with this kind of massive operation. These technicians—production designers, cinematographers, at least thirty in all—are in demand. If Levine waited till he had a script, the chances were strong that the crew Attenborough needed would be busy on other pictures.

But he went ahead, took the risk, and hired them. If my script stunk, if it was unusable, they had to be paid. Not only that, preliminary production had to start.

Without a word on paper, Levine was now in for over two million dollars. . . .

Obviously, every writer feels pressure when he tries to make something work. But I've never felt as much pressure as when I went on trying to figure out *Bridge*, because I'd never had as much of one man's money riding on anything before. (Everyone, I think, was affected by the personal financing of the film. The crew in Holland, when we got to shooting, talked of it all the time. They hustled their tails off—I've never seen a crew work as hard.)

A movie, as a rough rule of thumb, runs a minute per page of screenplay. So I had to write approximately 175 pages of script, far more than I'd ever previously done. The length made so many new and different problems. Climaxes could not come at the same intervals as in something of more normal length.

Another rule. In a screenplay you always attack your story as late as possible. You enter each scene as close as you can to the end (movie scenes are, for the most part, terribly short compared to scenes in novels or even short stories). You also enter your story as late as you can.

But which story?

There were simply too many incidents that cried out for inclusion—*five* Victoria Crosses were awarded for heroism at Arnhem; that's England's highest military honor and it doesn't get awarded easily. Surely I needed those five.

Bridge was also intended to lure an all-star cast. So I had to try to write a bunch of parts that might appeal to stars—

—problem—

—none of the main characters in the Ryan book died. Well, you can't have an antiwar movie where all the leads live. So I began to fiddle with trying to make small roles, roles that would be instantly sympathetic—so that I could have someone to kill in the story.

Goddammit, though, which story?

Yes, I had problems, problems of time, problems of story, problems of length, on and on—but there were some problems I was lucky enough not to know about—

—for example, gliders.

When the air armada that opens Ryan's book took off from England, there were five thousand planes of various kinds involved—plus twenty-five hundred gliders. Most of the troops were carried into Holland via gliders. Well, when I finally got around to writing that sequence, I had a gay old time, going from this glider to that, one to another, inside then outside, whatever I wanted. What I didn't know when I wrote it was this—

—there weren't any gliders. Not anywhere. No matter how hard people tried to find one, they had no luck. (Gliders are meant to crash land, and that accounted for their absence.)

Well, if I'd known that we would have to build maybe one glider *in toto* and parts of some others and the rest would have to be made by movie magic, I don't know if I ever would have gotten started.

What finally untracked me was this: I lucked into the structure.

There was a scene I knew we had to have where a British general explained to his armored commanders what was about to happen, how they were about to belt across all these bridges the paratroopers had taken and wheel into Germany. I fiddled with his speech and it went like this at the end:

```
                    GENERAL HORROCKS
          I like to think of this as one of
          those American Western films--the
          paratroops, lacking substantial
          equipment, always short of food--
          these are the besieged homestead-
          ers. And the Germans, naturally,
          are the bad guys.
               (he pauses; then--)
          And we, my friends, are the caval-
          ry--on the way to the rescue.
```

That was the light bulb at last going on. Because I realized, for all its size and complexity, *Bridge* was a cavalry-to-the-rescue story—one in which the cavalry fails to arrive, ending, sadly, one mile short.

That was my spine, and everything that wouldn't cling I couldn't use. *All five* Victoria Cross stories fell out of the picture. Super material went by the boards. But it had to.

The first draft was done by November and was well received. Shortly thereafter, Levine began one of the most remarkable weeks in his long, remarkable career. . . .

In order for his gamble to pay off, what he needed were stars. For two main reasons:

(1) Movies are no longer a local operation; they are, all the most successful ones, international. And stars still have meaning in foreign markets.

(2) In foreign countries, there are still giant theatre chains and distribution companies, and they are wildly competitive with one another because of a continual shortage of product. What that means is, if Japan represents five percent of the world movie market, a

smash can do a tremendous amount of business. (*Tow-ering Inferno*, for example, took in over sixteen million dollars in Japan alone, more than the entire cost of the picture.)

Well, if my chain bought *Towering Inferno*—and I could only get it by outbidding your chain—that means that my theatres take in all that money and you are stuck playing Bruce Lee imitation contests.

What Levine planned to do was to try to assemble a package that would eventually prove so appealing to the chains and dis-tributors that they would pay him record-breaking sums of money in advance of receiving the film, and with those ad-vances he would pay for the film as it went along.

Obviously, there were bobby traps. Like (a) what if he couldn't assemble an appealing enough cast? Or (b) what if the distributors wouldn't come up with the sums he needed? Or (c) what if they did come up with enough and then the picture got into trouble and ran wildly over budget—there was no one to turn to, he would be stuck with the overrun.

In early January of '76, Levine and Attenborough went to Los Angeles for the talent raid. Certain English performers were already set—Dirk Bogarde, Anthony Hopkins, Laurence Olivier—but the crucial American performers were nonexis-tent.

By "crucial" the foreign distributors meant two names: Rob-ert Redford or Steve McQueen.

Levine felt he had a decent shot at them: Redford was famil-iar with the project and had let it be known that he looked on it not unfavorably. McQueen was not familiar with it, but he and Attenborough had known each other for years, since they'd act-ed together in *The Great Escape* and *The Sand Pebbles*.

They arrived on a Monday and set to work. Redford agreed to meet on Friday. Attenborough got the script to McQueen, who agreed to read it overnight and have lunch the following day.

Now two problems arose, the first involving paying stars per-centages for their agreeing to work. All stars get profit percent-ages, and the biggest ones work off gross.

Levine knew he couldn't pay any percentages because he

needed too many stars. So he had to make up for that lack with salary. The figure of a quarter of a million dollars a week was agreed on, half a million a week for either Redford or McQueen.

Those numbers were, at the time, gasping, and news of the project did not go unnoticed among the agents of Hollywood.

But now came an unexpected crusher: The agents demanded guarantees. What Levine had hoped to do was take the actors' acceptances and use them to flush out the foreign distributors. In other words, pay the actors as he got paid for them.

Many agents doubted the project would ever happen. Levine was not young, he had been away, etc. And they demanded protection for their clients. "Did I scream," Levine said. "I never screamed louder in my life. I'd never given in to a guarantee before, I swore I never would—but I didn't have much room to maneuver; if I did, I didn't see it." So anything Levine agreed to pay out now, he was legally bound for. Himself.

They met with McQueen the next day at the Brown Derby in Beverly Hills. McQueen was prompt, courteous, terrific.

But he said no.

Permanently.

This was Tuesday, and now the Friday meeting with Redford was the shooting match. On Wednesday, Jimmy Caan said yes. Gene Hackman too. So did Elliott Gould. By Thursday they had Sean Connery and Michael Caine. That night they got word that Ryan O'Neal was in.

Friday, they went to the Burbank lot where Redford was getting *President's Men* ready for an April opening. He was interested but he was exhausted; there was still a ton of work to be done on the Watergate film. He asked for the weekend, promising to give them an answer by Monday.

That weekend, McQueen came back in.

Or wanted to. But there was now only one star part left and it had been officially offered to Redford.

The reason for McQueen's change of heart had to do with another film that was casting at the same time and which had raised their money on the promise of delivering him to star. When he refused, they kept upping their offer and he kept refusing. Finally they reached three million and he said no.

Then someone got the idea of doing the two films back-to-back—McQueen insisted on both or nothing—and he would play three weeks in one, three weeks in the other.

McQueen's representatives and the other film's lawyers begin flooding Levine's hotel rooms. They explain that McQueen is now available. Levine explains that he has no part to offer. It's all up to Redford now.

"You'll never get Redford," McQueen's people assure Levine. "I know one thing and it's that you have no chance in this world to get Redford and I don't think you ought to take the chance of passing up McQueen."

But there is no part to offer McQueen.

"You're not listening," McQueen's people say. "You will not get Redford. Not possible. Now do you want to know McQueen's terms? Three million for three weeks. He'll do the two pictures, you'll schedule them so he doesn't have any time in between, six million for six weeks."

Anything else? Levine wonders.

"He has some people he'd like to take along."

How much for the friends? Levine asks.

"Fifty thousand maybe."

Levine nods.

"Then there's the house in Palm Springs."

The what?

"Steve's house. He's got a place in Palm Springs he can't get rid of. So you'll buy that."

That's very nice of me, Levine says. How much do I get to buy the house for?

"$470,000."

The demands go on and on, the madness building, until the weekend is over and Redford says yes, he'll do *Bridge.* Levine is on the next plane out, the raid done. He's been there for nine days, the longest stay of his career, but he's got his cast.

And he's also personally on the line for well over ten million dollars. Was he worried? He said, "You've got to remember a couple of things about me. First, I've always been a gambler. Second, I'm not exactly on my first time around. I've set some records no one'll ever touch, no matter what they do. When I did *Jack the Ripper*—this was after *Hercules*—I bought *Jack the Ripper* and I booked it into 643 theatres across the country and I gave a luncheon for all the major exhibitors.

"And I borrowed a million dollars—cash—for half an hour. Had a lot of trouble getting it, too, but finally it arrived at this luncheon—one million dollars—a thousand thousand dollar bills—is that a million?—I think it is. Twenty Brink's guards move into this room with all these exhibitors and they're to bring me the bills—cost me nine thousand dollars to borrow the million. Anyway, I took those bills—*and I held them high in the air*—and I said to those exhibitors, 'the next time you see this million it's going to be working for you—TV ads, newspaper ads, billboards—that's what I'm spending on this picture.' And I spent it too. Every penny. And we opened across the country—643 theatres at once—*and we dropped dead in every one!* You'd think somewhere, a small town maybe, someplace, it would have done business. But no. That's a record they'll never come close to. I've got a lot of them." He pauses. "Was I worried? You think I'm crazy? I couldn't sleep. Well, that's not saying a lot because I don't sleep anyway very much. But if I could have slept, I couldn't sleep."

That Levine was able to get any rest at all during the six months of shooting was due to two factors: the weather (it turned out to be the driest summer of the century in Holland, and the picture never lost a full day due to rain) and Richard Attenborough.

Richard Attenborough has had a most unusual career. He became a British stage star before he was twenty, playing the lead in the adaptation of Graham Greene's novel *Brighton Rock*. This was in 1943, and after the war, he became a British film star in the movie version of that book. He has remained a star in England ever since. He has won their equivalent of the Oscar for male actor, and he was the star of the original production of Agatha Christie's *Mousetrap*. He has also produced and starred in several marvelous films, *Seance on a Wet Afternoon*, among others.

He was knighted during the production of *A Bridge Too Far*. True story as to how he found out about his knighthood. Attenborough loves painting, and the ambition of his life has been to be placed on the board of trustees of the Tate Gallery in London. One morning he's going through the mail and there's a letter from the prime minister. He opens it.

And there it is—he has been invited to join the board. Now,

Attenborough is known as a very emotional man. He will cry if you tell him the wind is changing. Naturally, news like this reduces him to rubble. He's about to go tell his wife the news when he sees, on the bottom of the pile, yet another letter from 10 Downing Street. He opens this one and it tells him he's going to be knighted.

His reaction is right and proper: He is convinced he has totally lost his sanity.

His wife, Sheila, in an upstairs room, sees her husband come through the door, gripped by tears, holding out these letters to her, muttering, "Please—you've got to help me; do these letters say what I think they say?"

Having suggested on occasion that many film directors are given more credit than they are always due, I would like to talk about the one thing involved with the job that no one gives them credit for.

It's *hard*.

I don't mean hard like it was hard for Van Gogh to fill a canvas or for Kant to construct a universe.

I mean hard like in coal mining. Directing a film is one of the most brutally difficult occupations imaginable. We are not aware of this particular facet of the job because, in the first place, we only read about directors in tranquillity—when they are moving around the country selling their films. And they are only sent on these junkets when the studio feels the product has a chance to be, or has already proven to be, commercially successful.

In other words, we most often hear from directors when they are reflecting on success. But that man—the director in the Sherry Netherland sipping Scotch while he chats with an envoy from the *Times* or *New York* magazine—that man isn't a director anymore, he's no longer an artist, he has taken off that hat. He is a salesman now. And the reason that's the only man you see, and not the person trying to function in crisis, is because when he's directing, that's *work*, and the last thing anyone needs on the set is interruptions from outsiders.

How hard, as Mr. Carson would ask, is it to direct a film?

In the first place, for a major film, it is terribly time consuming. When *A Bridge Too Far* opened, in June of '77, Attenborough had spent more than twenty-four months of his life focused entirely and relentlessly on one single piece of material.

Remember our earlier division of the making of a film into three equally important parts: (1) preparation of the script and casting, (2) shooting the film, (3) editing and scoring. The writer is usually present only for the first part, the performers for the second, the composer for the third.

The director, if he cares, and all the good ones care desperately, is as involved in script talks as he is in dealing with the composer over a year later. He doesn't write the script, any more than he composes the score, but he imparts what he hopes you can get down. He has to maintain both passion and objectivity over a long period of time.

In Attenborough's case, it wasn't just twenty-four months; it was twenty-four months, seven days a week, for an average of eighteen hours per day. (When shooting was finally finished, Attenborough went to bed and literally slept around the clock for three days, waking up to eat, then back to bed again, very much dead to the world.)

There was also a great deal of travel involved. He lives in London, the producer and writer were in New York, many of the actors were in Los Angeles, and the movie was shot in Holland. If this wasn't enough, there was constant shuttling all across Europe for casting—nine trips to Germany alone.

For over ten months of 1976, he lived on the second floor of a small (twelve-room) hotel in Deventer, Holland. On an average day, he would be up by six, be on the set well before the morning start time of eight or whatever it was, stay till late afternoon when shooting was done.

Then he would go back to a factory the company had found empty and turned into a construction area and cutting rooms. There, in a makeshift theatre, he would watch the rushes of the previous day's shooting. Then a meeting with crucial staff people—the production design staff, the special-effects staff, the location heads—whoever was vital for the next day's shooting, because you've got to try to get your problems ironed out before you're shooting.

Following this, at nine, ten, whenever, he would return to his hotel and have a bite of dinner along with more meetings— production problems, cost problems, staff problems—and after *that* meeting, eleven, twelve, whenever, he would go to his room, try and study whatever the shooting could cover tomorrow, make notes for himself—

—then to bed.

Now, this kind of thing is obviously wearing on anybody, but in the case of a film director there's one additional element always present: the pressure of failure. Studios (or in this case, Levine) are very aware of two things: what a picture grosses (Attenborough had never had a hit, remember), and sometimes, even more importantly, what it costs to make.

And the pressure of cost was never as heavy on Attenborough as during the Million Dollar Hour.

The Million Dollar Hour was the hour from eight to nine in the morning, Sunday, the third of October, on Nijmegen Bridge.

To explain just why this was so, I've got to backtrack again a moment. Nijmegen (pronounced "*nigh*-maygen") is one of the biggest bridges in Europe. If you want to think of San Francisco's Golden Gate or New York's George Washington in this country, you're dealing with the same scale.

We needed to shoot on Nijmegen Bridge. The climactic action involving the Redford part took place there in 1944, and since authenticity was vital in every aspect of this production, the use of Nijmegen Bridge had to be cleared for the company.

Well, you just don't call up the Nijmegen Town Council and say, "Hello there, we're making this war movie, close the bridge for us, please." They *use* their bridges in Holland and you can't just shut something off to suit a movie company's needs, not anything the size of this bridge, because if you did, the traffic jam would likely spread into neighboring countries. What was finally agreed on, after negotiations that literally went on for half a year, was the following: They would close the bridge for one hour only, starting at eight in the morning, for several successive Sundays.

October 3 was to be Redford's last Sunday. Which meant that if the weather made shooting impossible, we could not duplicate the conditions until the following Sunday, *if* the good people of Nijmegen could be talked into letting us have the bridge an extra hour a week down the line.

Redford was actually contracted to work till Wednesday; he

was getting out ahead of schedule. So, since we needed this sequence, if the weather stopped us again, Redford would have to stay over the extra days, Thursday, Friday, Saturday, until we could shoot again the following Sunday.

There is a word in the movie business and it is called "overage." It refers to what you pay an artist if you go beyond the boundaries of his contract. (People are hired for specific lengths of time, and if you need them for longer, assuming they are available, you have to pay them for it, usually a percentage of their weekly salary.)

Well, considering Redford's weekly salary, his overage would come to $125,000.

That's per day.

Multiply that by four, and keeping him till next Sunday means half a million dollars.

That's just for him.

This is also the end of the giant part of the production. There were three days left, but they were basically two scenes involving Dirk Bogarde. The movie was due to finish Wednesday. That was the final day of shooting; everyone was paid only until then.

There were 275 people working that morning. And if we couldn't shoot, it meant that all of them would get extra salary (and meals and lodging and whatever else you can think of) to wait around to shoot the following Sunday.

If we could get the bridge the following Sunday. (The feeling was we couldn't.)

And *if* the weather, which was bad and getting worse, would be shootable a week down the line. (The guess was that it probably would not be.)

So when this was called a Million Dollar Hour, that's speaking conservatively. Everyone was standing around in the dawn chill, hoping. The unit call had been for six in the morning on location at the bridge, which meant that you had to get up hours before that. As well as being cold, it begins to look like rain. A lot like rain. And there is a terrible cutting wind. Personally I have never, on a movie set, felt anything close to such tension.

Attenborough's feeling the tension, too, more than any of the rest of us. *But he can't show it.* (A crew on location is wildly

mercurial—they can go from happy efficiency to sullen plod-
ding in a wink. Attenborough has a marvelous relationship with
his crew because he's genuinely good with people. And he also
always helps—if there's any kind of move to make from one
kind of shot to another, he's always grabbing heavy equipment,
lugging it along, and when the crew sees that—the director
hustling that way—there's not much they can do but join him.

A director on location is very much like a military leader and
he has to behave in like manner so the men won't mutiny.
There was a moment earlier in the shooting when Anthony
Hopkins, who portrayed Colonel Frost, the hero of Arnhem,
was playing a scene where he had to run from his building to
the rest of his troops, headquartered across the street, and the
street was in control of the Germans; there was constant sniper
fire. It was not a safe place, that street, and Hopkins did the
scene, running rapidly while the Germans fired at him.

The real Frost happened to be on the set that day, and after
the first take, while they were getting ready to try it again, the
real Frost said to Hopkins, "Ah, you're running too fast," and
Hopkins said, somewhat stunned, "Too fast?" and Frost answered, "Yes, you would never run that fast. You have to show
the Germans and your own men your contempt for danger.")

Well, Attenborough standing there on Nijmegen Bridge with
the Million Dollar Hour approaching wasn't about to show
fear, either, so he does what he always does in moments of
stress: He whistles Handel and walks around in little mystic pat-
terns that may have meaning to him, certainly to no one else.

Eight o'clock is coming nearer and nearer and things seem as
if they're starting to break. Everything's got to work because
there's no time to go back and do things over but the weather
seems as if it's going to be clear enough to shoot and now Redford's in position and the stunt men portraying German soldiers are climbing high in the girders of Nijmegen Bridge,
roping themselves in, not for safety but because that's what the
Germans did there in their final defense, and then the signal
comes that all the stunt men are secured and you can begin to
see the confidence flowing into Attenborough, because there
can't be anything wrong on this shot, he's thought so much
about it, covered it from every angle the mind of man can come
up with, and as crew members come running up to him with

last-minute questions he's snapping back the answers crisp and fast, "Is the machine gun nest all right like that?" and "Yes, fine" from Attenborough without a pause, and this questioner runs off while another comes up, going, "Will you see the sentry box emplacement in this shot?" and the immediate "We will, thank you," takes care of that and "Have the Sherman tanks been positioned properly?" and Attenborough quick takes a look, and says, "The Sherman tanks are splendid as you have them," and now an assistant director comes up behind with "The corpses, Sir Richard," and even though that's not a complete question, Attenborough knows precisely what to say and he says it, "The corpses must keep their eyes shut at all times, all corpses will be visible in this shot," and that cry echoes along the bridge as the assistant takes a megaphone and shouts to the extras playing dead Germans, "Corpses—listen now, you corpses—all corpses will keep eyes shut at all times while the cameras are rolling—you got that?—*not one bloody blink from one bloody corpse and that's final!*" and shooting time is almost on us now, and the rain *is* going to hold off, and now another assistant runs up, asking, "What about the smoke pots?" and Attenborough, on top of his game, replies, "You may start the smoke pots now, thank you very much," and right then, this trusted aide comes roaring up, excitedly saying, "What about the jeeps in the orchard, sir?"

I was standing by Attenborough and for a moment his eyes glazed over and he had to be thinking that suddenly the world had gone mad or was the world sane and the mistake his—had he forgotten—forgotten something vital? He was standing on a freezing bridge—what orchard? what jeeps? Was there some part of the shot that he'd neglected, something involving an orchard and jeeps, and here he was, with smoke pots going and, high in girders, guys hanging and a star ready to shoot and 275 people waiting but this question must be answered because what if it ruins the shot and if the shot's lost a million dollars are lost and—

—then he smiled very sweetly to his aide and said, "We will not require jeeps in the orchard at all, thank you so much for reminding me." This, it turns out, referring to the last half of a later scene to be shot afterward, the first half having been shot days before, all this in another location, and what this trusted aide had done was pick this particular moment to inquire if Attenborough's camera angle for this future sequence would require the placement of jeeps in the distant background in order to match what had been done before.

The weather held, the shooting on the bridge went quickly, the last major disaster had been averted. As we left the bridge, there was a genuine feeling of exultation. Attenborough was cheery as usual, no more whistling needed that day. Later, perhaps, but not then. There are always "laters" lurking in the lives of film directors, jeeps in the orchard that need tending to.

As I left Nijmegen Bridge that morning, with everybody on a high, I thought back to an earlier morning, two years before, when I had been walking along the street with Levine after he'd gotten a terrible piece of news—I forgot what, exactly, maybe that we couldn't use the bridges in Holland, which would mean we couldn't make the picture in Holland but probably in Yugoslavia, which has lots of tanks but no bridges, which would mean he would have to build his own bridge and keep reusing it under different disguises, except you couldn't build an entire bridge, only half, and only shoot from certain angles, and whatever it was, it meant the whole shooting match was up for grabs.

He was moving slowly on his cane along the street and everyone was in a rotten mood and I remember asking him why he was involved in something when he didn't need it, all the grief, what was the point?

And he whirled on me and he took his cane and pointed it dead between my eyes and his voice got very loud there on the sidewalk with people eddying by. "I'm seventy years old," he said. *"I'm seventy years old and I want to do this thing."*

He did it. . . . Incredibly, *Bridge* was brought in on schedule and under budget.

And then, as I said at the start of all this, the reviews came out. Or more precisely, the American reviews.

I have long since given up trying to predict the reaction to a film, one I've been involved with or anybody else's. But in the case of *A Bridge Too Far,* I just knew one thing: The critics were going to love us.

I knew that for a lot of reasons: (1) I had enjoyed the whole two-year experience so much, I couldn't conceive of anybody spoiling our party. (2) I genuinely believed the film was that good. (I still do; *Bridge* and *Butch* are, for me, the two top films I've been involved with.)

(3) And this is the main reason: It seemed to me before we opened that half the civilized world had already seen the film and everybody went crazy.

This last was unusual—most films are done in as much secrecy as possible. But because of the way Levine sold the film, it seemed to me almost like an open shop. Cutting rooms were set up in Holland, and as soon as ten minutes of film were done, they were available to be viewed by anyone interested in buying the film. (Levine realized early on the quality of what he was getting, so he held off taking offers, confident that those offers would increase as time went on. He was right—*Bridge* was four million dollars into profit long before it was released; that might have happened before, but believe me, not often.)

When forty minutes of film were done, they were there for anyone to come to see. When we were halfway through, people would troop to Holland and take in the hour and a half.

And the word of mouth would not stop building.

These were tough professional movie people and they all were knocked out by what they saw. The size of it all, the fabulous photography by the late Geoffrey Unsworth, the performances, everything. (Maybe the most remarkable thing about the enterprise was this: All of the stars behaved impeccably. They arrived on time, knew what they were supposed to do, did it adroitly and well, and, when they were done, left happily. No ego displays whatsoever, and this with fourteen stars involved.)

When the movie was finally finished, everyone was flying. Convinced that we were going to have it all—the public and the critics flocking to us. (Commercially, by the way, the movie did well around the world—one of the most successful pictures of its genre ever. And in England we were nominated for a bunch of their Oscar equivalents and won several. Generally, the reception, outside of the United States, was very strong.)

But we did not make it with most of the important American critics. And I was stunned. Not that the critics were wrong. But the main thrust of the negative comments seemed to me amazing—

—they didn't believe us.

The reason that amazed me was it was one line of attack we never in this world expected—because *nothing* dealing with the spectacularity of the film is invented. All those incredible heroics were true. *Bridge* is at least as authentic as *All the President's Men* and everyone took that film as sooth.

Three quick examples. Dirk Bogarde played the role of a British general and one of the things he did was send British troops into a supposedly unoccupied area. Except he had information that German troops, heavily armed, had taken over the area. But he disregarded the information and sent the men to be slaughtered.

Didn't believe that.

The Jimmy Caan part involved perhaps the most extraordinary incident. He was a sergeant whose captain had been killed. What he does is he takes the corpse and drives a jeep wildly through German lines until he finds an Allied emergency medical area. And he carries the dead captain and puts him on an operating table. And a medical officer says, "Get that man out of here." And what does Caan do? He pulls out a gun, points it dead at the officer, and commands him to operate.

And it turns out his captain was alive.

Now, an enlisted man threatening an officer over a corpse, actually taking out a weapon and commanding the officer to obey him—I'd never heard of a thing like that.

Yawn.

I guess John Wayne had done that so often nobody gave it a second thought. Just another piece of phony Hollywood theatrics.

A lot of people didn't believe Ryan O'Neal in the role of General James Gavin—O'Neal was so obviously too young to play a top paratroop general. Well, O'Neal was too young—but so was Gavin; O'Neal when he acted the role was the same age as Gavin when he took part in the Arnhem battle. Gavin was, I think, the youngest general in the Army at the time. Now, if I could have written a scene explaining that, it might have gone like this:

BRITISH OFFICER
(quietly, to one of Gavin's
aides)

```
          I'd expected Gavin to be a bit more
          mature a fellow.

                    GAVIN'S AIDE
          A lot of people are surprised,
          sir--but they don't know that Gav-
          in's the youngest general we have.

                    BRITISH OFFICER
          Oh, very good, carry on.
```

Well, that would be like telling the audience, "Don't think about pink elephants." If I'd written the scene, everybody would have assumed it was there simply to explain the miscasting of Ryan O'Neal. Perhaps we should have tried for George C. Scott in the part—he would have been wrong, but maybe people would have believed him.

But this movie, depicting this famous part of modern British military history, could not and would not be anything but dead-on accurate. Attenborough would never have permitted it; he had too great a sense of responsibility. I've never been involved in a project where authenticity was more sought after and achieved. And in the end, as far as many American critics were concerned, that may have proved our undoing.

We were too real to be real. . . .

part three

Da Vinci

Introduction

A few months ago, when I was fiddling with the structure of this book, trying to figure what to put in and where, my nineteen-year-old daughter, Jenny, appeared holding a tattered paperback and said, "Do you know you're in this?"

I shook my head and asked her what the book was. She told me—a 1960 collection of essays, poems, and stories: *New World Writing #17*.

"There's a story of yours, called 'Da Vinci,' " she said then.

Now came a long pause. Mind totally blank. I was like some old toad blinking on a summertime log. Finally I said, "Oh yeah, I wrote that."

"*Obviously* you wrote it," she said. "What's it about?"

I hadn't the foggiest. She looked at me while I kept trying to remember. Finally, a flicker. "A barber," I told her.

"Well, I'm going to read it," and with that, she left me alone, trying to remember what in the world I'd put to paper half a lifetime ago. She came back a little later and tossed me the book. I asked her how it was.

"Not bad," she said. High praise, but then you'd have to know Jenny to realize that.

As a very strong rule, I never reread anything I've written. But now I was fascinated, because I'd never had the experience before of someone giving me something I'd done that I had so totally forgotten.

When I finished "Da Vinci" I was genuinely excited—not by the quality of the story, but because I realized it would make a wonderful subject for a short screenplay adaptation: It contains just about all the crucial problems that one has to deal with in translating a piece of narrative fiction into something fit for the screen.

What follows, then, is in four parts.

First: the reprinted short story.

Second: thought processes setting out some of the problems of doing an adaptation. The same processes I always go through.

Three: my screenplay adaptation of the story.

Four: comments from my peers—a production designer, a cinematographer, an editor, a composer, a director—concerning how they would like the material altered to improve it. Plus what *their* problems would be in order to make the material work.

My hope in this is that by the time we're done, we'll have taken a piece of fiction and seen it through all its various steps—not just mine, but everybody's.

In other words, fingers crossed, we're going to make a movie. . . .

chapter fourteen
The Short Story

Mr. Bimbaum arrived on the first day of marble season.

A light blue day, the middle of March. We were all out in the playground behind school. The earth was still hard, and here and there occasional puff piles of darkening snow dotted the ground. I was playing Little Pot with Porky McKee, running back, lagging up, then racing to see who was closer, when my father appeared, beckoning from the sidewalk.

"Go take a haircut," he called, his breath white in the pale blue afternoon.

"Now?" I said. "This minute? Can't you see I'm playing Little Pot with Porky McKee?"

"Go," he repeated, and he pointed down along the road. I waved good-by to Porky and ran.

My father was owner and proprietor of the only barbershop in town, a two-chair affair set in the midst of Main Street. Whenever he hired a new man, a filler for the second chair, I was the guinea pig. My father himself could not fulfill the function, being bald, totally, except for a fringe of fine white hair above his ears, which he handled himself.

I opened the barbershop door. The overhead bell squawked. The new barber rose. We eyed each other. Mr. Bimbaum was a small man, aging and paunchy, with long beautiful fingers. I jumped into the chair. "Hurry it up," I said. "I'm due back soon. I'm playing Little Pot with Porky McKee."

He did not answer, but stared silently, intensely. At my head. He bent down and looked up at it and stood on tiptoe and looked down at it and walked around it and placed his fingers on it and drew an imaginary replica of it in the air. Finally, he nodded and said one word.

"Spherical."

"What?"

"Head shape spherical," he announced. Then he reached for a clean striped towel and tucked it around my neck. "Name?" he asked.

"Willy," I said. He pumped the chair twice, adjusting my level. "Name?" I asked in my turn.

"H. Bimbaum," he answered.

I broke out laughing. I whooped, kicking my feet, doubling up, screaming. When I was finished, he took his time and carefully swatted me on top of the head with the flat of his hand.

"Hey," I said. "That hurt."

He nodded. "Was supposed to."

I looked at him. He was still staring at my head, tilting his own head this way and that, muttering unintelligible sounds. "What's the 'H' stand for?" I asked.

"That nobody finds out," he answered. "Nobody." He stood up on tiptoe and sighted along the part in my hair, squinting, one eye closed. "Some butcher gave you your last cut," he muttered.

"Yeah?" I said, and I pointed to the other chair. "Well, my father gave it to me."

He nodded again and leaned close. "Then your father is a butcher," he announced. "Now shut up and sit still."

With that he reached for his scissors.

A small pair, silver, with short rounded blades. He blew on the blades and rubbed them against his pant legs. Then he held the scissors high in the air and the silver caught the light, showering it about the room. I stared, listening as he brought the handles together, hearing the first soft "snip," and then, quickly, another "snip," and then another. I closed my eyes. The sounds made rhythms and I hummed silently along with "Jingle Bells" and "Put on Your Old Gray Bonnet" and "America the Beautiful." The blades never stopped singing as he moved around me, taking a tuft of hair, stepping back nodding, moving forward, taking another. I relaxed. The snips began to take on theme in addition to rhythm, and I stopped my silent humming, being content just to listen. I sat deeper in the chair; the music swelled, rolling in, filling the tiny shop, harmony now in addition to theme. It was a beautiful moment in my life; I sensed it then, although I didn't know why. I have felt it only one time since, when I first saw the village of Toledo braced before the storm El Greco had unleashed. I can describe it only as a moment of total calm, of complete relaxation, but a relaxation that has nothing to do with sleep. Rather, it is a respite born of the knowledge that the sign is up, "The Master is at work," and, at least for awhile, nothing is going to go wrong; no one is going to slip, stumbling on the everpresent banana peel that is always lurking just ahead of us as we walk along. Not this time, anyway; not just now.

"Done," Mr. Bimbaum said, as he floated the towel away from my body with a single rapid motion. I stepped out of the chair and eyed myself in the mirror. I looked, I thought, quite well.

"Thank you," I said. "You give a nice haircut."

"Nice!" and he snorted, picking up an old copy of *Liberty*, sitting down in the second chair. I waited. My father came in.

"He gives a nice haircut," I said.

My father walked around me, inspecting. "A trifle close, maybe," he began. Again the snort from behind the magazine.

"A trifle close," my father repeated. "But otherwise acceptable. Bimbaum," and the magazine lowered, "you got a job."

"Can I go now?" I asked. "I've got to get back to Porky McKee."

"Go," my father said.

I went. I ran out the door and down the middle of the street, across the railroad track, then up the hill to school. The marble crowd had dwindled but Porky was still there. He was playing Big Pot now, kneeling on the hard ground, concentrating on the half-dozen marbles left inside the chalked circle.

"Hurry up," I said. "Finish it off."

He did not answer.

"Come on, Porky. Hurry. Let's go."

He stared straight at the marbles, and I knew then he was mad. "Don't tell me hurry," he mumbled. "I'm taking my time."

"What's the matter with you?" I said. "I just got a haircut was all."

"Yeah?" he said. "Well, you been gone almost two hours." I looked up at the school clock over the main door. He was right. It had taken two hours.

"I'm sorry, Porky," I said. "I don't know what happened."

He glanced at me and was about to say something, but instead he stopped and stared. "Willy," he said finally, "that's a beautiful haircut. A really beautiful haircut."

"New barber," I answered. "Named Bimbaum."

We both started to laugh. . . .

The lure of Little Pot kept us more than occupied throughout the remainder of the darkening afternoon. But finally, when the cold dusk winds began and we could no longer see the circle from the lagging line, Porky and I called it quits and wandered home. I waved good-by to him at his front door and ran past the intervening trio of houses to mine. Walking inside, I shouted greetings to one and all. My mother answered, as always, from the kitchen.

Even today, years after her thoughtless and more than abrupt departure, I still think of my mother as waiting for me in the kitchen. She inhabited it completely, leaving it only for such mandatory tasks as shopping or sleeping or playing casino on alternate Thursdays with the Weinsteins, who lived down the block. She was forever cooking, baking, tidying up, so that the room always glistened, no matter how high the stack of pots and pans piled one atop the other in the sink. My mother believed in the curative power of food. Catch a cold? Have some chicken broth. Break your leg? Have a dumpling. And so it went. She was a good woman, kind and less obtuse than most of us, and I know that if they had ever given a Nobel Prize for *kreplach*, my mother would have won it every year.

"How's the new one?" she said to me, her eyes marking the progress of the rich brown stew bubbling on the stove.

"Look," I said and I walked forward, intercepting her gaze.

"Willy," she said. "My God, you're beautiful."

"His name's Bimbaum," I told her.

My mother nodded. "Nice name." She paused, staring at me. "Turn around slow."

I did. "Father's already hired him. I was there."

"Of course," she replied. "The man is obviously a craftsman."

"You want to know what he said about Father? He said Father was a butcher."

My mother shrugged. "That's strong language. Your father ain't exactly a butcher. But he ain't exactly a craftsman either. Why did he say such a thing?"

I was about to explain when the back door opened and my father appeared, accompanied by Mr. Bimbaum. "Ho, ho, ho," my father said, embracing my mother. "Have I got a surprise. Bimbaum here is renting the spare room. For a small fee. Meals extra. Bimbaum, this is my wife, Emma. Emma, say hello."

"Hello," my mother said.

Mr. Bimbaum nodded.

"You gave my son Willy here a fine cut," she went on.

"Of course," he answered. And then, "Where's my room?"

"Up the back stairs," my mother said. "Where's your luggage?"

"Luggage is here," and he held up a small, battered brown suitcase.

"That's all you got?"

"What am I?" he snorted. "A princess in a fairy book? No, I ain't no princess. I'm a barber. A barber needs scissors. Inside here I got scissors. What more luggage?"

"Up the back stairs," my mother repeated, louder this time. "My son Willy here will show you."

"I'm so blind I can't find it?" Mr. Bimbaum said, stopping me. He walked to the stairs. "If I shouldn't be able to locate it for myself, I'll yell for help." He went on muttering to himself a moment more, laughing and shrugging his shoulders. Then he stopped. "Food is when?"

"Food is when I say so," my mother answered.

"Equitable," Bimbaum nodded. "Very equitable." He disappeared up the back stairs. We waited in the kitchen, listening as the door to the spare room opened and closed sharply. With that, my mother turned and faced my father.

"Ho, ho, ho," she said. "Some surprise."

"Don't you like him?" my father asked, smiling very hard. "I thought sure you would like him. I said to myself, Emma is sure to like Mr. . . . ."

"Since when do we run a boarding house?" my mother interrupted.

"Since when do you object to making a little money? Business ain't so good."

"Business is the same as always. And that man got the manners of a pig."

"Well," my father shrugged. "Maybe he ain't sociable. And maybe he ain't refined. But Emma," and he came closer to her, taking her hands, "Emma, you should see him cut hair. This afternoon. I watched. This afternoon he did Mr. Dietrich, the postman, the one with a head that looks like a nose. In ninety minutes, Mr. Dietrich was beautiful. The man's an artist, Emma. A real artist, don't you see? Where else should he live?"

"I don't know," my mother said. "But he's here now."

"Then you don't mind?"

In answer, she walked quickly to the foot of the stairs and cupped her hands around her mouth. "Hey, you!" she hollered at the top of her voice. "Hey, Bimbaum! Food!"

And so Mr. Bimbaum came to live with us.

Until his arrival, ours had always been a happy home. Nothing idyllic; just happy. We all got along well, kept our squabbling to a minimum, and managed to laugh a good deal. But right from the start, the addition of Mr. Bimbaum changed everything.

For the better. He and my father would leave together for the shop in the morning, each carrying a brown paper bag which held two thick meat sandwiches, a sprig of parsley (my mother was always a great believer in parsley), and some kind of fruit. Each night they returned and we had supper together, and then they would retire to the living room to talk about cutting hair. Sometimes my mother and I would join them, but more often we chose to remain in the kitchen, playing casino, but with the doors wide open so that the rhythms of Mr. Bimbaum's scissors could come through. What they did in the living room seemed to me to be nothing but an endless discussion of head shapes, scalp diseases, and scissors technique; but to my father, there was never enough of it. For always it was Bimbaum who terminated their talk, hurrying through the kitchen, nodding to us, then up the back stairs to bed. My father would join us soon after, singing some Polish folk song or other, his face contorted with rich emotion, always accompanying himself on an imaginary mandolin. Whenever my father sang, it was a good thing, showing inner contentment. But unfortunately he was tone deaf and the sounds, sincere as they were, were not particularly pleasant. "Better he should be a little sadder," my mother took to muttering. "If he sings those high notes again my ears will pop." But he sang the high notes, bravely, not flinching, his face a picture of passion or longing or joy. It was irresistible. We found ourselves laughing louder, longer, and life was nothing but peaches and heavy cream.

For two weeks.

It was evening. Roast and dumplings simmering on the stove, my mother and I watching. Mr. Bimbaum appeared, nodded, and hurried up the stairs. A pause. One minute. Five minutes. Ten. My father walked in. No sound. No singing. Walking past us without a word, he went to the living room. We could hear the sounds of the evening paper.

"No songs?" my mother called.

No answer.

"What is it?" I asked.

"Bad," my mother answered. "Something bad." She hurried out of the kitchen and I heard whispering, then silence, then more whispering. Then my mother was back.

"That Porky McKee," she sighed. "And I thought he was supposed to be your friend."

In a minute I was out of the house running. When I got to Porky's, I rang the bell. The door opened.

"I knew it would be you," Porky said. "I just knew it."

"Porky," I said, "what happened? My father won't talk. My mother won't tell me. What did you do?"

"It was your fault, Willy. Some of it was."

"What did you do, Porky?"

He paused, his voice getting softer. "I had Mr. Bimbaum give me a haircut."

"What's so bad about that?"

"You don't understand, Willy. Your father. His chair was empty. Bimbaum's was busy."

"No," I said. "You didn't do it."

He nodded, whispering now. "I did. I did. I waited for Bimbaum."

"How could you do such a thing, Porky? Don't you know my father got feelings?"

"I had to, Willy. I just had to. You been talking so much about that Bimbaum. I had to find out for myself. And you know what? You were right. Look," and he turned around. "Some haircut, huh?"

I nodded. "You never looked better. What kind of head shape you got?"

"Semi-triangular."

I nodded again. "You're right," I said. "It was my fault. I got a big mouth."

"I'm sorry, Willy. You know I didn't mean anything. It's just that I had to do it. You explain that to your father, will you?"

"Sure," I muttered. "Sure." We waved good-by. I walked home.

I did not sleep well that night, my eyes would not close. I stormed and tossed and stared out the window. I turned on the bed light and read half of a Hardy Boys book. I turned on the overhead light and played Big Pot by myself on the rug. I had wild thoughts. My stomach ached. Twice I raided the icebox, stuffing myself. It was a bad evening.

But the ones that followed were no better. I slept little. In school I misspelled "Illinois," and Porky kept clobbering me in Little Pot. Each day I grew more and more nervous. I confided in no one, not even Porky, which was silly; he would have understood.

Because haircut time was coming around again and I wanted Mr. Bimbaum to do it.

By the end of the fourth week, I was shaggy; the tops of my ears were disappearing behind the underbrush. I knew that I had to do something. I suggested to my mother that she and my father take a trip some place, any place, for a day's vacation. She laughed at me. I watched my father closely, hoping he would catch a cold; he was as healthy as a cow.

Finally, in desperation, on a Saturday afternoon, I spoke to my mother about it.

She handed me a cake of soap. "Go wash your mouth," she said.

"But you don't understand," I began. "You ..."

"Stab your father in the back," she interrupted. "My own little Judas."

"OK," I said. "OK."

"Go take a haircut," she commanded. "This minute. No haircut, no food. Now go."

It was a long walk downtown. I carried on a semiaudible conversation with myself most of the way. "Don't you see, Father ... Of course I see, son ... Then you don't mind, Father ... Of course not, son, you just go right ahead ..." It was after two when I turned left down Main Street, creeping on tiptoe. Then I was there. I peeked through the glass window.

Disaster. Both chairs were empty. I waited. Five minutes. A man walked into the shop. I peered again. Double disaster. Bimbaum was cutting the man's hair. I waited. Three o'clock. Ten after three. Bimbaum still snipped.

Final disaster. It started to rain. That was too much. I stood there in the rain, hoping for something, some miracle, any miracle.

No miracle. The rain increased. I was soaked. I stuck my hands in my pockets and shivered. I sneezed. Again. A third time.

Then I walked inside.

I took off my jacket and hung it over a hook. Bimbaum was finishing.

"Hop up," my father said.

I did not move.

"Hop up," he repeated, slapping the back of the black leather chair. I stared at the floor.

"I think I'll wait for Mr. Bimbaum," I said finally.

Chaos . . .

I was the first one home. I walked into the kitchen and stood, turning around slowly while my mother inspected. "Very nice," she nodded. "Your father is definitely improving."

"Oh, yes," I said.

"Go change into something dry," she said. I did. Then I came back to the kitchen. Bimbaum appeared, gave his customary nod, and disappeared.

"Where's your father, Willy?" my mother asked.

"I don't know," I said. It was the truth. I didn't know. He had stormed out of the shop as soon as I sat down in Bimbaum's chair.

"Must be busy at the shop," she went on.

"Must be."

We waited. She idly turned the chops over in the frying pan and lowered the flame. Then we heard footsteps out in back. Accompanied by loud mutterings. Then my father was standing in the kitchen, pointing a finger at me.

"Stabbed in the back!" he roared. "By my own son, stabbed in the back!" With that he vanished into the living room.

My mother turned to me, pale. "Tell me you didn't," she pleaded.

There was nothing I could say.

Abruptly, she left the room and hurried out to my father. I took off my shoes and crept to the hallway, pressed against the wall, watching and listening.

"He's only a boy, Morris," my mother was saying. "Remember he's only . . ."

"Boy, schmoy," my father cut in. "The little pecker knifed me in the back. Here. Feel. Put your hand on. The blood is still dripping."

"Morris," my mother soothed. "Morris."

"That goddam Bimbaum anyway," my father ranted on. "Him and his goddam head shapes. Who the hell does he think he is, Leonardo da Vinci? What right does he got living in my house, eating my food, slopping up my gravy?"

"Does your head ache?" my mother asked. "Are you hungry? Can I get you a little something to *nosh* on?"

"I don't want food," my father shouted. "I want revenge!"

"Morris, don't lose control."

"Bimbaum," he went on, shaking his fist. "I tell you this. You are one washed-up barber. In this town you're dead."

"You can't go firing him for no reason," my mother said. "You want to look like a fool to your son?"

That stopped him. "You're right," he admitted, after a pause, his voice softer now. "I can't fire him without no cause." He smacked his forehead. "Cause, cause, who got a cause?"

"You don't want Willy thinking bad things about you, Morris. Bad things like maybe you was a small man, or worse, that you was jealous. You wouldn't . . ."

"You got any chicken broth?" my father asked. "I could use a cup chicken broth to clear the head."

"In the box. It heats up in a second." She stood. I ducked out of sight. I heard her crossing to the kitchen. Then my father's voice, shaking with emotion.

"Bimbaum," he was saying. "Bimbaum old pal. Your days are numbered!"

And they were. From then on, it was only a question of time.

But it did not happen right away. The days passed, days full of quiet bickering and quiet meals and tension, always tension, mounting steadily. It was three weeks later before the end began.

We were finishing dinner, the four of us, racing to see who would be the first one done and excused. My father cleared his throat and glanced quickly at my mother.

"Business is terrible," he announced.

No one said anything.

"Yes," he went on. "Business is terrible. But not in the way you might think."

"What do you mean by that, Morris?" my mother asked, I imagine on cue.

"Well," he expanded, "it ain't so much that the shop lacks customers so much as it is that the customers ain't getting service."

"What do you mean by that, Morris?" my mother repeated, a trifle mechanically.

"I mean that Mr. Bimbaum takes too goddam long cutting hair, that's what I mean."

"Oh, surely that is not so," my mother said.

"Oh, but it is so," my father replied. "Just today he took a hundred and three minutes to cut the hair of old Mr. Hathaway, who is practically bald to begin with."

"Well, well," my mother said. "Just imagine that."

"A hundred and three minutes!" my father exploded, talking directly to Mr. Bimbaum now. "I timed it myself. Who can make money in a hundred and three minutes, I ask? Answer: not me. I can cut three heads in that time. Maybe four."

"That's because you're a butcher," Mr. Bimbaum said. "What does a butcher need with time?"

"This particular butcher," my father answered, tapping his thumb to his chest, "this particular butcher happens to own the particular shop in which you are employed. Or should I say were employed."

"Meaning?" Bimbaum asked.

"Meaning that unless you get a little speedier, you get out and I find somebody who ain't such a slowpoke."

"Butcher," Mr. Bimbaum said again. "Money-grubbing butcher."

"Perhaps so," my father said. "Perhaps not. But at least I am fair. Tomorrow we time you. If you can cut a head in, shall we say, forty-five minutes, you stay. If not, out. Vanished. Gone."

"What head?" Mr. Bimbaum asked. "You going to pick Mr. Dietrich? He got a head like a nose."

"I said I was fair. You need a guinea pig. I got a guinea pig. I happen to be its father."

"Me?" I said.

"You," he said.

With that the discussion ended.

So bright and early the next morning we trooped downtown, my father, Mr. Bimbaum and I. My father carried a big, round alarm clock. Mr. Bimbaum carried his silver scissors. No one spoke. We entered the shop and I jumped into the second chair. My father set the alarm clock. He and Bimbaum looked at each other.

"You got forty-five minutes," my father said, and he left the shop.

I waited in the chair. Mr. Bimbaum stared at my head. He bent down and looked up at it and stood on tiptoe and looked down at it and walked around it and placed his fingers on it and drew an imaginary replica of it in the air.

"Spherical," I whispered. "It's spherical, Mr. Bimbaum. Don't you remember?"

"I never forgot a head shape in my life," he said. "But sometimes, especially with the young, the head shape changes."

"Well, mine hasn't changed, Mr. Bimbaum. It's still spherical. Now will you hurry up."

He closed one eye and sighted along the part in my hair. Then he redrew the imaginary replica in the air and squinted at it. "Still spherical," he announced and he tucked the striped towel around my neck.

"Forty minutes," my father said, appearing suddenly in the doorway. "Forty minutes to go, Bimbaum," and he was gone again, pacing the sidewalk in front of the shop.

Mr. Bimbaum took out his scissors and blew on them, holding them up to the light. The room grew brighter. He snipped them together a few times.

"Come on, Mr. Bimbaum," I said. "Please."

"Shut up and sit still," he answered.

Grudgingly, I did what he said. He put his fingers against my head and snipped. A few scattered hairs fell into the towel. He walked slowly around me. Snip. A few more hairs fell. He stepped back and looked at me, his head tilted to one side.

"Hurry, Mr. Bimbaum," I said. "Please hurry."

"Thirty-two minutes," my father announced, again in the doorway. "Almost one-third gone, Bimbaum."

The scissors were in continuous motion now, and again the rhythms began. But this time the songs were different; these were softer songs, sadder songs. "The Minstrel Boy to the Way Is Gone" and "Red River Valley" and . . .

"Twenty-one minutes," my father said from the door.

"Come on, Mr. Bimbaum," I muttered. "Come on. Please come on."

"I should ruin a lifetime in twenty-one minutes?" he said.

Now it was "Shenandoah," and the sound of it poured in, filling the tiny shop. "Away, you rolling river. Oh Shenandoah, I long to see you. Away. I'm bound away . . ."

I closed my eyes; my father came in again but I did not bother opening them. The sound was too beautiful. I just sat there listening, listening to the distant chants of the boatmen, to the mighty rolling waves pounding steadily in against the shore. The sound swelled, grew richer, louder, even louder, louder still.

Then it stopped.

The alarm clock went off. My father was standing in the shop. "Time's up, Bimbaum," he said.

Mr. Bimbaum said nothing. He walked quickly to the alarm clock and with one swipe of his beautiful hand knocked it senseless to the floor. Then he turned to my father. "Get out, butcher," he said. "I'm cutting this boy's hair."

Meekly, my father left.

"I'm sorry, Mr. Bimbaum," I began.

"Shut up and sit still," he ordered.

I turned to face him. "I'm really sorry," I began again.

"I told you once already," he said, and he swatted me on top of the head with the flat of his hand.

"Anyway," I finished, sitting still, "it's my fault and I'm sorry."

"Fault!" he snorted, snipping away. "Why is it your fault? No time. Nobody's got no time. Whose fault is that?"

"What I meant . . ."

"Shut up," he repeated. He took another snip of hair. "The butchers. The butchers are taking over. You mark my words. By the time you grow up, the goddam butchers will own the world. You'll see. Goddam little brat anyway."

He snipped steadily. I closed my eyes. Snip. Snip. Then no more.

"There," Mr. Bimbaum said. "Done."

With that, he yanked the towel from around my neck, crumpled it in his hands and threw it on the floor. Holding his scissors to the light, he blew on them, one time. Then, without a word, he walked from the store.

He was gone by the time we got home that night. Bag and baggage, gone. We sat down to supper, the three of us. No one spoke. I cleared away the soup dishes and brought in the roast. My father cut the slices and put them on our plates. Still silence. Then my father turned to me.

"He was a fine barber, Willy. You understand that. No one ever said any different."

I nodded. "That's right. But he took too long."

It was my father's turn to nod. Then my mother spoke.

"Hush and eat your dumplings," she commanded.

We obeyed.

chapter fifteen
Before We Begin Writing

In any adaptation—in any screenplay, really—the make or break work is done before the writing actually begins.

The writing is never what takes the most time. It's trying to figure what you're going to put down that fills the days. With anger at your own ineptitude, with frustration that nothing is happening inside your head, with panic that maybe nothing will *ever* happen inside your head, with blessed little moments that somehow knit together so that you can begin to visualize a scene.

Normally, to fill those terrible preparatory days, I tend to do a lot of research. Now, in the case of "Da Vinci," there isn't a whole lot of research I can do. But I've read and reread the story. (I haven't written the screenplay yet; as you read this, for all intents and purposes, I'm not really sure how it will begin or end. Or how long it will be; if I had to guess, it would be between thirty and forty pages, but if it comes out longer or shorter, it won't surprise me much.)

If I haven't actually written, I have made my marks in the margins of the book. On the first page, for example, the second longish paragraph is inked every time—that's where we learn Willie's old man owns the town barbershop, that he's bald, and that the kid is the guinea pig. That's basic plot, I think I'll need that.

And as well as making my marks, I've asked myself a bunch of

311

questions, which I'll get to now. "Da Vinci," obviously, is not going to be a full-length screenplay—your eyes would glaze over if you had to read a book and then a screenplay of the book.

But these questions, the ones that follow, are what I ask myself before I begin. Always, always. And many times over. The answers change as the material shifts in your head. But not the questions.

They may seem obvious or irrelevant, and perhaps they are. But not to me. I must know what I am doing before I begin doing it. I must be able to give myself satisfactory answers or I'm nowhere.

With screenwriting, as with a gift, it's the thought that counts. . . .

(1) WHAT'S THE STORY ABOUT?

There is no right answer for this question. No single right answer. Even though "Da Vinci" is not material of Dostoevskian complexity, there are still various legitimate opinions as to what it's about.

Maybe it's about a family that almost fragments. A visitor appears, causes troubles, tensions, problems. But in the end, the strength of the family endures. The story, after all, ends with the family together, happily following the orders of the mother, perhaps the true strength of the unit.

Or—

Maybe it's about a kid learning there is more to life than dreamed of in his philosophy. Bimbaum is clearly something unusual and different for a marble player to have to deal with.

Or—

—enough *or*'s. I can put down half a dozen others I don't believe, just as I don't believe the two above. For me, the answer is simply this: *"Da Vinci" is about a guy who loses a job.*

You may not agree; fine. You may be correct. And if you wrote the screenplay, you would handle the material your way. But in my version, that's the story line I'm going to use.

Now, many times when you see a movie of a book you've read, you will find they have little or nothing to do with each other. The same can be true here. (Producers often acquire material for crazy reasons. They like a character, or they think if you tuck in a part for Bo Derek, it can be a blockbuster. There was one producer in the not so long ago who bought three books purely for their locations—he had never been to New Zealand, so that was one purchase. He wanted to go around the world at the studio's expense.)

Okay. Let's make some changes—"Da Vinci" can be an action movie. Easy. Bimbaum is a spy, a spy on the run, and the Russian secret police find him and he has to enlist the family to survive. May make an okay picture.

It can be a story of passion: Make Bimbaum Burt Reynolds, the mother Jane Fonda, and let them have an affair seen through the eyes of the kid. Maybe the father finds out. Maybe only the kid knows his old man knows. May not make a bad picture.

It could be a *Catcher in the Rye*–type piece—a story of adolescent sensitivity and pain. Porky McKee dies, unfairly of some miserable disease, and the kid, Willie, has to deal with the existence of an unjust God. Make Willie older, sign Tim Hutton, watch the teenyboppers cry. May make a good picture.

None of this is meant to be facetious. Bigger changes than any of the above are made in adaptations every year.

But for any screenwriter, personally, I feel they are death.

All I have, when I start an adaptation (and I don't think this can be repeated too often, which is why I'm going to repeat it too often), is my emotional connection with the source material. If I had been offered James Kirkwood's novel *Some Kind of Hero* with the proviso that, oh, yes, we're going to keep it just as it is with one teeny-weeny change—we're going to make the main character black so we can nab Richard Pryor—I couldn't have done it. Kirkwood is a fine writer and Pryor is a dazzling talent, but when commercial matters dictate a total subversion of the source material, we are in, as the French say, deep shit.

Not the happiest of habitations.

(2) WHAT'S THE STORY REALLY ABOUT?

"Da Vinci" says this: *There is no place for the artist in the modern world.*

I've got a leg up on this answer, since I wrote the story. But even if I hadn't, there are clues. For example, the title. It isn't called "New Guy in Town" or "The Filler of the Second Chair."

And the father calls Bimbaum an artist.

And everything about Bimbaum indicates that he takes his work with artistic passion.

But he takes too long. Even when his job is on the line, he takes too long. So he's canned. You don't tell Michelangelo, "Hey, I need the ceiling done by Saturday."

Look, none of this "artist" talk is meant to be pretentious. We're dealing with a little story. But it wasn't written about a starving sculptor or the tragedy of Schubert getting canned and dying, his songs unsung. Part of the hoped-for charm of the piece was the fact that the character's occupation was the reverse of what you might have expected.

(3) WHAT ABOUT TIME?

There are really two "times" involved here—the time *of* the story (the period) and the time *in* the story (the duration).

Taking the period first—I don't think this screenplay should be set in the past. Since it's about the fact that there's no place for the artist in the modern world, it's a cheat if we don't set it in the modern world.

Now, with the duration, we start getting into potential alterations. "Da Vinci" takes place over three haircuts for Willie: the test; the second, where he double-crosses his father; and the last, when Bimbaum gets fired.

Do we need three haircuts?

Movies are compression.

Can we get by with two? If we do, what do we gain and what do we lose?

Think about that.

(4) WHO TELLS THE STORY?

Now things are really getting sticky. Because "Da Vinci" is told in the first person. The kid narrates the story. Perfectly fine for fiction.

Not so good for movies.

Characters talking directly to the camera are, for many reasons, off-putting. *Alfie* got away with it successfully. Maybe a few others. But very few. Maybe we're one of those few. If we were to open with the marble scene, it might go like this.

FADE IN ON

A SCHOOLYARD. Spring. TWO KIDS are playing Little Pot, a marble game where you lag a great distance toward a small chalked circle with marbles inside. Whoever lags closest gets to shoot first. Now one kid--his name is PORKY McKEE--lags. As he runs along following his marble toward the chalked circle, the second kid, WILLIE, looks at the camera, starts to talk.

> WILLIE
>
> I was playing Little Pot with Porky McKee when Mr. Bimbaum butted into my life.
>> (he turns away from the camera, concentrates on making his lag, when we--)

CUT TO

A BALD MAN, moving across the schoolyard. It's MORRIS, WILLIE's father.

> MORRIS
>
> Go take a haircut--

> WILLIE
>> (looks up)
>
> Now? This is for the championship.

> MORRIS
>> (in no mood to mess around)
>
> Go.

> WILLIE
>> (he sighs, looks at his father)

```
            Okay.
                 (he turns toward Porky)
            Back in a little.
                 (now he looks at the camera
                     again)
            My father never understood the im-
            portance of marbles.
                 (as he starts to run across
                     the schoolyard--)

     CUT TO
```

Cut to whatever you want, I'm not crazy about it. It would work, probably, but there's something as I write even this fragment that's bothersome. Forget the specifics of the dialog or the event. Talking directly to the camera presents problems in a movie. You can do it in the theatre—*Our Town*, for example—and I can do it here. But in a movie you don't tell people things, you show people things. And writing *Da Vinci* with a ten-year-old kid talking to us throughout doesn't fill me with a whole lot of enthusiasm.

But—

—how's if we got a little stylish? Let's keep the first-person narration, and let's keep Willie as the narrator, but let's make it material recollected in tranquillity. I'll show you what I mean.

```
     FADE IN ON


     A SCHOOLYARD IN SPRING. TWO KIDS are deeply in-
     volved in a fierce game of marbles.

     CUT TO


     A NICE-LOOKING, WELL-DRESSED GUY OF THIRTY. He
     walks toward the competitors. As he comes closer,
     we can hear the rat-tat-tat of their talk. 'Quit
     fudging--'    'I'm    not--'    '--are,    are--'
     '--shut up, you're just trying to make me miss--'
     '--you'll miss anyway, now quit fudging--'
```

THE NICE-LOOKING GUY is right up near them now, but they pay him no attention. He stops, looks at them a moment, then stares around at his surroundings.

> NICE-LOOKING GUY
> (shaking his head, bemused)
> The battles this schoolyard has seen.

CUT TO

ONE OF THE KIDS--WILLIE--kneeling by the chalked circle, concentrating hard, getting ready to shoot.

NOW THE NICE-LOOKING GUY kneels alongside him, assumes the same position. He tries to make his hand mime the proper form for marble shooting. His fingers are clumsy.

> NICE-LOOKING GUY
> I've even forgotten how to hold a shooter.

WILLIE keeps concentrating, as if he hasn't heard the NICE-LOOKING GUY speak. And of course he hasn't heard him--because as we look at them, now we see the resemblance of the two: The guy talking is WILLIE grown up.

> NICE-LOOKING GUY
> It took something of earth-shaking import to break up our games.
> (and now he points off--)

CUT TO

A BALD MAN hurrying across the schoolyard.

> NICE-LOOKING GUY
> (indicating the bald man)

Now <u>he</u> was of earth-shaking import.

                    BALD MAN
Go take a haircut.

                    WILLIE
                (looking up)
Now? This is for the championship.

                    BALD MAN

<u>Go</u>.

                    WILLIE
But Daddy, I'm winning--
                (the bald man points stern-
                ly back in the direction he
                came)

CUT TO

THE NICE-LOOKING GUY. As WILLIE sighs, stands, he
stands, too, at the same time.

                    WILLIE
Back in a little, Porky.
                (and as he starts to hurry
                away--)

CUT TO

OUTSIDE A BARBERSHOP IN A SMALL TOWN. The NICE-
LOOKING GUY stands casually on the sidewalk,
watching as WILLIE rounds the corner up ahead,
runs toward the shop.

                    NICE-LOOKING GUY
                My father ran the only barbershop
                in town. Whenever he hired a help-
                er, I was the guinea pig, since my
                father, bald from his twenties,
                couldn't fulfill the function.

```
WILLIE has reached the shop now, and as he throws
the door open, rushes inside--


CUT TO


THE NICE-LOOKING GUY. He sits in a corner, watch-
ing as WILLIE comes to a stop, eyes the new barber.


                    NICE-LOOKING GUY
          I was not in the best of moods when I
          met Mr. Bimbaum. I didn't know it
          then, but Mr. Bimbaum was never in
          the best of moods.
```

And now we would cut to Bimbaum and describe him and like that.

Well?

Those two pages wrote easily enough. (Remember, I haven't written the screenplay yet. And there is a very good reason for that—I'm not sure how. Believe that. What I am doing now is the one thing all writers are masters of: putting off doomsday.)

I think it is more stylish than having Willie tell the story as a kid. And one of the reasons that a narrator would be a huge help in this material is this: It's not just a first person story, a great deal of what happens is interior. There's not that much dialog to lift.

One of the things that drives you mad, if you are lucky enough to have a novel bought for a movie, is people are constantly asking you which you wrote first, the book or the screenplay? (Curses on Erich Segal.) *Marathon Man*, for example, was difficult to turn into a screenplay, because only one scene—Olivier in the diamond district—was a totally exterior scene. You could just lift it almost shot for shot.

Okay, back to the problem of the narrator in *Da Vinci*. Another way of doing it would be simply to use the technique of voice-over. We would see the scenes, but the bridging material of interior stuff would be told us by a voice, maybe Willie the kid, or just an unnamed person who would serve as storyteller.

Or we could get rid of the narrator altogether and have it move from scene to scene like most movies do.

Think again now. If you were going to tell the story as a screenplay, how would you go about it? And why? And what would you gain?

And what would you lose?

(5) WHERE DOES THE STORY TAKE PLACE?

Easy. Just where it does. A small American town. Unspecified. I'm from a small Illinois town (or it was small when I was growing up in it), so I guess that's where it takes place.

I mean, why change it? You can. No problem. Set it in the South or in a city or outside of London—but what do you gain?

When you make a locale shift, you are moving away from the author's intention somewhat. And it's imperative, when you do an adaptation, to stay as close as you can to the author's intention. One little shift here, another there, and suddenly you'll find the material fragmenting on you.

Sure you can shift it. But you better have a goddam good reason. Better than just, say, that the producer always wanted to visit New Zealand.

(6) WHAT ABOUT THE CHARACTERS?

Getting toward the crunch now. Lots of thoughts involved. Have we enough characters to tell our story? Have we too many—can we cut some or amalgamate? Shall we change them? How? Older? Younger? Make them more appealing? Sweeter? On and on.

Let's get specific. *Da Vinci* has five people. Here they are and we'll talk about them one at a time.

> Willie
> Morris—his father
> Emma—his mother
> Porky—his friend
> Mr. Bimbaum

Willie

Obviously, since somebody has to get the haircuts, we've got to keep Willie. I think we like him in the story. (At least I know we're *supposed* to like him.)

He's certainly not memorable, like Phoebe in *Catcher*. But that's probably okay, the story isn't about a memorable kid. What we've got is a marble player, a prepubescent who cares more about sports than girls.

What about girls, though? If we up Willie just a couple of years in age, we can add the brush stroke of adolescent problems. He can *want* to look better so he can impress someone of the opposite sex. (That would help buttress his actions when he double-crosses his father in the second haircut.) But what about the difficulties of adding a girl character?

We don't have to *add* one.

We can just switch Porky's sex.

Sex switching has been done in movies before, most brilliantly in the Cary Grant–Rosalind Russell version of *The Front Page*, retitled *His Girl Friday*, where Hildy Johnson went from being a male to a lady without even a change in name.

Porky can be a tomboy who is dealing with the same body changes that Willie is going through. And we can take their relationship through that pain of her going from pal to female to see if their world can withstand such a shaking.

Problem: Porky gets a haircut from Bimbaum. A girl wouldn't likely do that.

Possible solution: Do we need Porky's haircut? Can Willie's need alone be a sufficient drive? Especially since he now, for the first time, *cares* about his looks.

My instinct at this point is not to mess around with any of this—for the same reason, essentially, as I didn't want to switch locales. It reshifts the story, certainly more than a little, and Mr. Bimbaum may end up being this extra thumb. Who cares if he loses a job or not? Whether Willie and Porky survive takes center stage.

Okay. Enough about Willie for now. But this kind of questioning is the kind of thing you must leave your mind open to. Most free-associating ideas end up like toothpaste. Sometimes they don't. Is this one of those sometimes? Make up your own mind.

Morris and Emma

Again, not memorable creations. But the story functions pretty well with them along, the story's not about them, and they provide (again, were meant to provide) a feeling of family warmth against which Bimbaum operates.

But do we need them both?

One of them absolutely—someone's got to run the goddam barbershop.

What if we knock off the mother? Would that make the Willie–Morris relationship closer and, again, buttress Willie's double-cross?

But Emma has some helpful exposition. And the feel of the house, the warmth of the kitchen, is her doing. Yes, we can get rid of her, but I don't think the game is worth the candle. I say keep her.

Getting rid of Morris is also possible. But it presents credibility problems. I mean, how many lady barbers are there in small towns? Some, sure. But it throws a weight where you don't want it—you've got to think about extraneous things as you go through the screenplay: It's all kind of weird having a lady doing that kind of work when her kid's growing up.

And as screenwriters, damn near the last thing we want is our audience thinking extraneous things. We want to put blinders on them—we want them looking where we need them to look—and the minute they begin contemplating matters that are not our concern, we're in terrible trouble.

We are trying to tell *our* story. There's no time in a screenplay where we can lose them. Because movies keep going, going, going—it's not like a novel where you can go back and reread a section or a paragraph. We must grab them and make them listen to *us*. Once their mind begins wondering about matters foreign to our story, we've lost them. And once we've lost them, even for a long blink, the game is gone, we may as well pick up our baseball and head home.

So I say keep the parents.

Porky

Well, can't we get rid of somebody? Porky has the smallest part, we've already said we can probably sneak safely home without his haircut. Willie doesn't have to be playing marbles when Morris comes to get him, he can be shooting baskets alone or be home doing schoolwork. Do we need, do we *really need*, Porky McKee?

Please think about that seriously.

All right. If you think we can get rid of Porky, you have made, for me, a grievous and damaging error.

Why?

Three things about this material that have been stated before can be put together here: (1) This is the story of a guy who loses a job; (2) the guy happens to be a barber; (3) our particular barber happens to be an artist.

What does Porky have to do with all this?

Porky is the first one who *tells* us that something strange and different has appeared on our horizon. He carries perhaps the most important single piece of expository information in the entire piece.

He's been playing marbles. The game is interrupted. For a haircut. He waits. And waits. For *hours*. And he's pissed. When Willie returns he lets him know he's ticked about the wasted time. And in that angry state, what does he do next?

He tells Willie, "That's a beautiful haircut. A really beautiful haircut."

Boy, do we need that.

Because kids don't talk that way to each other.

He is a peer. An angry very young man. But such is Willie's transformation that he loses his anger and just stares before commenting on the cut.

Later, Willie's mother echoes the thought, but that's bullshit, that's meaningless. That's what a parent says to a child. My God, how many parents do we know with homely children who *believe* their offspring are glories? So a mother, a parent, a loving one, who compliments a child, that tells us nothing.

But when Porky McKee says "beautiful," that's gold.

Mr. Bimbaum

He's our man, he's our story, there's no way we're going to dump him.

But he sure isn't very likable.

And we don't know much about him.

What about that?

One of the constant comments screenwriters listen to is this: Nobody gives a shit about the main character. You get that from executives, producers, directors, you certainly get it from stars.

And there's a point to it—they're not dumb. If we are doing a gangster flick—say, for example, a great one like *White Heat* with Cagney—the problem of likability doesn't arise much. Cagney was meant to be repugnant but fascinating, and he sure was. I doubt anyone suggested an added scene where he saves an orphan from drowning.

But audiences do want to identify. We all crave heroes. So what do we do about the unyielding crustiness of H. Bimbaum? Can we make him more sympathetic? Sure we can.

Should we?

That brings us to the final and most important question that must be answered before a screenplay can be begun.

(7) WHAT MUST WE CLING TO?

In an adaptation, you have to make changes. In any adaptation. You simply must. If a novel is four hundred pages long and a screenplay runs a hundred and thirty-five, how can you remain literally faithful? Obviously, you can't. Same with a play. If you just shot the stage play, the audience would go mad with boredom. There were many pleasant comments concerning *All the President's Men* centering on how faithful we were to the book. Of course we were—but the movie also ended halfway through the Woodward and Bernstein effort.

So changes must occur.

Which changes, though?

While you are altering, you must also remain faithful to two things: the author's intention and the emotional core of the original work as it affected you.

So we've got to make changes with "Da Vinci." *Which* changes, though? What do we change?—

—*and what must we cling to?*

The fate of any adaptation hinges on how the screenwriter answers that question.

Mr. Bimbaum is just a bitch of a problem. He makes no attempt to enlist our sympathies. He swats Willie on the head, snorts at Emma, calls Morris a "butcher."

How are we supposed to like a man like that? One answer would be if he had a decent relationship with somebody. And I think the logical person would be not the parents but the more central figure of Willie. Can we structure that into the story? The reason for all this is simple enough: If Willie cares about the old guy, Bimbaum's departure would be a more emotional moment. If the kid cares, *we* ought to care.

Easy enough to set up. Let's say it's evening or it's a Sunday, the shop is closed, and the kid's folks are off somewhere—a celebration maybe, anniversary, birthday, whatever. All we need is a moment in time when the kid and the old guy are alone.

Now, once they're alone, we can't make it too easy—they shouldn't fall into each other's arms. So try this—just an example, you can come up with any number that are better, but what if the kid is making himself a sandwich, peanut butter and jelly, but the house is out of peanut butter, so the kid says that he's off to the store, can he get the old man anything, and the old man snaps, "What, I'm so old I can't go to the store myself?" And the kid is hurt, which you see in his eyes, or he snaps right back, "Boy, you never make anything easy, do you?" and he slams his way out the door.

Then we cut to a full jar of peanut butter and the kid making himself lunch, and Bimbaum comes in and watches or busies himself so that his back is turned to the kid and he mutters something like "I never been able to," and the kid, concentrating on his sandwich-making, says, "Able to what?" and Bimbaum answers, "Make anything easy," and then quick to cover his embarrassment he scowls and says, "How can you eat that junk?" and the kid says, stunned, "Junk? You call peanut butter and jelly junk? Are you crazy, it's better than anything," and the old guy seems dubious and says, "I wouldn't put stuff like that in my stomach," and now the kid, really stunned, says, "You never had peanut butter and jelly? Never *tasted* it, even?" And he may hold out the sandwich and the old man grunts "No" but the kid insists and as the old man relents and takes a bite—

—we cut to the two of them at the kitchen table, both eating peanut butter and jelly, and the old guy is wolfing his, you can tell he really likes it—only, of course, he'll never admit such a thing—and finally he says that his wife was a stickler for healthy foods and now the kid is shocked—"*You?* You had a *wife?*" and Bimbaum snarls yes, yes, he had a wife, a good woman and a stickler for what you put in your stomach, only maybe she died or she left him, he was such a crank, the point is, he's alone.

And then he rambles about how that changed him, how he became obsessed with hair after that, and he talks about what his life was like before, gives details, and the kid is fascinated (if we can do the details well enough) and as he goes to make himself another sandwich he can see Bimbaum wants another, too, so he makes them both seconds and while he's doing that he casually asks what the *H* stands for in his name and Bimbaum answers and the kid admits that his first name is a stinker, too, and we fade on the two of them eating quietly, with a sense of pleasure. Bimbaum and the kid, sort of together—a bond formed over peanut butter and strawberry jam.

Well, what do we think of that? Probably a bit contrived, but since we want to know about Bimbaum, again, probably the scene will hold. Also, the sequence is sentimental, but this isn't *Death Wish II*, what's wrong with a little decent sentiment? The sequence serves the function it was designed for: It draws the two main characters together to give emotional punch to the firing and departure of Bimbaum.

So do we add it in? Is it a good idea? Well . . . ?

YUK!!! It is a putrid idea. It is not only putrid, it is something much more damaging than that: It is *wrong*.

Why?

Two reasons. One: Bimbaum is a sour pickle of a man. The minute we turn him into Cuddles Zacall, he diminishes. Dickens can make Scrooge cute and we love it. That's a Christmas story about a tight financier.

But Bimbaum is an artist! He is *strange*. He has and *must always have mystery*. He appears out of nowhere on the first day of marble season, disappears two haircuts later. Strange things happen when he works on you: Time vanishes, wonderful sounds and thoughts fill your brain.

How does he do it?

That's the mystery we must protect. And the minute we find

out *anything* about his past, *anything at all,* we are ripping at the heart of our material, changing it, *ruining* it forever.

Van Gogh was an artist. An artist, a genius, and a mystery. The basis of his madness has got to stay out of our grasp, beyond our comprehension. Once we say, "Well, yes, Vinnie was a weirdo, but consider the traumas of his childhood," and then we outline the essential why of his career, the mystery is gone. One of the reasons the critics can never nail down Shakespeare is we don't know anything about him. A few dates—he was born here, left for London *X* years later, had his first success *X* years after that—but that's all. He remains a mystery and that is part of his legend.

Bimbaum better remain a mystery too. Or we are left with sentimental garbage.

Nothing is bulletproof.

Believe that. *Jaws* could have been *Orca*—they were both about angry monsters; *The Thing* could have been *The Attack of the Killer Tomatoes*—they were both about angry vegetables.

Gone With the Wind could have been a disaster; during shooting, the creators of *Casablanca* were convinced that it *was* a disaster.

You think *Gone With the Wind* couldn't have been *Mandingo?* Wrong. The creators of the Mitchell classic made some genuinely remarkable decisions. Here's one, for example. *Gone With the Wind* centers around the time of the Civil War. Well, one thing that movies have always done well is action. Big battle scenes. Great hordes of soldiers doing and dying, cannons blasting away.

Well, there isn't a whole lot of that in the movie. Some, sure, but it would have been easy, even logical, to add in twenty minutes, say, of surefire battle stuff and cut twenty minutes of Scarlett and Rhett. But they didn't. What did they cling to in *Gone With the Wind?*

Scarlett and Rhett.

And we must cling to Bimbaum, just as he is. Cranky, cantankerous, weird, arrogant, different. He is what's special about the material. And somehow, we must try to keep that special quality and, at the same time, make the audience give a damn.

Easy money at the brick factory. . . .

chapter sixteen
The Screenplay

FADE IN ON

A MARBLE AS IT ROLLS ALONG THE GROUND. It's moving pretty fast and WE STAY right with it. Then, as it starts to slow--

PULL BACK TO REVEAL

A SCHOOLYARD on an agonizingly beautiful spring day. TWO SCRUFFY-LOOKING KIDS are engaged in a fierce game of Little Pot. (Never mind what the rules are, they don't play it for long.)

PORKY McKEE runs alongside his marble toward the target--a small chalked circle with a bunch of smaller marbles nestled inside. As his marble comes to rest no more than twelve inches from the circle, he is pleased--this is evidenced by any number of things: He whoops out loud, jumps in the air, clasps his hands above his head like a triumphant fighter.

CUT TO

THE OTHER KID--it's WILLIE--and he holds his lagging marble in his right hand, stares at the small chalked circle many yards away. He concentrates, slowly starts his lagging motion, bringing his arm back with care--at which point PORKY begins a wild rat-tat-tat of talk.

                    PORKY
          (nonstop)
     You'll never beat me, never beat me,
     jinx--jinx--give up, why don't you?--
     jinx--

WILLIE does his best to ignore it all, lags and--

CUT TO

HIS MARBLE, rolling along, WILLIE chugging right beside it, eyeing its progress.

CUT TO

THE SMALL CHALKED CIRCLE and PORKY's marble. Now WIL-LIE's comes into view, goes past PORKY's, finally stops no more than a couple of inches from the target.

CUT TO

WILLIE AND PORKY. PORKY just stares, then grabs a pre-tend knife, stabs himself in the heart, falls groaning to the ground.

WILLIE looks at PORKY. They have lived next to each oth-er for eight of their eleven years, have been best friends for six of those eight. But this is <u>marbles</u>.

> WILLIE
> (John Wayne was never tougher)
> I take no prisoners, McKee.

Now he kneels beside the chalked circle, picks up his marble, expertly brings it into shooting position, takes a deep breath, when--

> MAN'S VOICE (<u>OVER</u>)
> Go take a haircut.

As WILLIE looks up--

CUT TO

A BALD MAN standing on the sidewalk not far from them. His name is MORRIS.

> WILLIE
> (plaintive)
> Now? Daddy, this is for the world's cham-pionship--<u>and</u> <u>I'm</u> <u>winning</u>.

                              MORRIS
                Go!
                    (he points off)

CUT TO

WILLIE. He sighs, stands.

                              WILLIE
                Back in a little, Porky.

And with that, he takes off. And the minute he does
that--

CREDITS START TO ROLL.

What WE SEE, as WILLIE runs along, is the world he inhabits. It's a small town, the time is today, but probably
if you looked at it thirty years ago, you wouldn't have
seen much difference. A tv aerial here and there may
just be the biggest changes. Probably, a few miles away,
there are shopping centers and parking problems and
progress. But not here, at least not now, and maybe not
ever.

Music starts, too, but not rock. Rather what we have
here is something closer to Copland. The kind of wondrous Americana tune that can be played sprightly and
fast, and it works that way; but when you slow it down,
orchestrate it fully, it's terribly moving. For reasons
that will become clear before we're done, the music will
be referred to as ''Bimbaum's Theme.''

CUT TO

WILLIE, tearing away from the schoolyard, going up a
hill.

CUT TO

THE CREST OF THE HILL as WILLIE reaches it. The town,
what there is of it, is visible in the distance.

CUT TO

A RAILROAD TRACK as WILLIE approaches, slows, glances
both ways before darting across.

CUT TO

THE TOWN SQUARE as WILLIE runs along. A FEW PEOPLE wave
to him on his journey; he waves back, never breaking
stride.

CUT TO

THE MAIN STREET IN TOWN NOW. WILLIE passes a bus station, a FEW PEOPLE waiting idly on the sidewalk.

CUT TO

A BOARDED-UP MOVIE HOUSE as he whizzes by. The music is
reaching a peak now and WILLIE at last starts to slow as
we

CUT TO

A BARBERSHOP at the end of the block. As WILLIE reaches
it, throws open the door--

CREDITS COME TO AN END.

CUT TO

INSIDE THE SHOP as the overhead bell on the door
squawks. WILLIE steps in, shuts the door. The bell
squawks again.

We are a long way from the world of Vidal Sassoon. The
shop is small, a few benches and some magazines piled on
a couple of tables. Two barber chairs, two sinks, calen-
dars with photographs on the walls.

Seated in a corner, his hands folded in his lap, is a MAN.
He stands now, and as he does--

CUT TO

MR. BIMBAUM, CLOSE UP. Small, aging, ageless. He wears a
rumpled suit; even if it came directly from the dry
cleaners, it would still look rumpled on him. He's a
little paunchy now, and he was never Tyrone Power. But
his eyes are bright. When Mr. Bimbaum stares at you, it
is very hard not to look away.

CUT TO

WILLIE, hopping into the nearest chair.

> WILLIE
> Okay, let's get it going, I'm destroying
> Porky McKee.

Now this geyser of information bursts from him; as he
speaks, he points quickly to various drawers and
shelves.

> Shears are there, clippers are there, ra-
> zors there, towels there, shampoo's
> there--

BIMBAUM hasn't moved--what he seems to be doing is just
staring at WILLIE's head.

> BIMBAUM
> An expert, huh?

> WILLIE
> Whenever my father hires anybody, I get
> to be the guinea pig, so . . .
>> (now he stops, a bit confused as
>> we)

CUT TO

BIMBAUM, advancing slowly toward the chair, his eyes
fixated on WILLIE's head. He walks around it slowly,
bends down, looks up at it, stands on tiptoe, looks
down.

CUT TO

WILLIE, watching the old guy.

> WILLIE
> What're you doing?

BIMBAUM makes no reply. He places his hands on WILLIE's
head, fingers wide apart.

> Something wrong?

CUT TO

BIMBAUM. Again no answer. He is concentrating deeply.
Now he takes his hands from WILLIE's head, makes an
imaginary replica of it in the air.

> BIMBAUM
> (finally nods to himself, says one
> word)
> Spherical.

> WILLIE
> Huh?

> BIMBAUM
> Head shape spherical.

CUT TO

THE SINK, as BIMBAUM turns on the spigots, adjusts them
to his liking.

> BIMBAUM
> Name?

> WILLIE
> (watching as Bimbaum takes a bar-
> ber's cape, pulls it over his
> chest)
> Willie.
> (as Bimbaum knots the cape behind
> his neck)
> Name?

> BIMBAUM
> H. Bimbaum.

And on that piece of information--

CUT TO

WILLIE, and he can't help it, he just breaks out laughing.

> BIMBAUM
> That is funny why?

                         WILLIE
                  (trying for control)
               Well . . . it's just--I mean, if the
               ''H'' is worse than the ''Bimbaum'' it
               must be a really horrible name.
                  (and he laughs again)

CUT TO

BIMBAUM. Thoughtfully, he stands there, and when WIL-
LIE's laughter is done, he swats the kid on top of the
head.

                         WILLIE
               That hurt.

                         BIMBAUM
               Was supposed to.

He goes to the sink now, gestures for WILLIE to bend forward. He looks at WILLIE's hair a moment, shakes his
head.

               Some butcher gave you your last haircut.

CUT TO

WILLIE. Looks up.

                         WILLIE
               Yeah?
                  (and he points to the other bar-
                     ber's chair)
               Well, my father gave it to me.

CUT TO

BIMBAUM. He leans in TOWARD THE CAMERA, speaks very distinctly.

                         BIMBAUM
               Then your father is a butcher. . . .

And with that, he reaches for some shampoo as we

CUT TO

SOMETHING SILVER IN EXTREME CLOSE UP.

HOLD ON IT.

We don't know what it is, but that's okay, we're not going to stay on it forever--

--now there seem to be two slivers of silver and they're
at right angles to each other as we

PULL BACK TO REVEAL

BIMBAUM'S SCISSORS. He holds it up to the light, studies
it a moment, concentrating deeply.

CUT TO

WILLIE, watching the OLD GUY, not knowing quite what to
make of it.

CUT TO

THE SHOP, and as BIMBAUM's scissors catch the light, it
seems for an instant as if the walls and ceiling are
filled with dots of brightness, a shower of sparkling
dots and

CUT TO

BIMBAUM, as now, still holding the scissors, he works
the blades--they make a rhythm--snip-snip-snip.

CUT TO

WILLIE, watching, as BIMBAUM makes the rhythm again--
snip-snip-snip. It's the same rhythm as the start of the
first three notes of ''Jingle Bells,'' and under his
breath WILLIE, almost without knowing it, hums that
tune. ''Jingle bells, jingle bells, jingle all the
way . . .''

CUT TO

BIMBAUM, as he moves close to WILLIE now, the scissors
continuing their snipping sound, and he takes some hair
between his long beautiful fingers, gradually moves the
fingers down to just the tips of the hair, makes a first
snip and

CUT TO

A few tiny bits of hair falling and

CUT TO

BIMBAUM, moving around the chair, making another almost
imperceptible snip and

CUT TO

WILLIE, shifting in the chair, getting comfortable and

CUT TO

BIMBAUM in motion, another snip, another and

CUT TO

MORE HAIR FALLING, just the smallest amount imaginable,
and

CUT TO

THE SCISSORS, snip-snip-snip, and

CUT TO

WILLIE, relaxing, humming ''Jingle Bells,'' and

CUT TO

THE WALLS as the bright dots dance and

CUT TO

WILLIE watching the dots--there's a calendar on the
wall of a beautiful springtime shot of a river and rocks
and grass and great green trees, and as the dots move
across the scene--

CUT TO

BIMBAUM'S EYES--bright, and as he moves gracefully
around the chair--

CUT TO

MORE SNIPPETS OF HAIR falling away and

CUT TO

WILLIE, deeply relaxed now, a kind of daydreamy look on his face and we

CUT TO

THE SCHOOLYARD, only it's all kind of hazy and WILLIE is aiming his shooting marble at another marble an impossible distance away, and PORKY is waving his arms, trying to distract him, and a CROWD OF PEOPLE watches as WILLIE casually shoots his marble and it flies through the air and bingo--a perfect hit and the CROWD is amazed and

CUT TO

THE DOTS, continuing their dance as ''Bimbaum's Theme'' begins again, lilting and lovely and

CUT TO

THE SCHOOLYARD again, again kind of hazy, and the CROWD is bigger and WILLIE has to make an even more impossible shot, the marble is much too far away to hit, and as PORKY stands there WILLIE moves his arm behind his back and does the shot that way and again--bingo, another perfect hit and this time PORKY is amazed, too, along with the CROWD, which is much bigger now, and they start to clap and WILLIE modestly acknowledges their admiration as PORKY walks over to him, carrying a gigantic golden trophy that is inscribed ''Champion of the Known World,'' and he hands it to WILLIE, who graciously accepts it, bows to the CROWD, which is huge now, and they shake their heads in wonder as they continue to clap away and

CUT TO

BIMBAUM, fierce in his concentration now, his beautiful fingers always moving, his silver scissors snipping away and

CUT TO

WILLIE, eyes starting to close as he looks at the calendar photo of the river and the trees and ''Bimbaum's
Theme'' is louder than before, louder and more beautiful and

CUT TO

THE CALENDAR PHOTOGRAPH OF THE RIVER, only now the river
starts to flow, and the sound of the water foaming
around the rocks begins to build--and now the great
trees start to bend in a spring wind, and that sound, the
wind sound, joins the rush of the water, and it's so
lovely, so perfect and lovely, all you want to do is lie
down by the water's edge in the thick grass and stare at
the blue sky with the white clouds and the giant green
trees gracefully moving as the wind passes through and

HOLD ON THE FLOWING RIVER. And the trees and the sky as
''Bimbaum's Theme'' reaches a climax--

CUT SHARPLY TO

THE BELL ABOVE THE BARBERSHOP DOOR as MORRIS enters.

                          MORRIS
           Done?

CUT TO

BIMBAUM, floating the cape away from WILLIE's body.

                          BIMBAUM
           Done.

CUT TO

MORRIS. He glances at WILLIE, moves to BIMBAUM, who
stands by the sink. (We haven't seen WILLIE yet--not
clearly. We don't know what he looks like.)

                          MORRIS
           The haircut is maybe a trifle close.

BIMBAUM snorts, turns away, puts the shampoo back.

As I said, a trifle close--but otherwise acceptable. Bimbaum--you got a job.

And on that--

CUT TO

WILLIE out the door and gone and now

A SERIES OF QUICK CUTS--

but not of WILLIE, of his shadow as he retraces his steps back to the marble game--

--the boarded up movie house as the shadow flits by--

--the shadow racing across the town square--

--now the railroad tracks as the shadow pauses, darts across--

--faster than before, the shadow races up the hill and now--

CUT TO

PORKY McKEE alone at the schoolyard. PORKY is playing a game of Big Pot by himself, carefully shooting marbles out of a large chalked circle.

> WILLIE'S VOICE (<u>OVER</u>)
> (coming closer)
> Prepare to die.

PORKY says nothing. He is clearly steamed about something.

> C'mon, let's go, hurry it up.

> PORKY
> Don't tell me hurry--you've been gone almost two hours--
> (and he points off--)

CUT TO

A CLOCK high on the wall of the school. It reads almost five o'clock.

CUT TO

PORKY. Continues to shoot marbles. Angry as hell.

>   PORKY
>   It was maybe three when you left.
>   (louder)
>   I think it stinks, disappearing like
>   that--

And now, as he turns, looks up at WILLIE--

CUT TO

PORKY. CLOSE UP. And the anger goes, replaced by surprise.

>   PORKY
>   (soft)
>   Willie . . . that's a beautiful haircut.

And now, at last--

CUT TO

WILLIE, and what PORKY says is true: The scruffy figure
that left the playground two hours ago has been replaced
by a great-looking kid.

>   WILLIE
>   . . . it is? . . .

CUT TO

PORKY. He makes a nod.

CUT TO

>   PORKY
>   You look fantastic.

CUT TO

A SCHOOL WINDOW as WILLIE takes a long look at himself,
PORKY reflected alongside. There is a pause, then--

                    WILLIE
           (a little nod)
         I guess I do. . . .

Now, from the TWO of them reflected in the window--

CUT TO

THE TWO OF THEM jogging home, dusk. The street is lined
with ordinary-looking houses. PORKY waves, veers off
into one. WILLIE waves back, heads for the next. He
slows as he approaches it, reaches into a pocket, takes
out a small harmonica. He tries playing ''Jingle
Bells,'' doesn't do it very well, shrugs, throws open
the back door, and we

CUT TO

CHUNKS OF CARROTS being plopped into a large pot of
thick, bubbling stew.

PULL BACK TO REVEAL

THE KITCHEN as WILLIE enters. His mother, EMMA, is working the stove like Toscanini, moving from burner to oven
and back. She's a slightly pudgy woman, probably the
same age as her husband--mid-forties.

                    EMMA
           (stirring the stew)
         How's the new one?

                    WILLIE
           (moving close, turning for in-
            spection)
         Take a peek.

                    EMMA
           (delighted)
         Look at the glamour boy.

                    WILLIE
         His name's H. Bimbaum--

                    EMMA
         --nice name--

> WILLIE
> --father's already hired him.

CUT TO

EMMA, pulling open the oven a speck, checking on the progress of some freshly baked bread.

> EMMA
> Naturally. The man is obviously a crafts-
> man.

CUT TO

WILLIE. His voice going soft.

> WILLIE
> You want to know what he said about Fa-
> ther? He said Father was a butcher.

> EMMA
> (shrugs)
> That's strong language--your father
> isn't exactly a butcher--but he isn't a
> craftsman either.

There is the sound now of the front door opening and closing.

> MORRIS'S VOICE (<u>OVER</u>)
> Everybody is where?

> EMMA
> (calling out)
> Give a guess.

CUT TO

MORRIS actually bounding into the kitchen--he seems very excited.

> MORRIS
> Ho-ho, have I got a surprise--
> (now he gestures behind him)

CUT TO

BIMBAUM, a small battered suitcase in hand, standing behind MORRIS.

>   MORRIS
> --Bimbaum here is going to rent the spare
> room, meals extra. Bimbaum, my wife,
> Emma.

They nod.

>   EMMA
> You gave my Willie here a fine cut.

>   BIMBAUM
> Of course; where's my room?

>   EMMA
>   (points toward the back stairs)
> Where's your luggage?

BIMBAUM holds up his small bag.

>   That's all?

>   BIMBAUM
> What am I, a fairy princess who needs a
> ball gown? I'm a barber. A barber needs a
> few clothes and a bunch of scissors. What
> more luggage?

>   EMMA
> Willie will show you the room.

>   BIMBAUM
> This place is so big I can't find it my-
> self?
>   (he goes to the back stairs)
> If I get lost, I promise to holler for
> help.

CUT TO

EMMA, staring as he disappears. Now she turns on MORRIS.

>   EMMA
> Ho-ho, some surprise; since when do we
> run a boardinghouse?

                         MORRIS
          Since when do you object to a little extra
          money--business ain't so hot.

                         EMMA
          Business is the same as always--and that
          man got the manners of a pig.

                         MORRIS
          Maybe he ain't sociable, but, Emma, you
          should see him cut hair.

CUT TO

MORRIS, going to her now, taking her hands.

                         MORRIS
          This afternoon, he did Mr. Dietrich, the
          postman, the one with a head like a nose.
          In ninety minutes, Mr. Dietrich was cute.
          The man's an artist, Emma, a real artist.
          Where else should he live?

EMMA hesitates, then takes a big wooden spoon, digs out
a chunk of beef, gives it to MORRIS.

                         MORRIS
                  (eating the peace offering)
          Perfection. . . .

HOLD ON the TWO of them, then--

CUT TO

A PORCH OUTSIDE THE LIVING ROOM. WILLIE and PORKY are
playing checkers. Some time has passed--WILLIE's hair
is longer than before. It's night. EMMA joins them.

                         EMMA
                  (sinking into a chair)
          I couldn't take any more.

                         WILLIE
          They still at it?
                  (he turns, looks inside--)

CUT TO

THE LIVING ROOM. BIMBAUM and MORRIS are visible--MORRIS
watching as BIMBAUM moves his scissors through the air,
as if demonstrating something. MORRIS is studying everything BIMBAUM does.

CUT TO

THE PORCH.

>   EMMA
> Ten nights in a row--what's so fascinat-
> ing about scalp disease? How long can you
> talk about head shapes?

Now the sound of a mandolin and MORRIS's voice raised in
song. He is not Caruso. EMMA shakes her head.

> Worse and worse.

>   WILLIE
>   (making a double jump)
> He only sings when he feels good.

MORRIS is singing louder now.

>   EMMA
>   (she sighs)
> Better he should be a little sad-
> der. . . .

As the singing goes on--

CUT TO

More music--equally lacking in calibre--WILLIE is in
his room, practicing his harmonica. He lies on his bed,
eyes closed, doing his best. The room is small, dominat-
ed by posters of sports heroes: Reggie Jackson, Bjorn
Borg. Another week or so has gone by--WILLIE's hair is
that much longer. It's late afternoon.

>   BIMBAUM
>   (appearing in the open doorway, a
>   towel in one hand)
> Why do you make that sound?

                         WILLIE
                  (quickly stopping)
              I'm sorry--

                         BIMBAUM
              --answer.

                         WILLIE
              I thought maybe I might want to be a musi-
              cian, so I asked could we have a piano? My
              father bought me this instead--
                  (holds up harmonica)
              --he said if I got good on this then he'd
              get me a small guitar, and if I got good on
              that, then he might get a piano.
                  (dubiously looking at the instru-
                    ment)
              I don't see a piano in my future.

                         BIMBAUM
              Play me your best tune.

CUT TO

WILLIE. He hesitates, then starts ''Shenandoah''--''Oh
Shenandoah, I long to see you, away, you rolling
river...''

CUT TO

MR. BIMBAUM, watching, listening.

                         WILLIE
                  (breaks off)
              Not so good, huh?

                         BIMBAUM
              Not so good? Terrible.

                         WILLIE
                  (stung)
              You said to do it.
                  (he puts the harmonica on the bed)

                         BIMBAUM
              Don't be such a sensitive. Everyone was
              terrible once. At the start, we all
              stink.

                    (he looks at Willie a moment)
          Even I wasn't always great.
                    (he moves out of sight down the
                      hall)

CUT TO

WILLIE. He thinks a minute, shuts the door, tries
''Shenandoah'' again. Not so hot. But he goes gamely on
as we

CUT TO

THE KITCHEN, a few nights later. Roast and dumplings
simmering on the stove. WILLIE and his MOTHER stand
guard. There is a sound behind them and as they turn--

CUT TO

BIMBAUM. He hurries through the kitchen and disappears
up the back stairs. Not so much as a nod.

CUT TO

EMMA. She looks at WILLIE, is about to speak, thinks
better of it, turns her attention back to her cooking.
Silence. Then the slamming of the front door. Hard. A
pause. Then the heavy sound of trudging footsteps. Coming closer and closer and

CUT TO

MORRIS. He stands in the kitchen door with the look of a
stricken samurai warrior on his face. After a moment he
goes into the living room, sinks heavily onto a sofa.

CUT TO

EMMA AND WILLIE in the kitchen.

                         EMMA
              (calling out)
          No songs.

No answer.

                         WILLIE
          What is it?

                              EMMA

          Something bad.
                    (and with that she leaves her post
                    by the stove, hurries into the
                    living room)

CUT TO

WILLIE. He stands there alone a moment. He moves the
dumplings around. Then he stops, walks to where he has a
view of the living room.

CUT TO

THE LIVING ROOM. EMMA is kneeling by MORRIS and they
whisper to each other.

CUT TO

WILLIE, riveted.

CUT TO

MORRIS AND EMMA. They whisper a moment more, then she
rises, moves back toward the kitchen.

CUT TO

WILLIE. Waiting.

CUT TO

EMMA, pale, in the kitchen doorway. She shakes and
shakes her head. Then--

                              EMMA

          That Porky McKee--
                    (a sigh)
          --and I thought he was supposed to be your
          friend.

As she finishes, stands there, WILLIE turns, dashes out
as we

CUT TO

THE FRONT OF PORKY'S HOUSE, and WILLIE, jamming his finger against the bell. As the door opens--

CUT TO

PORKY, standing inside his house. A screen door separates the TWO of them, so we can't see PORKY clearly, but it looks like he's gnawing on a leg of fried chicken.

               PORKY
   I just knew it would be you.

               WILLIE
   What happened?--my father's groaning, my
   mother's turned pale, what did you do?

               PORKY
    (pauses, then--)

   I had Mr. Bimbaum give me a haircut.

               WILLIE
   There's got to be more.

               PORKY
   Well . . .

               WILLIE
   <u>What?</u>

               PORKY
   Your father--his chair was empty. Bimbaum's was busy.

CUT TO

WILLIE. Stunned.

               WILLIE
   You didn't do it.

CUT TO

PORKY, still behind the screen door.

               PORKY
   I did, I did, I waited for Bimbaum--
    (in a rush now)
   --I had to, Willie--the way you been
   looking I had to give it a try, and was it
   ever worth it--

>   (and now he opens the screen door,
>   steps out)
>   Some haircut, huh?

PORKY, need it be said, has improved vastly in appearance.

>   WILLIE
>   (nods)
>   You never looked better. What kind of
>   head shape you got?--

>   PORKY
>   --semi-triangular.

He offers WILLIE a bite of the chicken leg; WILLIE
shakes his head no.

>   I'm sorry, Willie--tell your father I
>   didn't mean anything personal; explain
>   that to him.

CUT TO

WILLIE, exploding.

>   WILLIE
>   Explain it? The man's got feelings, Por-
>   ky--you should see him--a wreck--he may
>   never get over it--for all I know he's
>   just going to lay around like a lump for
>   the rest of his life--I mean, who knows--

>   PORKY
>   (cutting in)
>   --take it easy--it was just a one-time
>   thing--it'll never happen again--

>   WILLIE
>   --it will, it will, you don't under-
>   stand . . .
>   (and now it bursts from him)
>   --I wanna do the same thing!

CUT TO

THE TWO OF THEM, standing in silence for a moment.
Then--

                    PORKY
              (softly)
         Oh, Willie . . . .

                    WILLIE
              (such guilt)
         I want that Bimbaum again.

                    PORKY
              (helpfully)
         Maybe your father will get sick--
              (as Willie gives him a sharp
              look--)
         --not really sick, I don't mean serious,
         but he could catch cold--

                    WILLIE
         --he's a horse--

                    PORKY
         --then maybe some cousin might get mar-
         ried and they'd have to go, or maybe--

                    WILLIE
         --I only got one shot. When haircut time
         comes up I'll ask my mother to help me.

                    PORKY
              (nods)
         Great.

                    WILLIE
         You think?

                    PORKY
              (gnawing on his chicken)
         Mothers always understand.

Now on the word <u>mothers</u>--

CUT TO

EMMA, grabbing a bar of soap from the kitchen sink. And
she's not smiling.

                    EMMA
         Go wash your mouth.

PULL BACK TO REVEAL

WILLIE, scruffy as when we first saw him, standing in the kitchen with her.

>   WILLIE
>   But listen--

>   EMMA
>   Stab your own father in the back? My own
>   little Judas.

>   WILLIE
>   Please--

>   EMMA
>   You need a haircut, your father will give
>   you a haircut--<u>now</u>.

And as she takes him by the arm, marches him toward the kitchen door--

CUT TO

THE MAIN STREET IN TOWN. It's cloudy. WILLIE trudges slowly along. A COUPLE OF PEOPLE nod hello. He kind of grunts back, continues on.

CUT TO

THE BARBERSHOP as WILLIE slows, creeping now along the sidewalk. He slows, stops, looks toward the heavens.

CUT TO

THE SKY. Darkening.

CUT TO

WILLIE. He reaches the edge of the glass window in front of the shop, quickly peeks in--

CUT TO

INSIDE THE SHOP. MORRIS and BIMBAUM sit on benches, looking off in different directions. No customers. The shop is empty.

CUT TO

WILLIE, pulling his head back out of sight. He begins to knead his stomach. From the distance now: thunder.

CUT TO

WILLIE. He looks up as another crash of thunder is heard. His face is as gloomy as the bleak sky. Now he turns quickly as we

CUT TO

AN OLD GUY who obviously needs a haircut. THE OLD GUY walks slowly toward the shop.

CUT TO

WILLIE, watching him, and now there is a flicker of hope showing.

CUT TO

THE OLD GUY. He stops in front of the shop, as if making up his mind.

CUT TO

WILLIE, praying almost for the GUY to go in and--

CUT TO

THE GUY. He takes a step away, changes his mind, enters the shop.

CUT TO

WILLIE. He waits a moment. Another. Finally, when he can't take any more, he quick grabs another peek inside the shop.

CUT TO

INSIDE. THE OLD GUY has gone into BIMBAUM's chair. MORRIS is still sitting idly on the bench, staring off.

CUT TO

WILLIE, out of sight again, shaking his head. Whatever
torment he is going through, it's not lessening as time
goes on.

CUT TO

THE SIDEWALK. The first dainty drop of rain splashes
lightly down.

CUT TO

WILLIE, standing huddled on the sidewalk. He wears just
a T-shirt and jeans and already his shoulders are a little wet.

CUT TO

THE SKY. EXPLODING. It's like someone has switched on a
spigot and a torrential spring rain unloads.

CUT TO

WILLIE, alone, rocking back and forth. He's soaked but
he just keeps on rocking. He glances inside the shop.

CUT TO

INSIDE. BIMBAUM is determining his CUSTOMER's head
shape.

CUT TO

WILLIE, walking around in a kind of mystic circle.

CUT TO

THE HEAVENS. You never saw such rain.

CUT TO

WILLIE, drenched; he grabs another look inside.

CUT TO

INSIDE. BIMBAUM is just reaching for some shampoo.

CUT TO

WILLIE. Whipped but still standing there. He looks like he just stepped from a bathtub.

CUT TO

THE SKIES AND MURDEROUS THUNDER. It rumbles on and on and the rain, hard as it was before, only increases in tempo.

CUT TO

WILLIE. He closes his eyes, takes a deep breath, then goes to the door, walks into the barbershop.

CUT TO

INSIDE. MORRIS rises, goes to his empty chair.

> MORRIS
> Perfect timing.

WILLIE doesn't move. MORRIS pats the back of his chair.

> Hop up.

CUT TO

WILLIE. CLOSE UP.

> WILLIE
> (finally mumbling it out)
> I think I'll wait for Mr. Bimbaum.

And the instant he's said it—

CUT TO

MORRIS. Erupting—

> MORRIS
> (huge)
> Not in this shop—not in my shop—out—
> Out!—OUT!!!—

CUT TO

WILLIE, fleeing out the door, into the storm. . . .

HOLD ON WILLIE. Then--

CUT TO

EMMA IN THE KITCHEN, working her magic at the stove.
WILLIE silently enters. Outside, the rain still rages.

> EMMA
> (glancing at him)
> You didn't take a cut.

> WILLIE
> They were jammed--I'll come back tomor-
> row.

> EMMA
> Good, good.

She smiles, returns to her labors. WILLIE slinks upstairs as we

CUT TO

WILLIE IN HIS ROOM. He lies on his bed, dry now; different jeans, a clean T-shirt. He stares at the unrelenting
rain. It's early evening.

Now he hears footsteps hurrying up the stairs. He goes
to his door, looks out, catches a glimpse of BIMBAUM going to his room down the hall.

WILLIE returns to his bed, picks up his harmonica, tosses it back down.

Now he hears the raging voice of his FATHER. Again he
heads for the door as we

CUT TO

THE LIVING ROOM, MORRIS storming around, EMMA in pursuit, doing her best to pacify him.

PULL BACK TO REVEAL

WILLIE, crouched on the screen porch, listening.

> EMMA
>
> Morris--my God, remember, he's only a
> boy.

> MORRIS
>
> Some boy.
> (clutching his heart)
> Here's where the knife went in--feel--
> the blood is still dripping--

> EMMA
>
> --let me get you something nice to eat--

CUT TO

MORRIS. Louder now.

> MORRIS
>
> I don't want food, I want revenge. That
> goddam Bimbaum anyway--him and his head
> shapes--who does he think he is, Leonardo
> da Vinci?
> (and now he stares up at the ceil-
> ing, shakes a fist toward it--)
> In this town, Bimbaum, you're a dead man.

CUT TO

WILLIE, watching his PARENTS. If he seemed miserable
waiting out in the rain, he looks worse now. . . .

CUT TO

THE FOUR OF THEM AT DINNER THAT NIGHT. Dead silence, except for the clink of utensils scraping plates. They ALL
eat quickly, no one looking at anybody else. MORRIS finally puts his fork down, glances at EMMA quickly, then
sighs audibly.

> EMMA
>
> (right on cue)
> Whatever is the matter, Morris?

> MORRIS
>
> Business. Business is bad.

                         EMMA
Truly?

                         MORRIS
Yes, business is terrible--but not in the
way that you might think.

                         EMMA
I wish you'd explain that to me, Morris.

                         MORRIS
Well, it ain't so much that the shop
doesn't have customers, it's that the
customers ain't getting service.

                         EMMA
What do you mean?

                         MORRIS
I mean that Bimbaum here takes too goddam
long cutting hair.

                         EMMA
Oh, surely that is not so.

                         MORRIS
Oh, but it is so--just today he took one
hundred and six minutes to do old Mr. Den-
zel, who is practically bald to begin
with. Who can make money that way? Answer: Not me. I can cut three heads in a
hundred and six minutes.

CUT TO

MR. BIMBAUM, eating steadily away.

                         BIMBAUM
That's because you're a butcher--what
does a butcher need with time?

CUT TO

WILLIE, watching the TWO MEN.

                    MORRIS
This particular butcher happens to own
the shop in which you are employed. Or
should I say, were employed.

                    BIMBAUM
        (puts his fork down now)
Meaning?

                    MORRIS
Meaning that unless you get speedier, you
get out and I hire someone who ain't such a
slowpoke. Not that many jobs around, Bimbaum.

CUT TO

BIMBAUM. He nods.

CUT TO

MORRIS, staring at him.

                    MORRIS
You work for me, you work my way. Tomorrow
you get timed: If you can cut a head in,
say, forty-five minutes, you stay; if you
can't, good-bye.

                    BIMBAUM
What head? You'll probably pick Mr. Die-
trich--he's got a head like a nose.

                    MORRIS
I may be a butcher, but at least I am
fair--you need a guinea pig, I got a guinea pig--I happen to be its father.

CUT TO

WILLIE, glancing quickly at his father.

                    WILLIE
Me?

                    MORRIS
Oh yes, you.

                         WILLIE
              I don't think I want to be there.

                         MORRIS
              Guess what, sonny boy--what you want and
              what you get ain't always necessarily the
              same. . . .

HOLD ON THE QUARTET sitting silently at the table.
Then--

CUT TO

THE MAIN STREET IN TOWN. The next morning. Church bells
off in the distance. It's Sunday and a beauty.

MORRIS, WILLIE, and BIMBAUM troop down the empty
street. MORRIS, stalking ahead, carries a large alarm
clock. BIMBAUM is behind him, wearing, as always, his
rumpled suit. Bringing up the rear, slowly, is WILLIE.
As they move toward their appointed destination--

CUT TO

THE ALARM CLOCK being placed firmly on a shelf. MORRIS
finishes setting it. It ticks loudly.

CUT TO

BIMBAUM AND WILLIE watching him--we're inside the shop.

                         MORRIS
                   (moving toward the door)
              You got forty-five minutes.

And as he leaves--

CUT TO

THE CLOCK. It reads 11:15. And counting.

CUT TO

WILLIE, the instant his FATHER has gone. He dashes to a
shelf, grabs a cape, throws it around his body, hurries
to BIMBAUM's chair, jumps up, turns, and

CUT TO

BIMBAUM. Staring, staring at WILLIE's head. In a world of his own.

>   WILLIE
>   (gesturing for Bimbaum to get
>   started)
>   It's spherical, Mr. Bimbaum. Don't you
>   remember?

>   BIMBAUM
>   I never forgot a head shape in my life. But
>   sometimes, especially with the young,
>   the head shape changes.

>   WILLIE
>   Well, mine hasn't changed--I promise
>   you--now c'mon--

CUT TO

WILLIE IN THE CHAIR as BIMBAUM advances slowly, his eyes always on WILLIE's head. He walks around it, bends down, looks up, stands on tiptoe, looks down. Now he places his fingers on WILLIE's head, takes them off, draws an imaginary circle in the air.

CUT TO

MORRIS, in front of the shop, pacing back and forth, back and forth.

CUT TO

BIMBAUM. Finally nods, satisfied.

>   BIMBAUM
>   Still spherical.

CUT TO

WILLIE, a sigh of relief; he sits straight in the chair, ready. Then he almost groans--

>   WILLIE
>   You're not.

CUT TO

BIMBAUM. He is fiddling with the faucets in the sink.

> **WILLIE**
> Forget the damn shampoo.

> **BIMBAUM**
> A barber only works on clean hair.

> **WILLIE**
> Make believe mine's clean--can't you do
> that?

CUT TO

MORRIS, sticking his head in from outside.

> **MORRIS**
> Forty-one minutes to go, Bimbaum.
> (then he is outside again, pacing)

CUT TO

THE SINK as BIMBAUM fiddles with the faucets, getting
the temperature just right.

CUT TO

THE CLOCK, ticking away.

CUT TO

WILLIE, his head in the sink now, as BIMBAUM expertly
applies shampoo, gets a wonderful lather built up.

CUT TO

MORRIS, on the sidewalk, doing his sentry duty.

CUT TO

DOTS OF LIGHT dancing off the walls of the shop.

PULL BACK TO REVEAL

BIMBAUM holding his silver scissors high, blowing on
them, getting them ready.

CUT TO

MORRIS, head in the door again.

>   MORRIS
>   Thirty-six minutes, Bimbaum. Nine gone
>   so far.

CUT TO

BIMBAUM. It's as if he hasn't heard. He snips the scissors a couple of times, turns then to WILLIE.

CUT TO

A FEW HAIRS, slowly falling.

CUT TO

BIMBAUM, stepping back from WILLIE, squinting a moment, moving in again, gracefully. He reaches out, makes another tiny snip.

>   WILLIE
>   A crew cut, Mr. Bimbaum--I've always
>   wanted one. I know you could give a great
>   crew cut if you wanted.

>   BIMBAUM
>   Don't you ever say a thing like that.
>   again.

>   WILLIE
>   But there aren't that many jobs--Father
>   told you that last night--

CUT TO

MORRIS. In the doorway.

>   MORRIS
>   Twenty-nine minutes to go--one-third
>   over.

CUT TO

WILLIE as his FATHER moves back outside.

                                WILLIE
                            (turning)
                    Did you hear that? Did you <u>hear</u> it?

                                BIMBAUM
                    Shut up and sit still.

CUT TO

THE DOTS OF LIGHTS, dancing.

CUT TO

BIMBAUM, moving more gracefully than ever, taking a
snip here, another snip there.

CUT TO

WILLIE, his eyes just beginning to close.

CUT TO

MORRIS, looming in the doorway.

                                MORRIS
                    Twenty-five minutes to go, Bimbaum--

CUT TO

MORRIS, again in the doorway.

                                MORRIS
                    Twenty-one minutes to go, Bimbaum.

CUT TO

MORRIS, back in the doorway.

                                MORRIS
                    Fifteen minutes to go, Bimbaum.

And he exits as we

CUT TO

WILLIE, soft, throat dry.

                         WILLIE
          Just for God's sakes please do it.

                         BIMBAUM
                    (squinting along the part in Wil-
                    lie's hair)
          I should ruin a lifetime in fifteen min-
          utes?

CUT TO

AGAIN, THE DOTS OF LIGHT.

CUT TO

BIMBAUM, another small snip, another, a third.

CUT TO

THE CALENDAR ON THE WALL. The river and the rocks and the
great green trees.

CUT TO

BIMBAUM, eyes bright, concentrating fiercely, snipping
away, his beautiful fingers in constant motion and

CUT TO

WILLIE, eyes closed now and

CUT TO

BIMBAUM, moving like a dancer and

CUT TO

THE RIVER, as again it comes to life, starts to flow, and
we hear the water boiling over the rocks and hear the
wind in the trees--

--and now the glorious theme of ''Shenandoah'' becomes
clear, starting soft, getting stronger--''Away, you
rolling river''--and now

CUT TO

THE ALARM CLOCK going off and MORRIS in the doorway, talking over the jangling sound of the alarm.

> MORRIS
> High noon, Bimbaum. Time's up.

CUT TO

MR. BIMBAUM. He says nothing. For a moment he just stands frozen. Then he walks to the still-ringing alarm, and with one swipe of his beautiful hand he knocks it senseless to the floor. Silence. Now he turns toward MORRIS.

> BIMBAUM
> Get out, Butcher. I'm cutting this boy's hair.

CUT TO

MORRIS. He tries to return BIMBAUM's stare, thinks better of it, turns, meekly leaves, closing the door behind him.

CUT TO

WILLIE, as BIMBAUM comes back to the chair--

> WILLIE
> Listen, Mr. Bimbaum--

> BIMBAUM
> --shut up and sit still--

> WILLIE
> (turning to face the old man)
> --I'm sorry--

CUT TO

BIMBAUM.

> BIMBAUM
> I told you to sit still--

                    (and with that, he swats Willie on
                    top of the head with the flat of
                    his hand.)

CUT TO

WILLIE, sitting still, staring straight out.

                         WILLIE
                    Anyway, it's my fault and I'm really sor-
                    ry.

                         BIMBAUM
                    Fault? Nobody's got no time. Why is that
                    your fault?

CUT TO

BIMBAUM. CLOSE UP.

                         BIMBAUM
                    The butchers. The butchers are taking
                    over. By the time you grow up, the butch-
                    ers will own the world, you'll see. God-
                    dam little brat anyway.
                         (and now as he goes back to work--)

CUT TO

THE CALENDAR ON THE WALL.

And now for the last time, it comes to life--and now
again, the sound of ''Shenandoah,'' just like before--

--only it isn't like before--because suddenly the river
changes from a lovely stream to something majestic, a
giant of a waterway, maybe it's the Amazon or the Nile or
the mouth of the Mississippi, but whatever it is, it's
awesome, it just makes you gasp--

--and ''Shenandoah'' changes, too, it's booming now,
the sound just as awesome as the sight, and on and on they
go, the glorious song, the mighty river, and as they
climax--

CUT TO

BIMBAUM. He blows on his scissors, says one word.

                    BIMBAUM
          Done.

CUT TO

WILLIE, blinking in the chair, watching as BIMBAUM,
without a glance back, walks out of the store and gone.

HOLD ON WILLIE a moment, alone. Then—

CUT TO

WILLIE, still alone, walking along a railroad track,
using his arms for balance. Sometimes it's fun; you get
the feeling it isn't that just now.

CUT TO

WILLIE, hands stuffed into his jeans pockets, walking
alone across the town square. A couple of KIDS wave to
him. He doesn't wave back.

CUT TO

PORKY playing marbles in the schoolyard. He looks up,
sees WILLIE standing on the sidewalk. PORKY gestures
for WILLIE to join him. WILLIE shakes his head, walks
on.

CUT TO

MORRIS AND EMMA IN THE KITCHEN by the stove as WILLIE enters, stops, looks at them.

                    WILLIE
          Gone?

                    EMMA
          Bag and baggage.

CUT TO

WILLIE. He nods, heads for the stairs.

                    MORRIS
          Willie?

WILLIE stops.

          He was a fine barber. No one ever said any
          different.

                    EMMA
          That's right. But he took too long.

WILLIE makes no reply, leaves them--

CUT TO

THE BACK STAIRS as WILLIE trudges up.

CUT TO

THE LANDING as he reaches it, turns.

CUT TO

HIS ROOM as he enters, looks around. It's the same as before. Reggie Jackson and Bjorn Borg on the walls, his
little harmonica on the bed--

CUT TO

WILLIE, stopping suddenly, staring as we

CUT TO

THE BED. Because not far from the harmonica is a small
pair of silver scissors.

CUT TO

WILLIE. He walks to the bed, looks at the scissors,
picks them up. He lies on the bed, puts the harmonica on
his chest, studies the scissors he holds in his hands.

CUT TO

THE SILVER SCISSORS as WILLIE makes them move, three
times--snip-snip-snip. It's the rhythm of ''Jingle
Bells'' and he hums the three notes. Again three snips,
again he hums the three notes.

CUT TO

WILLIE, and now he pauses a moment, then makes a different rhythm: snip--snip-snip--snip. He does it again:
snip--snip-snip--snip. It's the start of ''Bimbaum's
Theme.'' He picks up the harmonica now, plays the first
notes--not very well. He stops, wipes the harmonica on
his T-shirt, tries again. Maybe a little better. But
this time he doesn't stop, he goes right on playing, and
as he does--

CAMERA STARTS TO MOVE

Out the window and down the side of the house. MORRIS and
EMMA are visible now, by the stove, close together, in
the kitchen. She takes a wooden spoon, gives him a taste
of what she's cooking. As always: perfection.

HOLD ON THE TWO OF THEM BRIEFLY--

--because the harmonica is still playing ''Bimbaum's
Theme'' only now it's something to hear--Larry Adler on
his best day never sounded this good as we

CUT TO

THE BARBERSHOP. Empty, shut--

--and now a wonderful guitar sound joins the harmonica.
''Bimbaum's Theme'' goes on, the two instruments playing perfectly together as we

CUT TO

THE SCHOOLYARD. Empty. No marble games--

--and a piano beautifully joins guitar and the harmonica. The three instruments blend and build as we

CUT TO

THE BUS STATION. A single figure stands waiting on the
sidewalk. It's BIMBAUM, holding his battered suitcase.
He stands there in his rumpled suit, fierce, sour,
alone--in other words, absolutely unchanged.

The piano and the guitar and the harmonica continue to work their magic as the

CAMERA MAKES ITS LAST MOVE--

--up toward the blue, blue sky. . . .

FINAL FADE OUT.

Interviews

Designer: Tony Walton

Tony Walton was born in England but has worked in America
for the past twenty years. Unusually versatile, he not only does
sets and/or costumes for movies but on Broadway as well (*Pip-
pin, Chicago, Sophisticated Ladies, Woman of the Year*). His first film
was *Mary Poppins,* which earned him an Oscar nomination for
Best Costume Design. With Philip Rosenberg, he won an Oscar
for Art Direction on *All That Jazz.* Among his other films are:

> *A Funny Thing Happened on the Way to the Forum*
> *Petulia*
> *Murder on the Orient Express*
> *The Wiz*
> *Equus*
> *Prince of the City*

□□□

ON DESIGN

The production designer is responsible for the visual elements
of the film—hand in hand with the cinematographer and, of
course, the director. There are some directors who are visually

very powerful, some who are less so. When you've worked with a director before, you tend to develop a shorthand with them, and I suppose there's more liberty, more trust.

ON WORK HABITS

One of the first things I like to do, and I imagine it's frequently done, is to take a film, more or less scene by scene, and try to picture what it would be like just in terms of the color palette of the whole film, so that if it needs to be soothing, it's keyed a certain way; if there's a need for jarring moments, it can be helped enormously by the use of jarring color or an unexpected contrast in coloration.

Ideally, I come on very early, frequently early enough to participate in the decision of who's to be cinematographer. Six months before filming isn't unusual. In a complex film, a film that requires a tremendous amount of building, then it would be much longer than six months.

ON DESIGN EMPHASIS

The emphasis shifts, depending on what the film is. For example, with *Prince of the City*, one of the major problems was the astounding number of characters, many of whom appeared for such brief moments that it was obviously going to be very hard for an audience to follow who was who at any given moment. So one of the tasks on my end was to try and make the environment of each of those people as blindingly clear as I could without caricaturing it so that it drew attention to itself. It was important to have a sense, not necessarily of remembering the name of the character, but of knowing whose team, what side he was on—white hat, black hat, or whatever—whether he was a bureaucrat or a street person. All of this, of course, with a strong level of believability.

In *Murder on the Orient Express*, a level of believable reality is not what we were after; it was a contrived, fluffy affair, and we wanted the people to have a movie-movie feeling. So the costumes were not broken down to look real or worn. And the sets permitted a certain kind of glamorization. People can talk about the train and how lucky we were to be able to shoot on the real *Orient Express*, but actually it was entirely made in the studio, using some key "museum pieces" from the actual train. People who had traveled on the real train said, "Oh, how nice to see it again," but actually it was an almost absurd glamorization of what the real thing was. If we had done the real thing accurately, it would probably have looked just a hair tacky.

ON *DA VINCI:* STUDIO OR LOCATION

Da Vinci centers on a remarkable event in a very normal environment.

If there were a practical way to do it, I think it would be best to find real locations and try to bend the technical problems to make them work within the real environment. I'm not saying you can't create a real environment on a set, obviously you can, but there's something about using reality that forces everyone's approach to be more believable.

And I think I would use the strangeness of Bimbaum and his abilities to be a really powerful counterbalance to the surrounding normalcy. So that even in looking for a small town, I think it would probably be a good idea not to look for anything too picturesque but rather for something that is like the square root of small towns.

ON *DA VINCI:* WIGS

The haircuts themselves obviously present a problem for the costume designer and hair and makeup people—I would think almost certainly you'd need wigs for the two kids. That's a very dangerous thing—wigs have a tendency to look, well, wiggy, so you'd have to be sure to have someone who really does wigs beautifully.

The reason for wigs is that you don't want to be controlled in the scheduling by the length of hair that the kids have at any given moment. It might just be possible to do so, but it would be terribly complex—especially in the shooting of the time-passage sequences. So it would be valuable to be able to control that up front.

ON *DA VINCI*: BIMBAUM'S COSTUME

My first impulse would be to go for maybe one or two imperceptible pieces of perfection about him.

Maybe a hard color in a little immaculate bow tie. Or perhaps the nature of the cuffs on his shirt would give a very precise fine touch to his general bagginess. Or maybe a totally unexpected pair of shoes—which, of course, you don't see in films too often. But there might be an opportunity in his almost balletic movements around the barbershop chair to see that his shoes are very particular, very strange.

ON *DA VINCI*: THE ENDING

I felt the ending slightly unresolved. Perhaps that shot of Bimbaum that then traveled up to the sky accounts for it, and I wondered if there might be some value to our being left with some sort of image of Bimbaum—that left him unchanged but in some way gave a slightly heroic sense to him. You know, that it wasn't a defeat, that there was a little victory left behind—I'm hopeless at suggesting any way of achieving that.

ON *DA VINCI*: THE HAIRCUTS

This is all off the top of my head, but might it be possible, in addition to the calendar on the wall, to have some magazines lying around? Perhaps the one on top might have an autumnal scene, a lot of clouds, so that for one of the fantasies the ceiling could have kind of a floating quality and you could see that Willie's drifting off and the clouds are wafting by, as opposed to your repeating of the water imagery.

I'm really mucking about now, but I wonder if the rushing water might be related to the shampooing part—the haircuts are obviously a sensual experience.

The massiveness of switching to the Nile or Amazon or

some kind of giant waterway might be out of scale for the story itself and might give a risk of pretentiousness to the last moments of the final haircut.

Again, on those last haircut moments—perhaps the film could be agonizingly slowed up so as to make our sense of anxiety about Bimbaum's lack of speed more provoking. Perhaps leaves, falling so slowly from trees—perhaps that could help us share Willie's wanting so much for Bimbaum to speed up somehow.

One last thing—it might be worth making a small equivalent of a teeter-totter, but instead of being on a one-way hinge, it would be on a sort of ball-bearing gimbal. And an operator would be down out of camera view and able to shift it, so that Bimbaum would literally be able to float a little bit. His movements would become imperceptibly unreal, and I mean imperceptibly. I would hope you wouldn't be quite conscious of where the effect was coming from—but it might add to the magic quality of the haircuts.

□□□

I never thought a whole lot about production design when I was working on *Da Vinci*. I tend not to fret overmuch on most technical aspects of a finished film when I'm writing. But when Walton began discussing the problems of wigs, I realized again just how much we are, all of us on a film, dependent on each other.

I have no way of knowing how fresh his comments were to you, but they sure as hell were enlightening to me. And helpful. For example, his notions on how to make the haircuts work.

None of those changes are remotely threatening to a screenwriter because nothing threatens me unless the alterations affect the spine of the piece. The haircuts I wrote can be executed any way at all—just so the magic stays. The magic is what's crucial. And what I was writing was the best I could do, but all it was was an indication to the other technicians of what the thrust of the sequences were to be.

Clouds on the ceiling, leaves in agonizing slow motion—wonderful, I say. I don't care if we go to the Nile or the Amazon—all that shot was meant to say was this: We're *building*, we're heading toward climax.

And speaking personally, I'll never think of the haircuts again without seeing old Bimbaum, scissors in hand, concentrating fiercely, and at the same time floating, floating somehow, as if he was subject to special and different laws than the rest of us plodders down here. . . .

Cinematographer: Gordon Willis

Gordon Willis began to learn his trade while in the Air Force. He shot documentaries and, when he got out, in 1955, became an assistant cameraman. His first feature was *End of the Road* in 1969. Since then, he has been constantly busy, and among his films are:

> *The Godfather*
> *The Godfather Part II*
> *The Paper Chase*
> *Klute*
> *All the President's Men*
> *Annie Hall*
> *Manhattan*

ON THE FUNCTIONS OF THE CINEMATOGRAPHER

The lighting of a scene is certainly my chief function. The setup of the shot is my other main job, and that's done in tandem with the director.

If you have ten places to shoot an actor in a room where he's doing something, the ideal thing is to make the right choice of setup. Once you make the right choice, that's ninety percent of what you're doing. In other words, the shot will do the job.

ON WORK HABITS

For the director to get the most out of me and for me to be able to do my job well, I should come on a minimum of a month before shooting. If it's a complicated picture with a lot of locations and things to discuss, it should be more—say, six weeks.

During that time, you generally have fragmented talks with the director. And you constantly discuss things with the production designer. A lot goes on—a lot of time gets sucked up going to locations, studying them, coming back. And then generally there are budget problems here, so stuff gets cut or added or whatever. The more you know about it, the better you're able to function.

ON THE "LOOK" OF A PICTURE

Every picture that I photograph ends up with a "look" because that's what I do. I mean, I'm visually oriented. But that "look" comes out of the story reference. It never comes out of "Let's give this picture a *look*."

ON WORKING WITH DIRECTORS

Ideally, you want to go through the script with the director scene by scene. It's really a visual editing process. The director will say, "This is what I want to achieve here and this is how I want to achieve it," and I'll discuss what I think.

You've got to find out what he wants to do first of all, and then, second of all, you've got to discover if it physically functions. Has he put himself in a position where the logistics make it impossible to accomplish the movie? That happens.

A good director and a good cameraman are supportive of each other—they're constantly giving each other information. Essentially, you're working as an extension of the director.

What you're trying to do is fulfill the idea, fulfill the vision, then extend the idea to the best possible lengths—you want to make the movie wonderful.

ON "DUMP TRUCK" DIRECTORS

There's a lot of what I call "dump truck" directing. That's when you take a long shot and a medium close-up and a close-up of every actor and every angle of the scene. You end up with a dozen pieces of film over and over again but you don't have a vision of how anything is supposed to cut together, no vision of what the movie is supposed to be at all.

Then you dump all that film in the editor's office and they make the movie. I don't think you can make a good movie that way, because it doesn't come from the ground up. That's not directing, that's just coverage.

THE TRICK

Generally, the trick on a movie is to take something that's often very sophisticated and reduce it to something very simple. So that it reads out in a good way to an audience. That's hard, because not too many people understand simplicity: They equate it with "no good."

ON INTENT

I think it would be smart for the screenwriter, just on a flyleaf, to include a page about his intent. That one page could be very helpful—what the intent is, what the story is.

Because sometimes, during shooting, people get lost. They think they understand but they lose their reference points somewhere in the middle of a movie. One thing I'm proud of about myself is that I generally don't get confused because I set my sights on something before we start. Then maybe in the middle I'll say, "This wasn't the idea before, it's not the idea now, we're going the wrong way, we're making another movie."

Shooting is a difficult time—there are a lot of people around, a lot of last minute decisions to be made, it's easy to get lost, and it's physically very tiring. I always say that making a movie is digging coal, but people don't understand that.

ON *DA VINCI:* SHOOTING THE HAIRCUTS

The haircuts would require a great deal of thought. How do you make them magical? The director might say, "Well, I want hair flying everywhere," but that would be wrong, I think; that's not it. The second haircut, that's a sequence I would have to chew on for a long time.

I've got an idea for the first haircut though; I may be wrong, it's just a notion, but what if you didn't see Bimbaum at all?

You deal with the kid and you deal with the haircut but you never see the barber. All you hear is his voice. You see the scissors and you see his hands. The scene goes on like you have it—Willie's having the conversation with Bimbaum. And you're hearing Bimbaum. And all the slaps on the head and that business, the measuring the head shape.

But all you see are the scissors and the pair of hands. The hands coming in and out. The voice discussing it. The hands should be different—short and stocky or long or whatever. Wonderful hands.

If you did it that way, I hope it would still be magical and you'd have someplace to build for the second haircut. You wouldn't have any special effects this way, no sparklers or opticals. But maybe you'd have introduced something strange and magical. The magic might come out of what you don't see. You haven't done anything creative yet—it's what's written, except you've selected a way of showing it. Scissors, hands, a man talking. Isn't that already interesting?

ON *DA VINCI:* SHOOTING BIMBAUM

I think Bimbaum should be shot always a little off.

For example, if you went with the notion for the first haircut, then you don't actually see him until the kitchen scene that night. I wouldn't do anything to intrude here—rather than lighting him differently from the others, maybe the shot structure would be different.

What I mean is, shoot the family in close-ups or medium close-ups and the talk goes on—"Guess what, we have a boarder and he's going to live upstairs," whatever the dialog is. But maybe I'd keep Bimbaum in the doorway and shoot him full-length, head to toe. So you see him, but he's not one hundred percent there. He doesn't have the same presence in the kitchen that everybody else has. But you'd have to be careful that he didn't become an intruder, he shouldn't be threatening. Just slightly different.

If you wanted, you could go the opposite way in the kitchen scene at the end where he's told he's got to speed up. They're all sitting at the table, and you could shoot the others with their plates in front of them—your average three-quarter eating shot. But when you go to Bimbaum, you could shoot him from under the chin up, so that now he has a full head and they're more distant.

The danger in *Da Vinci* would be getting it too complicated. You want to keep it always as simple Americana, structurally and visually. But you also want to keep Bimbaum, without drawing attention to it, slightly different, always a little bit strange. . . .

□□□

I'd never met Gordon Willis before our interview, but I'd followed his career more than any other cameraman, I suppose, because he's been involved with so many outstanding pictures. And he sure didn't disappoint me when we talked.

Of all of us who work in movies, the world of the cinematographer remains for me the most mysterious. Of course, I'm not around much during principal photography, but even if I were, it's beyond me. But they are always—the good ones, at least—crucial. I've always felt, for example, that Willis's shooting of *All the President's Men* was the basic reason the movie worked.

And I don't know about you, but I'd love to see the first haircut done his way. Just Bimbaum's voice, and his silver scissors, and those hands, moving in and out of frame, making their magic. . . .

Editor: Dede Allen

Dede Allen began her editing career with Columbia Pictures in the early forties. It was not till 1959 that she was given the opportunity to edit a feature film, *Odds Against Tomorrow*. Since that time, she has edited the following films, among others:

> *The Hustler*
> *America, America*
> *Bonnie and Clyde*
> *Rachel, Rachel*
> *Alice's Restaurant*
> *Little Big Man*
> *Slaughterhouse-Five*
> *Serpico*
> *Dog Day Afternoon*
> *Slapshot*
> *The Wiz*
> *Reds*

□□□

ON EDITING

Editing is not taking out, it's putting together. It's taking a story, which has been photographed from many different angles and, very often, in many different takes, and making it play in the best possible way that it can.

I'm sure it's very much like the process of writing. I can't do anything unless I know what I'm doing and why I'm doing it. In other words, how do you cut a scene until you know what the scene's about and why you're putting it together in the way you are?

ON CONFIDENCE

I start every picture thinking that I'll fail, that I'll never be able to do it, that I'll forget how to cut. I won't know how to do it, I'll let it down. You get very moody when you're working on a picture. Certain things you can cure and certain things you can't—I'm fifty-eight years old and I still bite my fingernails.

ON THE FIRST CUT

I like to come on a film as early as possible. I like to come on when they start shooting and I like to edit the film as it shoots. The first cut for me is the most important. I like to have that done within a few weeks of when the film has finished shooting. It may be half an hour longer than the final film will be. You start with this amorphous first cut, which is usually lugubrious, long, terrifying—it sends the director home with the shivers. You've got everything in there and it's atrocious from a story-telling point of view, because everything's said over and over and over.

ON THE ATMOSPHERE IN THE CUTTING ROOM

The cutting room is a place where an atmosphere can be created in which a director can be as insecure as he is ever going to be or could possibly want to be, and know he's not going to be exposed to anything but people who want to help solve problems.

On any film, problems develop in the writing of the screenplay and the shooting of the film that eventually have to be solved. The cutting room is the last place where any problems of story or acting or directing that have accumulated along the way can be fixed. The buck stops in the cutting room.

Every picture has what I call a "soft underbelly." There are always areas of difficulty where we flounder, and I think the director has to be given the right to go ape-shit crazy—and they've got to be given it with no smart-ass solutions of "Ah-hah, so you didn't know." In other words, they've got to feel comfortable being insecure. Just the way you might have to feel insecure in your writing.

ON *DA VINCI* IN GENERAL AND MORRIS IN PARTICULAR

I think Morris, the father, came off as a much richer character in the story. In the screenplay, I had very little feeling for Morris emotionally. I miss a feeling of loss on Morris's part.

Small point—wasn't it the postman who had the head like a nose and Bimbaum made him beautiful? That's the word Morris uses in the story: "beautiful." In the screenplay, you changed it—here he says, he made him "cute." That alters the meaning. "Cute" is a slightly downputting remark on the part of Morris.

Look—Willie gets a marvelous gift from Bimbaum. But he also gets a gift from Morris that I can see so clearly in the story but not in the screenplay, which was that *Morris really understood what an artist was.* In the story there are days and days spent in the living room where they're discussing haircutting—the father wants to be an artist, too, he wants to be more than a technician. And he isn't. But you get the feeling that maybe he could have been. Otherwise, why would he spend all this time talking with Bimbaum? In the story, that's one of the strong sequences, where the father is so excited about this artist he's brought home, this nasty old man.

I think the feeling of loss would be greater if Morris had given more of himself to his relationship with Bimbaum in the screenplay—and then deprived himself. Because what he's doing is cutting himself off from his son. He's going to have a son who's going to grow up and be Bimbaum.

ON THE PORCH SCENE

I would want to try and strengthen Morris; I would like to give the feeling that he's more than just a fixture there in order to hire and fire and get mad.

That scene on the porch, the one where Willie's playing

checkers with his friend and Emma comes out and says she can't take it anymore in the living room. "Ten days—how long can you talk about head shapes?"

I don't like Emma just *telling* me what's going on in the other room. If it were shot exactly as your screenplay indicates, we couldn't do much.

But I would like there to be coverage so we could shoot where the real life is—inside. We don't have to play the porch scene as crisply as you've written it. I want to see Morris. I want to give Morris credit for having the potential so that when we know that Willie is going to become an artist, that there was something about Morris that also could have gone that way but didn't. I never got that feeling because of the way the screenplay concentrated on the foreground.

□□□

As I listened to Dede Allen talk, it was a wonderful moment for me—because I think she's dead right, I had damaged Morris.

And as she went on, a whole bunch of images, images I'd never imagined in the writing, hit me. What if the porch scene began where it does—but then concentrated on the living room?

—what if Morris were holding his scissors at a certain angle, and Bimbaum came over, slightly adjusted the angle of Morris's arm? And Morris tried to get it right. But no, another slight arm adjustment.

—or what if we were looking at a bunch of roughly drawn head shapes and Morris pointed to the wrong one and Bimbaum shook his head, corrected, pointed to the proper one, and we could see Morris's frustration. He's trying, he's trying like a son of a bitch, but it just eludes him.

—or what if, during the final haircut, instead of just being inside and Morris storming through the door, announcing how many minutes to go, what if we punch up those "pacing" shots of Morris to show just how difficult a moment this was for him? He was suffering just like Willie was suffering, just like maybe even Bimbaum was suffering.

All that may help. I don't think it can hurt.

I didn't mean to weaken Morris, but when you make an adaptation, you're bound to lose things, some of which are unintended.

I was writing about this guy who loses a job—that was the structure I was following. So I tightened the material—three haircuts to two—and Morris's reactions changed. In the story, he lets Willie have the second haircut after the rainstorm—in the screenplay he just shouts for Willie to get the hell gone.

A different screenwriter might have kept the long living-room sequence in the story, might have let there be three haircuts—but I didn't know how to do it without the whole piece unraveling.

I'm not sure I ever would have come up with Dede Allen's suggestion—something in me says that's an editor's mind at work. They have such knowledge of how you can play a scene, so that it works on the screen but might be confusing on the printed page.

I also envied her relationship with directors—she's in a sense the end of the relay race and she and her director share one certain knowledge that binds them in a way no screenwriter can ever be: They both know they're on the *Titanic* together. . . .

Composer:
David Grusin

David Grusin is a distinguished jazz pianist as well as a record producer. His first movie was *Divorce, American Style*, in 1967. Since then he has worked on the following films, among others:

> *The Heart Is a Lonely Hunter*
> *Tell Them Willie Boy Is Here*
> *The Graduate*

Three Days of the Condor
The Electric Horseman
Heaven Can Wait
Reds
Absence of Malice
On Golden Pond

ON MOVIE SCORES

It really isn't important how pretty the music is. The film isn't about music; the score isn't about music. What matters is how helpful the score is to the film.

ON MYSTERY

I think the function of a score is subliminal and psychological. I believe there's a mystery about the emotional response a listener gets from a piece of music. I can't define how it works, but it's there in some way. How you respond to a Mahler symphony will certainly differ from your reaction to a Donna Summer record, but in both cases something happens to you. You're maybe not even aware of it.

What we try to accomplish in film scoring is to channel those responses in an organized way, so that an audience can be moved in one direction or another without actually knowing why. I believe that's the most functional use of film music.

ON THE TUG OF WAR

By the time the composer gets hired, the battle lines are drawn. Usually, the composer comes on very late, after the film has been rough-cut. There may already have been three years of work on the project with a producer, a director, a writer, and others being involved. And if there are differences of opinion, which there frequently are, usually I find the producer on one side and the director on the other. And not just about music— about the project in general; maybe one wants a scene left in and the other doesn't. When I show up, there's a preconception of getting me on one side or the other. In other words, I'm often in a tug of war. The director might say about the producer, "Don't listen to him, listen to me, he doesn't understand the film, I'm the only one who understands it." And the producer might take me aside and say the same thing. I don't mean to imply that this happens every time out, but it's happened to me often enough by now to make me think maybe it's not an uncommon disease.

ON THE PROBLEM

I'm convinced there are at least a half dozen ways to successfully score almost every film; I mean radically different ways with radically different styles of music. So the crucial problem becomes: Which way is the very best? That's the problem I roll around on the floor with.

ON FIRST IMPRESSIONS

The best situation for me is to see the cut of the film the first time without other people around. I really think that one of the biggest contributions a composer can bring to a project is simply this: The composer is one of the few people involved at that point who has never seen the film before. And on his first viewing he truly sees the reality of it. He doesn't see the script as it was before the rewrite, he's not seeing the earlier cuts before all the scenes were changed, he's seeing exactly what's on the screen *now*. There is a certain objectivity that lasts for that first running. And for me, that first impression is terribly important—because when I see the film that first time, I'm the audience.

MUSIC FOR *DA VINCI*

I don't think *Da Vinci* should have a big score at all. I mean, the orchestra should not be large—I think I'd try to use as few instruments as I could get away with. I'm not speaking of the *amount* of music here, I'm talking about the *kind* of sound.

Less can really be more in film scoring. That's why so many art films are so impressive musically: They are sometimes scored with just a few instruments (frequently because of a lack of budget), and that sparseness is artistically quite pleasing. Personally, I find that kind of thing terribly appealing.

And I think basically that *Da Vinci* requires a two-motif score—the kid's and Bimbaum's.

ON MUSIC FOR BIMBAUM

When we first meet him in the shop, and through the dialog, I don't think we need music for him. The haircut is what makes him an artist, so I'd like to introduce his theme once he's got the scissors in his hands and we can see the man at work.

We want to set him apart, he's unusual, and maybe we could do that with some kind of dissonance. But not too much; we don't want to make him scary. It's all a matter of degree.

I think the scissors are a specific, wonderful sound. Hopefully, they could be used as they exist, at the start, but then gradually we might change the reality of the sound by "bending" it electronically, or perhaps filtering it in some way.

I wouldn't want to get cute with the scissors—for instance, by making a waltz out of the scissor tempo. But I think they might be superimposed over some instruments to become part of the music—some high, shimmering kind of texture. I hear high sounds for this scene; maybe the first instrument would be a harpsichord, riding high over some mid-range muted strings. I don't know for sure, but I think I'd like a kind of hard-edged sound for Bimbaum. I'm not sure if his music should be melodic, but perhaps angular, with unusual intervals; not unpleasant, but harmonically and melodically different.

ON MUSIC FOR WILLIE

For Willie, I think one might just pick an instrument, and that would become his sound. It's an old device; I think it came from ballet and opera, where a character is identified by a specific instrument.

I don't know why, but at this point I hear the kid as a clarinet.

ON THE ENDING

I don't know if the ending can work musically the way you have it working in the script. You've got the music making a kind of an unusual plot point; it's supposed to take us into the future and let us know that Willie becomes an artist like Bimbaum.

Music is frequently asked to do things for film for which there are no ironclad guarantees of success, and this may be one of those times. You're also asking a lot from an audience, because they're not conditioned to think of music as carrying the plot in this way. They may be listening to the melody, and perhaps the orchestrations, etc., but are they really going to be able to absorb the idea of the kid becoming an artist, *solely* through the score?

I think things are further complicated by having him first fumble with the harmonica, then get better, then adding the guitar, and after that the piano.

Maybe a good way to start would be this: When the guitar enters, the harmonica stops. And when the piano takes over, the guitar stops. Maybe that way we could make the story point. In other words, when the guitar enters, the "harmonica" part of his life is finished. He's moving on. And he's done with the guitar when the piano begins—he's growing, getting older. At the very end, we could perhaps bring the three instruments together, but certainly not till then.

I'm not saying this solution would work; maybe, maybe not. The problem's still there: Audiences aren't stupid, but we're asking them to do things they're not accustomed to.

For me, the ending would be *the* challenge of the score. Before trying to write it, there would be a lot of rolling on the floor.

□□□

The Grusin interview reminded me again of one of the basic truths of filmmaking: *We are all at each other's mercy.*

Look, I know the producer's going to get killed by the studio and the director's going to be eaten alive by the star; I realize that just when the cinematographer has spent hours beautifully lighting a romantic garden scene, it's going to rain; I am aware that the production designer will be told, the morning he was supposed to shoot in the Sistine chapel, that he won't be allowed to use the Sistine chapel.

Well, tough about them, I've got troubles of my own.

I'm the screenwriter and my constant trouble is that my screenplay is toothpaste but my specific problem with *Da Vinci* was this: I couldn't figure out the ending.

The ending of the story centered too much on the family. I wanted the influence of Bimbaum to be what we were left with.

How, though?

Finally I get the notion for the scene where Willie is playing the harmonica and Bimbaum tells him everyone was terrible once. And in that scene Willie says how if he masters the harmonica he'll get a guitar and if he masters the guitar, then he'll get a piano.

So I blithely write the ending with that thought in mind. It's so easy—I just type a few words. The music goes from crummy harmonica to good harmonica to guitar to piano. Final fade-out.

Then Grusin tells me what you've just read about the ending—that I'm asking music to accomplish something that it may not be able to do. And of course, he's dead on the money. What I wrote was a *literary* conceit, and sometimes they don't shoot so hot.

The point is, if the ending can be made to work, it won't be because of me, it will be because the composer, in this case, finds a solution. For me to be at my best, I need everybody. We all, always, need everybody.

One last thing—I don't know about you, but as far as I'm concerned, now and forever, Willie's going to be a clarinet. . . .

Director:
George Roy Hill

George Roy Hill studied music at Yale and acting in Ireland. He began directing for live television—*A Night to Remember, Judgment at Nuremberg.* For a time he worked on Broadway, and the first play he directed, *Look Homeward, Angel,* won the Pulitzer prize in 1957. Among his dozen films are:

> *The World of Henry Orient*
> *Hawaii*
> *Butch Cassidy and the Sundance Kid*
> *Slaughterhouse-Five*
> *The Sting*
> *The Great Waldo Pepper*
> *Slapshot*
> *The World According to Garp*

☐☐☐

ON DIRECTING

The principle job of a director is to first get his script and get it right and get it playable and get it almost foolproof. Then his job is to cast it as perfectly as he can.

If he does those two things, he can phone in the direction, because it doesn't make any difference, his work is eighty percent done. The fact is that no director with a poor script that is badly cast can make it work through his direction. On the other hand, if he gets the script right and the actors right, then he can invent, then the rest of it is fun—I don't mean it's all fun, it's partly a pain in the ass, but I mean, then you have a solid basis on which you can create.

ON SHOOTING

The most anxiety-producing time is the actual filming, because by that time you have the picture in your head. And to make the scenes all correspond to what's in your head is very difficult.

Because there's nothing more artistically devastating than the atmosphere of a movie production. There are so many people around, so many people bothering you, asking you questions, actors wanting to know what tie they're going to wear—you're in constant danger of being fragmented, and the vision you have of the scene gets eaten away by a thousand different problems. It's a physical drain—I exercise and get into shape, but shooting is always a very, very tough time for me.

ON STUDIOS AND STARS

If I went in tomorrow and said I wanted to do, say, *David and Goliath*, the studio might send out a research organization to find out if the public wanted a biblical film.

And if they got back certain replies they might say, "All right, do it, but we want to have a star play David or Saul" or what have you.

That's perfectly all right with me if the name values fit the movie. But if I go in and say, "Look, I've found this wonderful kid for David and an old actor who's been working in regional theatre and I want him for Saul," they might say, "All right, we'll do it, but we won't give you more than X million dollars."

Then you have to make up your mind. If you want to, you can do it for X million dollars, or you can compromise and take a star and get a bigger budget. But this is a constant, it's a continual give-and-take proposition when you're preparing a film.

Once I get the go-ahead, I never hear from them again; I don't know if that's unusual or not, but I don't get bothered by them. Except in the case of *Hawaii*, where things were disastrous.

ON *DA VINCI:* THE ARTIST AS SHIT

What you've done here is take a story that works pretty well on paper, but you really make some fundamental errors in your screenplay—and since you are very glib and very clever and very able, you have covered up those errors and masked them so that most people would not see them. But I would, I think, be inclined to unmask you.

Da Vinci is an allegory and I don't much like allegories—I agree with Mrs. Malaprop that allegories should stay on the banks of the Nile.

This story, as you yourself say, is about how an artist cannot survive in the modern world—you claim it's about a guy losing a job but that's not really accurate. And if it is accurate, it's pretty damn dull.

This guy loses a job because of his integrity, his artistic integrity. Fair enough. But you also make him a shit, which is a cliché—that in order to have integrity you must behave like a shit. Shaw did it first, I think, with Dubedat in "Doctor's Dilemma," and since then it has become a popular dramatic concept. I don't buy it. The people I've known with the greatest artistic integrity are usually the most professional and the most considerate, while I've unfortunately run into a few second-rate artists who behaved like shits in the belief that this somehow automatically endows them with talent and integrity.

ON *DA VINCI:* THE ARTIST AS A BARBER

The first thing to say, the artist as a barber is a very tough visual thing to do. You have, in some of your more purple prose, described the effects of these haircuts.

Well, you've left the poor fucking director saying, "Jesus Christ, this kid gets a haircut and everybody falls down." Now I've seen lots of kids and lots of haircuts, but I've never seen a haircut that made me want go "Ooh—ooh—ahh," especially in a small midwestern town.

It just doesn't happen—unless you let him have a fright wig in the first scene or a hairpiece of snakes, like Medusa, and then you clean him up. In which case, it's going to be fairly obvious.

And then when Willie gets the haircut and Porky sees it and says, "What a beautiful haircut"—you say in your notes that kids don't talk that way. Well, you're right there, they sure as hell don't. I mean, you could have Willie back-lit and you could have the Hallelujah Chorus coming in and have a close-up of him through gauze and you'll create an effect, but in fact, you're striving to do something that's false. No kid's haircut is going to bring the world to an end.

In the story, you accept this, because you don't have to deal with the visuals, but in the screenplay, you run smack into them, and there's your director saying, "What the hell can I do?" I would sure try and pull every trick I knew—have the kid back-lit, have his hair a kind of glowing nimbus—but I'm going to have to light him through the whole movie that way, and it's going to take for fucking ever.

So you've got a very basic problem in the fundamental visual concept of the piece—and you're on very thin ice when you start accepting a haircut as a great work of art.

ON *DA VINCI:* THE HARMONICA SCENE

In your notes you say it would be phony, bad, dangerous, to write a scene that establishes a relationship with the boy and Bimbaum—and then you go ahead and write one. The very thing you say is bad, you write. The thrust of that scene where he's playing the harmonica is to give something to the old man. He softens his attitude toward the boy for one moment. It's the crotchety but dear old man—that's the artist saying what every young artist wants to hear. You know what I've written in the margin beside that scene? "Ugh." Enjoying this, Bill?

ON *DA VINCI:* WILLIE'S BEHAVIOR

He knows he's going to destroy his father—he's a cretin if he doesn't know he's going to destroy his father, because Porky's already done it. So this kid is so vain about how gorgeous he looks in his new haircut that he can't bear to have his father touch his head—is he suddenly Narcissus, in love with his haircut? Is that your basic sympathetic character? I'd boot the little kid's ass from here to doomsday.

I'm not suggesting this, but if he had a girl friend who, instead of Porky saying, "My God, you're beautiful," said, "Come on, I'm taking you to bed," and then later said, "I'm not taking you to bed anymore because you don't look so good," that would give him motivation to go get the haircut. Granted, a girl who behaves that way may not seem a girl with outstanding qualities, but we don't all pick the best, particularly when we're young. Then the boy is in the grips of an overpowering emotion—sex, which we all know drives people to all kinds of desperate things. Of course, this would change the balance of the story—it would now be about a boy who destroys his father because he wants to get humped. And Mr. Bimbaum goes floating away.

ON *DA VINCI*: HYPE

This script as written has things in it that set a director's teeth on edge. Look at your opening page—"Pull back to reveal a schoolyard on an agonizingly beautiful spring day." Well, the studio executive reads that and he says, "Oh, an agonizingly beautiful spring day, that's great." The director says, "When have I ever agonized over a spring day?" Then he says to his cameraman, "Get me an agonizingly beautiful spring day."

It's all hype—you write it, the executive reads it, and after I've shot it, everybody looks at it and says, "Wait a minute, that isn't agonizingly beautiful, why isn't it?" It's the director's fault.

More hype—when we see Porky after his haircut, you say, "Porky, need it be said, has vastly improved his appearance." Well, what the hell can I do to improve his goddam appearance, I've only got hair. I've got to make everything suddenly wonderful, with hair!

One of your more egregious examples of hype is in the second haircut—where the river isn't like before, it's the Nile or the Amazon—"but whatever it is, it makes you gasp." Jesus God.

I wonder what Shakespeare would have read like if he wrote this way? "And it's the most agonizingly beautiful dawn you've ever seen and the ghost appears and it's the most staggering-fucking-looking ghost anybody ever saw."

ON *DA VINCI:* CONCLUSION

A lot of the questions I ask, a lot of my attack on a property, is to tear it apart and see if it can stand up under really rigorous assault. Because you're going to be attacked later on, you might as well be your own attackee.

As far as *Da Vinci* is concerned, when I was in live tv, I worked on lots of worse things than this. . . .

□□□

Pretty withering.

But pretty helpful too. Because Hill has as good a story mind as any director I've come in contact with.

Which is not to say he is without flaw. He does hate what he calls hyping the script—a lot of directors do. John Schlesinger didn't like the hype I stuck into *Marathon Man*—but he took the job. Hill was driven almost mad by some of the hype in *Butch Cassidy.* I remember him being furious about the way I wrote the entrance of the Superposse—where I had half a page about the camera zooming like a racing car toward this stopped train. But again, he took the job.

And I don't think he's right at all about the harmonica scene—it's meant to be stern and tough. That's Bimbaum at his most arrogant, not Captain Kangaroo befriending a puppy.

There are a lot of things I disagree with in what Hill said—

—but he may be right.

I don't think Bimbaum's a shit and I don't think the artist as shit is a cliché—

—but Hill may be right.

I don't think this is a screenplay about a kid who knifes his father in the back—

—but Hill may be right.

And I think the haircuts can work, I think they can be magical. I think a lot of things in opposition to what's been said here. But when somebody very smart gives you the benefits of his wisdom, you better listen. Of the *Da Vinci* interviews, Hill was alone in much of what he felt. But that doesn't make him wrong. And if the others had agreed, in part or in whole with his insights, that wouldn't necessarily make *me* wrong. But it just may.

If enough people tell you you're drunk, it's not inadvisable for a screenwriter to consider lying down. . . .

chapter eighteen
The Relay Race

Inherent with every screenwriting job is a moment of mourning. This moment has nothing to do with the quality of the work experience. It's there, if I am replaced (*Charly*) or rewritten (*The Stepford Wives*) or still writing even after the completion of principal photography (*A Bridge Too Far*). And I'm not sure if the moment exists in any other kind of narrative writing—I don't believe it happens with plays, and it never occurs in any books I've been involved with.

The moment involves a terrible sense of loss.

It's possible to conceive of the making of a film as a relay race. A long one, two to three years long. The starter of the race, usually, is the producer. He acquires the property. Then, again usually, he hires the screenwriter and the race is on.

When a producer hires me, what he is buying, rough rule of thumb, is six months of my life. That's about the length of time from when I first read the property to when I deliver the first draft.

Most writers, when they are at work on a project, any project, become interested, and then involved, and then obsessed. And when we are in the obsessive phase, our personalities split. We may look the same, act the same, but a very large part of our brain is cut away, intent only on the project at hand.

We never know when help is on the way. An example from this book: One night I had insomnia and was watching very late-night tv and *The Blob* was on and I stared at it until that scene, mentioned earlier, where Steve McQueen has that dopey moment in the car with the girl. And suddenly you sit there, thinking, "Shit, I can use that." I didn't know then I was going to write a section on protecting the star, but I knew that car moment was *something*.

Not only don't we know when help is coming, we don't know where. A remark by a cabdriver may spark a thought. A book title seen a thousand times may suddenly take on a useful meaning. Help can come from any direction, so we have to stay on the lookout, because we all need, do I have to add, all the help we can get.

In the months when I'm not writing, sometimes I hear or see things and consciously think, "I ought to remember that, that may come in handy sometime." And then the next instant it's gone. But when I'm in the obsessive stage, I'm a sponge. And not a whole lot of use to anybody. Wherever I am, obviously that's where the physical part of me inhabits space. But always, a large part of my mind is where I am right now, staring at white paper, wondering how in hell to fill it with words.

Until I have filled enough pages, there is no movie.

As I said, filling those pages is six months of whatever time I have left. And those first months are as full of research as I can make them. I read and reread the source material, and I fiddle. I interview people and jot down what I hope will help. I read and reread other material that may deal with the same or a similar subject. I listen to music that may jog something. Music is becoming increasingly important to me. I've been alone in my pit for a quarter century now and I can't take the silence anymore. So I constantly put on a stack of records and let them play in the background. For *Bridge*, to take an example, I bought a bunch of military-oriented records—Sousa marches, etc.—and had them on quietly all day; for *Waldo Pepper*, pop tunes from the twenties.

All this, of course, is building up to the moment of actual writing. I am getting myself as full of the material as I possibly can. When I can't stand it any more, I try and write. If the writing goes well X weeks later, I have a first draft. And then I have it mimeoed. And then I get it back and look at it.

And at that point, I know more about the movie than anybody else in the world. I stand there holding the script, and of course I'm pleased that something exists, and of course I'm frightened that it stinks. But running along with those emotions is the knowledge of my knowledge—I know so much. I've made so many decisions about what to save and what to pitch—I could have written a five-hundred-page screenplay if I'd wanted-ed. I am, as I stand there, the movie.

And then comes the moment of mourning. Because the relay race must go on and my lap is ending; I must pass the baton to the other technicians.

And when you give it away, the loss, of course, is the end of your imagination. The movie in my head is going to leave me. Other people's fantasies are going to take over. As they must.

Generally speaking, at his time of greatest knowledge, conceivably at the time of his greatest usefulness, the screenwriter is cast aside.

That's the way movies are made.

I'm not a whiz at transcribing interviews; I have no idea what your reaction to them was. But I can tell you my two reactions and I was totally unprepared for both. They filled me with elation and they filled me with despair.

Elation because their suggestions improved my screenplay.

Despair because their suggestions improved my screenplay.

The elation I think is easy enough to understand—anytime anyone can help you, can make your work better, whether it's a friend reading a book or an editor making cogent comments, that's terrific. We all, I think, want whatever we do to have as much quality as possible.

The despair I felt comes from this simple fact: Talks such as I had on *Da Vinci* are simply inconceivable in the actual world of making a movie.

I have been at the craft for almost twenty years now, and until the past weeks, I've never spent five minutes alone with an editor. Or a production designer. Or a cinematographer. I've never *met* the composer on any film I've ever done, except once, and that was long after the score was completed.

Yes, I've met with directors. Often fruitfully. But it's not the same as here.

Because he has secrets.

He is fighting wars I never know about. Maybe the producer hates my script and wants to bring in someone else. Maybe the director hates my script and wants to bring in someone else. Maybe the studio is insisting on the use of a star who is suddenly available. Maybe the director took the job because he needs the money or the work or he's always wanted to do a movie on the subject matter I've written about and so he grabbed the script before someone else could make a movie covering similar ground.

From the very beginning, I have had an ambition in dealing with a director. I've wanted to do the following: sit down and discuss the script from the point of view of my particular intention. Not shot by shot. But scene by scene. I've wanted to go through from fade-in till fade-out and say, "Here's what I meant by scene one. I did it this way because this is what I was after." And then scene two, etc. Such a talk may take four hours, it may take eight.

Well, forget about it.

Never happens. And that's dangerous, because often, when a scene is sludge, it's because the intention of the script wasn't the same as the intention of the director when it went on the floor.

Now, when I say I wanted to give my intention for each scene, that doesn't mean I want the director to sit there and grunt agreement. Often, very often, I may intend something in a scene, it's clear in my head, but what I put on paper veered off. He would point that out to me. I could change it, fix it maybe.

Never happens.

Once we pass the baton, we become, and I don't know why, this weird *thing*, some vestigial lump, like a baby born with a tail. Get rid of it.

We are not held in much esteem. Most of us don't deserve to be. But there is an attitude toward us maybe best exemplified by Sam Goldwyn, who used to sneak to the writers' building and listen and get angry if he didn't actually hear typewriters clacking.

Few of the powers out there know what a cameraman does, but they know they can't do it. Occasionally, a cameraman gets replaced, but not often. The same for the other technicians.

They don't know what we do, either, but they do know the alphabet, and they also have lists of dozens of other writers who can change what we've done.

The attitude toward us continues after the picture has finished shooting. I've never seen a rough cut of a picture I've written. And I rarely get invited to sneaks. *Marathon Man* is a good example, because there were two sneaks, in California. And I live in New York so it's expensive to bring me out. Except I was in California at the time. Wouldn't have cost a whole lot to have me along. I mention *Marathon Man* because it was a picture that, I suspect, was grievously damaged by the sneak reactions.

Probably I couldn't have helped. The movie was no longer mine, and many others knew much more about the film than I did.

But no one knew more about the *structure* of the film.

No one ever does or ever will. You keep that inside you. And often the screenwriter will know why a section of the movie is just lying there, gasping for air. He may not be able to fix it, but he may at least be able to articulate the reason for the mess.

But we are not called on to articulate. We are, after our lap is finished, for the most part, mute. Usually, they don't want us around. As I said, I don't know why, but it's odd.

And in movies, the screenwriter is the odd man out.

But there is a trade-off. That beginning lap we run, regardless of what happens later—that lap is ours. We have the privilege, if you will, of the initial vision.

We're the ones who first get to make the movie. . . .

Final
Fade-In

I am ending this book—it's now June of '82—at the greatest time of panic and despair in modern Hollywood history.

A desperate agent said to me yesterday, "It's like living underwater out here." This past January, when I began, is already looked back on with some nostalgia.

How could things be worse? Remember these?

> *The Border*
> *Personal Best*
> *One from the Heart*
> *A Stranger Is Watching*
> *Shoot the Moon*
> *Making Love*
> *Cannery Row*
> *Evil Under the Sun*
> *I'm Dancing as Fast as I Can*
> *Deathtrap*
> *I Ought to Be in Pictures*
> *Cat People*
> *A Little Sex*
> *Wrong Is Right*
> *Partners*

And that's a selective list. The fact is that, in the first five months of this year, only *Porky's* was a runaway hit.

Events are taking place out there—or *not* taking place, to be a bit more precise—that were unheard of a year or two ago. Just one example: I know of a best-selling piece of nonfiction that a studio developed. A first-class script was written. The script attracted a world-famous award-winning director. And one of the hottest young stars also committed.

And the studio put it in turnaround.

I am not talking about an introverted art film—this is a movie with action, adventure, rich characters. The director is so anxious to get it off the ground that he has agreed to defer his entire salary.

And no one will touch it.

The summer is upon us now—thirty-nine pictures will open from the major studios between now and Labor Day. Some feel the summer will be big and the studios will get active again. Some feel the summer won't be big and the studios won't get active again.

I suppose I'm perverse, but I think the summer will be huge—the biggest in the history of Hollywood—and the studios will still remain immobile.

Their confidence factor is simply gone.

They will make sequels—*Jaws III* was announced today. And they will make rip-offs—sixty clones of *Halloween* are for sale today from all around the world if anyone in Hollywood wants to buy them.

There is nothing new about this. After his first film proved successful, Broncho Billy Anderson made 375 more just like it. And we never minded the Andy Hardy movies; I didn't, anyway.

But that was when Metro alone was turning out fifty films a year. Now the entire industry doesn't make a lot more than twice that many altogether.

They are not waiting for Godot out there, they are waiting for HBO instead. Cable will save them—not by just buying pictures, but by becoming a giant financial contributor to the actual making of movies.

That's a theory, anyway.

I have no idea as to its eventual accuracy, but I believe that we will soon have again what we have come to take for granted—the most vital and vibrant film industry of any country in the world.

Hollywood has been desperate before, but up till now it's

been a technical advance that's brought salvation—sound or color or CinemaScope or Smell-O-Vision. But I don't think so this time.

This time I think it's going to be talent. Young talent.

I have just spent the past two days looking at short films made by graduates and undergraduates at the NYU Film School. There were, needless to say, no masterpieces. And probably only two of the ten I saw would be good enough to go into the theatres immediately.

But they were all so goddam gifted.

I think there's a wave of talent rising now. Thousands upon thousands of young men and women who literally love film. I realize this is a book about Hollywood, so obviously there has to be a happy ending. Only I'm not tacking this on. I believe that wave is upon us and that it's not going to be stopped. And to all that talent let me say, where the hell have you been and I wish you joy . . .

. . . and may you ignore the critics when they attack you, and pay no attention to their praise . . .

. . . and may you please remember when your scenes are sludge, that screenplays are structure . . .

. . . and may you have peers as willing to improve your project as you must be; treat them kindly, for they will save your ass many times over . . .

. . . and may you always remember "it's only a movie" but never forget there are lots worse things than movies—like politicians . . .

. . . and may you be lucky enough and skilled enough to make some glorious moments for all those people sitting out there in the dark, as earlier craftsmen created such moments for you . . .

. . . and finally and most of all . . .

> . . . may all your scars
> be little ones. . . .

January–June, 1982
New York City

index